On the Rim of the Caribbean

On the Rim of the Caribbean

Colonial Georgia and the British Atlantic World

PAUL M. PRESSLY

The University of Georgia Press   *Athens and London*

Set in Adobe Caslon Pro by Graphic Composition, Inc., Bogart, Georgia
Cartography by David Wasserboehr, Flying W Graphics
Manufactured by Thomson-Shore, Inc.
The paper in this book meets the guidelines for
permanence and durability of the Committee on
Production Guidelines for Book Longevity of the
Council on Library Resources.

Printed in the United States of America
13 14 15 16 17 P 5 4 3 2 1

Library of Congress Cataloging-in-Publication Data

Pressly, Paul M.
On the rim of the Caribbean : colonial Georgia and the British Atlantic world /
Paul M. Pressly.
p. cm.
Includes bibliographical references and index.
ISBN-13: 978-0-8203-3567-4 (hardcover : alk. paper)
ISBN-10: 0-8203-3567-3 (hardcover : alk. paper)
ISBN-13: 978-0-8203-4503-1 (pbk. : alk. paper)
ISBN-10: 0-8203-4503-2 (pbk. : alk. paper)
1. Georgia—Economic conditions—18th century. 2. Georgia—Commerce—West
Indies, British—History—18th century. 3. West Indies, British—Commerce—
Georgia—History—18th century. 4. Plantations—Georgia—History—18th century.
5. Georgia—History—Colonial period, ca. 1600–1775. I. Title.
F289.P74 2013
975.8'02—dc23   2012033964

British Library Cataloging-in-Publication Data available

In memory of my parents,

William Laurens

Alice McCallie Pressly

And in honor of

Jane, Bill, and Nancy

Contents

Preface

In the early summer of 2006, I led a group of residents from the community of Pin Point, outside Savannah, to Ossabaw Island to look at the remains of the North End Plantation, including three tabby cabins that the Georgia state archaeologist has described as the best preserved in the state. As head of an education alliance, I knew that some of the community members were descended from enslaved people who had labored on the plantations of this island, now a heritage preserve with twenty-six thousand acres of marsh and maritime forest accessible only by boat. We were not prepared for their reactions. Several of the older members became excited when they stood before those tabbies constructed of oyster shells, lime, sand, and water. They had lived in the cabins as children during the 1940s, when their parents had worked for the owners of Ossabaw, and pointed out details of the living arrangements that re-created for us a way of life that seemed closer to another time. They retain a strong feeling for this island, which has been a part of their families for over two centuries. In an interview, Bo Bowens told how people often asked him about his accent and whether he was from the Caribbean. He would reply, "No! I am from someplace special and beautiful. I'm from Ossabaw!"

On the coast of Georgia, the eighteenth century is closer than one would think. Pin Point has ties to the enslaved people who first came to the islands from Africa in the 1760s to grow indigo, herd cattle, and build ocean-going vessels. My work in helping to interpret the stories around the North End Plantation provided an essential spur to this book. Motivated by this experience, I pulled together a symposium about African American life and culture in the Georgia Lowcountry from the eighteenth century to the twentieth. Out of that effort came a gathering of distinguished scholars, an audience of several hundred people, and a book that fills a gap in the subject matter. What also emerged were close working relationships with people who have extended extraordinary help to me in this enterprise.

I would like to thank Todd Groce and Stan Deaton of the Georgia Historical Society, who together have redefined public history in the South while stimulating primary research. Deaton's unfailing encouragement helped me over the initial hurdles and kept my focus on the principal theme. Neither the symposium nor this book would have materialized without the support of John Inscoe, Saye Professor of History at the University of Georgia and former editor of the *Georgia Historical Quarterly*. His friendship helped me to concentrate on significant issues in local history, and his willingness to come to Ossabaw Island and think about how to tell the story of the tabby cabins was one of the seeds that led to the symposium.

Philip D. Morgan served as the editor of the book that came out of the symposium on African American life on the Georgia coast. Assisting him throughout the process was worth at least one and maybe two graduate courses. His accessibility meant much, and our brief conversations about the relationship of the Caribbean and the Lowcountry were vital to shaping this work. Erskine Clarke, who knows the coast of Georgia through his exploration of the thousands of letters of the Charles C. Jones family, imparted his wisdom and extraordinary sensitivity to people and their feelings while advising on an Ossabaw project funded by the National Endowment for the Humanities.

Serving on the advisory council of the University of Georgia Press gave me a great appreciation for the work of its staff and most especially Nicole Mitchell, Nancy Grayson, Derek Krissoff, John Joerschke, and Beth Snead. Their craftsmanship, hard work, passion, and energy provided inspiration. Craig Barrow, owner of Wormsloe Plantation in Savannah, continues his family's legacy of nurturing and supporting the press. His commitment to the history of the Georgia coast serves as a model, and his friendship brought me into contact with relevant scholars through his new initiative, the Wormsloe Institute for Environmental History.

Others who have influenced the shape of this work include Betty Wood, Jacqueline Jones, Allison Dorsey, and Charles Elmore, historians; George McDaniel, director of Drayton Hall; Deborah Mack, museum consultant; Emory Campbell, chair of the Gullah Geechee Cultural Corridor Heritage Commission; and Dan Elliott, archaeologist. The anonymous reviewers gave me much more than their honorariums commanded. I am grateful for their professionalism. The Ossabaw Island Foundation accorded me remarkably generous time to complete this work. A special thanks to the executive director of the foundation, Elizabeth DuBose, whose love of history and historic preservation is unmatched.

Allison Hersch, a writer, made insightful comments on every chapter and served as a cheerleader par excellence. Special thanks to Nora Lewis and Lynette Stout of the Georgia Historical Society, Anne Smith of the Georgia Archives, the archivists at the old Public Record Office in London, and those at the National Archives of Scotland in Edinburgh. I am grateful for the service I received from the staffs of the Perkins Library at Duke, the Southern Historical Collection at UNC-Chapel Hill, the National Archives and Records Administration in Morrow, Georgia, and the Library of Congress.

My wife, Jane, has given me unfailing support throughout the project, traveled with me to distant places, and run interference at crucial moments. The Madeira Club of Savannah has gathered for the past sixty years to celebrate the virtues of that drink and to listen to papers of a historical bent. The comments of its members are much appreciated.

I close by expressing how meaningful it has been to be involved with the men and women of Pin Point. It is impossible not to be captivated by the way their ancestors moved from indigo cultivation, cattle herding, and shipbuilding in the eighteenth century to Sea Island cotton in the antebellum period, to tenant farming in the late nineteenth century, and finally to crabbing and oystering in a community on the mainland in the twentieth. Today, they have fully entered into the mainstream of American life as architects, teachers, longshoremen, and members of the military. Theirs is not simply an African American story or even a Southern story but a fully American story.

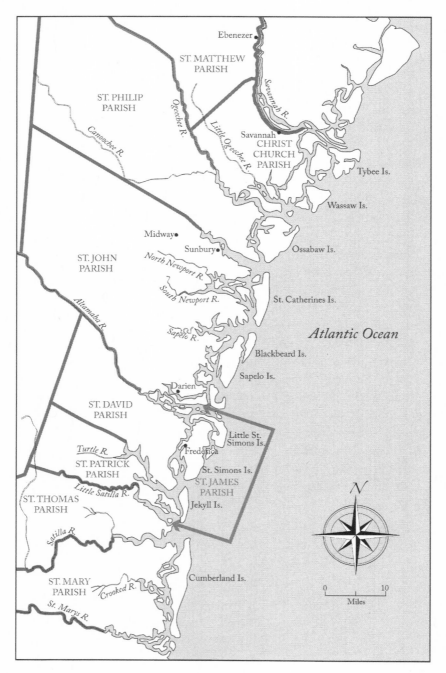

Coastal Georgia, 1775.

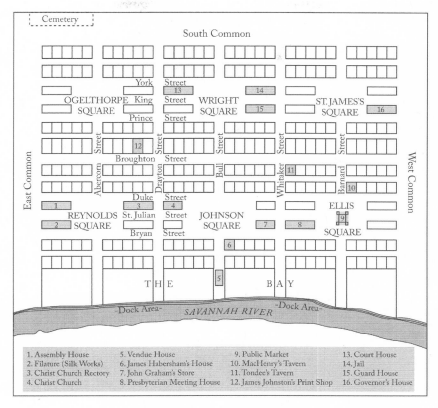

Cemetery

South Common

York Street

13

14

OGELTHORPE King Street WRIGHT 15 ST. JAMES'S
SQUARE Prince Street SQUARE 16 SQUARE

12

Broughton Street

11

10

1 3 4 ELLIS

REYNOLDS St. Julian Street JOHNSON 9
2 SQUARE SQUARE 7 8 SQUARE
Bryan Street

Duke Street

6

T H E 5 B A Y

Dock Area SAVANNAH RIVER Dock Area

East Common

West Common

Abercorn Street

Drayton Street

Bull Street

Whitaker Street

Barnard Street

1. Assembly House   5. Vendue House   9. Public Market   13. Court House
2. Filature (Silk Works)   6. James Habersham's House 10. MacHenry's Tavern   14. Jail
3. Christ Church Rectory   7. John Graham's Store   11. Tondee's Tavern   15. Guard House
4. Christ Church   8. Presbyterian Meeting House 12. James Johnston's Print Shop 16. Governor's House

Savannah, 1770. Based on a plan by Thomas Shruder, deputy surveyor general, submitted February 5, 1770.

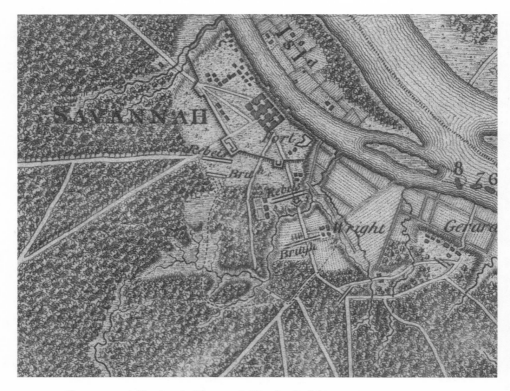

Yamacraw neighborhood of Savannah. The detail of this 1780 map captures many of the buildings that made up this subcommunity to the northwest of Savannah, which served the maritime trades. The front section consisted of warehouses, stores, and a shipyard. The middle portion was a noisy collection of taverns, boardinghouses, and other places where sailors and black people could find a more tolerant atmosphere. The back section, also known as the village of St. Gall, included houses belonging to the collector of the port, artisans, carpenters, and others from a lower-middling background. British defensive lines are also visible. By Archibald Campbell, engraved by Willm. Faden, 1780 (Hmap1780cop2). Courtesy of Hargrett Rare Book and Manuscript Library, University of Georgia Libraries.

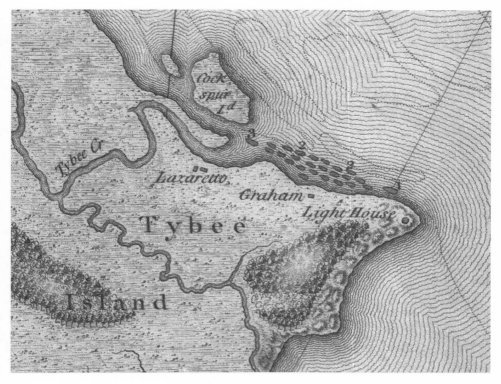

Entrance to the Savannah River, 1780. This map shows the relationship between the lighthouse on Tybee Island, Cockspur Island where vessels anchored before making their way to Savannah, and the lazaretto, where Africans were held in quarantine before being sold in Savannah. British naval vessels are depicted in the south channel. By Archibald Campbell, engraved by Willm. Faden, 1780 (Hmap1780 3copy2). Courtesy of Hargrett Rare Book and Manuscript Library, University of Georgia Libraries.

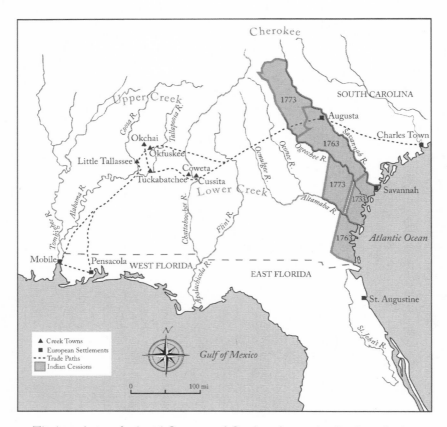

The boundaries of colonial Georgia and Creek trading paths. Creeks and other
natives made cessions of land in 1733, 1763, and 1773. The majority of deerskins
passing through Augusta came down the Savannah River by boat and was shipped
from Savannah to Britain or carried to Charles Town for export.

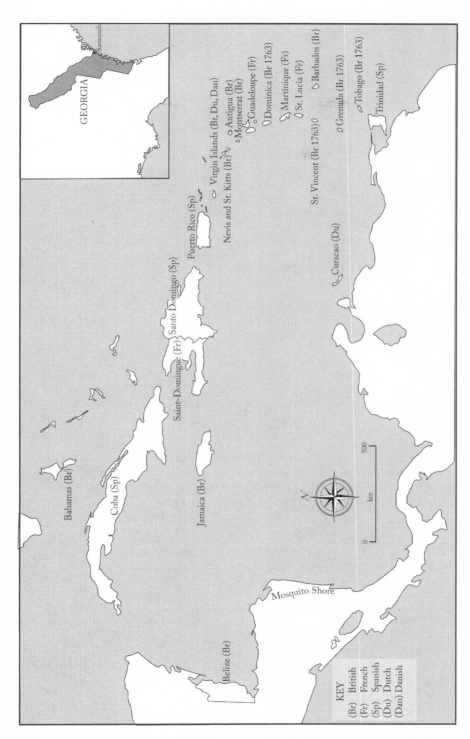

The Caribbean in the eighteenth century.

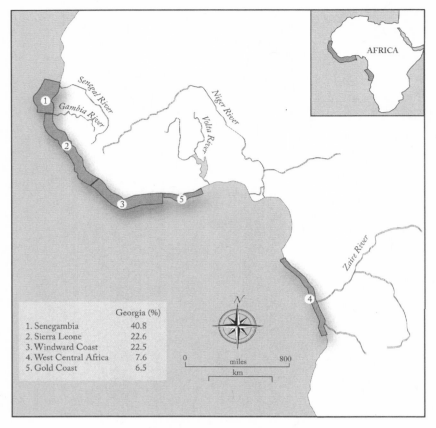

	Georgia (%)
1. Senegambia	40.8
2. Sierra Leone	22.6
3. Windward Coast	22.5
4. West Central Africa	7.6
5. Gold Coast	6.5

Coastal origins of slave shipments from West Africa, 1751–75. As a slave port, Savannah imported a high percentage of Africans from the regions of Senegambia, Sierra Leone, and the Windward Coast. Traders valued the agricultural skills, especially in rice cultivation, that many brought. Nevertheless, the diversity of enslaved people reflected an immense geographic range, the influence of Islam, the protracted movement of slaves from the interior to the coast, and the preponderance of small group purchases. Trans-Atlantic Slave Trade Database, CD-ROM, 1999.

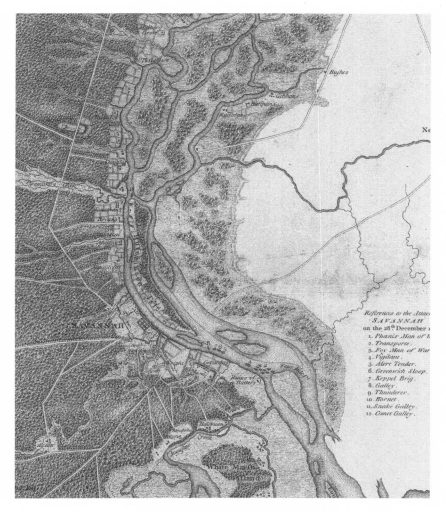

Rice plantations on the Savannah River, 1780. This detailed map prepared after the British reoccupation of Georgia offers several important features: the layout of individual rice plantations, the names of prominent merchant-planters, the buildings that comprised Yamacraw to the northwest of Savannah, British fortifications around the town, and the relatively undeveloped nature of the land behind the river. "Sketch of the northern frontier of Georgia: extending from the mouth of the Savannah River to the town of Augusta." By Archibald Campbell, engraved by Willm. Faden, 1780 (Hmap1780 3copy2). Courtesy of Hargrett Rare Book and Manuscript Library, University of Georgia Libraries.

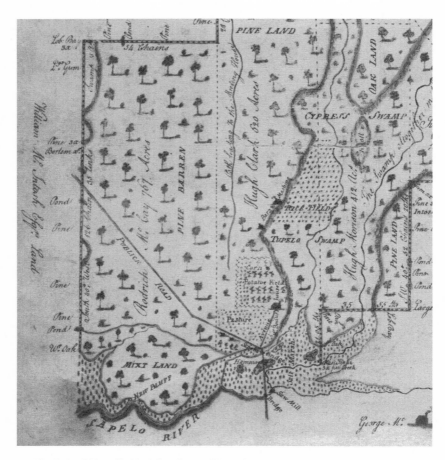

"An Inland Rice Field: After Survey Plat of Robert Baillie, John Douglas, 1772. Surveyor-General Office." Two small creeks that passed through cypress and tupelo swamps were dammed to contain enough fresh water to irrigate the rice field at appropriate moments during the growing season. The "inland swamp" method was vulnerable to both drought and flooding in comparison to the method used on Savannah River plantations, where the flow of the tides drove fresh water onto the fields. Courtesy of the National Archives and Records Administration, Morrow, Georgia.

On the Rim of the Caribbean

Introduction

How did colonial Georgia, an economic backwater for much of its existence, find its way into the burgeoning Caribbean and Atlantic economies where trade spilled over national boundaries, merchants reacted to rapidly shifting conditions in multiple markets, and the transport of enslaved Africans bound together four continents and three races? Scholarly interest in comparative and interdisciplinary approaches to studying the past has produced a deep and rich understanding of the role of the Carolina lowcountry within the British Atlantic economy. Considerably less attention has been paid to placing Georgia within that same context, in part because its coastal area seemed a simple extension of the Carolina lowcountry. As a recently created colony, Georgia seemed to contemporaries and historians alike to be a peripheral region, a "fledgling province" of little weight, more acted upon than an active participant in colonial affairs, as one scholar has so well phrased it. Created as a utopian experiment for redeeming the "worthy poor" of England, it ended its first nineteen years nearly bankrupt. Thereafter, it lagged behind developments elsewhere in North America and only reluctantly embraced the American Revolution. Yet the colony was also a microcosm of broader forces at work in the Atlantic world. Its experience speaks to the spread of a plantation system that reflected the greater Caribbean world, the growing importance of the African Diaspora in transforming the lowcountry, the emergence of a merchant community that had its roots in a transatlantic world, and the continuing importance of the deerskin trade in knitting together the West Indies, native towns, and the London leather market.[1]

Georgia sat on the outer edge of a plantation complex that dominated the Caribbean and reached from the rivers of Brazil in South America to the southeastern coast of the North American mainland, one of the last territories in that vast area to be incorporated into the larger whole. When James Oglethorpe and a band of like-minded philanthropists obtained a charter from the Crown in 1732 to found a colony for humanitarian as well as military and mercantilist reasons, they were swimming against the tide. The worthy poor gathered from the urban centers of Great Britain, together with German peasants deeply rooted in a simple Pietist culture, presented a striking contrast to the hypercompetitive, grasping emigrants from Barbados who had been so instrumental in the founding of South Carolina in 1670. With a steadfast sense of purpose, the colony represented a resounding repudiation of that Caribbean world: the prohibition of slavery and rum; the commitment to subsistence farming; a population composed primarily of artisans, minor officials, and indentured servants; the deliberate choice not to produce an exportable commodity—in short a refusal to participate in the Atlantic economy, while being deeply engaged in the Atlantic world. Members of the charter generation, about two thousand strong, made their way into the royal period, and if most were ready for the change, their frame of mind still reflected their earlier experiences. How Georgia's original population merged into the new order after the adoption of slavery is an important part of a larger story.

In the years after 1750, it is not too extreme to speak of the "Carolinization" of Georgia as a model of plantation development took hold that was rooted in the West Indies and transformed by South Carolina. That colony owed its social and cultural system to Barbados, cradle of the sugar revolution in the mid-seventeenth century and "cultural hearth" of the British West Indies. The Barbadians who settled there were a potent mix of planters, adventurers, artisans, indentured servants, and enslaved people who faithfully replicated their world: capitalist exploitation of land, intensive slave labor, a highly stratified society, and the production of a staple commodity for export. From there, a lowcountry cultural core radiated from Charles Town, stretching north to include the Cape Fear region of North Carolina and into coastal Georgia. The end of the prohibition of slavery in 1750 opened a fresh chapter. David Chestnutt has described the migration of 359 Carolina planters across the Savannah River in successive waves between 1746 and 1766, carrying with them a work force and capital that primed the growth of rice plantations. If South Carolina was the colony of a colony, then its younger sibling could claim an even longer lineage through a succession of three colonies.[2]

Because the raw and young Georgia was influenced by multiple cultural and economic forces, it is important to put the Carolinization thesis into perspective. While describing a fundamental reality, the image is an oversimplification. Carolina's influence on the new rice frontier was enormous, but how this influence operated is a complex story involving the merger of people from different backgrounds to form a new planting elite (or, more properly, elites); a black labor force assembled from local, regional, and Atlantic markets; a shipping and marketing infrastructure with unusually strong ties to the Caribbean; and a commitment to building alliances within the multicultural world of the deerskin trade. In discussions of the Lower South as a whole during the colonial era, historians typically mention South Carolina and Georgia in the first paragraph of their essays and then settle down to talk about Charles Town and the surrounding lowcountry. Younger and smaller, Georgia becomes lost in the shuffle.[3]

Of the many changes the colony underwent during its first fifty years, the most remarkable, historian Jack Greene thought, was its sudden rise to prosperity. From the days when the second governor arrived to find the population small and mostly "so very poor that they but barely subsist themselves" to the moment a few years later when it became evident that the colony was "Making a very rapid Progress towards being an Opulent & Considerable Province," Georgia increased in production, credit, shipping, wealth, population, and settlements.[4] Many valuable studies have opened new doors to understanding the nature of this new world, from Betty Wood's dissection of informal slave economies and Mart Stewart's thoughtful study of landscape as the mediation of culture and nature to Ben Marsh's examination of frontier women and the works of John Juricek and Julie Anne Sweet on colonial Georgia and the Creeks.[5]

The colony's entry into the Atlantic economy offers yet another avenue for approaching the basic building blocks of that fledgling society. There is a need to consider the markets for its commodities; the ships, sailors, and sea captains who filled its ports; the wide range of people who participated in the export and import trades; Savannah's struggles to establish commercial independence from Charles Town; the slave trade in the context of fresh research and new perspectives; the retail network within the province; and the sources of credit that fueled the expansion. On a broader level, there is an even greater need to touch on the effects of the larger world of trade on the internal structure of the colony: the impact of the Caribbean on the timber industry, the way in which plantations spread within individual parishes, the dramatic growth of consumption, and the role of Savannah in the deerskin trade.

That story, too, must be placed in a larger setting. The geographer D. W. Meinig distilled much of the thinking behind the idea of an Atlantic history when he described the successive transfers of people onto American shores as a vast interaction between traditional societies in the Americas, myriad cultures on the African continent, and migrating communities of European settlers, the whole functioning as "a sudden and harsh encounter between two old worlds that transformed both and integrated them into a single New World."[6] Georgia was not entering a self-contained sphere of trade. In its broadest sense, Atlantic history extends beyond empires to look at what historian David Hancock described as the "decentralized, net-worked, and self-organized world" that grew up in the cracks and nooks, the interstices, between empires.[7] His classic study of Madeira wine dem-onstrated the porousness of empire, the way this beverage linked Portu-guese peasants, French brandy merchants, and Swedish lumbermen to an international group of traders with a large market on the North American continent. Patterns in the rice, sugar, and tobacco trades followed more of a linear model as shippers in peripheral regions like Georgia transported most of their surpluses to the core, or metropolitan, areas. Yet the "two-region" staples approach, with a colony that provided natural resources and a metropolis that provided labor and capital, has given way to an immensely complex picture rooted in geographic, economic, and cultural diversity.[8]

In the contemporary view of Atlantic history, empires retain their role as a basic organizing principle—but as a way of understanding people, trade, and cultures in the process of being reshaped rather than as a coherent institutional entity. The Spanish Atlantic created a "New World" that was not entirely European, Native American, or African as rising amounts of racial mixing created a diverse social and cultural landscape. Silver mining remained the cornerstone of the imperial economy.[9] The Portuguese empire was a phenomenon of the South Atlantic, with a slaving frontier in cen-tral Africa that kept moving farther eastward and a plantation frontier in Brazil, the major destination for Africans transported to the Americas. On both sides of the ocean, the walls between African and Portuguese cultures were porous.[10] The French Atlantic included the vast expanse of Canada, a strategic position on the Lower Mississippi anchored by New Orleans, and the single wealthiest colony in the Caribbean: Saint-Domingue with its sugar, coffee, and indigo plantations. While French colonization in North America took the form of an "intercultural alliance" between fur traders, missionaries, officials, and Native Americans, in the Caribbean it centered on the importation of more than 1.1 million Africans.[11]

After a late start, Britain carved out an empire that by the middle of the eighteenth century was second only to Spain's in size and importance. Because of ever-expanding trade and the movement of people, Britain's Atlantic world was far larger and more complex than its formal Atlantic empire, as much black as white, as much an extension of Africa as of Europe, and with the economy of British North America tightly intertwined with that of the West Indies.[12] By 1760, some twenty-three colonies with 1.3 million whites and 646,000 blacks, plus a portion of the Native Americans who lived in the continent's interior, made up a world that reached from Ireland to the North American mainland to the Caribbean and to the slaving stations of the African coast. Historians have typically grouped the colonies of British America into distinct if loosely defined regions, including the Atlantic islands, the New England colonies, the Middle Atlantic colonies, the Chesapeake Bay, the Lower South, and the West Indies.

Approaching matters from the point of view of wealth and population, historian Trevor Burnard suggested an important variation. In his view, the colonies from Delaware to Massachusetts, which were the least wealthy of British North America, with 60 percent of the population and 30 percent of the total wealth, formed one distinct group. What he called the "South," from Maryland through North Carolina, enjoyed the best claim to be the middle of British America with over one-third of the population and nearly 30 percent of the total wealth. The economy of the Carolinas, and by inference Georgia, was more nearly similar to that of the West Indies and a counterpoint to that of the more northern colonies: poor in people, especially white people, but rich in property. On a per capita basis, including all blacks and whites, South Carolina and the West Indies were two and a half times more wealthy than the people in his definition of the South.[13] If the lowcountry was in fact an intimate part of the mainland whose diverse people shared considerably more in terms of values and practices than they differed, the region must nevertheless be understood as a society shaped by forces that pulled in sharply different directions.

Beginning its odyssey as a virtually bankrupt colony, Georgia came into its own as a plantation economy at the very moment when the British West Indies reached its golden age of prosperity.[14] The sugar islands were the most dynamic, wealthy, and diplomatically significant part of the empire.

The sugar revolution had transformed the small strings of islands forming the Greater and Lesser Antilles into producers of the single most valuable commodity imported into Great Britain. The plantation complex represented huge capital investments, massive concentrations of Africans, a relentless monoculture, and an orientation toward exports that meant an economic life dependent on shipping and marketing. The region became the "forging ground" for the institution of slavery, and its larger towns were the primary destinations for Africans. Modestly endowed North Americans looked on the wealthy planter oligarchy that dominated life in the islands with a sense of awe and wonder. A high percentage of the richest became absentee proprietors in England, and the average wealth per white person towered far above that for the mainland, a stunning £1,042 versus £46.[15]

The plantation complex that stretched from Brazil to the Lower South sank deep roots into Georgia's soil within a very short period of time. Philip D. Morgan went a step further when he asserted, "While lowcountry Georgia possessed the territorial extent of a mainland colony, it bore many of the features of a Caribbean island."[16] The culture and example of the sugar islands, especially those of the Lesser Antilles, exercised a profound influence over the province. As Jack Greene argued, slavery in the lowcountry followed a model worked out in the sugar culture of Barbados. At the same time, the lowcountry developed its own distinct features. Georgia's entry into the British Atlantic was not an uninventive imitation of the Carolina experience, as if there were only one approach to the challenges of settling the lowcountry. The colony necessarily borrowed institutions and practices from different periods of Carolina's history and combined them in creative and freewheeling ways. The distinctive features of the Georgia lowcountry may have been a matter of nuances and shadings, but these subtle and not so subtle differences with Carolina combined to create a powerful new reality.

Chapter 1 begins by asking what groups made up Georgia during the late 1740s, how they were distributed, and their relationship with the transatlantic economy. Those questions are vital because there was not one Georgia at the end of the trusteeship period but three distinct economies, three types of interaction with the Atlantic world, three sets of aspirations built around Savannah, Augusta, and Frederica. The end of the trustees' charter was a moment of high expectation and genuine fear on the part of the artisans, former indentured servants, shopkeepers, and minor officials who were the inhabitants of the colony. How elements of this diverse population made their way into the new planting elite after 1750 is the subject of chapter 2. Attracted by the prospect of rich new rice lands, ambitious and tough Carolinian planters brought precious labor, capital, and expertise, but veterans of the trustee period remained in control of the process of land distribution and selected not only Carolinians but Georgians and West Indians.

As it embraced the plantation model, the Georgia lowcountry faced an awkward dilemma. Laying the foundations for rice plantations was not a quick process, and during those early years little rice was exported. For a colony with no maritime tradition, the beginning of overseas trade was problematic. Chapter 3 discusses how the Caribbean provided the engine of economic growth and remained critical to the involvement in trade of a broad spectrum of people, from planters and timbermen to petty retailers and backcountry farmers. The lure of the West Indian market drew a wide range of Georgians into the use of Africans for timbering, and the trade offered a means for spreading a modicum of wealth throughout the colony. During the royal period, commerce with the Caribbean accounted for one-half of the colony's shipping, and the waterfront of Savannah, with its high percentage of black sailors, reflected that reality. Chapter 4 considers the capital as a town that reflected traits characteristic of the Caribbean in terms of waterfront, occupational profile, and relationship of blacks to whites and suggests that, economically and culturally, lowcountry Georgia faced south and east rather than to the north. Unlike the commercially prosperous South Carolina, Georgia was considerably less integrated into the North American mainland.

Chapter 5 takes up the question of who led the colony into overseas trade and how connections in the Atlantic world were made. Savannah may have begun as a commercial outpost of Charles Town, but it showed considerable independence in developing its own set of relationships. Although a thin layer of merchants and retailers stepped out of the trustee period, the import-export merchants in Savannah and Sunbury were primarily recent arrivals, mostly Scots, who felt part of a wider world and never acquired strong ties with their counterparts on the North American mainland. Connected throughout the Atlantic, they represented an elite that proved adaptive to local culture but remained loyal to a larger vision of the British empire and its benefits. During the last decade of the colonial era, they were importing Africans at a higher rate than traders in either Virginia or Maryland, so that Georgia emerged in second place next to the largest slave mart in North America, Charles Town. Chapter 6 considers what can be learned from this frontier outpost about the components of supply and demand for black slaves in transatlantic markets. Seen through the eyes of the newly empowered merchant community, the challenge was to balance the supply of labor from Africa, the West Indian market, and Charles Town with the inflow of enslaved labor from migrating planters. Savannah traders controlled few of the decisions about supply and had to react to what British slavers and West Indian merchants thought about demand in this newly developed outpost. Yet they juggled myriad factors and managed the inflow of malnourished and physically damaged "cargos" to ensure a rough equivalence of supply and demand while guaranteeing the precious outflow of hundreds of thousands of pounds sterling from the debtor colony.

Chapter 7 compares Georgia's experience in creating plantations with that of the British Caribbean and describes how the colony followed a similar evolution. The true frontier in terms of rice culture in the lowcountry was the Savannah River, always difficult to manage and late in being developed. Savannah's merchants played the lead role in introducing the costly and involved tidal flow method of cultivation, which changed the nature of class relations in the lowcountry. Open to new technology, they were instrumental figures in a highly adaptive economic culture. A related issue concerns the question of African agency in the development of rice culture. That question takes on a different meaning in a colony where one-quarter of the black population came from an adjacent province and were experienced cultivators while the planters who carried them were knowledgeable farmers. The Georgia experience does not fit neatly into the image of the transfer of an entire rice culture from the west coast of Africa as opposed to what was more likely a pragmatic fusion of practices and technology both African and European in origin.

The emergence of a rice market in Savannah gave export merchants unusual leverage within the economy and produced a system that differed in several respects from that in Charles Town. Chapter 8 considers the contrasting features and how a small town in the lowcountry inserted itself into the great international rice market at a fortuitous moment. The export of rice, together with deerskins, generated a veritable flood of goods from Great Britain. How a mass market for imported manufactures came into existence in Georgia touches on the larger issue of mass consumption in North America. Chapter 9 focuses attention on the kinds of goods imported compared to South Carolina, characteristics of the distribution network, and different types of consumers within the colony. Expressed in terms of the individual white person, Georgians were purchasing quantities of British merchandise on a level close to that of South Carolina, a puzzling development in a frontier province that in no way approached the wealth of its neighbor. Unraveling that conundrum holds the key to other issues. Chapter 10 considers the importance of the trade in deerskins in terms of its percentage of total exports, imports, and credit in London. In Georgia, rice and hides went hand in hand, each serving the other. Together they supported the rising stream of merchandise flowing out of Britain. The chapter argues that deerskins provided the necessary margin that floated the entire economy and made possible the high levels of consumption for whites as well as serving the demand of Creeks. Within that trade, the large import-export merchants came to rely on rum as a necessary ingredient in the exchange, tying sugar plantations, natives, and English consumers into one vast network. How the deerskin trade ballooned into an important underpinning of Georgia's overall web of credit is part of that story.

From 1750 to 1775, Georgia's population grew from two thousand people to more than forty thousand, in rice exports from a few hundred barrels to over twenty-three thousand, and in shipping from fifty-one vessels to well over two hundred.[17] "Such a rapid progress in population, agriculture, and commerce, as no other country ever equaled in so short a time," the chief justice of Georgia wrote from the confines of a tiny room in London at the climax of the Revolution. Anthony Stokes was puzzled and angered by the ingratitude of Georgians who had lived in a land where "justice was regularly and impartially administered—oppression was unknown—the taxes levied on the subject trifling—and every man that had industry became opulent."[18] The story of Georgia's rapid growth holds lessons on many fronts: the way a colony created to replicate distinct features of British society reinvented itself in a short space of time and acquired many of the characteristics of the British Atlantic world; how a frontier where Carolinians played so large a role earned its own distinctive character; the manner in which its commercial leadership, benefiting from a lack of counterbalancing forces within the colony, pushed the economy further and deeper into the Atlantic world than could have been anticipated; and the degree to which the Georgia lowcountry was oriented to the West Indies and the Atlantic as opposed to the North American mainland. In chapter 11, the story concludes with the argument that the American Revolution initiated the process of bringing the lowcountry more fully into the orbit of the North American mainland, a process that would extend well beyond the Revolution. While the Georgia lowcountry remained tied to the West Indies and to the models it offered, the Revolution and its aftermath effectively nationalized this part of the world in terms of outlook, connections, and structures.

A colony that seemed to many a peripheral region, a fledgling province of little weight, serves as an important bellwether of the larger processes of integration into the British Atlantic. However, the telling of this story presents a special challenge. For the royal period, the records for understanding Georgia's relationship with this larger world are comparatively few, the sources vague, and references often contradictory. But new information has become available, old sources are now more accessible, and, together with the wealth of studies that have appeared on the Atlantic world, it is possible to create a coherent story. The goal has been to combine vignettes of people or specific incidents with a better defined statistical portrait of colonial Georgia. This book has limitations, however, and perhaps none greater than the relative absence of women. My focus on the trade and commerce conducted by wholesale merchants makes it difficult to do justice to their role. Yet, this book opens a door on related issues like the consumption patterns of Georgians, the impact of trade on specific ethnic and social groups, and regional variations in the way planter families settled the lowcountry. As consumer products flooded the American markets, Georgians retained their orientation of looking to the south and east rather than to the north. The Anglo American world of commerce that emerged after 1750 involved the whole of British America, not merely the North American mainland.

Chapter One

The Three Georgias

In 1749, a former miller and part-time bricklayer, Isaac Young, was one of the few farmers still actively planting on the Savannah River, and he continued year after year in adverse conditions on marshy soil. Most settlers nearby had ceased operations years before when the death or flight to South Carolina of their indentured servants created a desperate shortage of labor and the cost of cultivation proved exorbitant. Arriving in 1736 with a wife, seven children, and one indentured servant, Young was technically an "adventurer," someone who paid his own way over, but his resources were modest. Granted acreage on a small tract by the London-based trustees, he and his family fell sick, a child died, and the rest survived because a nearby planter with means took pity and supplied them with food while Young found work as a bricklayer. Asking for assistance from the trustees, he gamely pledged, "I hope yet to gett a Livelihood in ye Colony my family being most of them able to work and are bred up in Countrey Business from their Cradle." Marginal figures like millers seemed condemned to failure in a setting where, if disease did not consume them, the marshy riverbanks of the Savannah, ill suited to European farming techniques, were sure to do so. The nearby planter soon decamped for South Carolina and an agricultural system based on slavery. With virtually no white labor available at an affordable price, Isaac Young made ends meet by buying horses in South Carolina as an agent for the colony and by laying bricks in town.[1]

While New England was enjoying a boom in fishing and trade, while the Chesapeake Bay region was entering its golden age with tobacco, while South Carolina had developed rice into a cornucopia of "Carolina gold," and while the Caribbean had become the wealthiest region in British America thanks to sugar, the youngest colony in North America, Georgia, found itself struggling for existence. Since its creation in 1733, the province had labored to feed itself, had few large farms much less plantations, suffered from the expense of white labor, possessed no commercially viable crop, and enjoyed little place in the deerskin trade other than as a conduit of skins to its next-door neighbor. The irony was painful. Born out of a philanthropic vision, Georgia was meant to be not merely a model colony but a model society for Britain where the "decayed tradesmen" and "worthy" poor of the mother country would become a society of yeoman farmers who found moral redemption in subsistence farming.[2] In 1732, James Oglethorpe and other philanthropists in London seized on long-current ideas for planting a colony south of the Savannah River and obtained a charter from King George to accomplish goals that were at once humanitarian, military, and commercial. Twenty-one trustees gained extensive powers over this courageous if ill-conceived experiment. Instead of a plantation economy focused on high returns, the maximum exploitation of labor, and the commercialization of staple commodities, the new colony represented a commitment to small farms, white labor, and a heavy-handed paternalism, a stunning rejection of the Carolina and Caribbean models. By the close of the 1740s, it stood in a lonely spot. Of all the colonies in British North America, this frontier province was the only one to forbid chattel slavery, the only one to place strict limitations on land ownership, the only one to lack a genuine provincial government.[3]

The dilemma was exacerbated by the fact that there was not one Georgia in 1749 but three distinct entities that coexisted uneasily, two of them vying to maintain their autonomy, the other seeking to assert its dominance. Three different economies existed, three types of interaction with the Atlantic economy, three sets of aspirations. The first centered in Savannah, a struggling town of artisans, shopkeepers, and minor officials that lacked an economic rationale and barely kept afloat with hard currency flowing from London. The second centered in Frederica on St. Simons Island, where a regiment of His Majesty's troops resided whose expenditures anchored the economy in the southern part of the colony. The third was a tiny enclave built around Augusta, a frontier trading post located up the Savannah River whose Indian merchants, traders, and packhorsemen were effectively Carolinians working for Charles Town merchant houses. Georgia was no more than a strip of coastal marshland that stretched from the mouth of the Savannah River to that of the Altamaha, a distance of sixty-five miles, and extended into the interior only as far as tidal waters influenced the flow of rivers, some twenty-five to thirty miles. Augusta in turn was an isolated settlement perched on the convergence of trading paths one hundred fifty miles up the Savannah and existed only by the tolerance of native peoples, knowledgeable consumers of English merchandise. When the trustees removed the ban on slavery the following year, the colony was supremely unprepared to embrace a plantation economy based on the Carolina and Caribbean models.

Located on a forty-foot bluff overlooking the Savannah River about seventeen miles from the ocean, the town of Savannah remained true to the principal reason for the creation of Georgia—the generous impulse to provide a safe and prosperous haven for the poor and dispossessed of England and for persecuted European Protestants. In February 1733, Oglethorpe had arrived with sixty-eight men, including a miller, carpenter, baker, cordwainer, apothecary, "Peruke-maker" and joiner; forty-four women; and twenty-two children. The women were overwhelmingly wives, mothers, and daughters.[4] Sixteen years later, Savannah was still an extension of this vision. Although its population was now over seven hundred, most were former "charity settlers" and indentured servants sent out at the expense of the trust, and "adventurers" who had paid their own way over but had few resources. Walking along Bay Street facing the river, where the best commercial property was to be found, one would have encountered the owners of lots who reflected the relatively flat profile of the population: a successful carpenter, a mariner who deftly moved between legal and illegal activities, a simple laborer, a clerk to the governing council, a "victualler" and shopkeeper, a shipwright, and "Mother" Penrose, who ran a tavern serving sailors, travelers, and locals while trading goods secured by her husband.[5] Artisans, craftsmen, and minor officials dominated the scene to the detriment of the shopkeepers, merchants, and others who usually made up the mercantile sector of an eighteenth-century town. The ineffective trustees wrung their hands and decried Savannah's "decaying condition."[6] "Let our miserable circumstances speak," the leading merchant quietly observed.[7] The royal surveyor of the southern colonies recalled of his arrival in 1751 that he "might have bought at that time with twenty Pounds Sterling near half the City," and if he was exaggerating to make a point, there was substantial truth to his charge that the town was economically stagnant.[8]

Constructive engagement with the Atlantic world was no easy matter. Although by 1749 the War of Austrian Succession was over and Spanish Florida no longer posed a threat, the economy remained stagnant, no crop was grown for export, and little shipping occurred at the lone public dock.

In a town of several hundred people, shopkeepers existed by retailing a limited number of goods at high prices or simply by bartering their wares. One of the first Jewish settlers, Abraham Minis, retreated from a venture with Jacob Salomon of New York City to concentrate on providing food, drink, and merchandise in a combination tavern, inn, and store.[9] Lending a touch of the Caribbean world, Captain Caleb Davis sailed his vessels into town from nearby Beaufort, South Carolina, brought needed provisions, carried lumber to the West Indies, and at one time advanced cash to the general's regiment on St. Simons.[10] Davis set up on one of the best lots on Bay Street a trading store run by a dark-skinned woman thought to be a slave. The secretary to the trustees noted that she laid out his cloths, looked after his linen, and effectively ran his life, "and whenever he ordered any Parcel of Silver to be weighed out for any Use," she carried out the measurements.[11] Placed in a store on the Bay and "having obtained good Knowledge of his Business," this woman helped control the access of Savannahians to imported articles. Davis defied conventions in a town more interested in his West Indian goods than his reputation as a part-time pirate.

One partnership showed signs of being able to compete in transatlantic trade. Coming to Georgia as a missionary with the evangelist George Whitefield at age twenty-three, James Habersham was one of the few to possess experience in the Atlantic economy and to understand how networks of merchants, traders, and entrepreneurs operated.[12] As a teenager, he had been apprenticed to his uncle, a wholesale grocer in London, and served as manager of two sugar refineries. He negotiated for hogsheads of sugar from West Indian suppliers, serviced markets on three continents, and knew something of bills of lading, customs receipts, and how to write letters to suppliers and customers. Habersham's able direction of Whitefield's Bethesda Orphanage for children in need, the largest capital project in the colony, demonstrated his extraordinary skill at working with limited resources.[13] Francis Harris had ventured to Georgia as an aspiring merchant in the employ of the trustees and served as manager of the public store. In 1744, Harris joined with the twenty-nine-year-old disciple of Whitefield to purchase a schooner from Bethesda and set up a store near the Bay where, according to one observer, they "[kept] large Stores, as well as dry Goods and eatable provisions, and [made] great profit."[14] The partners' prompt payment of invoices in Charles Town impressed merchants accustomed to the difficulties of collecting debts in this notoriously uncreditworthy province;

their ability to arbitrage money bills coming out of Frederica for Carolina currency spoke to their grasp of the intricacies of currency transactions; and their search for a correspondent in London demonstrated their commitment to direct ties with the homeland.[15]

Not only had the trustees crippled the development of trade with their restrictive policies but a booming Charles Town exercised an iron grip over the commercial life of Savannah, consciously and unconsciously preventing the emergence of a balanced economy. In supplying the hoes, axes, cloth, and foodstuffs the colony needed, Carolina merchants charged as much as a 60 percent markup during the war years and converted Savannah's shopkeepers into glorified commission agents who could do no more than tack on a modest 2.5 percent commission. A disgruntled customer accused the largest store in town, Harris & Habersham, of being run by men "who buys [*sic*] everything at Second Hand of the Merchants in Charlestown, Having never imported a Shillings worth themselves from any part of Europe, or from any where else that I ever heard of."[16] When goods were purchased in a town like Philadelphia, Savannahians were forced to order through a Charles Town merchant or pay the cost of shipping to Charles Town and having the goods unloaded and stored in a warehouse, and then pay an additional insurance premium when they were carried to Savannah.[17] "It is difficult and sometimes dangerous to have things brought from Charles Town," the Reverend Bolzius, pastor of the German settlement of Ebenezer, grumbled, "because the ship crews are generally careless with the goods entrusted to them. They bring everything in open boats or pirogues; and, because they are sometimes fourteen days underway from Charles Town to Savannah, much is spoiled or damaged by the rain."[18] Once in Savannah, the story did not end. The lone wharf was too short, poorly maintained, and lacked store or shelter for cargos in transit. Goods had to be immediately carted up the forty-foot embankment for storage. Seventeen years after the founding of the colony, Savannah remained a primitive location for trade.[19] The agricultural sector, built around small farms, indentured servants, and charity settlers without farming experience, remained in shambles. Faced with poor harvests in 1744, 1747, and 1749, the colony was unable to feed itself and humbly supplicated South Carolina for grain and cattle.[20]

Frederica represented a vastly different world. The southern part of Georgia, from the Ogeechee River to the Altamaha, constituted a semi-autonomous region and acknowledged the rule of Savannah not only with ill grace but at times with open defiance. In setting up the town of Frederica on St. Simons Island in 1736, James Oglethorpe had assumed power over every phase of civilian and military life, and when he returned from England as the commanding general of a regular army regiment, he made Fort Frederica the hub for British military operations along the southern frontier. Less than pleased with Oglethorpe's independent ways, the trustees called into being a governing body in Savannah, awkwardly named the Board of the President and Assistants, and appointed as its head their hardworking but ineffectual secretary, William Stephens, and the three bailiffs of the town. For the next several years, a strong military presence confronted a weak civilian government, and Oglethorpe's successor, Major William Horton, became the dominant authority in the Southern District.[21]

The commander of the Forty-Second Regiment of Foot, stationed on St. Simons Island, was polite in his communication but resistant to obeying orders emanating from Savannah. The governing magistrates complained about Horton's refusal to honor summonses from Savannah courts, his private diplomacy with the Creeks, the illegal privateering sponsored by the commander, the questioning of the magistrates' authority at every turn, and indeed the fact that the Southern District conducted itself like an autonomous region.[22] The major commanded approximately five hundred men whose presence represented nearly 20 percent of all whites in the colony; the expenditures of his regiment pumped thousands of pounds sterling into the local economy; and he enjoyed the loyalty of settlers on the nearby mainland, who looked to him for sustenance and support.[23] The boom town of Frederica had grown up in the shadow of the tabby fort, with approximately 150 inhabitants, including blacksmiths, wheelwrights, carpenters, shoemakers, bakers, shopkeepers, and especially merchants, who exercised considerable power given the volume of provisions and supplies required by the regiment.[24] During those heady days, St. Simons merchant Henry Manley reproached the citizens of Savannah "for a Pack of Fools to stay and starve, when at Frederica there was money enough, and everybody paid their money upon asking."[25] His auditors may have privately agreed. A sloop from New York sailed into the capital with a full offering of merchandise and provisions: "Wherefore, after some few Things of least Value were taken off his Hands, [the master] designed to proceed with the Bulk of his Loading to the Army in the South, consisting of Flour, Rice, Biscuit, strong Beer, Wine, &c," the secretary of the trust growled.[26]

While Savannah struggled to gain its economic footing, the redcoats enjoyed an artificial prosperity, entertained grandly, and consumed quantities of precious corn, peas, rice, flour, and clothing. Not only did the regiment constitute the largest single market for goods and services, but the commissary at Frederica possessed the means to settle accounts. The commanding officer issued paper known as "Oglethorpe's money notes," bills to be redeemed by the War Office and bearing the government's imprimatur. The notes constituted the largest source of currency in the colony and traded at par value in Savannah, Charles Town, and the northern colonies.[27] In addition to the regular troops, the British government made extensive payments to boatmen, rangers, laborers, a company of Highland Independent Rangers drawn from the settlement at Darien, Creek Indians, and suppliers of food, who lined up to feed the garrison. Boat builders cheered when Oglethorpe purchased virtually every boat along the coast and employed Georgians for the crews. If South Carolina's merchants had scooped up the bulk of the lucrative trade in provisions during the war years, Georgia's shopkeepers were now sharing in the cornucopia. The regimental commander allied himself with Mary Musgrove Matthews Bosomworth, daughter of an English trader and Creek mother, who was struggling to balance the competing roles she had played earlier in the life of the colony—interpreter and negotiator for Oglethorpe, cultural broker, Indian trader, businesswoman in an age when few women dared enter the counting room. When Mary Bosomworth claimed ownership of an extensive stretch of Indian land—Ossabaw, St. Catherines, and Sapelo islands—Horton gave his wholehearted endorsement, to the consternation of Savannah's magistrates, who were appalled at the violation of a British law forbidding the alienation of Indian territory to private citizens.[28] The artificial prosperity, however, could not last. Once the War Office began scaling back its financial commitment, the balance of power between Frederica and Savannah began shifting, and the governing magistrates could turn their attention to the longer-term relationship with the upcountry.

The third "Georgia" resided in the frontier trading post of Augusta, on the Savannah River 150 miles in a direct line from the capital and some 230 miles following the snake-like turns of the river, at a point where the upper and lower trading paths into Creek territory intersected. The post existed at the express desire of the Creeks as a way of satisfying their growing demand for an increasingly sophisticated array of British, continental, and Asian goods. James Oglethorpe had founded the modest trading prost as a way to stake out a position in the leather trade and cut into South Carolina's commerce, which was instrumental in providing that colony with precious earnings for investment in a plantation economy.[29] Once London ruled that half the traders working in the new province must hold a Georgia license, companies based in Charles Town shifted their operations from New Windsor on the Carolina side of the river to this area where several key trading paths converged. Its settlers were mainly Carolinians who changed nothing in their mode of operation. Hundreds of men, one trader claimed with exaggeration, gathered at Augusta for the spring rendezvous of the traders returning from Indian country with their packhorses piled high with hides. Large boats carried their pelts directly to Charles Town, sailing past Savannah with scarcely more than a glance at the pathetic condition of the port.[30] Ironically, the colony's wealth was centered in Augusta, not Savannah, in the primitive warehouses of a frontier trading post where the inventories of deceased traders during the 1750s spoke to the high stakes involved: Daniel Clark at £2,969 sterling; William Sludders at £1,714; John Pettygrew, £1,063; and Lachlan McIntosh, £1,097.[31]

Essentially a warehousing center from which traders took off with loaded packhorses for native towns, Augusta was the sign and seal of the frontier economy that dominated the upper part of the colony. It was also a visible expression of the Carolinian stranglehold on commerce that extended to the banks of the Mississippi. The seven largest firms, all Carolinian, combined into one loosely organized "monopoly," Brown & Rae, to set the terms of trade in a fundamentally chaotic business. Competition in the upcountry was cutthroat, and the abuses of traders notorious. In a world where few rules existed and the system of licensing was widely abused, Brown, Rae and Company assigned traders to specific towns, established a standard for dressing deerskins, attempted to limit the abuse of rum, and set the expected rate of exchange.[32] "The powerful Company at Augusta seem[s] to look upon the whole Trade of the Creek Nation as their undoubted Right," one competitor grumbled, "and whatever Part they are deprived of they are apt to imagine an Encroachment upon their Property and that in all Matters regarding the said Nation, their Advice and Opinions ought to be decesive."[33] The authorities in Savannah were in agreement and accused the company of monopolizing the Indian trade. The partners studiously avoided Savannah and Savannahians, and, in return, the magistrates of Savannah threw their efforts into convincing London that no storekeeper or merchant in Augusta should have a license to trade, only traders who went into Creek or Cherokee country.[34] If Frederica exemplified the strategic reasons for creating Georgia and if Savannah stood for the humanitarian aims, Augusta underlined the commercial advantages inherent in a new outpost on the margins of the British empire. While deerskins were not silk or wine as envisioned in the original plan, they represented the kind of commodity London's merchants coveted, all the more so since a significant market existed on the continent.

At the end of the decade, Georgia's population bespoke a crippled economy. It remained at 1,700 white people and an estimated 300 blacks, essentially where it had been at the beginning of the decade, at least in terms of whites.[35] While South Carolina's white population had grown by two-thirds in size during that time, its neighbor's barely held even. Milton Ready estimated a mortality rate as high as 30 percent for the population as a whole during the early years and presumably higher for charity settlers and indentured servants, who suffered from lesser access to nutritional foods.[36] The population deserted the countryside for the towns and large villages where people who were originally bakers, carpenters, and wheelwrights struggled to reestablish their earlier occupations. As many as two-thirds of the white residents in the colony now resided in Savannah, Frederica, and Augusta or the villages of Darien and Ebenezer, an estimated 1,150 out of 1,735 people, leading to the irony of a frontier settlement concentrated in urban areas.[37] To a greater extent than in South Carolina, each Georgia town reflected a radically different slice of the Atlantic world: a lifestyle built around the needs of a full regiment of the royal army in one town; in another, Scottish Highlanders who spoke their own language and created a fiercely self-contained society; in a third, a faithful re-creation of German peasant culture; in the largest settlement, an English town flavored by a heavy German presence; and, in the fifth, a frontier trading post where traders of a rough-and-tumble background lived and worked within two vastly different cultures.[38] Each reflected a particular economy not duplicated elsewhere.

By the early 1740s, the coast of Georgia was virtually free of a native presence. Decades before, Carolinians had allied with a succession of natives to conduct slaving expeditions against the many bands that populated the Southeast, and then turned on each in cynical fashion, from Westos and Savannahs to Yamasees and Muskogees. The Southeast became a "shatter zone" as small groups disappeared or sought refuge in sturdier units. In 1715, the Yamasee War produced alliances between various native groupings that killed over four hundred Carolinians and ended with the deaths of substantially more natives. The depopulated strip of land from the Savannah to the St. Marys River served as mute testimony to the far-reaching effects of this latter-day version of the "Columbian cataclysm."[39] Alongside the kaleidoscopic mix of Europeans in the 1730s were over one hundred Yamacraw natives who lived for a time at a village not far from Savannah, a handful of Uchees located above the German Salzburgers at Ebenezer, a small village of Chickasaws below Augusta, Muskogee hunters who wandered close to the coast and were not reluctant to shoot cattle rather than deer, and occasional native women whose function was clearly that of permanent servitude.[40] The Yamacraws whom the settlers first encountered were a collection of refugees, outcasts, and opportunists primarily from among the Lower Creeks, whose venerable leader Tomochichi became a trusted friend and councilor to Oglethorpe.[41] When he died in 1739, his followers scattered to other locations.

The coast bore a stark resemblance to the islands of the Caribbean where Old World diseases and the ruthless commitment of Europeans to enslave and export Indians had decimated the native population. White Georgians along the water's edge lived in a demographic cocoon that kept them ignorant and uncomprehending of the complexities of native societies on the periphery of their small region. When Mary Bosomworth and a band of Lower Creeks descended on Savannah to claim a share of the presents sent by Britain as its stake in intercultural diplomacy, residents were thrown into terror. The ensuing scene, a mixture of bathos and fear, bespoke the failure of the local magistrates to comprehend the cultural world of Native Americans, their inability to conduct negotiations in the way that Carolinians had long mastered, and their all-consuming desire to marginalize a mustee woman whose utility had lessened.[42]

In these early years, Georgia was a place of casual borders and blurred lines of authority, where differing cultures, communities, and individuals intermingled in ways not yet hardened into unchangeable categories. The condition of European women illustrated the unusual flexibility that characterized this setting. The trusteeship proved to be a liberating experience for some women who were involved in a wide range of vocational pursuits, including retailing, tavernkeeping, winding silk thread, and laboring on garden farms. Social systems were supple, and lines of authority were indistinctly drawn in a world where labor was a scarce commodity.

Women were a little more than a third of the immigrants recorded between 1731 and 1741; most came in family groups; and death was ever present. Marriages often ended quickly and cohabitation outside wedlock was a frequent occurrence. Tolerance for relationships that fell outside the European norm was high, creating opportunities for low-status women to marry above their rank in the Old World. Yet marriages were, in the words of historian Ben Marsh, irregular, distorted, and unconventional. Families became diffuse, ethnically mixed, and fragmentary and, if a woman could not find a mate, she was exposed to the harsh economic realities of the time.[43]

The year 1749 was a moment when people sensed that economic realities were causing those categories to take a more definitive shape. Bit by bit the colony was making connections in the Atlantic economy that went well beyond the flow of hard currency from the home country, spilling over the boundaries of empire. Mariners and merchants who supplied the colony were among the first to intrude into the self-contained world designed by Oglethorpe and the trustees. "Many a merchant deals in contraband goods with Spaniards and Frenchmen in the West Indies without bad conscience," the Reverend Bolzius reported to his superiors in Germany.[44] From nearby Beaufort, South Carolina, Savannah attracted Captain Caleb Davis, an ambitious, unscrupulous man who made the town his base for carrying lumber to the West Indies and returning with sugar and molasses. In between, he traded with the enemy in St. Augustine and allowed the Spanish governor and other officials to run up debts—including a former slave, Captain Francisco Menendez, leader of the free blacks who had fled Carolina to form the community of Gracia Real de Santa Teresa de Mose, the only home for free blacks in North America.[45] In Savannah, where slavery was banned, he kept a mulatto mistress for all to see. In Beaufort, he dealt in slaves for profit, buying and selling for the local market. In St. Augustine, he traded with a free black community organized to fight the British. These were not compromises that could be sustained for long. After being imprisoned in Savannah, he spent part of the 1740s privateering on behalf of the British commander at Frederica off the Florida coast and in the Caribbean. He still had a store on the Bay in the 1750s, and he sailed to the West Indies in search of cargo, his very presence a reminder of the fluidity of territorial boundaries and social conventions as well as the opportunities that awaited the colony in southern waters.[46]

The Caribbean, where the sugar revolution had transformed Britain's colonies into the richest in British America, provided the logical market for Georgia. The increasing monoculture of most but not all of the islands denuded the interior hills of scarce wood and restricted the amount of fertile land devoted to provisions. The West Indies had long since turned to North America to meet its needs for wood products and to satisfy the growing demand for food to maintain the fast-expanding slave population. Georgia's prohibition of the importation of rum, at the behest of Creek headmen as well as to satisfy Oglethorpe's obsession with keeping colonists from "Debauchery and Idleness," prevented the colony from participating in the trade for foodstuffs.[47] One adventurer nevertheless laid down plans for bypassing the spirit of the law. In the 1730s, a merchant from Bristol set up a store in Savannah to gain an edge in supplying the colony with hardware and clothing. His ultimate aim was to export lumber to the West Indies and import slaves, if not rum, through his brother on St. Kitts. After the tumultuous battles of the early 1740s when he and other advocates for slavery, dubbed "Malcontents," were checkmated by the uncompromising trustees, Robert Williams moved across the Savannah River to the safety of nearby Beaufort, where he resumed his business.[48] In 1747, the trustees relented and authorized the importation of rum as a way to make it easier for West Indian shippers to pay for Georgia lumber.[49] The most serious proponent of the lumber trade, the firm Harris & Habersham, spent the last half of the 1740s trying to create a market for the lumber milled by the Salzburgers at Ebenezer. James Habersham attributed their failure to do so to the poor conditions of the port, where overflowing water caused boards left on the wharf to twist into unusable shapes, to the absence of shippers willing to carry cargo of such low value, and to the firm's lack of knowledge of market conditions. Shippers avoided the port, he pointed out, because the few items that could be loaded were insufficient to generate enough revenue to cover insurance and freight costs: "We have no Corn, Pease, Rice, Pitch, Tar, Beef or Pork for Exportation. On the contrary we have not yet raised enough for our own consumption."[50]

From the moment he set foot in Georgia, Habersham realized the futility of the system of agriculture and deplored the lack of an export crop. Politically astute, he refrained from openly criticizing the trustees, who clung to their foundering vision. Inspired by hopes of a new beginning for England's underclass, the trustees had thought to plant charity settlers and indentured servants on fifty-acre farms scattered strategically throughout the coastal lands and to provide sufficient resources to enable them to become subsistence farmers. They were to re-create the traditional English farming village while serving as an easily assembled militia to combat Spanish troops and recapture Carolina slaves headed to St. Augustine. Critics found ample material to scoff at. Of the 2,009 charity settlers and servants sent at the expense of the trust by 1747, less than 12 percent had occupations related to husbandry. A high percentage of the immigrants were women, many of them in their late thirties and forties, who were unlikely to provide the labor necessary for the fields and past their prime years for producing children.[51] The fifty-acre plots were too small to become viable farms in wet soil while the predilection of London for assigning settlers to tiny hamlets created as military outposts sealed their fate.[52] "Decayed tradesmen," cosseted by the arcane and often petty regulations of the trustees, struggled to make sense of a terrain that was alternately sandy and marshy, subject to extreme heat, full of pesky insects, and periodically visited by hurricanes.[53] Most of the villages disappeared within the first ten years, and a high percentage of their first residents sought refuge in the few urban centers of the colony. The trustees had created a public store to provide provisions on credit. By 1738, the store's indebtedness exceeded £5,000.[54]

In addition to charity settlers, the trust recruited another kind of immigrant, the adventurer, who could afford to pay his own way across, brought indentured servants, and was thought to possess ambition and determination. Contrary to impressions, Georgia had room for the enterprising and energetic. The granting body in London assigned up to five-hundred-acre tracts to those who committed to provide a servant for every fifty acres awarded. In that first decade, when hopes ran high, 239 adventurers and 685 indentured servants landed in Savannah, a precious addition to the nascent colony where the shortage of labor was crippling.[55] The results were meager. Adventurers put money and labor into large farms on both the Savannah and Ogeechee rivers only to see a few dozen acres come into production, their labor force decimated, and their capital exhausted. Planters blamed the disappointing yields on the poor quality of their indentured servants, although servants could tell another story of mistreatment at the hands of planters. In the early years, many servants died within months of arrival, others fled across the river to South Carolina for better opportunities, and those who remained proved ineffective at laboring in the harsh conditions.[56]

During those difficult years, the colony survived solely because of an extraordinary inflow of capital that was without precedent in the history of British North America. Georgia's role as a defensive buffer against Spanish Florida and the first line of defense for the Carolinas in the lead-up to the War of Jenkins' Ear had emboldened a traditionally parsimonious Parliament to vote £108,000 sterling in the first decade of the colony's existence.[57] With that money, the trust financed the passage of almost two thousand settlers across the Atlantic and provided for the multiple costs of the early stages of settlement. After a chaotic start made all the more difficult by Oglethorpe's erratic spending, the trustees began issuing bills of exchange drawn on an account at the Bank of England; known as "sola" bills, they were thirty-day sight drafts upon the trustees payable within six months of presentation. Between 1738 and 1747, the trust deposited £88,000 in grants made by Parliament and issued £47,000 in sola bills, a conservative model but one that ultimately failed. The bills were never made legal currency and, as soon as they were issued, tended to disappear from circulation in payment of imports. Initially suspicious of these promissory notes, Charles Town merchants accepted the bills only when the process of redemption for pounds sterling proved straightforward. The great beneficiaries were the handful of boat captains who carried over several thousand people, the manufacturers and brokers of dry goods and tools in England, and the mercantile community of Charles Town.[58]

Last on the receiving line were the colonists who worked directly or indirectly for the trust. The list was long: bailiffs, constables, tythingmen, rangers, boat pilots, schoolmaster, public midwife, the "cowpen keeper," and the apothecary. In addition, the local magistrates had to pay the costs of maintaining one hundred or so indentured servants who worked on public projects and provide generous bounties for those engaged in silk production. The magistrates subsidized as many as one-third of Savannah's residents. The shipment of sola bills was invariably delayed, and the shortage of paper currency threw laborers, artisans, shopkeepers, and merchants into crisis.[59] To avoid being financially overextended, Harris & Habersham eventually cut off credit to those holding paper notes from the magistrates, provoking one magistrate to accuse the partners of pawning off secondhand goods, jacking up prices, and reducing credit to "cause an universal Clamour among all People of this part of the Colony and stir them up to an Insurrection."[60]

With the Spanish defeat at Bloody Marsh in 1741 and the demoralization that came in the wake of the debate over whether slavery should be permitted, the extraordinary largesse of Parliament dried up. Over the following five years, Parliament approved a considerably smaller amount, £16,000 sterling for the whole period, and in 1748 and 1749 made no appropriation. The colony was financially adrift. The loss of Parliament's backing was accompanied by the shifting of philanthropic interest of private individuals in Britain, a decline in immigration by adventurers with their servants, and, inevitably, a reduction of the financing that George Whitefield had been able to bring into the colony to underwrite the Bethesda Orphanage.[61]

As shown in Table 1, only the copious defense expenditures flowing out of the War Office forestalled bankruptcy and provided the essential resources for rebuilding the economy. The saving grace was the continuing military spending to maintain the Forty-Second Regiment of Foot on St. Simons Island and, even more important, to keep the militia and irregular units in service after the war had wound down. If the cannons, muskets, powder, and uniforms represented funds disbursed in England, the food, provisions, and salaries paid to soldiers represented money that typically remained in the Lower South. More significant were the continuing payments to irregular troops like the Highlanders; numerous boatmen, sea captains, and their crews; Lower Creeks; and those who supplied food to the army. According to a report submitted at the end of the period, the cost of maintaining the royal troops was around £20,000 per annum and of maintaining the extensive irregular forces, an astonishing £19,500.[62] The military notes that found their way into many a pocket via the Highlanders, boatmen, and storekeepers floated an entire population, at least in the Southern District, and provided substantial support for the Northern District. When the subsidy for "additional troops" drew to an end, Pastor Bolzius rejoiced that "young men [will] have no longer an opportunity to live a loose life at the fortifications, or on the reconnaissance boats. Rather, they will earn their living in a better way by useful work. Maybe it will be easier from now on to find fieldhands for hire."[63]

The disbanding of the regiment in 1749 threatened to unhinge the creaky financial edifice on which the colony rested. In May the final trooping of

TABLE I   Capital Inflow into Georgia, 1733–49, in Pounds Sterling

	Parliamentary Grants	Gifts	Private Capital	Bethesda Orphanage	Defense Expenditure
1733–37	46,000	16,036	20,700	—	—
1738–42	62,000	1,608	7,020	3,358	121,000
1743–47	16,000	800	8,640	2,153	95,000
1748–49	—	—	5,000	N.A.	20,000
Totals	124,000	18,444	41,360	5,511	236,000

Sources: Taylor, "Colonizing Georgia," 121–22; "An account of Oglethorpe's Expenses in America, 1738–1743," James Oglethorpe Papers, Perkins Library, Duke University; "An Account of Money Received and Disbursed for the Orphan House in Georgia by George Whitefield, A.B. Late of Pembroke College, Oxford, 1741" and "A Brief Account of the Rise, Progress, and Present Situation of the Orphan House in Georgia," 1746, both in DeRenne Collection, Hargrett Library, University of Georgia. Total military expenses by the War Office for Georgia were reduced to account for the percentage spent in England on weaponry and supplies.

the colors was held on the parade grounds. Although the governing magistrates offered generous land grants to soldiers who remained, only fifty-two of the several hundred chose to tempt their fate. In addition, the three independent companies of South Carolina militia stationed in Georgia were to be discontinued. Harris & Habersham had contracted for two vessels to sail from London with dry goods and to take on local produce for the return trip, the first time in the history of the colony that vessels had been chartered to carry exports.[64] The firm's calculations were finely calibrated. Habersham planned on a brisk sale of dry goods to the king's regiment on St. Simons and payment in valuable military notes to be used to purchase rice in South Carolina, which was necessary to make up a complete cargo since Georgia had only limited produce to ship. As King George's War wound down, the flow of military supplies and men began to dry up, and in April 1749 came official news of the regiment's disbanding. The final formation at Frederica in May knocked plans askew. Not only did the market on St. Simons disappear, but Harris & Habersham were under contract to purchase a hundred thousand pounds of Indian corn from the Salzburgers of Ebenezer, to be sold to the regiment. Demand for goods at their own store in Savannah shriveled as the entire economy contracted in the face of the regiment's disappearance. Habersham informed the alarmed trustees and reiterated to the accountant for the trust that if they did not pay the sola bills owed, "we must absolutely sink under the Load."[65]

Although James Habersham had reason to worry, he had an insider's knowledge of a hoped-for change. Long an advocate of slavery, he was well aware that the trustees had softened their position and initiated transatlantic conversations that would result in the lifting of the ban. If Georgia were to pass through much the same stages as the sugar islands of the Lesser Antilles, it would do so within a matter of months rather than decades. The jump from indentured servanthood to slavery as a system of labor took place as a result of a single decision made in London by men increasingly disinterested in a colony that had failed to live up to expectations, rather than as a gradual, drawn-out process as planters experimented with supply and demand. Rumors that the trustees were thinking seriously of removing the prohibition on slavery had already sparked a renewed sense of opportunity. Immigrants were beginning to reappear and trade was slowly improving as the lower middling groups in the colony showed resilience and stamina in the face of adversity. Most Georgians, whatever their background, accepted as self-evident the harsh judgment delivered by a leading Malcontent in the heat of battle that "it is as clear as Light itself, that Negroes are as essentially necessary to the Cultivation of Georgia, as Axes, Hoes, or any other Utensil of Agriculture."[66] The fiercely antislavery Salzburgers in Ebenezer and the Highlanders of Darien faded into the background. A schoolmaster loyal to the trustees phrased the reigning attitude simply, "My Lord they are stark Mad after Negroes."[67]

Tragically, the Malcontents had spoken a brutal truth. Newly enslaved Africans were more productive than indentured servants. Blacks could be housed and fed for much less than a white servant, as low as one-quarter of the cost; and, although a servant cost less, about £6 versus roughly £30 for a slave, this difference was more than offset by the short tenure of that servant and the higher productivity of enslaved people. In a classic study, Betty Wood and Ralph Gray compared the economics of servants versus slaves in order to determine the potential profitability of the two labor systems. Not surprisingly, the rate of return for slave-operated farms was considerably higher.[68] The vision of creating a colony based on indentured white labor capable of serving as a military deterrent to the Spanish was not economically viable.

The reality was that blacks had never been completely absent from Georgia.[69] The deerskin merchants and traders in Augusta, a group enjoying a fair degree of autonomy moving goods between that trading post and Indian towns in the interior, carried on their business without reference to London's philanthropic gentlemen and employed an estimated one hundred blacks in the deerskin trade.[70] Below Augusta, in what later became St. George Parish, blacks functioned as drovers and cowboys, herding cattle in the woods or on the trails from the Edisto River in Carolina to the Altamaha. Sent by their masters in Carolina, they rode through the pine barrens rounding up heifers heavy with calves, bringing in cattle ready for slaughtering, and living on their own in the woods for weeks and months at a time.[71] The situation in Savannah spoke to the importance of enslaved labor in maritime activity. Blacks possessed by Carolinians manned the rafts, piraguas, schooners, and sloops engaged in the coastal trade, and there was little way of telling who was free or enslaved and, if enslaved, who belonged to whom. Captain Caleb Davis turned over the management of his store on Bay Street to his mulatto mistress and applauded when she pummeled a first mate who insulted her. According to one source, the trust employed blacks as indentured servants with the intention of releasing them from service at the end of their time.[72] Then too there were Maroon colonies along the banks of the Savannah River made up of slaves who had escaped from their Carolina owners and established encampments, which eluded detection and from which they mounted raids for supplies.[73] In the South, the situation was more defined. Blacks served officers of the Forty-Second Regiment and worked at the manual labor involved in maintaining a fort. Some officers apparently employed black "servants" on private farms they acquired on the mainland.[74]

Africans in Georgia numbered an estimated three hundred people, many of whom were jack-of-all-trades rather than prime field hands or skilled artisans. That total equaled about 17 percent of the white population.[75] For a few brief years, Georgia was a society with slaves rather than a slave society like South Carolina, a place where blacks were one of several forms of labor. In the late 1740s and even into the early 1750s, the enslaved people in the colony constituted a charter generation in the sense that Ira Berlin proposed the term: first arrivals who enjoyed considerable autonomy and acquired a certain familiarity with their owners.[76] Only in a few cases did they function as field hands on plantations. Patrick Mackay, a former

Malcontent who had advocated the introduction of slavery, surreptitiously brought his slaves back across the Savannah River from his Carolina plantation, worked them on his Georgia lands until local magistrates investigated, then hurriedly ferried them to the other side.[77] Some Georgians were willing to accord blacks limited rights. Savannahians bought rum, sugar, molasses, and food from Davis's woman on the Bay without asking questions. When a merchant on Frederica purchased a free black of Curacao who had been captured on the Spanish Main and sold him as a slave, the authorities in Savannah, backed by James Habersham, intervened to secure his release and filed suit against the merchant.[78] According to at least one historian, free mulattoes and mustees intermarried with the Jewish population and with other whites, and their offspring inherited property, received grants of land, and became naturalized British citizens. Negroes purchased as servants by the trust had no more restrictions on their manumission than whites, and their treatment seems to have been equally as benign.[79]

When, in the second half of 1748, the trustees conceded that slavery was inevitable, they ordered local magistrates to assemble a council of notables to discuss the conditions under which the institution might be introduced. In one fell swoop, the grand dream of a white men's colony in the Lower South was pronounced dead. The two councils that met in January and October 1749, although weighted toward Savannah, represented a fair cross section of Georgia's settlers: those on the ship *Ann* with Oglethorpe, military officers from St. Simons, hard-nosed planters from South Carolina, shopkeepers, artisans, James Habersham and Francis Harris, and the Reverend John Martin Bolzius, a notable opponent of slavery. Also among the members were a former miller, a millwright, a shopkeeper, a former linen draper, a mariner, and a surgeon-turned-planter. In recommending the lifting of the ban on chattel slavery, Georgia's leaders pointedly declined to embrace the Carolina model, retaining the illusion that they could manage the number of blacks under white supervision and prevent the "Africanization" of the countryside. The humane and generous spirit that had animated the thinking behind this colony still tugged at consciences that had already made the decision to commit Georgia to the kind of plantation economy that stretched from Brazil to the Lower South. In answer to the question of whether planters should have unlimited power over their slaves, the answer was "unanimously agreed that they should not." On being asked the appropriate punishment for anyone who "maliciously Murders, Dismembers or Cruelly and Barbarously uses a Negroe," the answer was that he should be tried and subjected to the same pains and penalties, "as if he had committed the Crime upon the person of a White Man."[80]

The Reverend John Martin Bolzius, leader of the Salzburgers at Ebenezer and a long-time opponent of slavery, and James Habersham, his patron, exercised a leading role in shaping the replies. Their fingerprints were on the concluding statement: "it is our Inclinations to make the condition of Slavery as easy as may be consistent with the Safety of His Majesty's Subjects, by putting them under the protection of the Laws" and by hoping that people in other colonies would imitate those laws. They saw the new Georgia as a beacon for the rest of North America. On the critical question of the proportion of "labouring white men" to the number of working slaves, the answer was one white to five blacks, a testimony to the desire to avoid creating districts where the ratio was one to eight or nine. The artisans of Savannah, the dominant social group, played a crucial part. They argued that blacks should not work at semi-skilled trades other than as coopers and sawyers on plantations and in the export of produce, but "no Negro Sawyers [were] to be employed in Towns." Nor would an "Artificer, except a Cooper" be permitted to take a black man as an apprentice or instruct him in a trade. Making barrels of rice was approved but not carpentry or other activities that bespoke skilled labor. Composed as recommendations to the trustees only nine years after the implementation of the harsh South Carolina Code, they denoted a society that intended to keep its own identity.[81]

When James Oglethorpe embarked for England for the last time in April 1743, it was with a mixture of frustration and relief: frustration at the repeated blows he had so stoically absorbed and relief that he could put the doomed experiment behind him. Settling into life at his country estate, he scowled at the news about the movement toward slavery and the declining interest among his fellow trustees. However, had he ventured to return in 1749 he would have found much that was recognizable. The average size of land grants for the trustee period through 1749 was still a relatively small eighty-six acres, hardly enough for a planter to establish a viable plantation amid marshland and maritime forest. Significant changes in land tenure had moderated the requirement of tail-male, but a free market in land did not yet exist.[82] While the Spanish threat had disappeared, relatively few enslaved people were within the colony, much less on plantations, despite the frequent finger pointing of officials about their numbers. The much-feared "Negro merchant" of South Carolina remained a distant figure. The one significant industry was the manufacture of silk thread, much as the original philanthropists had envisioned. Mulberry trees dotted the landscape, and hardworking German women of Ebenezer earned good money for their expertise at winding thread. Although the general population had evolved well beyond the "decayed tradesmen" of England, Georgia remained a colony of white men and women of exceptionally modest means; artisans and tradesmen were still the dominant figures in the social landscape. However, three questions that would have thrown Oglethorpe off his stride loomed large. The first was how this atypical population, unaccustomed to crass commercialism, would integrate slavery into a social and economic structure at such variance with Carolina's. The second was how a new set of planters, with profit on their mind and slavery in their plans, would fit into this setting. The third concerned how government would deal with the tenacious regional spirit within the colony and the ways it repeatedly resisted efforts at reform.

Chapter Two

Merging Planting Elites

In March 1750, the Georgia Trust reluctantly bowed to reality and converted all land grants made during the trusteeship from tail-male, or inheritance by the eldest son, to "absolute Inheritance," clearing the way for the emergence of a free market in land. In April, the trust approved a request to the Privy Council to repeal the ban on slavery and permit the "Importation and Use of Negroes" in Georgia.[1] With scarcely a murmur, the central pillars of the plan that once divided the colony into warring factions vanished. In excited tones, word ricocheted around the Atlantic world, from Charles Town and the Caribbean to Britain and beyond. Planters and merchants took note of a likely new frontier modeled on the rice plantations of the Carolina lowcountry and weighed the possibilities. Not surprisingly, they gave only a modest cheer. They well knew that Georgia was an impoverished land, which had no government yet in place and none of the infrastructure necessary for trade.[2] In the months after the long-expected announcement, few settlers would push across the Savannah River. Fewer still came by boat.

Alexander Wylly, from the tiny island of Tortola, was the exception. When he stepped onto the public wharf in Savannah in that year, he came prepared to establish a trading house in a province that had as yet no trade, an audacious act for even the experienced and a foolhardy act for someone in his early twenties. If residents were justified in smiling at his brashness, he possessed two things rare for this fragile colony: capital and connections. Wylly's Scottish uncle figured prominently in the deerskin trade in Augusta and had promised to advance him goods to finance his start. Too, the young man belonged to a network of merchants and retailers who had left Britain for the New World and retained links with each other throughout the Caribbean and North America. His father, a storekeeper in the market town of Colerain, Ireland, had taken the family to Tortola in hopes of breaking into the sugar trade as a supplier of dry goods.[3] If nothing else,

Wylly counted on acting as a conduit for goods shipped up the Savannah to his uncle and taking advantage of that town's potential for cutting into Carolina's deerskin trade. As he marched up the steep incline to the top of the bluff, however, he might have had second thoughts. There was no building under the bluff where captains, crews, and "Negroes" could regroup after a voyage.[4] Nor were customs officials on hand to establish the contents of his schooner on arrival. That function was exercised by the wharfinger, Mrs. Fitzpatrick, a former tavernkeeper who pulled out a sheet of paper with the duties scribbled on it while she checked the goods transported. Hers was a sometime job. As late as 1752, only fifteen vessels entered the colony during the whole year, scarcely more than one a month. The bluff itself, or the Bay or Strand as it was popularly called, remained a broad expanse of sandy soil bordered by an uneven collection of shops, taverns, and private homes, most of them relatively crude structures.[5]

The success of Wylly's bet ultimately depended on the colony's ability to recruit planters and their enslaved workers to transform coastal marsh into productive rice plantations and to compete on international markets. While South Carolina created a planting elite through land grants to waves of immigrants over eighty years, the interim government of Georgia would shape the contours of that colony's elite during a four-year period from 1751 to 1754. In those crucial years, a small body of men made awards while governing Georgia with no legislative check and little direction from London until the first royal governor arrived. Their rise to power was as rapid as it was astonishing. In 1747, James Habersham had been on the outside of political power. He infuriated the magistrates of Savannah individually and collectively by cutting off their credit and criticizing their financial ineptitude as well as by gently suggesting to the trustees that the policies of the trust were misguided.[6] In 1749, the increasingly desperate trustees appointed the thirty-five-year-old merchant to the Board of the President and Assistants. With the resident secretary of the trust as president and the bailiffs of Savannah as his assistants, the board was a weak, timid group, never fully able to establish itself in making grants of land, acting as a local court of justice, or performing basic administrative tasks.[7] Led by a seventy-eight-year-old verging on senility, assisted by a former linen draper who drank too much, and with only one member versed in agriculture or finance, it was a government adrift.[8]

Habersham's standing had risen as the trustees' desperation increased and their recognition of hard realities set in. In the letter conveying news of Habersham's selection, the secretary of the trust lavished praise on how the merchant had demonstrated that "Habits of Virtue, and Industry may be as easily got, as Habits of Vice and Laziness," holding him up as a model of diligence and self-improvement for the rest of the colony.[9] Appreciative trustees elevated this plain-spoken realist to the position of secretary of the province, charged with serving as the eyes and ears of the trust and providing monthly reports.[10] The turnaround was swift. Working behind the scenes, Habersham persuaded London to force into retirement the worn-out president, remove a headstrong member of the board who had supported the Bosomworths, and appoint his own partner, Francis Harris, as well as a long-time ally, Noble Jones. Having arrived on the ship *Ann* with Oglethorpe, Jones possessed impeccable credentials: a master carpenter who became surveyor of land for the province, a surgeon on occasion, captain of the militia, and owner of significant property and slaves. His military insights were well received by Oglethorpe; his land surveys were the basis for the towns of Augusta and Ebenezer; and his surgical work was dictated by common sense and experience. When a purged member muttered that matters "carried the Face more of an Arbitrary Government than a Civil One," many wondered how much truth there was to the charge.[11] They did not have long to wait.

The first challenge to the board came when the trustees called for the election of a representative assembly to discuss the future of the colony in January 1751. It was an unprecedented step for a body that had long resisted calls for self-government.[12] With delegates from Darien, Midway, and Augusta demanding to be heard, regional agendas were very much in evidence. After thirteen of the sixteen delegates appeared, Habersham engineered the election of Francis Harris as speaker, then turned around and secured the removal of three delegates judged to be unfriendly. When remaining delegates showed "some disagreeable Humours," members of the board invited small groups to dinners in their private homes "where they might have a freer Conversation than in Publick, and be a Means of keeping up a good Understanding."[13]

Half-hidden from view was the single most important battle—the question of who was to receive grants of land now that a free market had been established. The calling of the assembly sparked a flood of petitions, many of them submitted by small freeholders who saw the dawning of a new age. Expectations ran high. Certain "independent-minded" deputies, who Habersham grumbled "were weak enough to think they had a power to provide for themselves and Friends too," actively encouraged settlers to lobby the board during the February session. The opening of the political process prodded humbler levels of society—artisans, laborers, simple farmers, and minor officials—to claim their share of the prizes. Petitioners went so far as to ask the assembly to make no grants to "Strangers" until they and their children were provided for: Georgians first, no matter their status, then Carolinians and others. "We have for some Time past been pestered with these unreasonable Petitions from People who we well knew had neither Ability or Inclination to cultivate a Foot of Land," James Habersham told London with uncharacteristic gruffness. He warned that his board was resolved not to make any grant until it knew how far petitioners were capable of improving land and to do so only "in Proportion to their Ability, which has given great Umbrage to many, but a greater Satisfaction to others, who see the Ill consequence to the Province of granted Land lying unoccupied."[14]

The members of the board intended to use their tight control of public land to recruit an elite capable of transforming coastal Georgia into a plantation economy modeled after South Carolina's and to do so as rapidly as possible. It was not an easy or simple process. James Habersham and colleagues on the board were compelled to deal with the demands and needs of Georgians in the colony before 1750 and to smooth over the regional tensions so much in evidence during the preceding decade. The Scots around Darien still constituted a self-contained society, separated from the rest by language, dress, and cattle raising.[15] The army officers from the Forty-Second Regiment of Foot on Frederica who elected to remain behind formed another stubborn special-interest group. Minor government officials in and around Savannah could not be neglected nor could the shopkeepers and more entrepreneurial figures in the town. Around the growing frontier post of Augusta were merchants, traders, and would-be settlers anxious to claim land in a territory that technically did not fall within the boundaries of the colony, although the Creeks chose to look the other way for a time in recognition of the vital role of that post in providing British merchandise.[16]

Despite appearances, these Georgians were not without resources for purchasing enslaved people and making a start in carving out at least modest plantations. As poor and economically bereft as the colony was, small pockets of capital existed. Those precious funds came from the military expenditures that the War Office had made for over a decade along the Georgia coast and were held by a wide range of people, including militia members and boatmen, shopkeepers and government officials.[17] Captain Daniel Demetre, commander of the colony's chief galley, possessed twenty-three slaves in 1755.[18] Moreover, capital was to be found among the deerskin traders in Augusta, who possessed more disposable wealth than any other group in the colony and were acquiring Africans at a rapid rate to man their warehouses and herd their cattle. During those critical years, the board awarded land grants to 130 Georgians who had been present in the colony before 1750, or 42 percent of the 324 petitions received before 1755.[19]

Regional rivalries and local politics were very much in play when the board made its decisions. The district around Darien and Frederica had long been a section whose independent ways were rooted in the society of Highlanders, the autonomy traditionally enjoyed by Oglethorpe's regiment, and widespread support for Mary Bosomworth and her claim to the three islands off the coast. Resentment of Savannah remained very much alive. In a memorial, the Scots around Darien complained bitterly, "We are harassed with Warrants, Judgments, and Executions, not only to the Utmost Rigor of the Law, but sometimes in a very Illegal Manner," and they claimed no settlers had come to their region for two years and no decent outlet existed for crops since it was costly and time-consuming to carry produce to Savannah.[20] The board responded with uncharacteristic diplomacy and made extensive grants of land to the men who signed the memorial, notably members of the families that led the migration from the Highlands in the mid-1730s. Captain John Mohr McIntosh and his three sons, Lachlan, George, and William, emerged as prime beneficiaries.[21] Other Highlanders whose names were on the memorial, most of them illiterate, received favorable treatment. When Angus, William, and Hugh Clark petitioned for large tracts for their cattle farming operations, the minutes of the council broke into an almost lyrical celebration of "Children nursed in, and innured to the Colony."[22]

Twenty officers from Oglethorpe's regiment received five-hundred-acre grants along the Medway and Newport rivers, the very men who had sustained a defiant position toward Savannah during the previous decade.[23] The board noted that three recipients from Frederica were "all Gentlemen of easy Fortunes and very capable of cultivating the Same."[24] Like most officers of the eighteenth century, they possessed independent means typically derived from their families' estates in the homeland. Captain Mark Carr had the wherewithal to establish two plantations in the 1740s, with brick houses, outbuildings, and "servants,"[25] while Captain James Mackay claimed kinship with and perhaps the patronage of the Lords of Reay in Sutherland County in Scotland.[26] If the officer corps was becoming less an aristocratic preserve throughout the eighteenth century, Mackay of Strathy Hall lived up to that image. Becoming one of the largest slaveholders in the colony, he eventually found a seat on the governor's council, tangling with the Habersham clique at a later date. Captain Carr donated the land for the town of Sunbury to create a port that would help planters bypass what he considered the suffocating grip of Savannah.[27] Other officers became pivotal figures in the southern portion of the province.[28] Most never shook off the natural arrogance of the eighteenth-century British officer.[29]

North of the Ogeechee, a very different scene existed. The senior magistrates and their allies in the colony set the tone by helping themselves to generous amounts of land to create an enclave along the Little Ogeechee River, eight miles west of Savannah. Habersham left his mercantile business for Silk Hope plantation, ironically christened for the trustees' dream of producing silk thread, and added two plantations, Forest Dean and Beverly. Other members of the inner circle obtained grants there or along the Savannah River. Knowledgeable Georgians were annoyed and upset by the way the Habershams, Joneses, and others bypassed the limitation of land grants to five-hundred-acre tracts by making claims on behalf of children or relatives.[30] Such hypocrisy did not sit well. Most of the children were under age; some of the relatives never existed. Self-dealing was the coin of the realm for these insiders. When Henry Parker, briefly president of the board, solicited acreage on the Little Ogeechee for his son William Henry Parker, filial pride shone through. "The Board having for some Time past been pleased with the Behaviour and Industry of this Eldest Son of Georgia," the minutes noted, "and believing that it's [*sic*] Patrons would think him intitled to a Birth right, they granted his request."[31]

In evaluating petitions for land, the members of the Board of the President and Assistants did not have the luxury of confining grants to the strong and powerful. They were faced with the necessity of identifying entrepreneurial qualities and backing talented individuals, whatever their origins. Using their knowledge of people, they supported veterans of the trustee period in making the transition to a slave-based economy, men like Isaac Young, a former miller who had despaired of being able to feed his family; Peter Baillou, a shopkeeper who amassed several hundred acres and six enslaved people before his early death; and Peter Morel, a French Swiss Protestant, militia captain, and tavernkeeper on the Bay. The board granted Morel a five-hundred-acre estate on the Savannah River, deeming him a "Man of Resolution."[32] When an artisan vowed that he "designed to leave off his Trade of a Carpenter and employ his whole Strength for the Benefit of his Wife and four Children in the Cultivation of Lands," the board was pleased to grant him choice acreage on the Little Ogeechee.[33]

A few less fortunate received special consideration. When the Salzburgers voiced their fears that they would be eventually swallowed up by the "Great 500-acre Gentlemen late of South Carolina," Habersham intervened to secure them additional land.[34] However, the board had no hesitation about aggressively pruning requests for land from those whom it did not consider "worthy." Arriving in 1744, Englishman Robert Luden served as an indentured servant on the farm of Isaac Young for his term and earned good marks, but when he applied for three hundred acres near Savannah, the board cut him back to one hundred, enough for survival as a yeoman farmer, but far from enough to enter the ranks of planters.[35] With few exceptions, the board held tightly to its position of penalizing "marginal" figures in the land-granting process.

Land grants for Georgians had a defensive reasoning behind them—to mitigate old differences and rivalries and to create a new elite willing to invest in a plantation economy. The grants that the board extended to those outside the colony had a simpler rationale—to attract men of talent and ability who knew rice culture, commanded enslaved workers, and possessed valuable experience in cultivating the marshy terrain of the coast. Emerging from the depression brought about by King George's War, Carolina planters were shipping over fifty-five thousand barrels of rice at a time when Savannah was fortunate to see five hundred cross its lone wharf.[36] Indigo, the blue dye made from the indigo plant, had caught on as a supplementary crop on plantations and become a major commodity for export when it was still virtually unknown in Georgia. Importations of slaves resumed after the lull of the 1740s and were averaging between one and two thousand people a year during the first half of the decade. Charles Town emerged as the largest slave market in North America while Georgia was too new to the trade to make more than a timid appearance in the slave pens of its neighbor.

James Habersham and the board awarded grants to 119 men from South Carolina, or 39 percent of the total in the period 1751–54.[37] For two decades, Carolinians had eyed the lands in this province with a view to claiming choice rice acreage when slavery was legalized. As signs multiplied that the trust was in retreat, several took out grants to test the waters, smuggled blacks into the colony, and, after halfhearted protests from Savannah magistrates, returned to South Carolina or lay low in the inaccessible tidelands. The year 1752 marked the first wave of immigration when Carolinians filed 103 petitions for land.[38] A newly arrived German engineer, William Gerard De Brahm, helped several groups to survey territory around the Newport River and later recalled the "many rich Carolina Planters" who followed their example.[39] If the engineer badly overestimated the number of enslaved people coming into the colony—one thousand by his estimate—he was off only because of the length of time it took to relocate a work force, typically two and sometimes three years or more.

Whether large or small, Carolina rice planters carried with them a unique culture that had evolved out of a common set of experiences. They had learned their craft by laborious experimentation and a willingness to set aside examples based on the English farm. They came to view the soggy swampland of the coast as fertile wetland soil that could be made productive by controlling the water that pooled in swamps. They learned from Africans whose ancestors had been growing rice for centuries and acquired techniques and technology first applied along the rivers and floodplains of Senegambia and Sierra Leone. As historian Max Edelson emphasizes, these planters were persistent experimenters who respected the improvisational character of American farming and willingly fused differing traditions. They were keenly motivated to cut costs and offered the enslaved people a degree of autonomy in the form of time to plant their own gardens, raise fowl, and catch fish in return for pushing responsibility for their own food supply onto their shoulders. Practical men, they walked the swamps, mastered the details of the terrain, and showed themselves willing to exercise direct, managerial authority over their plantations.[40]

The majority of the Carolinians who came by 1755 were Congregationalists, descendants of New England Puritans who had founded the small town of Dorchester on the Edisto River. Ecstatic upon learning of their interest, James Habersham reported to London, "We have had an extraordinary Character of them from All Quarters, which I believe they very justly deserve."[41] During the late seventeenth and early eighteenth centuries, the proprietors of South Carolina had made a vigorous effort to attract oppressed Protestants to the southern parishes, which were lightly inhabited and threatened by the Spanish and their native allies.[42] Answering the call in 1695, the New Englanders established farms where they pursued a modest agricultural agenda, focusing on cattle, timber, and provisions. Of fifty-two families of Dissenters in 1725, forty were small slaveholders.[43] By mid-century, larger planters were taking up surrounding rice lands while younger sons of the Puritans were establishing plantations beyond the area served by the church, threatening the integrity of the community. In 1752, members of the Congregational Church at Dorchester traveled to the swampy marshes between the Medway and Newport rivers to investigate the suitability of the land. When they returned with a glowing report, several dozen men promptly signed a petition asking Habersham and the board for grants.[44] Most were small planters leaving behind an assortment of farm lots of forty-five or fifty acres in exchange for plantations that ranged from two hundred to five hundred acres.[45] Women were among the early planters. Lydia Saunders, a widow with ten slaves, received a grant for five hundred fifty acres, purchased another five hundred, and even when she remarried, she kept her estate distinct from that of her husband.[46] Despite the size of their farms and small plantations, Congregationalists brought with them 326 enslaved people, the largest number of any group from South Carolina, averaging 7 slaves per family. As their first act, they created the Midway Church and set about building an insular community distinguished for its hard work, plain living, and intellectual engagement.[47]

Of the 119 Carolinians who petitioned for land by 1755, only a handful represented the type that the Board of the President and Assistants most prized: the entrepreneurial, freewheeling individual with a large number of enslaved people for whom maximizing profit and status was a high priority and speculating in a broad range of activities was a way of life. The most significant was Jonathan Bryan, a man who had assisted in the founding of the colony, a devoted supporter of Habersham's mentor, the evangelist George Whitefield, and a planter and land speculator of formidable talents.[48] Bryan had been born in St. Helena Parish during the early eighteenth century when its economy still revolved around the deerskin trade and raising cattle was the most prosperous form of agricultural activity. Growing up during the Yamasee War of 1715, he was accustomed to the alarms triggered by natives coming out of Spanish Florida to raid plantations well after the war had drawn down.[49] At age twenty-five, as commander of the Port Royal scout boat, he had greeted Oglethorpe on the banks of the Savannah, provided the settlers on the ship *Ann* with cattle and provisions, and accompanied the future general on his first tour of the islands. Once enslaved Africans were permitted, he was among the first to appear before the Board of the President and Assistants, where James Habersham, linked to him through their mutual involvement in Bethesda Orphanage, looked after his interests.[50] Transporting sixty slaves in 1752, Bryan established what was arguably the first genuine rice plantation on the Savannah River, Walnut Hill, while keeping an active interest in his Carolina holdings.[51] A person of immense energy and limitless ambition, Bryan stood at the beginning of a career that brought him a total of thirty-two thousand acres by grant and purchase in Georgia and South Carolina and more than two hundred fifty slaves whom he worked at one time or another.[52]

Accompanying Bryan were other planters who represented families that had moved into the parishes below the Combahee River after conditions became relatively stable: the two Deveaux brothers, who were sons of a Huguenot from the West Indies instrumental in the introduction of indigo; Stephen Bull, from a prominent political family and grandson of a leading deerskin and Indian slave trader during the early eighteenth century; John Mullryne, a merchant-planter from Montserrat who had settled in Beaufort; the Gibbons brothers, sons of a settler from New Providence in the Bahamas; the tightly knit Butler family whose Baptist faith gave them a special identity; and the Bourquins, French Swiss from the failed Purrysburg settlement forty miles up the Savannah River.[53] Virtually all were Dissenters. A small number of merchants left Charles Town for Georgia, perhaps no more than four or five in those first years after 1750. Having typically failed in their businesses, they were looking for redemption on the Georgia frontier. They brought invaluable contacts, considerable expertise, and, in the case of three of them, mortgaged slaves.[54]

In January 1753, the governing board read aloud a petition of Lewis Johnston, "late of the Island of St. Christopher's, setting forth that he was desirous of settling and improving Lands in this colony, and to that End he intended to remove his Wife and Negroes from St. Christopher's as soon as possible."[55] One of the first inhabitants of the West Indies to appear before the board, Johnston electrified his listeners with the announcement that he was bringing a number of slaves and that he represented others eager to obtain tracts. It was a moment whose significance no one in the tiny room misunderstood. Georgians well knew the importance of the Caribbean to South Carolina's economic success and their own impotence by comparison. The trusteeship period had represented a resounding repudiation of the Caribbean world: a commitment to yeoman farming; the absence of Africans; a population composed primarily of artisans, minor officials, and indentured servants; an urban orientation; and the lack of an exportable commodity. By way of contrast, immigrants from Barbados had settled South Carolina and brought with them a social and economic system based on the production of a single commodity, a slave-powered plantation system, a highly stratified social structure, great disparities in wealth, and a high ratio of blacks to whites. In the eyes of the board, Johnston had much to recommend him. From a distinguished Scottish family, he held a degree from the University of Edinburgh, a beneficiary of the best medical education available in the British Isles. Like his father, he had served as a surgeon in the Royal Navy and, then, settling on St. Kitts, married the niece of a well-to-do planter.[56] The board members liked what they sensed of the man—a risk-taking entrepreneur, a God-fearing Calvinist, a physician who still practiced medicine. They responded to his vision for integrating Georgia into the Atlantic world.

An influential group led by Johnston came from St. Kitts, where opportunities were fast shrinking. Unlike Barbados and Jamaica, the Leeward Islands had shown no tendency to turn away from the relentless drive toward sugar monoculture and bore the consequences of an unhealthy concentration in landholdings and a consequent fall in productivity.[57] Johnston came with three other Scots. The following year, Clement Martin Jr., son of a slave trader and sea-captain-turned-planter, left the island for a tract on the Newport River while John Hamm settled on the Savannah. In their train came Clement Crooke, a wealthy planter and merchant who died before the move, but his determined widow, daughter of a Charles Town merchant, took land on Bermuda Island, today Colonel's Island, proved an able planter, and married her daughters to the colony's elite.[58] One young merchant, Robert Baillie, came from Jamaica.[59] During the colonial period, Lewis Johnston and Clement Martin sat on the governor's council, Alexander Wylly served as speaker of the house, and Baillie sat in the assembly. An Anglican missionary sent from England to catechize slaves noted that owners in Georgia were adamantly opposed to his efforts, "especially those who resort to us from ye West Indies," because they believed that "a slave is ten times worse when a Xn, [than] in his State of Paganism."[60]

The development of plantations in the Georgia lowcountry followed a different rhythm than in its northern neighbor. In South Carolina, development took place over a period of eighty years and unfolded in a series of concentric circles that moved progressively outward. The first plantations had formed an original core around the four rivers flowing past or around Charles Town—the Ashley, Cooper, Stono, and Wanda. By the early eighteenth century, planters had begun growing rice and were simultaneously raising much of the produce that fed the town. By the second decade, planters were developing land along a secondary zone constituted by the Edisto and Santee rivers, including the branch of the Edisto known as Pon Pons, the source of so many Georgia planters.[61] It was in these river basins that rice growing became so profitable. In the 1730s and afterward, the more adventuresome and the landless with access to capital were moving into a sparsely settled frontier zone roughly forty to one hundred miles from Charles Town on both the northern and southern coasts. The Beaufort District that abutted the Savannah River initially attracted a type of planter willing to take outsized risks and unafraid of frontier conditions.

In Georgia, plantation development followed a different logic. As seen in Table 2, most of the migrants from South Carolina passed over the Savannah River, where land titles were complex and technology not yet up to the task of subduing its currents, and established themselves south of the Ogeechee River. The processes of settling the several river systems proceeded simultaneously rather than beginning with a core around Savannah that moved outward. As shown in Table 3, the extended Butler and Bourquin families, the Gibbons and Deveaux brothers, Jonathan Bryan, and certain Charles Town merchants brought approximately five hundred sixty captives into Georgia, an infusion that represented the introduction of large-scale slaveholding into the province.[62] Most settled on the Savannah, Little Ogeechee, and Ogeechee rivers and along the numerous tidal creeks feeding into them. On the Savannah, the average plantation between 1755 and 1760, as seen in Table 2, held thirty enslaved people; on the Little Ogeechee, twenty-seven;

TABLE 2   Enslaved People on or near Lowcountry Rivers, 1755–60

	Planters	Bondspeople	Average Number of Slaves	Percent Slaves
Savannah River	17	519	30.5	20.4
Little Ogeechee River	16	432	27.0	17.0
Ogeechee River	27	421	15.6	16.6
Medway River	24	290	12.0	11.4
Newport River	87	881	10.1	34.6
Totals	171	2,543	14.9	100.0

Source: Based on petitions for land in *Colonial Records of the State of Georgia*, vols. 7 and 8, and on the table correlating land petitions and estate inventories in Statom, "Negro Slavery," 167–69. Since this method does not account for births, deaths, purchases, and sales, it indicates only the relative importance of the slaves on each river, not actual numbers. Multiple petitions by the same person were reconciled.

and on the Ogeechee, sixteen, where the number is skewed by the presence of small planters farther up the river as opposed to those closer to the ocean. Principal carriers of the Barbadian tradition, they demonstrated a mastery of the sophisticated technology necessary for rice cultivation, the capital to purchase Africans, a desire to amass thousands of acres of land, and the social habits of wealthier families with tightly constructed marriages within a narrow band of people, access to political power, and a social world that quickly erected barriers to entry. Jonathan Bryan's spouse epitomized the changing expectations for wealthier women in the new social order. Mary Williamson, the stepdaughter of his brother Joseph, had little involvement in her husband's business or political life, addressed him formally as Mr. Bryan, and accorded him the respect that a southern patriarch demanded. And yet women did not necessarily play a passive role in the Bryan family. Mary's widowed mother followed her daughter to Georgia and became a planter in her own right. And Mary's own daughters were given an income independent of their husbands.[63] Through these families, marriage became a critical instrument of class formation.

South of the Ogeechee, plantation development evolved in a different fashion as planters, made up of pre-1750 Georgians and religiously motivated Carolinians, established themselves. The largest numbers of both

TABLE 3 Estimated Number of Slaves Brought from South Carolina, 1751–55

Congregationalists	326
Butler families	210
Gibbons brothers	49
Jonathan Bryan	66
Deveaux brothers	89
Bourquin families	35
Charles Town merchants	114
Small planters	100
Total	989

Sources: Based on petitions for land in *Colonial Records of the State of Georgia*, vols. 7 and 8; and information in Chestnutt, *South Carolina's Expansion*. The Congregationalists included 71 families.

planters and enslaved people were to be found in the swampland around the North and South Newport rivers: 51 percent of all planters petitioning for land in the period 1755–60 and 35 percent of slaves. As seen in Table 2, eighty-seven planters held 881 bondspeople for an average of 10.1 enslaved people per plantation. The Newport area, virtually unsettled during the trustee period, became a focal point for the new economy, containing more blacks than the Savannah River area. The majority of its planters, whatever their origin, sprang from a modest world where hard physical labor fell to the master as well as the slave. The Congregationalists in particular found themselves in much the same position as in South Carolina, working shoulder to shoulder with their slaves in the fields or, at the very least, remaining on the farm to tend to the many details of raising a crop.[64] They were people on the make, ambitious, hardworking, and anxious to secure additional bondsmen, and they were cultivating rice on a small scale in the frantic effort to enter the ranks of more established planters. In one of the more productive rice areas in the lowcountry, plantations were not yet "plantations" but small- to medium-size farms. To think of an "aristocracy" installing itself in the swamps and marshes of southern Georgia is to miss an important point.

From the summer of 1750 until the first royal governor arrived in October 1754, the six members of the Board of the President and Assistants effectively managed Georgia's government with virtually no supervision or interference from London. Led by the strong-willed James Habersham,

they forged a consensus that withstood the shocks and stresses of a fledgling province only beginning to find its feet economically, politically, and
culturally. When Governor John Reynolds, a naval officer more accustomed
to commanding from the quarterdeck, assumed his post in October 1754,
he incorporated the members of the board into the new administration as
part of the governor's council.[65] Elections of the first legislative assembly
in January 1755 revealed the extensive fault lines that ran through Georgia's
body politic. The underlying regional and political tensions that dated from
the trustee period sprang into view while the election itself became a refer-
endum on James Habersham.

In the elections to that first assembly, long-standing resentments against
the dominance of the old board surged to the fore: the anger of the southern districts at their continued disenfranchisement, as seen in the fact that
only four seats were allotted to them; the old fears of Augusta and its Indian
merchants for their independence; the anti-Habersham faction in Savannah that was angry at its rough treatment in years past; and the would-be
settlers who had received less than their due in land grants, victims of the
arbitrary decisions made on "Land Days." Delegates from the Darien and
Midway districts, from the Ogeechee River, and from within Savannah rallied around the delegates from Augusta and spoke of their fears of the
centralizing trend of the government as well as of a now-dormant issue,
the treatment of Mary Bosomworth.[66] The blunt-spoken Reynolds aggressively backed his council, but when that body began to ask too many questions and demanded to see his royal instructions, he began to reassess the
political lineup. In a matter of months, he concluded that the Habersham
faction "appeared to be extremely Greedy of Power, and would fain have
all things Determined by Vote" within the council rather than act in an
advisory capacity.[67]

In the most decisive moment in the political history of the royal period,
Habersham and his allies were successful in persuading London to issue
a recall of the governor in October 1756. Reynolds departed but not before calling a new election for the legislative assembly, where his partisans
emerged dominant. The delegates immediately voted to authorize an as-
sessment of the state of the province aimed at discrediting members of the
old board of the trustee period.[68] Reporting in 1757, a legislative committee
indicted the Habersham faction for multiple wrongs during the interim
government: building sizable estates by giving large tracts to their own chil-

dren, denying grants to people "well able to Cultivate and Improve Lands," monopolizing trade in the colony, building a horribly expensive structure for weaving silk thread, and disenfranchising the southern part of the colony.[69] The financial benefits of being close to power were there for all to see. More than half of the public expenditures, from gifts for natives to supplies for silk cultivation, went through the firm of Harris & Habersham.[70]

The replacement for Reynolds, Henry Ellis, was the epitome of what the outspoken naval captain was not, a polished diplomat and politician who instinctively knew how to balance the powers of the royal governor with the need to recognize and mollify the established leadership of the colony. Appointed by Lord Halifax to calm troubled waters, he ended the factionalism that had torn the colony apart, soothed the Creeks who had for so long been neglected by Georgia, and put in place a thoughtful military plan to counter Georgia's weaknesses at the height of the Seven Years' War.[71] With a deft touch, Ellis mollified the members of the old board, kept them on the governor's council, and gave that body free rein in the distribution of land. In essence, the recall of Captain Reynolds paved the way for the council to consolidate its power and become an active partner of the next two governors for more than fifteen years.[72] The development made for a striking contrast with South Carolina, where the governor's council emerged from the political battles of that period a weak body that became weaker as time went on.[73] For the remainder of the royal period, the council in Georgia retained the look and feel of the old Board of the President and Assistants, where James Habersham, Francis Harris, and Noble Jones continued to play dominant roles.

By the end of the decade, Georgia stood at a remarkable point. The comment made by historian David Chestnutt that the Congregationalists at Midway absorbed the Georgians into their society rather than being absorbed by the Georgians rings true.[74] Throughout the lowcountry, Carolinians set the standard in terms of building a rice-based economy, controlled the majority of blacks, and brought an adventuresome, pioneering attitude, whether in the grand style of Jonathan Bryan or the more muted one of the small Congregationalist planter. But this image obscures the way that the pre-1750 Georgians inserted themselves into the emerging society and indeed controlled the pace and direction through the interim government. A dynamic process was under way throughout the whole of the lowcountry.[75] Among the many planters and farmers, Georgians enjoyed a well-entrenched presence. In St. Matthew and St. Andrew parishes, they were in the majority by a substantial margin, the Salzburgers forming an irreducible core of German-speaking peasants and the Highlanders around Darien still wearing kilts and speaking Gaelic, as much a separate world as the Salzburgers. Substantial planters would emerge from their numbers. In St. John Parish, Oglethorpe's former army officers brought status and capital that awed the Carolinians while other Georgians who had benefited from the military expenditures of the British government during the 1740s invested their funds in slaves. Along the Little Ogeechee, the enclave of magistrates, former magistrates, their children, and friends from the trustee period remained intact and exercised considerable influence in the life of the royal colony. On the Savannah River, some holders of land grants from the trustees developed their property like the former miller Isaac Young, who had once begged for food but now had twenty-five people enslaved. Capping this blending of old and new was the governor's council, with members from the trustee period continuing to set the pace.

Although Georgia was seeing a planting class emerging out of multiple traditions and seeing continuity in its leadership, the colony remained weak, with a still-fragile economy. The second governor judged Savannah to be "exceedingly ill supplied & very inconvenient for Trade" and recommended moving the capital to a not-yet-created town on the Ogeechee River. Shopkeepers had few sales and marked up their prices merely to survive, sending the little hard currency that came into their hands to Charles Town. Astonished at the lack of capital, the governor ventured to guess that there were not ten men in the province worth £500 sterling, and, although that may have been an overstatement, he could have added that fewer vessels cleared the port of Savannah in 1760 than had done so five years earlier, rice exports were stagnant, and shipments of lumber had fallen.[76] Yet the decade had seen valuable investments made on the backs of black labor as slaves struggled to transform coastal marsh into a new landscape that reflected the dominant values of white inhabitants. By 1761, there were sixty-one hundred whites and thirty-six hundred blacks, a 400 percent increase over the figures a decade earlier.[77] But the outstanding question remained the same as it had been ten years earlier: how to establish a viable shipping trade within the Atlantic economy and convert that trade into tangible economic growth so that all elements of society, large and small, Georgians and Carolinians, found a place. The path to expansion lay through the West Indies, as Habersham had suggested over a decade before, but how to initiate meaningful exchange remained an open question.[78] Georgia's relationship with the Caribbean was much more complex and involved than the simple importation of a "model economy" from the Carolina lowcountry.

Chapter Three

The West Indies, Cornerstone of Trade

With a wealth that far surpassed that of any other region in the Western Hemisphere, the West Indies offered Georgia a way out of its economic woes. Devoted to the production of sugar, molasses, and rum, the sugar islands were exporting to Britain over £3 million sterling of staples in an average year by the early 1770s. The island colonies outshone the mainland in ways that defined the emerging British empire. They were at the heart of the ever-increasing transatlantic trade in human beings; they supported a large merchant marine carrying enslaved people and sugar; they provided a ready market for British manufactured goods; and they were generating substantial accumulations of capital in Great Britain. North America benefited mightily. Sugar plantations were monstrous consumers of people and things, and economic logic dictated a close relationship between the Caribbean and the eastern seaboard. By the early 1770s, British North America was receiving £800,000 sterling per year from wood, fish, flour, livestock, and other products shipped to the south.[1]

Without an export crop and barely able to feed itself, trustee Georgia had little hope of breaking into this highly competitive game. The promotional literature that had branded the land as "the most delightful Country of the Universe" and painted for credulous readers a vision of fertile soil and virgin forests succeeded in luring many an unsuspecting soul into becoming a charity settler, but even the shrewdest merchants of Charles Town never found a way to cut lumber profitably in the new colony.[2] With his usual clarity, James Habersham explained to the trustees in 1747 that lumber was the logical place for the colony to make a start but the obstacles were many. The "Negroes" of South Carolina cut and sawed lumber more cheaply; the shippers of Charles Town offered rates as much as 50 percent less; New Englanders built vessels and sent them to the West Indies to be sold while transporting lumber at low rates to add to their margins. When Habersham applied to a New York factor in Frederica to hire a sloop to transport lumber, the factor set impossible terms because of his lack of confidence that a low-value item like wood would pay the cost of the voyage. Lumber alone would not do, the merchant lamented, and he underscored the importance of "mixed cargos." Georgia's lone merchant suffered the indignity of watching crews from Bermuda sail into tidal creeks and coastal rivers, offer a pittance to residents, and cut valuable cypress and cedar trees for shipbuilding.[3]

In the early 1760s, the British West Indies awoke to the rich opportunities that the colony offered as a major supplier of longleaf pine, also called yellow pine or heart of pine, which covered so much of the coastal plain and beyond.[4] Pine barrens extended on the flat coastal plains from the southern frontier of eastern Virginia to the Florida peninsula, bounded on one side by the foothills of the Appalachian Mountains and on the other by coastal marshes. Of matchless height, longleaf pines were ramrod straight with few or no branches and an open crown spreading outward at the top; the soil they grew in was mainly sand and gravel over clay; the undergrowth, mostly wire grass or broom sedge. Resistant to flames, the trees had an environmental advantage over other species in a region prone to fire set by lightning or by natives hunting deer. The general flatness of the land and the lack of underbrush enabled visitors to pass through miles of unbroken forest, described by some as like a "park" but characterized by a numbing uniformity. Hard, resistant to decay, and possessing great tensile strength, longleaf was ideal as a building material, whether used to frame a house or in naval construction, and was much sought after in the West Indies. In the brackish marshes and swamps along the coast were valuable cypress, white cedar, red bay, live oak, and tupelo gum.[5] Opportunities for a thriving lumber industry were at hand.

From 1761 to 1768, Georgia saw its exports of longleaf pine jump sevenfold, from 307,000 feet of lumber to 2.1 million feet. In 1761, it sent out 606,000 cedar shingles for roofing; seven years later, 3.6 million shingles, a dramatic sixfold increase.[6] The merchants of Savannah and Sunbury took heart. Shipping was now materializing in their ports; mixed cargos were easier to assemble; rum and slaves appeared in greater quantities on the wharves. The exchange of goods with the Caribbean would provide the critical boost to the colony's economy, the priming agent that led to Georgia's rapid economic growth. For the royal period, that trade served as the foundation for the colony's presence in the Atlantic world. Between 1765 and 1772, the percentage of vessels heading south averaged 48 percent of the total shipping outward from the colony while the percentage of tonnage, a critical indicator of the value of cargos, was virtually the same. By way of contrast, Carolina's shipping to the Caribbean never amounted to more than one-third of the total for most of the period; and, if one subtracts Bermuda and the Bahamas, the figure falls as low as 11 percent during the 1730s. In 1763, South Carolina began shipping substantial quantities of rice to the region thanks to a change in mercantilist legislation, and the figure rose to 33 percent for the year 1772. However, the tonnage, 22 percent of the total in that busy port, was far less than that of Georgia.[7] The trade with Britain and southern Europe commanded a much greater share of the cargo. South Carolina sent 143 vessels to the region during 1772, and Georgia was not far behind with 104. Charles Town merchants had reason to look over their shoulders.[8] The humble lumber trade was to reach into every corner of the colony and bind every level of society together in a way that no other commerce did.

Georgians put a deservedly high value on the lumber industry. When Parliament passed the Stamp Act, imposing a tax on all paper documents to raise revenue, it also placed an "Incumbrance" on the exportation of lumber that required a bond double the value of the lumber until the cargo was sold. The bond applied to transient sea captains, placing Georgia in a vulnerable position because so much of its shipping was transient in nature. In writing a polite but firm objection at the request of the legislature, James Habersham captured an essential truth. Wood products, horses, and livestock were "principally . . . the Means, whereby most of the Inhabitants have acquired the little property they possess."[9] The West Indian trade gave white Georgians their first precious taste of the Atlantic economy and put money into the pockets of a broad range of citizens. Loggers along the major rivers, planters clearing their first lands, upcountry farmers, speculators, cattlemen, small merchants, and even retailers found a footing in the lumber business. Everyone, it seemed, had a load of pine, cedar, cypress, or oak to deliver to a sawmill, and many purchased one or two African sawyers to prepare timber directly for the market. Sailing into Savannah, West Indians came with a bit of money, a few enslaved people, and hogsheads of sugar to offer in exchange for the valuable timber that grew in the pine barrens of the extensive coastal plain. While other colonies rushed to defend "ancient" British freedoms expounded by the Virginia Resolutions and the Circular

TABLE 4   Exports to the West Indies (Mean Pounds Sterling Value), 1768–72

	Georgia	South Carolina
Wood products	6,437	2,339
Rice	4,908	50,780
Livestock	2,873	1,477
Beef, pork	1,185	2,763
Indian corn	710	2,477
Bread, flour	51	2,159
Totals	16,164	61,995

Source: Shepherd, "Commodity Exports."

Letter of the Massachusetts House of Assembly, the youngest colony initially saw only the Stamp Act's potentially deadening effect on trade.

As Georgia's leading commodity in the West Indian trade, lumber accounted for almost 40 percent of the sterling value of exports dispatched to Jamaica, St. Kitts, and elsewhere. As seen in Table 4, the colony far outstripped South Carolina in the supply of yellow pine and cedar shingles and sent more livestock than its neighbor. The impact of the trade in wood products was profound. The chief surveyor of the Southern District stated what many considered to be a truism when he wrote: "Reducing the rough timber into boards is now the most common branch of business in the southern colonies, that comes under the name of manufactures."[10] Whether Bernard Romans was accurate is a matter of opinion. The mills that ground rice with water power or horse power arguably came closer to being an integrated manufacturing process than sawing boards, while tanneries produced cowhide leather, shipyards turned out a modest number of coastal ships, an occasional sugar refinery broke the landscape on the coast, and the production of pitch and tar in North Carolina involved a complicated production process. Nevertheless, the most prevalent feature in either lowcountry or upcountry that bespoke manufacturing was the ubiquitous sawmill. Along the coast, ample freshwater creeks and rivers provided power for the sawmills that came to dot the landscape during the 1750s and 1760s: along the Sapelo, Canoochee, Medway, upper parts of the Ogeechee, Newport, and Savannah rivers. Anxious to turn a profit, the less cautious and the careless sealed their fate when they constructed dams to power their mills on small streams. Water overflowed into the surrounding woods, became stagnant, and killed the root systems, making the ground into a sieve that drained the stream.[11] In the upcountry, sawmills congregated more tightly around the Savannah River and its principal tributaries: notably, the mouth of Briar Creek, Beaver Dams Creek, Black Creek, and Great Sweet Water Creek.[12] The mills were temporary affairs, made of wood and saw blades, so that the metal parts could be moved to the next location once the old site had been stripped of its pine.

"Manufacturing" lumber was something of a misnomer. The basic ingredient was the hard labor of African sawyers who, with or without the benefit of a sawmill, cut timber, prepared shingles, and shaved rough staves for the market. Virtually every plantation, every farm, every cowpen participated in this lucrative activity, often done in wintertime when plantation work stood still and the sap was down. African labor could be redirected to the surrounding woods and earn a valuable supplement. But a former deputy surveyor of lands for Georgia, Bernard Romans, made an important point in his remarkably detailed volume, *A Concise Natural History of East and West Florida*. Felling timber was serious business. Using the open pit method, two sawyers standing beneath a downed tree could cut 600 feet of marketable lumber per week, or 31,200 feet per year. If the boards were one inch thick, they might sell for 6 shillings sterling per hundred or £93 12s., per year. And if the boards were thicker or were scantling or ranging timber, the price was even higher. He estimated that, if hired out, such men would earn for their master close to £30 sterling each.[13] Romans explained that five enslaved people formed a stave-making gang in the wintertime: a logger, two to cross-cut the wood, a splitter, and a fifth person to shave, or "draw," the staves. As a semi-skilled sawyer, the slave engaged in heavy-duty, occasionally dangerous work; in compensation, he enjoyed more freedom and the opportunity to set his own pace in a wooded tract. Laboring next to a white timber cutter, he benefited from the shoulder-to-shoulder democracy that a joint effort entailed. Working with a large gang of sawyers and pushed by a profit-minded merchant or planter, he could find himself forced into a hectic schedule of slashing, cutting, and clearing a tract before rushing off to the next campaign. His peers on rafts that carried the lumber to market enjoyed relative freedom, setting their own schedules as the current carried them down the Savannah or other rivers. At the end of the venture, a gallon of rum awaited successful crew members.

Fueling this growing flow of lumber were first-generation planters anxiously clearing their land of trees and scrub, a valuable source of income in the first year or two of an arduous enterprise. "The moment they have got the water off, they attack the trees, which in some swamps are very numerous," an eighteenth-century observer described. "[T]hese they cut down at the root, leaving the stumps in the earth."[14] The more provident planters cut them in lengths and converted them into lumber. A number of men saw timbering as the first stage in generating the capital needed for a plantation. Thomas Peacock came to Georgia with four slaves and received a grant on the Newport River for timbering. Ten years later, he had fourteen slaves and requested additional land for "sawing lumber." He eventually established a plantation with twenty-five captives to cultivate rice but continued to seek grants of "pine barrens" to employ his sawyers. Petitions for land submitted to the governing council repeated the same formulaic justification: "the whole being Pine barren and for the particular purpose of sawing."[15]

The lure of the West Indian market drew a wide range of Georgians into the use of Africans for timbering and provided the means for spreading prosperity through many social and economic groups. The German peasants at Ebenezer, with their strong scruples against slavery, held out until well into the 1750s but eventually bowed to the economic reality that enslaved people made costs competitive with Carolinian lumber. Whenever Savannah's merchants needed an order of yellow pine or a special order of hard-to-reach cypress, they turned to their correspondents in St. Matthew Parish as the most dependable source, especially when a quick turnaround was necessary. Throughout the colonial period, the Salzburgers constituted one of the principal sources of lumber for the Savannah market.[16] The Scots around Darien brought previous experience of logging from the Highlands and, if they were skeptical about human bondage, acquired enslaved people as their modest means permitted.[17] Farther up the rivers, small-time settlers found timbering to be a profitable business. A young man on the make, Andrew Griner, came into the province with a wife, a child, and two enslaved people and received several grants for the purpose of erecting sawmills on creeks that ran into the Savannah River. By 1764, he had four children, owned six Africans, and was in an ideal location to capitalize on the demand for yellow pine.[18] Women who became widows were willing to pursue their husbands' timbering ventures. Mary Bevill embarked on a joint venture with three men to erect a sawmill on Brier Creek, relied on the nine slaves she had inherited, and apparently remained single.[19] If Georgia's claim to land between Ebenezer and Augusta was tenuous at best, that did not impede the governing council from assigning the best timberland along the connecting creeks of the Savannah River. Most claimants were modest people of English origin.

Wandering herdsmen and their Africans made a good living when timbering was combined with cattle raising. Not far above Griner's holdings, the naturalist William Bartram crossed the Savannah and rode through a pine forest until he came upon a house, stable, and cowpen. There he found a husband and wife superintending a number of enslaved women and children milking cows. His host explained that the men were at work squaring pine and cypress timber for the West Indian market. The two walked to the high banks of the "Majestic Savannah," stood at the timber landing, and found themselves surrounded by slaves who, according to the writer, bubbled with praise for the owner's "industry, humanity and liberal spirit." The landing was a broad area that overlooked a steep bluff rising up from the water about sixty feet below. Bartram marveled at the efficiency of the operation: "The logs being dragged by timber wheels to this yard, and landed as near the brink of this high bank as possible with safety, and laid by the side of each other, are rolled off and precipitated down the bank into the river, where being formed into rafts, they are conducted by slaves down to Savanna, about fifty miles below this place."[20] The heartwood trunks of longleaf were especially buoyant, floating lazily down the relatively flat, slow-moving Savannah River, except when the freshets came with spring rains.

Whether on the coast or in the upcountry, Georgians of whatever rank stripped the land nearest water unmercifully in the search to tap the profits that came from participation in the West Indian trade.[21] The cattlemen along the fringes of the frontier cut trees until the resources of their tract had been exhausted and then moved on. There was little or no concern for erosion or replanting and, if the nature of eighteenth-century tools limited the damage, the basic attitudes leading to the destruction of the environment were already in place. The Savannah authorities applauded. In 1764, the governor's council ordered no pineland to be sold unless there were sufficient "Negroes" to harvest the crop of trees: one enslaved person for every one hundred acres, four for every five hundred acres, and a sawmill or eight slaves for one thousand acres.[22] Letting land sit "unproductively" was the unforgivable sin. Nor were Savannahians out of step. One merchant left his failing business to take control of one thousand acres along the Savannah River owned by his father-in-law. Profoundly uninterested in rice cultivation, James Edward Powell had the wit to establish a major timbering operation on some of the richest acreage along the river, built a wharf at Savannah, and began shipments to the West Indies. A well-off merchant like Powell set the standard by the way he rushed in, cut trees, devastated the landscape, and moved on when there was little left but scrub.[23] The image can be overstated, however. There is a reasonable argument to make that colonists successfully adapted agriculture to the lowcountry environment and were creative as well as destructive as "environmental agents," as one historian argues. From a longer perspective, they would display a dynamic, adaptive relationship with the landscape.[24] Nevertheless, in the minds of most Georgians, land remained the second most valuable commodity after rice, and exploitation was the aim.

The explosion of output in timber was no accident. The merchants of Savannah were responding to sea captains looking for lumber to meet the voracious demand in the West Indies. Compared to other North American colonies, Georgia's output was small. Massachusetts was shipping roughly twelve million feet of lumber to the Caribbean compared to the two million feet of the southernmost colony.[25] However this colony of the Lower South had an edge. "The Pine timber of Georgia commands a price considerably higher in the sugar islands than any other kinds in the United States," a Georgian in the post-revolutionary period commented. In *Observations on the Commerce of the American States*, John Lord Sheffield concurred, "The lumber of the Southern Colonies is preferred, and is sold 20 perct. dearer; it is mostly for building."[26] Savannah's merchants were quick to capitalize on their ability to secure land grants and exploited the most easily accessible timber as quickly as possible. Some wanted ownership of the process from beginning to end. Johnston and Wylly, both from the West Indies, understood the stakes. They reserved two thousand acres "for the purpose of erecting a sawmill" in St. Matthew and St. George parishes along Beaver Dams Creek.[27] In yet another indication of Georgia's orientation toward the Caribbean, most of those who jumped into the lumber game were former West Indians or Scotsmen who enjoyed contacts in that world.[28]

The legislature had passed acts regulating the dimensions of boards, staves for making barrels, headings to cover the top of the barrels, and shingles for roofing and had created inspectors for the ports of Sunbury and Savannah, but merchants had to be as attentive to the need to fill an order quickly as to the quality of the wood. As a Jamaican correspondent told Edward Telfair about a schooner he sent, "You must know very well that vessels as small as she is can never do anything in the lumber way unless kept constantly going."[29] Telfair had little time to comply. The request from Jamaica came in August. If the boards were in Savannah, all well and good, but if they had to be floated down from Ebenezer or beyond, the low level of the river made rafting a virtual impossibility.[30] The most reliable contact for Joseph Clay was Johann Caspar Wertsch, a German immigrant at Ebenezer, who began as a young schoolteacher and became one of two principal merchants in that small peasant community. Involved on several fronts, Wertsch sold plantation tools, lent money to farmers, distributed bonuses for the growing of silk, and guarded the precious deed to the New Jerusalem Church. This entrepreneurial German held the key to much of the lumber industry in St. Matthew Parish, brokering the output of planters and loggers and meeting the needs of sawmill operators, carpenters, and coopers alike in the sparsely populated land.[31]

Despite the rising volume of exports of lumber and rice, most shippers still regarded Savannah as a young, marginal port good only for filling in dead moments in the trading cycle, picking up lumber when other higher-valued products were not available, and dumping cargo that could not be offloaded elsewhere. One of the first to discover its virtues came from the tiny island of Montserrat, thirty-nine square miles, nestled on the outer edge of the Leeward Islands. A Philadelphian and Quaker, Robert King operated from the capital of Plymouth as the largest commercial house. Montserrat represented the prime characteristics of most sugar islands: the near-monoculture in sugar, the concentrated character of plantations, and a black-to-white ratio of ten to one. Dealing "in all manner of merchandize," he utilized his base to conduct trade throughout the Caribbean, keeping several vessels moving from port to port. Although officially living in Philadelphia, King operated in a hands-on-fashion, carefully listening and evaluating inter-island talk, meeting vessels as they returned, supervising the quick discharge of cargo, and loading the ships again to dispatch them to a port of his choice. The *Providence* appeared in October 1764, the

TABLE 5   Lumber Shipments to the West Indies by Place of Origin of Ship
Owners, 1765–66

	Feet	*Percent*
Great Britain	729,836	27.0
Georgia	608,688	22.5
Northward colonies	561,165	20.8
West Indies	415,652	15.3
Bermuda, Bahamas	388,925	14.4
Totals	2,704,266	100.0

Source: Naval Shipping Lists for Georgia, 1765–66, CO 5/710, NA-UK. Northward colonies include the New England and Middle Atlantic provinces and Maryland. Virginia, North Carolina, and South Carolina did not participate in the Georgia trade. Vessels from the West Indies came almost exclusively from St. Kitts and Jamaica, with occasional schooners and sloops from Montserrat and Tortola.

Prudence in 1765, and the *Nancy* the following year. King's vessels would link Georgia to the sugar plantations of the West Indies, the slave castles of West Africa, the trade in deerskins through the importation of rum, and, indirectly, the commercial know-how and shipping of Philadelphia.[32] Although West Indians were a small proportion of the ship owners whose vessels carried wood products, their presence had multiple ramifications.

As shown in Table 5, the most important shippers were the English and Scots of Britain. Called before a parliamentary committee at the end of the Revolution, John Graham described how a handful of ships dispatched from Liverpool and Bristol delivered dry goods to the West Indies and, while waiting for the sugar crop to come in, made runs to the colony for lumber. Within three months, they were back on station. Called "seekers," as opposed to vessels that remained at one port, perhaps ten to twelve paid a visit each year.[33] During the second quarter of 1767, five British ships carried off 217,000 of the 330,000 feet exported.[34] By way of contrast, the northward colonies, from North Carolina to Massachusetts, played a relatively modest role. During the 1760s, a few vessels came from Boston and Salem in a triangular trade of sorts, with food products exchanged for lumber, rice, and tar, and these in turn converted into molasses and sugar for the voyage back to Boston.[35] Although New England would lose out in the coming years to Philadelphia, Georgia was never more than a niche market for the great commercial centers of British North America. With so much valuable lumber in their hinterlands, there was little incentive to include the frontier province in their shipping. The almost complete absence of Carolinians in Georgia's West Indian trade tells a parallel story. Charles Town merchants who engaged in the lucrative rice business with the sugar islands had little desire to dirty their hands with wood products, and those few who did found sufficient cargo in their own colony.

Bermudians represented an important lubricant to the trade. That small atoll on the edge of the Atlantic had long held a place in the sailing world out of proportion to its size.[36] The island enjoyed a well-earned reputation; and if the rise of South Carolina had reduced its importance, the colony still drew in a heady brew of sailors, sea captains, and vessels from two trading areas—the Chesapeake and its tobacco route, and the sugar islands. A small group of owners and captains displayed an intimate knowledge of the Georgia market and its possibilities, carrying almost as much lumber as vessels from the West Indies did. With a family in Bermuda, Samuel Stiles became a familiar face on the Savannah waterfront. He sailed Bermuda sloops around the Caribbean on behalf of Savannah merchants and enjoyed a mostly free rein in deciding what to purchase and in what quantities. "We leave you the liberty to invest the proceeds [of the trip] agreeable to the best of your judgment," Edward Telfair assured him. Stiles acquired partial ownership in his sloops, typically one-quarter, and sometimes went on "joint account," sharing the cost of the cargo. A hardworking and dependable sea captain, he enjoyed a certain standing within the colony. On his father's side were important family connections: the speaker of the Bermuda Assembly, a wealthy Philadelphia merchant, and the wife of a governor of that colony. Stiles bought a plantation in Georgia but left his family in Bermuda until after the Revolution.[37]

The surprise was the strength of Georgia's own shipping in the Caribbean trade. The 22.5 percent of lumber that went in vessels owned by Georgians, although modest, was still greater than that of northern, West Indian, and Bermudan vessels and only behind those of the English. At the heart of this presence were a handful of sea captains, many of whom came out of Beaufort, South Carolina.[38] Founded in 1712, tiny Beaufort was part of a tradition steeped in trading across imperial boundaries, employing crews of mixed color, changing loyalties, and indulging in privateering as the occasion demanded. While in his twenties, Captain David Cutler

Braddock had been captured off the Georgia coast by the Spanish, commanded a Carolina galley after his release, was accused of trading with
St. Augustine by a British officer, and freelanced as a privateer in the West
Indies. When, at age thirty, he acquired land in Georgia, he became one
of the few battle-tested mariners in the colony.[39] Braddock organized an
effort that brought his son-in-law, William Lyford Jr., together with seven
enslaved sailors, to Savannah from Charles Town to serve as pilots for the
Georgia coast. In an earlier time, Lyford had traded with the Spanish of
St. Augustine, turned privateer, and by the 1750s was one of the most active
of the Carolina sea captains in the West Indian trade.[40]

Other sea captains in Georgia hailed from northern ports, men like
Preserved Alger who made Savannah his home base after repeated stops
on the passage from the north to the Caribbean. Ownership of voyages
reflected the diversity of Savannah's maritime world: mariners who often
held a share, Scottish merchants, minor traders, Bermudans who used the
Georgia registry for purposes of convenience, traders, newcomers like the
star-crossed Button Gwinnett, and even the governor of Georgia. And
there was one woman who conducted a vigorous trade in the West Indies,
Elizabeth Butler, the widow of William Butler Sr. and owner of over a
hundred slaves and several plantations. Originally from Charles Town, she
operated with a Scotsman as partner.[41] As a group, the Georgian shippers
brought an entrepreneurial spirit to a colony decidedly lacking in one, and
that spirit had a distinctly West Indian flavor. At the end of the colonial
era, Georgians owned five ships, one snow, six brigantines, fourteen schooners, and nine sloops, some engaged in the coastal trade, most in the West
Indian, and two carrying rice to Britain.[42]

Lumber may have been the foundation for trade but other products
ensured the profitability of the voyage—notably, rice, corn, livestock, and
barrels of beef and pork. Planters, farmers, cattle herders, and even townsmen with a bit of land to spare earned precious pounds sterling through
supplying horses and cattle, in a greater absolute amount than did their
neighbors in Carolina.[43] Most of the revenue came from horses bred on
plantations and farms around Savannah; they were valued at £5 sterling
on the mainland and twice that figure in the sugar islands.[44] While 260
horses left the port each year on average, only 50-odd cows and steers did
so, a small number given the extensive herds of cattle; there were as many
as 25,000 head throughout the colony belonging to planters, farmers, and

herdsmen.[45] A significant percentage of the wealth of both slaveowners and non-slaveowners was tied up in stock, an asset that required relatively little labor.[46] Although few cattle went to the West Indies, barrels of beef constituted a more sought-after commerce. Planter John Morel advertised 150 barrels of beef available at his plantation on Ossabaw Island near Savannah; some of that was consumed in the Savannah market, but a good part entered the West Indian circuit.[47] An even larger number of pork barrels was sent, although Georgia's pork suffered by comparison with pork from the mid-Atlantic colonies.[48] The West Indian market represented a fairly modest outlet for Georgia beef, suggesting that most of the consumption was internal or for the markets of East and West Florida where a vigorous demand prompted herds of cattle to be moved overland.

The largest markets for Georgia cattle were found in two new colonies acquired from Spain in the wake of the Seven Years' War, East and West Florida, where military garrisons, indentured servants, deerskin traders, and black labor on indigo plantations required massive imports.[49] In the mid-1760s, two noted traders obtained a contract to supply beef to newly occupied Pensacola and were obliged to drive their cattle through lands where Creeks "never suffered any but oxen to pass."[50] When the governor of East Florida charged John Graham with securing one thousand head of cattle, the Savannah merchant at first opted for upcountry cattle because they fed on fields of cane at the edge of streams, had more meat than those "on the salts," and were reputed to be in better health.[51] When Graham worried about the potential loss on the long, exhausting drive to East Florida, he purchased a second herd of five hundred cattle from a planter in St. Andrew Parish for the same price. The two Floridas were a prized market for beef that complemented demand from the West Indies.

While the West Indian trade opened up markets for Georgia's products, it also brought the sounds, smells, and feel of the Caribbean onto the streets of Savannah: the potent rums of Jamaica and Antigua, brown sugar, the glistening bodies of recently oiled slaves about to be sold, casks of coffee, and piles of mahogany wood. Forty feet below the sandy bluff that fronted Savannah, a typical spring day saw a ship loading rice for London, a Philadelphia sloop discharging flour and bread, a schooner from Charles Town unloading dry goods, and as many as four vessels from the West Indies discharging hogsheads of muscovado sugar and rum, cocoa, mahogany, and "a few likely New Negroes." Women as well as men were on the wharf looking at the goods displayed in modest stores run by petty retailers, the jacks-of-all-trades in the mercantile world. Sugar was an important commodity, rum even more so. The taverns and tippling houses throughout the town depended on a steady supply; merchants kept ample stocks for their customers; deerskin traders bought in quantity; private homes kept rum in storage; rafters expected access to rum when they docked their lumber in Savannah; and the enslaved people on plantations routinely exchanged stolen goods for rum peddled from boats along the rivers and tidal creeks. According to official records, Georgians imported annually an average of 73,941 gallons of rum, both West Indian and North American, between 1769 and 1771. The figure is clearly understated.[52] According to a historian of the rum trade, John McCusker, the actual figure for total imports was closer to 99,000 gallons, a testimony to the vigorous illicit commerce that took place even in the Lower South.[53]

Smuggling was of relatively recent vintage. In an earlier time, Governor Wright, an astute judge of people and conditions, had assured the government there was little smuggling except for the occasional French vessel that appeared off the coast. But the growth of the population, the rise of the West Indian trade, and the new level of prosperity led Georgians to imitate their peers. In 1773, the collector of the port of Savannah gave a candid appraisal. Vessels from the West Indies chose one of the tidal rivers along the coast to unload cargo in almost complete isolation or, increasingly, were sailing up the Savannah River and deliberately running aground on one of the sand banks. The master would leave his crew to report the situation to Savannah and, upon his return, would find his cargo the lighter by several hogsheads of rum and sugar. Canoes or boats would suddenly emerge out of nowhere, take on a load, and then wait until night to run it up to Savannah. The collector speculated that goods went to South Carolina "through our creeks" because it was much more difficult to smuggle in front of Charles Town where the bar was within sight of the Custom House.

Alexander Thompson may have been making a pitch for a larger budget and a bigger staff, but he had a good case. There was no proper water guard, no way for him or his officers to patrol the creeks, no boats available for reconnoitering, no writs of assistance as in Boston, no visits from the king's vessels for a show of force, and, perhaps most serious of all, no way to easily obtain information "where all are more or less Connected."[54] Customs was impotent in this part of the world. Until 1769, that had not bothered the officers of the port or anyone else. The collector, William Spencer, was an impecunious veteran of the trustee period whose friendship with James Habersham and the old guard helped him keep a position that held his large family together. The man had lost his first wife and children during the 1740s in a raid by Indian allies of the Spanish and enjoyed enormous sympathy. His son-in-law Thompson, a Scotsman who had worked with the East India Company, brought a different temperament to the job.[55] Nevertheless, Savannah remained in a vastly different position from Charles Town, where relations between the Customs House and the merchant community had deteriorated to the point of open hostilities. Based on McCusker's figures, approximately twenty-five thousand gallons of rum were smuggled into Georgia on an annual basis.[56]

Drinking rum was the one activity that cut across cultures. Creeks and Indian traders could lie together dead drunk in the shadow of the trading post at Buzzards Roost on the Ocmulgee River. White sailors and black sailors could join together in drinks, cards, and a smoke in a Yamacraw tavern between voyages. White boat captains carried on a vigorous illicit trade in stolen goods in return for bottles of rum. But the drinking also showed sharp differences in values, habits, and cultural attitudes. Like most white North Americans, Georgians consumed a considerable amount of rum. One customs officer estimated that white Georgians, minus children or those too poor to afford the beverage, each drank approximately twenty-two gallons a year.[57] His assumption was off by a wide margin. Women drank considerably less than men; the population was larger than he guessed; and there were probably more children than he estimated. He also assumed that only sick "Town Negroes" were given rum. In a considerably more sophisticated analysis, John McCusker came up with almost exactly the same figure, twenty-one gallons a year, but for every white adult male rather than the white adult population as a whole. The typical white male in North America, he argued, drank the equivalent of seven one-ounce shots of rum every day of the year, or three pints of that heady brew per week.[58] Such a prodigious consumption reflected the fact that North Americans needed a diet high in caloric content to supply the energy to live and to work. The reshaping of the lowcountry, the creation of farms in the upcountry, and the activities of deerskin traders, sailors, sawyers, and craftsmen demanded a high caloric food. Jamaican rum, with 147 calories per ounce, was valuable in this frontier setting as the highest source of caloric value of all alcoholic beverages and, in Georgia, represented the second most common product after Antiguan rum.[59] Based on his estimates of consumption, white Georgians drank about fifty-four thousand gallons per year.

For blacks, the demand for rum was likewise prodigious and for much the same reasons, but access was an occasional matter, controlled by slave-owners, at least up to a point. That point was quickly reached in the tippling houses of Yamacraw, a raucous neighborhood of sailors and workers on the western edge of Savannah; on rafts carrying lumber down the rivers; and in the vast informal slave economy that connected plantation to plantation and the rural world to the urban. Blacks crewed and sometimes captained flatboats, piraguas, and canoes moving between locations on creeks and rivers with plantation goods or other commodities for the market. As Betty Wood noted in her study of the informal economies, "It was widely held that, whether white or black, free or enslaved, most rivermen had no compunction in accepting stolen property in exchange for the one commodity that bondsmen and bondswomen reputedly sought above all else: hard liquor."[60] Rum was vital for the celebrations of life and death, marriages and funerals. John McCusker assumed that blacks drank rum at the rate of one gallon per year per person, averaging women, children, and men together, or, for Georgia, the equivalent of ten thousand gallons in the period around 1770.[61]

More significantly, the rum trade tightly bound the Georgia lowcountry to Creek towns like Coweta, Cussita, Apalachicola, and Okfuskee. The drink had long been the bane of the deerskin trade, and Oglethorpe gained a special standing among Creek headmen when he banned its use. Kegs of the liquid nevertheless made their way into the nation with little difficulty. When the Proclamation of 1763 opened Indian territory to virtually any person who could post a modest bond, rum increasingly displaced the traditional exchange of hides for British merchandise. Native Americans did not drink alcohol on a regular basis because it was only occasionally available, but when they did, men and women of all ages found no reason to restrain themselves and abandoned the tight restrictions placed on them by clan etiquette.[62] "They often transform themselves by liquor into the likeness of mad foaming bears," a trader and frontier diplomat judged in his detailed account of the natives of the Southeast.[63] William De Brahm had witnessed enough to write that natives "love strong Liquors, especially Rum or Brandy, at all times, which they prefer to anything in the World, and this is the only Commodity, for which they exchange their Horses."[64] If whites in Georgia were consuming on average fifty-four thousand gallons and enslaved people another ten thousand gallons, natives were taking the remaining thirty-five thousand gallons, three and a half times the amount the customs officer gave as his estimate.[65] An even greater amount was going through South Carolina into native country, and the volume for Mobile and Pensacola in West Florida almost equaled that of Georgia, according to official records. John Stuart, the superintendent of Indian affairs for the Southern Department, reported that "for one skin taken in exchange for British manufacture," there were "five got in exchange" for rum.[66] Traders, especially the more marginal ones, knew that rum was cheap and always attracted plenty of customers.

Rum was profitable but the importation of slaves was even more so. A cargo of rum, molasses, and mahogany took on a new look when a dozen or so bondsmen, freshly acquired from a vessel completing the Middle Passage to Jamaica or another island, provided that extra margin of profit in the same bookkeeping spirit that horses or rice did for the Georgia merchant. A small market like Savannah fit ideally into the circuit of towns in the Caribbean where sloops or schooners stopped in search of a cargo or a market.[67] Robert King of Montserrat sent his two or three vessels shuttling between Dutch and French islands, like St. Eustatius, Guadeloupe, St. Croix, and Grenada, and Charles Town on the mainland. He was glad to expand the range of ports.[68] In August 1766, the sixty-ton schooner *Nancy* sailed into Savannah from Guadeloupe with a crew of six men and a small cargo of slaves. The captain, Thomas Farmer, supervised the unloading of five men and women in a ritual that caused little notice on the wharves of the port and led the dazed party to a holding pen. Robert King had learned his lesson. The year before, he had sent a vessel with seventy "New Negroes" to Savannah only to discover that no one was willing to take on so sizable a cargo at a time when the port had not yet entered into the African trade in a major way. Captain Farmer had pulled up anchor and headed to Charles Town, where he found a ready market.[69] Of the thirty-four voyages from the West Indies that ended in Savannah during 1766, the average size of the human cargo was fourteen people, making the sales that much easier for local brokers.[70] Entry into the trade was simple and the risk comparatively small. Merchants and storekeepers on the wharves of Savannah liked the odds. Planters and townsmen were likely to pay cash for one or two people. And, if purchasing enslaved people for resale was too risky, they could always act as a broker for West Indian traders. During the 1760s, the heyday of that commerce, some 2,262 enslaved men, women, and children came through Savannah and Sunbury, valued at almost £68,000, assuming an average price of £30 per person.[71]

While the sights and sounds of the Caribbean dominated the wharves of Savannah, the attitudes and habits of the sugar islands inexorably seeped into the white population. A black sailor on Robert King's sloop composed a literary masterpiece that is the only firsthand account of life in Savannah during the colonial era. Purchased in Virginia by an English naval officer, taught to read and write, sold to Robert King on tiny Montserrat, and freed after he bought his liberty, Olaudah Equiano produced an autobiography that captured pride in Africa and its people, his tireless opposition to the slave trade, and his seriousness about spiritual matters, including the early stages of Methodism. Newly uncovered evidence suggests that Equiano was born in South Carolina, not in Africa, and that his African identity may have been a rhetorical invention.[72] The meticulous and moving accounts of his five visits to Savannah are confirmed, however, by the existing historical records. The official naval shipping list records the sloop *Nancy* departing Savannah on October 9, 1766, with 20 oxen, 12 hogs, and 13 dozen poultry for Dominica. Writing twenty years later, Equiano recalled, "We were in haste to complete our lading and were to carry twenty head of cattle with us to the West Indies." He remembered the date of departure as "about November" and the destination as Montserrat, which was in fact the ultimate destination. That he could recall the approximate dates of arrival, the cargos for each of the voyages, and the names of the people whom he encountered makes all the more poignant the contextual details he gave in affirming that free blacks—he became one during this time—"live in constant alarm for their liberty, which is but nominal, for they are universally insulted and plundered without the possibility of redress."[73]

Equiano's narrative captured the doubled-edged freedom and openness that a black sailor could experience in Savannah. Unobstructed, he walked the streets and wandered along roads out of town; he commanded a craft going up rivers in search of lumber to assemble a cargo; he visited with an enslaved friend who had his own small house; or he stood at the city market selling wares he had imported, sometimes no more than oranges, sometimes packets of sugar, and occasionally English manufactured goods.

The appearance was deceptive. One Sunday evening, Equiano was mingling with some blacks in the yard of their owner on Wright Square. The master, Dr. Perkins, a "very severe and cruel man," came in drunk and, seeing a black seaman consorting with his slaves, joined with a second white man in attacking him. "They beat and mangled me in a shameful manner, leaving me near dead," Equiano related. "I lost so much blood from the wounds I received, that I lay quite motionless and was so benumbed that I could not feel any thing for many hours."[74] Perkins had him committed to jail the next day. Although Captain Farmer sought out lawyers, they declined to intervene. Dr. Brydie, who had earlier treated Equiano, stepped in and, fearing for the sailor's life, nursed him back to health. The physicians represented the two sides to medicine in the Caribbean. Both were planters. Both acquired wealth in the form of slaves. Both were there, like their colleagues in the Caribbean, to make money. Some, like Brydie, displayed a genuine interest in preserving human life. More typically, those like Perkins succumbed to the immorality of a profit-driven slave society.[75]

After a final voyage to Savannah, Equiano cast about for a vessel to the Caribbean but, before he left, a black woman with a dead child beseeched him to conduct a funeral service since no white person, much less a minister, would perform the service. After repeated entreaties, he complied: "As she was much respected, there was a great company both of white and black people at the grave. I then accordingly assumed my new vocation, and performed the funeral ceremony to the satisfaction of all present." With understated anger, he concluded, "I thus took a final leave of Georgia; for the treatment I had received in it disgusted me very much against the place; and when I left it and sailed for Martinico I determined never more to revisit it."[76]

In the process of making the West Indian trade the priming agent for Georgia's rapid economic growth, the lowcountry began to acquire the look and feel of the sugar islands. Even Savannah, a town designed to accord with humanist principles and populated by Englishmen and Germans foreign to that culturally distant world, was not immune.

Chapter Four

Savannah as a "Caribbean" Town

On February 11, 1765, the *Prudence* from Montserrat appeared off Tybee Island, made its way over the relatively deep bar, and anchored to secure a pilot for the tedious journey seventeen miles up the Savannah River. Its owner, Robert King, was making a risky bet in the search for new markets. In addition to rum, coffee, and cocoa, seventy "New Negroes" from West Africa were crowded into the sloop, the largest shipment of slaves in the history of the port up to that time. Around the final bend, Savannah rose up out of a vast expanse of marsh as the landscape began to acquire a modicum of elevation. Ahead were high banks climbing forty feet from the river, crowned with a flat top that Georgians were proud to call a bluff. Captain Farmer arrived on the same day as two other vessels from the West Indies, the *Friendship* from Jamaica with a suspiciously small cargo that suggested smugglers had already lightened her load, and the *Nancy* from St. Kitts with rum, sugar, salt, seven slaves, and barrels of limes. Thirty-two vessels entered the port during the first quarter of the year: fourteen from the West Indies, two from Britain, seven from Charles Town, seven from the northerly colonies, and two from West Florida.[1] For a small town beginning to find its footing, the impact was considerable. Arriving in Savannah on a tour of British North America only three months before Farmer, Lord Adam Gordon had scribbled in his journal: "Georgia will become one of the richest, and most considerable Provinces in British America, and that in a very few years, provided peace continues."[2]

Prescient though he was, he could not have foreseen the consecutive years of economic boom that no other colony, not even South Carolina with its staggering wealth, would be able to match.[3] Between 1755 and 1772, shipments of rice went from 2,300 barrels to 23,500; deerskins from 50,000 to over 200,000 pounds; and lumber from 300,000 feet to 2.2 million feet.[4] In his report on the state of Georgia, William De Brahm, an engineer fascinated with numbers and typically accurate, calculated that the colony had exported over sixteen years 140,000 barrels of rice, 2.1 million pounds of deerskins, 1,747 horses, 452 cows, 6.3 million staves, and 24 million shingles.[5] Shipping jumped from 52 to 218 vessels entering the port. James Habersham, not one given to exaggeration, enthused that, at the moment he composed his letter, forty square-rigged vessels lay at the foot of Bay Street: "from the Situation I am now in, you must suppose, I am loaded with Business."[6] That growth also bore a special imprint. Savannah had to look to the Caribbean as its engine of economic growth, and the waterfront emerged as an emblem of a world that more nearly fit the sugar islands.

That image sat uneasily with the fact that Savannah as a town represented the classical ideals of proportion, harmony, and balance in a design that probably had its derivation in the evolving pattern of London's West End, where a succession of newly created squares provided ample inspiration for Georgia's trustees.[7] Oglethorpe may have been influenced by his experience on the parliamentary committee that supervised the building of Hanover Square in London, and he apparently carried the design with him when he left England.[8] Whatever the source, he laid out the town around four, then six, public squares, with forty town lots on two sides of each square, and four "trustee lots" reserved for public buildings on the other sides. Each lot had a street in front and an alley behind in rigorous symmetry.[9] Surrounded by cottages, shops, and public buildings and with a water pump in the center, the squares placed public space on an equal footing with private space, fostered a sense of community, and artfully blended with the environment on the bluff high above the gracefully winding river. At its founding, Savannah stood out as a quintessentially European town. The first inhabitants were English charity settlers and indentured servants, primarily from London and other urban centers, together with Protestant Germans and French, who faithfully replicated much of their experiences. If early Charles Town unfolded in the disorderly fashion of a medieval European city, its neighbor reflected eighteenth-century aspirations.[10]

By 1771, six years after Farmer's voyage, the town boasted a population of 1,996 people: 1,175 whites and 821 blacks.[11] The settlement was the largest south of Wilmington, North Carolina, with the exception of Charles Town, and compared not unfavorably with the smaller ones of the Chesapeake Bay region, where the network of rivers precluded the need for commercial distribution centers.[12] In the Lower South, St. Augustine in East Florida was still a predominantly military garrison despite British control.[13]

In South Carolina, Beaufort and Georgetown, dismissed as "inconsiderable villages" by one contemporary, were small if thriving centers for rice production without the people or the shipping of Savannah.[14] One hundred ten miles distant, Charles Town, with approximately 10,887 people in 1770, stood as the fourth largest city in North America, outranked only by Philadelphia, New York, and Boston, and the wealthiest of any town. Its shipping tonnage exceeded that of New York while the monetary value of the rice, indigo, and deerskins sent to England represented 29 percent of the value of all exports from the North American mainland.[15]

Savannah and Charles Town resembled towns in the Caribbean in terms of their central role. In no other section of North America did two centers so thoroughly dominate the areas they served, in part because of the high ratio of coast to land, where travel time was reckoned in "boat hours." Charles Town monopolized the export of staples; Savannah did the same although it had to share a part of that market with a growing Sunbury; both towns controlled the distribution of goods and services in their colonies; and both contained a remarkably high percentage of the white population within the lowcountry.[16] In the coastal strip that stretched from the Black River in South Carolina to the Altamaha in Georgia, few stores existed outside the limits of these two towns as was common in Pennsylvania, New York, or Massachusetts.[17] In the West Indies, the principal towns centralized functions to an even greater extent.[18] Because of the ratio of coast to land, plantations had easy accessibility to the principal port, with "droggers," or small boats, picking up hogsheads of sugar on plantation wharves. A high percentage of the total white population of 18,700 on Jamaica resided in the two towns of Kingston and Savanna la Mar.[19] The centralization of functions in the principal towns of the lowcountry, however, reflected another reason. Unlike sugar, which was sold on commission in Britain by specialists, the relatively unvarying quality in the rice bought and sold in Charles Town and Savannah meant a lesser role for the overseas specialist. Planters and export merchants in the Lower South found that a single market in each colony best served their needs.[20]

The presence of a large black population reinforced the similarities. By the end of the colonial era, Savannah's growing population contained 821 blacks out of a total of 1,996 people, or 41 percent of the total.[21] They were unskilled laborers, domestics, skilled artisans, hucksters, sailors, workers living independently, and vendors in the food market—a range of people who, far from servile, often appeared self-confident and gregarious.[22] Balancing this appearance were the half-hidden instruments of urban social control: an active slave market for Africans, frequent sales and separations of seasoned bondsmen, night patrols, arbitrary displays of power, and the fear of blacks by the white population. Widely distributed throughout households, blacks lived side by side with whites in small numbers. Many were stuffed into attics, back rooms, and outbuildings on the same property as their masters, if not in the same house, but avenues for escaping close supervision opened up even within these narrow confines.[23] Savannah mirrored its neighbor. Charles Town had a population that was 54 percent African and African American, men and women who performed a wide array of functions and were not loath to apply pressure to enlarge their economic independence.[24] Although in New York blacks formed 21 percent of the population in 1750, that figure had begun to decline, and the corresponding figures for Philadelphia and Boston were far less.[25] The lowcountry stood apart, approaching the ratios found in the larger towns of the West Indies. Charles Town paralleled the experience of the sophisticated, multilayered Kingston, Jamaica, where 55 percent of residents were black and "free colored." In the Leeward Islands, the population of blacks in urban parishes ranged from 60 to 90 percent.[26] Savannah may not have been Basseterre in St. Kitts or St. John's in Antigua, but it was firmly part of a Lower South that looked to the Caribbean in terms of racial makeup.

As late as 1760, Savannah was no more than a commercial outpost of Charles Town, clumsily and sometimes desperately trying to find a way to gain a modicum of independence while emulating its example. When he arrived in 1757, Governor Henry Ellis deplored the fate of shopkeepers forced to pay exorbitant prices for English goods shipped through its neighbor and earning no more than a token commission. At least half of Georgia's rice crop, he estimated, was taken out of the colony on small boats via the many tidal creeks and floated up to that shipping center, bypassing both customs and the Savannah market.[27] In 1760, only 37 vessels cleared outward, 16 percent of the volume departing the Carolina port. Within five years an explosion in trade brought Georgia to life as a serious player in the Atlantic economy. Shipping more than tripled. In 1766, the town handled 154 vessels compared to Charles Town's 385, or 40 percent.[28] Overnight, this scruffy little stopping point was producing numbers that commanded respect. The mean size of its vessels was less than its neighbor's but still undeniably competitive, and the turnaround time, so crucial to generating profits for ship owners, was in line. The majority of the vessels were small single-mast sloops, quick and nimble, averaging thirty tons, or double-masted schooners, slower, more stable, averaging thirty-eight tons, the workhorses of the Caribbean and the North American coast. By 1772, Georgia's vessels clearing outward still represented 40 percent of South Carolina's shipping despite the latter's rapidly expanding trade. But Savannah's tonnage was no match for Charles Town's, only 29 percent, a more realistic measure of the relative strength of the two ports.[29]

The town had become a competitive port only after 1759, when a New York merchant, Thomas Eatton, announced to the governor's council that he was bringing family and friends "from the northward" to begin a timbering operation for the West Indies. He faced a considerable challenge. The river was notoriously shallow with sand bars constantly appearing and disappearing. Lighters typically carried barrels of rice or lumber to Cockspur Island at the entrance to complete the loading.[30] For almost thirty years, the town had been without suitable docking space due to lack of funds, export crops, and commercial know-how. Vessels endured archaic procedures on short, poorly constructed docks, with local merchants paying expensive demurrage to sea captains for too many days spent loading while cargo rotted and lumber stored at dockside twisted into unusable shapes when spring tides and flooding inundated them.[31] Eatton contracted with William Gerard De Brahm, a German engineer who had already set a standard with his design of the fort surrounding Charles Town and his professional maps of the region.[32] A virtual stampede ensued, and by 1763, four years later, twenty-five wharves stretched more than a half mile in front of the Bay. The importance of the Caribbean was apparent. On the east side of Bull Street, owners included two mariners in the West Indian trade, the West Indian firm of Johnston & Wylly, several Carolinians now living in Georgia, a London factor, a merchant coming out of trusteeship Georgia, and two women from the powerful Tannatt family of St. Kitts, who showed their entrepreneurial skills when they staked a claim to not one, but two, docks. On the west side of Bull Street, a similar assortment could be found.[33]

Once the wharves were in place, Savannah showed itself ambitious and opportunistic in developing a trading pattern, as suggested by the figures in Table 6. While reflecting South Carolina's in a broad fashion, that pattern

TABLE 6   Outward Movement of Vessels from Georgia and South
Carolina, 1772

	Georgia	Percent	South Carolina	Percent
West Indies	104	47.7	143	26.3
South Carolina, Georgia	59	27.1	73	13.4
Great Britain	28	12.8	121	22.3
Northward colonies	18	8.3	129	23.8
Bermuda, Bahamas	9	4.1	39	7.2
Southern Europe	—	—	16	2.9
East and West Florida	—	—	20	3.7
Africa	—	—	2	0.3
Totals	218	100.0	543	99.9

Source: American Inspector-General's Ledger, 1768–72, Customs 16/1, NA-UK.

possessed its own signature. Georgia was sending over one hundred vessels to the Caribbean, the bread and butter of its commerce. Those vessels accounted for 49 percent of the total shipping tonnage going outward from the port, in contrast with 22 percent for South Carolina.[34] The second spoke in the wheel of commerce was the short haul between Charles Town and Savannah and Sunbury. In 1772, about one-quarter of Georgia's overall traffic covered the distance to the neighboring port, marking the continuing dependence of the youngest colony on its neighbor and the vital importance of Charles Town's merchants to the flow of goods. It was not all one way, however. Merchants in the two towns did restock their shelves from each other's warehouses, although the flow was mostly southward, including specialty items like a harpsichord or rare wines. The third spoke represented a long-sought triumph. In 1762, Governor Wright reported, "Hitherto all European Goods, consumed here, have been first carried to Charles Town in South Carolina, and from thence reshipped here."[35] Almost never did a vessel depart Savannah for the metropolis. Nine years later, twenty-eight vessels were heading to London, Cowes, and other ports, carrying rice, deerskins, and a small amount of indigo, a direct trade that made possible the structure of credit underlying the booming consumption of British goods.[36]

Unlike South Carolina, Georgia's shipping to the colonies northward was surprisingly weak in volume. In terms of inward traffic, the northern colonies provided foodstuffs, from flour and potatoes to salted fish and cheese, as well as New England rum, bar iron, shoes, candles, and iron pots, and accounted for about 8 percent of the colony's overall traffic. As for outward traffic, the colony was virtually absent from the North American continent other than dispatching schooners to Philadelphia. "But the Northern Trade is an injurious trade," Governor Wright complained, "as they take of but little of our produce and drain us of every trifle of Gold & Silver that is brought here."[37] Vessels stopped at Savannah to sell their goods and continued southward but rarely made a call on their return northward. South Carolina owned the commerce with Massachusetts, Connecticut, Rhode Island, New York, and especially North Carolina. The schooners and ships that sailed from New England and the middle colonies to the West Indies called on Charles Town for a return cargo, but not its neighbor. The commercial contacts of the Carolina lowcountry with the northern colonies highlighted the relative isolation of Georgia at a moment when British North America was in the midst of enormous upheaval.[38] The same held true for the Iberian Peninsula. The colony had virtually no presence in the Portuguese and Spanish markets that proved so lucrative for merchants like Henry Laurens, markets that built the capacity of Carolinians to operate independently of their factors in London or Bristol. By necessity, Georgia's merchants chose to tread traditional and seemingly unimaginative paths.

As Captain Farmer of the *Prudence* ascended the bluff to present his manifest, the crew stood on the wharf talking with dock hands and sailors while they took in the view from the water's edge: eighteen vessels floating alongside the wharfs that stretched the better part of half a mile; laborers loading barrels of rice; draymen hauling bulky casks, barrels, and hogsheads of rum; ship carpenters and caulkers going about their business; warehouse operators standing in front of their buildings; and men and women of the town who had walked down to buy salted cod, cheese, ship bread, and earthenware from New England ships or sugar, rum, coffee, and cocoa from West Indian vessels. In contrast to succeeding ages, women were an accustomed sight on the docks, their purchases fueling dozens of small transactions. At the dock where Captain Farmer's *Prudence* tied up, the owner, Thomas Lloyd, a country factor, or broker, advertised a "commodious wharf and stores" where he offered to sell "Country produce" like rice or indigo to merchants and sea captains, and rum, Madeira, "fine white powdered sugar," flour, and cheese to the general public.[39] Alongside him were merchants like Joseph Wood, originally from the West Indies, who owned a wharf 140 feet in width and 100 feet in depth, with a "crane-house" on each end for lifting hogsheads out of a vessel and with sufficient block and tackle "for hauling down" two vessels at once. Next to the bluff was his storehouse: four stories high, divided into ten rooms, and capable of holding two thousand barrels of rice, or so he claimed. When Wood advertised his real estate for sale, he noted that only two men were needed to "hoist and store a hogshead of rum." As many as sixteen of these multi-story buildings existed on the waterfront by the end of the period.[40]

The maritime population defined not merely the waterfront but the town itself. As illustrated in Table 7, approximately 1,300 men per year during the 1770s—or 325 tars on average per quarter—entered the port, almost half from the West Indies. In the busiest period of the year, from January through March when the rice crop came to market, the town saw close to 400 tars and masters discharging freight and, after several weeks of refitting and assembling cargo, loading their vessels and sailing on. Their numbers swelled the population of the town and, even allowing for the comings and goings during any given quarter, active sailors constituted 8.1 percent of the citizenry, and more if one counted those not under contract. In Charles Town, the figure was 4.5 percent. The Carolina town, wealthiest in North America, had a relatively broad and deep community, and while its waterfront with dozens of ships, hundreds of sailors, and thousands of barrels of rice made it the preeminent shipping center south of Philadelphia, the town could absorb these numbers. In Savannah, it was otherwise. The town was only eight streets deep, separated by four narrow lanes, and a width of five streets and six blocks. When the 325 sailors who arrived each quarter ascended the bluff to Bay Street and spilled over into Ellis Square or into the new neighborhood of Yamacraw, their impact was dramatic. Taverns filled up, the noise level soared, and streets took on added color from their distinctive dress, typically wide baggy breeches cut a few inches above the ankle, a checked shirt of blue or white linen, a gray or blue jacket, and gray stockings.[41] When boatmen, rafters, wharfmen, draymen, coopers, ship carpenters, chandlers, and caulkers are added to the count, the maritime community constituted at least one-quarter of the total population of Savannah and over one-half of adult males.[42]

If the heavy drinking and "dissolute" life of jack-tars produced a know-

TABLE 7   Estimated Number of Sailors in Savannah and Charles Town, 1772

	Sailors per Quarter	*Sailors in Port*	*Town Population*	*Percent*
Savannah	325	162	2,000	8.1
Charles Town	1,086	543	12,100	4.5

Source: Naval Shipping Lists, 1765–67, CO 5/710, NA-UK; American Inspector-General's Ledger, 1768–72, Customs 16, NA-UK; Clowse, *Measuring Charleston's Overseas Commerce.* The population of Charles Town is an average of the figures for 1770 and 1776 given in Coclanis, *Shadow of a Dream,* 114. Assumptions: an average of six sailors per vessel for Savannah and eight for Charles Town; one-fourth of the estimated number of sailors per annum present in a given quarter; one-half of the sailors in port present at a given moment.

ing shrug or frown on the part of middling Savannah, the reality that black sailors may have constituted as much as one-quarter of the total population of seamen aroused misgivings.[43] A common fixture of the maritime world in the West Indies, they were a source of unease in Georgia, a visible manifestation of autonomy that sat poorly with white people adjusting to becoming a slave society in the fullest sense of the word. On Montserrat, where shipping and boating were the lifelines of an export economy, sailors "were generally very scarce," according to Equiano, and owners like Robert King turned to enslaved labor and "free coloreds" to man their ships.[44] Attempts by the governing councils on St. Kitts and Jamaica to limit the role of black sailors ended in failure. The surveyor general of customs in Barbados recorded that the black seamen on his sloop were paid the same wages as their white counterparts during the 1760s.[45] By the mid-eighteenth century, historian Jeffrey Bolster judged that enslaved men and freedmen in the Caribbean virtually monopolized the maritime trades.[46] In her study of Curacao, Linda Rupert writes that black men dominated the labor force on regional sailing vessels and that by mid-century two-thirds were black.[47] On Nevis in 1765, about 3 percent of the black population was engaged in maritime activities as regular deep-sea sailors, occasional deep-sea sailors, boatmen, fishermen, and "wharf Negroes."[48] Many of the smaller vessels had all-black crews, whether on the droggers circling an island to load sugar and rum or on the schooners and vessels that engaged in inter-island trade. The Carolina lowcountry followed the same pattern. Historian Philip Morgan found that 8.6 percent of the enslaved people listed in inventories during the colonial era were "watermen," and on vessels engaged in river and coastal trade, crews were heavily black.[49]

Their travels made for an intricate pattern of connections. As historian Jeffrey Bolster has described so vividly, voyages from each Caribbean island radiated outward like spokes of a wheel: dead-end spokes like the daily expeditions of slaver fishermen, loops formed by the coastal trips of boatmen that connected the various parts of an individual island, bold lines connecting most islands to each other through the inter-island voyages of black and white crews, and the most prominent lines of all, between African, American, and European ports, voyages on which slaves and free blacks sailed.[50] Those sailors carried not just information and ideas but a shared outlook. Equiano's narrative amply confirms the observation made in the early nineteenth century: "Sailors and Negroes are ever on the most amicable terms. . . . [There is] mutual confidence and familiarity between them and in the presence of the sailor the Negro feels himself a man."[51] Bolster describes how black seafaring men wore a mantle of quasi-autonomy that the plantation slave never experienced. They found access to privileges, worldliness, and even wealth denied to most slaves. Voyaging between colonies, they were able to observe the workings of Atlantic society and open up the plantation world to outside influences.[52] In his encounters, Equiano experienced black and white comradeship in ports throughout the Caribbean, sailed to Philadelphia, walked the streets of Savannah and Charles Town, heard George Whitefield preach, and participated as a gunpowder courier in naval battles in the Mediterranean as a young boy.[53]

The waterfront worried white Georgians because ships and boats could serve as a pipeline to freedom and, ironically, for many that pipeline ended in the Caribbean. Many of the enslaved people on coastal plantations had a seafaring background. Billy had been a sailor, escaped from Savannah to St. Kitts, and was recaptured at considerable expense. Consigned to a sawmill with an iron chain fastened around his neck, he made another attempt to escape and headed to the coast to gain access to a vessel. Grimly determined, he slogged through the marshy terrain with a cloth around his neck to disguise the crippling metal chain.[54] The *Georgia Gazette* announced that "a Negroe Fellow, named Will; he is tall, . . . speaks very good English," had taken a canoe from Skidaway and made his escape to Savannah: "Having been used to the sea, he will probably attempt to pass for a free man, and endeavor to get on board some vessel."[55] A large percentage of runaway slaves headed for Savannah, some of them hoping to make it onto one of the vessels at dock. Elizabeth Deveaux, a wealthy planter, believed her runaway, Flora, had been enticed by sailors who were harboring her under the Savannah bluff.[56] Many of the runaways from inland plantations were part of the worldly and multilingual universe of those involved in sailing or in maritime activities in a port. Captain Mark Carr advertised for Bridgee, who had been imported from Africa by the Portuguese, sold to the Spanish, and spoke both languages. He had been captured in the Seven Years' War, purchased by Captain John Dunbar of Georgia, and sold by Dunbar to Carr. Bridgee represented a subversive force on a Georgia plantation, a man of several worlds, intimately familiar with the political discourse of the Atlantic empires, and eager to break free of the prison-like existence in a swamp.[57] Slaves like Bridgee were independent spirits who had tasted the wider world and wanted their share of it.

Ports of the West Indies and the lowcountry could be places of danger to the black sailor but also places of refuge. Returning to Savannah from Montserrat after buying his freedom, Olaudah Equiano was standing on the wharf beside the sloop *Nancy*, on which he was serving, when he was accosted by a slave belonging to James Read, a prominent merchant. Losing his temper, Equiano beat the culprit "soundly," presumably before an interested assembly of dockhands and passersby. The following day, the owner of the victim, James Read, descended on the wharf and demanded the captain deliver up the seaman "that he might have [Equiano] flogged all round the town, for beating his negro slave." Captain Farmer pointed out that his sailor was a free man. Read, a partner in the firm Read and Mossman and a member of the governor's council, shouted he wanted the jack-tar punished and, when Equiano was not delivered, stormed away, swearing he would bring out all the constables in town "for he would have [Equiano] out of this vessel."[58] For a brief moment, the sailor contemplated resistance: "for I would sooner die like a free man, than suffer myself to be scourged by the hands of ruffians, and my blood drawn like a slave." Persuaded by the captain that Read was a "spiteful" man capable of great mischief, Equiano left the *Nancy* and vanished into Yamacraw, a new neighborhood on the west side of town, a boisterous, noisy place of warehouses, lumberyards, taverns, cottages, boardinghouses, and a few shops.[59] He found refuge in the lodging where Farmer was staying, the house of a Mr. Dixon, as he recalled the name. For five days, Equiano hid indoors, "secreted," while the town's constables searched high and low to serve a warrant for his arrest.[60] The innkeeper apparently did not think it odd or particularly unusual for a black sailor to share quarters with his white captain.

Despite its subsequent reputation as a slum, Yamacraw, distinct from the long-defunct native village of that name, was three different communities, each with its own lifestyle.[61] The three were loosely grouped on the western side of town, several hundred feet from the boundary line. The first community was a waterfront area with warehouses, lumberyards, a shipyard, and storehouses, dominated by large merchants. "To be sold at Yammacraw," John Graham advertised, "a parcel of new Negroes, part of the cargo of the schooner *Fortune*," twenty or so enslaved people from Gambia by way of Barbados.[62] In a yard there, Robert Watts constructed the largest ship ever built in the colony. The second was a biracial neighborhood where black and white sailors found accommodations in the same lodging, where public houses catered to all comers, and where rowdiness and violence were standard. Sailors were fond of alehouse cheer, a short pipe of tobacco, spirits, rest, food, and dice. Brawls were not uncommon. "Last night, the carpenter of the brigantine *Antelope*, Capt. Thomas Paley, being in liquor, and endeavouring to get on board the vessel," the *Georgia Gazette* reported, "unfortunately fell into the river, and was drowned."[63] After returning from a voyage to London, Captain George Anderson saw his sailors "desert," or at least disappear, into the rum shops of Yamacraw.[64] The third community was the village of St. Gall, whose residents were laborers, carpenters, artisans, and even middling figures associated with the port, like the collector of customs. They held to their own. As a young girl Elizabeth Lichenstein, whose father commanded the colony's scout boat, moved from the Ogeechee River to Yamacraw to be with an aunt and attend school in Savannnah.[65] Within the relatively small space that later became Oglethorpe Ward, subcommunities could exist and thrive, each with its own identity and values.

In the port towns of the West Indies, neighborhoods like Yamacraw were common on the fringes of town but there they had an even more distinct character. In most islands, free people of color formed a significant part of the population, for example 14 percent of the residents of Kingston in 1773. It was not uncommon for "free coloreds," especially women, to run tippling, or drinking, houses and keep small shops in similar neighborhoods.[66] Blacks found the anonymity of the neighborhood reassuring.

When a slave by the name of Francois, "used to the sea," ran away, captains in Savannah were warned to stay clear of him. It is likely he followed the example of Equiano and found refuge there for a time.[67] Even known figures could fade into the landscape. Alexander Wylly warned that one of his slaves, a carpenter called Ismael, was "daily employed by Masters of Vessels" although he had no ticket and was frequently seen in the evenings playing the fiddle in tippling houses, presumably of Yamacraw. Ismael was pocketing the money and living on his own.[68] In March 1766, the Georgia legislature pointed its finger at white innkeepers and owners of tippling houses who "harbored" sailors and extended credit, "enticing" them into a life that disrupted the smooth flow of the waterfront.[69]

What of the town that lay beyond the wharves and docks and of the people who lived in large but simply designed two-story houses, trustee-era cottages, storehouses, huts, and attics, or who slept on stairways? When Captain Farmer walked up the bluff to file his papers with the Customs Office, he found a town not dissimilar to others he encountered in the Caribbean. Arriving in the same year, the naturalist John Bartram described the sand on the steep bank: "So that furious winds from ye river driveth loose white sand up ye declivity & lodgeth it on ye plain ground on which ye town stands."[70] He witnessed boys making a great game of jumping down the loose sand on the banks. The town had a recently settled, if not frontier, appearance. If Savannah clung stubbornly to its Palladian design, with symmetrical squares and small houses in the style of English cottages, its buildings were of wooden construction like those of the Leeward Islands. Brick remained a rare commodity except for foundations and chimneys, and colorful blue and red paint set off the modest structures, some 200–240 in the town proper and another 160 in two burgeoning suburbs.[71] The construction of many if not most homes conformed to the original simple plan: frame houses, sixteen feet by twenty-four feet, built close to the ground, with three rooms, one in front and two smaller ones in back, freestanding along the streets, with gardens to the sides and rear.

A post-revolutionary drawing of Bay Street shows a mix of buildings: a few simple frame houses from the 1730s, gable- or hip-roofed, and others that were two-story, comfortable looking but modest in appearance.[72] Few if any buildings in Savannah attained the level of a Charles Town double house, with its central hallway, brick construction, low-pitched roof, elaborate doorway featuring a portico supported by columns, a first floor set about ten feet above ground level, and the whole surrounded by forbidding wrought-iron fences. Merchant John Graham built a version of the single house so common in the West Indies: a two-story structure one-room deep, featuring a length-wise piazza to catch a cooling breeze. If the elegant and increasingly fenced homes of Charles Town, with their concern for social distance, more nearly resembled Kingston, Jamaica, the modest architecture of Savannah and the accessibility of its houses more nearly resembled Basseterre, St. John's, and other towns in the Leeward Islands.[73]

An analysis of the occupations of those who worked in Savannah, white and black, offers the most telling similarity with the towns of the Caribbean. In 1770, sugar, rum, and molasses represented 93 percent of the total exports of Barbados, 92 percent for St. Kitts, and 89 percent for Jamaica.[74] Rice and indigo accounted for 86 percent of exports from Georgia and South Carolina between 1768 and 1772.[75] Thousands of ships plied the Atlantic between England, West Africa, the Caribbean, and the lowcountry to serve that commerce while thousands of men unloaded merchandise and enslaved Africans, assembled the cargos to be shipped, and manned the vessels for the voyage outward. Export and import trades dominated the economic activity in urban centers. Historian B. W. Higman estimates that, in 1782, 41 percent of all male adults in Kingston were involved in maritime transport and external commercial exchange and only 13 percent in industrial activities, broadly defined. The latter sector included shipbuilding, leather working, cabinetmaking, metal working, and a range of other activities that required a degree of processing.[76]

Like the towns of the Caribbean, those of the lowcountry had a limited involvement in manufacturing. R. C. Nash found that three different sources of information for Charles Town produced figures for the working population involved in "industry" ranging between 13 and 15 percent of the total. Other than limited shipbuilding, there was a modest amount of tanning of hides, distilling molasses, and sugar baking. As a center of overseas commerce based on rice, slaves, and manufactured goods, the city depended on English merchants to an unusual extent. Yet Charles Town was more than a mere "shipping point," as has been charged.[77] It possessed a sophisticated and large mercantile community that sold rice in multiple markets on three continents, offered a wide array of British merchandise to a knowledgeable buying public, was able to tap much of the financing for South Carolina's development internally, and served as a processing center in the landing, buying, selling, and distributing of Africans on a massive scale.[78] Compared to Boston or Philadelphia, Charles Town may have had a much narrower profile of occupations, but the commercial and service sectors were fully developed.

Savannah was to follow in that mold. Although no available records permit an occupational profile of its residents in the eighteenth century, the register of deaths for the first decade of the nineteenth century is suggestive. The maritime and external commercial sectors accounted for 52 percent of deaths while the industrial sector, as defined by historian Jacob Price, accounted for only 9 percent. As a town that had realized its economic growth only in the last fifteen years of the colonial era, Savannah more nearly resembled the "shipping point" that Price described.[79]

In keeping with this profile, the dominant figures in Savannah were not planters but merchants. In Charles Town, the elites in the Carolina lowcountry invested heavily in handsome brick homes, expensive furniture and fabrics, and a social life that revolved around private clubs, societies like the musical St. Cecilia Society, and horseracing as well as other forms of gambling.[80] Large planters dominated the political life of the town, set the social calendar, and stoked the trade in luxury goods that kept shopkeepers and craftsmen in high demand. Savannah, however, was a different place. Although planters in Savannah represented nearly the same percentage of buyers of property as in Charles Town (14 percent versus 12 percent; see Table 8), their role was considerably more muted.[81] Some were small holders who had grown up during the trustee period and were struggling to become genuine planters. Others were transplants from the Southern District of the Carolina lowcountry, possessed a practical bent, and resented the social airs of their one-time brethren in Charles Town. They were more preoccupied with expanding their initial investments in land and slaves. Adding to this muted quality was the relative absence of lowcountry planters beyond Christ Church Parish.[82] The elites of St. John and St. Andrew parishes never embraced the town, partly for pecuniary reasons, partly because of a deeply rooted distaste for the town and its leadership. At times, it seemed as if the lower half of the lowcountry were boycotting the upper half, a division that dated back to the trusteeship period. The town itself never enjoyed the building boom that set the seal on Charles Town's unique spot in British North America.

Merchants rather than planters held pride of place in this rapidly grow-

TABLE 8   Sellers and Buyers of Property, Savannah, 1755–75

	Sellers	Percent	Buyers	Percent
Artisans, service workers	127	50.0	126	36.4
Merchants, retailers	40	15.8	77	22.3
Planters	27	10.6	49	14.2
Gentlemen	4	1.6	8	2.3
Women	22	8.7	36	10.4
Professionals	25	9.8	31	8.9
No status listed	9	3.5	19	5.5
	254	100.0	346	100.0

Sources: Beckemeyer, Abstracts of Georgia Colonial Conveyance Book. For the period after 1761, Conveyances c-2 (1761–66), S (1766–69), V (1769–71), x-1 (1771–72), x-2 (1772–74), Georgia Archives.

ing town. As exports grew in the early 1760s, merchants came to domi-nate Bay Street and Johnson Square and owned a good part of Ellis and Reynolds squares so that the front half of the town resembled nothing so much as an increasingly well-organized entrepôt.[83] Bay Street went from a rallying point for carpenters, sea captains, ship chandlers, small-time of-ficials, tavernkeepers, widows, and small shopkeepers to hosting the grand establishments of the larger merchants while retaining the more success-ful artisans and a sprinkling of widows.[84] The greatest change came in Johnson Square, where Oglethorpe and the immigrants on the ship *Ann* had first pitched tent and residents of the town still gathered to hear the news.[85] Habersham and Harris now controlled six prime lots for their op-erations, together with one on Bay Street; John Graham and John Simp-son operated large wholesale establishments; and John Rae, a Protestant of Northern Ireland who had fought his way up through the deerskin trade, opened a mercantile house across the way.[86] If that square bore an aura of hard-earned respectability, Ellis Square attracted a more unorthodox community: deerskin traders, Jewish merchants, and hard-nosed retailers accustomed to the cut and thrust of business in the trenches. The Nunes brothers, sons of a Lisbon physician, traded with the Creeks, lived in na-tive towns, acquired fluency in various Muskogee dialects, and without any sense of inhibition worked the margins of society.[87] An important firm with Bristol connections, Inglis and Hall, opened a store, as did a retailer from the trustee period, a mariner from Charles Town, and a retailer from England.[88]

Between 1750 and 1770, Savannah evolved from a community where modest artisans, shopkeepers, minor officials, and mariners dominated to a place where affluent merchants, well-to-do traders, well-off artisans, and successful planters set the tone. The town went from a society in which the lower middling orders had pride of place to one where wealth and economic power were increasingly concentrated in the hands of a few. The town saw clear lines of demarcation take root, both social and spatial, and a considerably less egalitarian world impose itself. And yet social boundaries, in keeping with the origins of the town, remained elastic. Many of the artisans and shopkeepers grew with the new opportunities and transformed themselves into men and women of substance and owners of slaves; others saw their sisters and brothers marry into families that were successful commercially; others found the rising level of prosperity reason enough to be satisfied. Carpenters and gunsmiths still worked alongside the wealthier merchants, and life on Savannah's squares retained their intimate quality. On Broughton Street, Abigail Minis's store and tavern attracted a steady stream of clients, and her stature in the community only increased as she and her sons became planters of modest standing.[89]

The social distance between export merchant and successful artisan in Savannah was considerably less than in Charles Town, a phenomenon with a parallel in the Leeward Islands. As wealthy planters decamped from St. Kitts, Antigua, and Montserrat, a certain leveling down of the white upper class had taken place. By the middle of the eighteenth century, as many as one-half of the wealthier planters had taken up residence in England to enjoy the benefits of life in the homeland, and they were followed by the more affluent of the merchants and professionals.[90] By mid-century, absentees made up a high percentage of the elite families of Antigua.[91] A visitor found St. Kitts "almost abandoned to overseers and managers, owing to the amazing fortunes that belong to Individuals, who almost all reside in England."[92] With fewer wealthy planters, the ranks were opened to managers and attorneys as well as to the merchants, physicians, and other professionals who remained. White artisans too found that independence could be purchased for the price of a few slaves to do their manual work. The distance between the lower ranks of the whites and the elite narrowed in response, a reflection as well of a growing sense of racial solidarity in an increasingly black world. In 1774, Janet Schaw noticed the absence of European snobbery and commented on the informality and friendliness that prevailed among whites, who all seemed intimately acquainted.[93]

In the case of Savannah, there was a related development that can be best described as a "leveling up." The town began as an ingathering of lower-middle-class artisans, minor magistrates, and charity settlers. The society that emerged at the end of the 1760s was not yet fully stratified and had room for the more successful artisans and shopkeepers or, at least, enjoyed closer relationships with people who had come through the same experiences. The levels of wealth and marriage patterns had not yet shut down the avenues of access. James Habersham's brother-in-law, Robert Bolton, could marry Susannah Mauve, daughter of a French-speaking shopkeeper, and see their children take pride of place in the town's mercantile elite in the post-revolutionary period.[94] One of the most important steps in transforming Oglethorpe's town was the skillful way that merchants co-opted artisans who came into the royal period full of suspicion and tentative about the change. Despite the legislative setback in 1757, when the assembly passed an ineffective bill limiting the use of slaves as artisans, the leading craftsmen of Savannah fared well in the new order, and most were more than ready to participate in the newfound prosperity.[95] Adrian Loyer earned enough as a gunsmith to purchase twelve enslaved people, hire out "Negroes and canoes," and invest in land on Skidaway Island and in South Carolina.[96]

Shipmasters who engaged in the West Indian trade had a significant impact on the ambience of the town and helped bridge the distance between artisans and shopkeepers, on the one hand, and merchants and adventurers, on the other. Mariners who sailed from island to island established themselves as owners of small retail shops, investors in real estate, and promoters of new ventures to the Caribbean. In the early years of the royal period, mariners like David Cunningham, Francis Goffe, Philip Hughes, Edward Carlton, Joseph Phillips, James Brooks, Andrew Elton Wells, and Isaac Martin owned their own vessels, brought trading relationships with them, and partnered with others onshore. As the years passed, some sold their property and faded from the picture, but others demonstrated remarkable staying power. Isaac Martin sensed where opportunity lay and left seafaring to take a lead role in developing Yamacraw as an important working-class neighborhood to the west of Savannah. David Montaigut held on to a choice lot on the Bay, kept his store, and became naval officer of the port.

Andrew Elton Wells left captaining his boat to found the one distillery in Georgia, located on the site of the old Trustees Garden and producing five thousand gallons of rum a year.[97]

Sea captains, artisans, and merchants tolerated much of the assertiveness of the Africans and African Americans around them because of the accompanying benefits. Many of those benefits revolved around the retailing of foodstuffs in the public market in much the same fashion as took place in the West Indies.[98] By the late 1760s, Ellis Square had become the official market for the town, sixty feet square with four small "houses" anchoring each corner and the stalls in between rented to vendors. African American women monopolized the flow of vegetables and fruits, set prices, and established an atmosphere remarkably similar to markets in the sugar islands and West Africa.[99] Ellis Square was the most successful combination of the popular with the mercantile in the whole of the town and the point where black and white cultures met and intertwined in ways not always predictable. "Huckster wenches" controlled the life of the marketplace, setting prices, dealing with "Country Negroes" for the purchase of their goods, and shaping the supplies available, much to the distress of the commissary of the market, the Scot George Baillie.[100] By the mid-1760s, the Georgia grand jury was already complaining about the "large bodies" of slaves who were making their way to Savannah, often on Sundays, to dispose of "corn, wood and other commodities, without ticket from their masters."[101] In 1774, an act required masters to obtain a license for their slaves "to sell Fruit, Fish, Garden Stuff or any other Commodities whatsoever in the Town of Savannah."[102]

Popular markets were a firmly entrenched feature of the urban economies of the sugar islands.[103] At Bridgetown, Barbados, a physician commented on "the sight of so many negroes on their way to town carrying on their heads baskets of fruit and vegetables in the market."[104] The whole town of St. John's in Antigua was supplied in this way.[105] Freedmen in the sugar islands could not compete with enslaved people because of their lack of access to land for which they did not have to pay rent. In the Leeward Islands, the markets held on Sundays could attract hundreds of blacks, who exercised one of the few vestiges of freedom which the slaves had in the plantation economy.[106] The hustle and bustle of the market provided an environment in which various kinds of clandestine activities could take place, like trading in stolen goods. In Charles Town, slave peddlers bought produce on their own account, traded with other slaves, and sold their own handcrafted objects. In 1772, an anonymous observer wrote, "Near that market, constantly resort a great number of loose, idle, and disorderly negro women, who are seated there from morn till night and *buy* and sell on their own accounts, what they please."[107] The women as well as male peddlers on the streets took advantage of the opportunities to engage in activities that alarmed whites: forestalling, selling at "exorbitant prices," trafficking with "Country Negroes," and harboring runaways.[108] They were taking on a role traditionally allotted to women in West Africa and the Caribbean. A historian of the dynamics of the marketplace in Georgia, Betty Wood, makes much of the spatial relationship with many West African markets, including those at Whydah in the kingdom of Dahomey, and Cape Corse in Guinea.[109]

Like in Charles Town, local hawkers and peddlers were to be found on most streets of Savannah offering cooked rice, oysters, vegetables, bread, and cakes; their singsong voices cried out in a variety of dialects that would later merge to become Gullah or Geechee.[110] Equiano recounted how he began by buying a glass tumbler at the Dutch port of St. Eustatius and sold it at Montserrat for a profit of a few pennies. Soon, he was buying jugs of rum and finding a particularly good market on Guadeloupe, Grenada, and the other French islands: "Thus was I going all about the islands upwards of four years and ever trading as I went." He brought bags of lime and oranges, earthenware, rum, and sugar—all salable items on Bay and Broughton streets.[111] Savannah became an extension of that West Indian exchange.

In the Caribbean, masters were in the habit of hiring out their slave labor to other white people to monetize their value. "I suppose nine-tenths of the mechanics throughout the West Indies," Equiano offered, "are negro slaves; and I well know the coopers among them earn two dollars a day; the carpenters the same, and oftentimes more; as also the masons, smiths, and fishermen, &c."[112] He was exaggerating to make the point that free people of color occupied an important place in the hierarchy of skills available for hire, and slaves formed an important element among the artisans and skilled workers of the main towns.[113] The enslaved people who worked for wages formed an elite. Whether in Bridgetown or Basseterre, Charles Town or Savannah, they enjoyed special privileges. Higman observed that the spread of self-hire throughout the Caribbean meant that many slaves were allowed to seek lodging apart from their owners' premises in huts they built on the fringes of town.[114] Those men and women found an opportunity to establish a measure of independence somewhere between bondage and freedom. The figures submitted by the rector of Christ Church in 1771 include forty black adults living on their own, paying their masters a weekly or monthly fee. Historian Philip Morgan estimated that this group represented as much as 10 percent of the adult black population, indicative of their importance in the town.[115]

Whether through self-hire or working for a master, the loosely constructed maritime world offered enslaved people considerable freedom of movement. Along the docks and in the shipyards, blacks worked as ship carpenters, blacksmiths, and coopers. Robert Watts, the premier shipbuilder in the colony, employed primarily enslaved people on his ships as did his brother in Sunbury.[116] When John Wand, Edward Telfair, and John Morel launched the eighty-four-foot *Elizabeth* from Ossabaw Island, the credit belonged to one master builder and thirty-odd slaves, including blacksmiths and ship carpenters brought from Antigua.[117] On the docks of Savannah, the swarm of "wharf Negroes" included many who had been hired out or had hired themselves out. When the *Crown* pulled into port, it took seven of their number a full week to unload the cargo. The captain paid out £5 16s. to their owners, not infrequently merchants themselves.[118] Even lowly porters and draymen controlled their time to a degree. There was money to be earned even if it were a small amount, and for those with genuine skills, there was good money to be made, if rarely enough to purchase their freedom.[119] Black boatmen enjoyed freedom of a sort in transporting rice and lumber from plantations, crewing for white captains engaged in the coastal or West Indian trade, manning canoes and small craft to sell provisions along the docks and to the ships, and steering rafts of logs down the Savannah River.[120] Often they set their own schedules, interacted with plantation slaves, and took advantage of opportunities to sell small goods as well as precious rum. Captain Adam Croddy worked his schooner up and down the tidal rivers and creeks of the coast with four black sailors.[121] Charged with piloting boats on the Georgia coast, Captain William Lyford maintained twenty-two black pilots, many of whom brought in ships from Tybee Island across the sand bars and shallow waters that made the river so treacherous.[122] Only in 1774 did the government introduce a badge system like that of Charles Town to control the activities of the enslaved people who hired away their time and enjoyed the relative freedom that came with it.[123] Very few black males in Savannah did not have some involvement in maritime activity at some point in their lives.

That pseudo-independence made the white community exceedingly nervous. In 1768, a resident complained to the Georgia grand jury that far too "many Negroes . . . are allowed to live so much at large . . . by which means a door is open to robberies and other bad practices."[124] Three years later, a grand jury repeated the same charge that slaves were "permitted to Rent houses in the lanes and Invirons of Savannah" and "in said houses meetings of Slaves are very frequent, Spirits and other liquors are sold and Stolen goods often Concealed."[125] When Equiano visited his friend Mosa in the latter's house, he expected an evening of sociability in secure surroundings. The night patrol ominously knocked on the door, came in to drink some freely offered punch, then arrested the sailor for violating an act that forbade lights in a slave house after 9 p.m. Flexing their maddeningly arbitrary power, the patrol took this free black man illegally to the workhouse for a whipping. The host was left undisturbed because of his master's protection.[126] It was a world full of ironies. Mosa may be the same person in the accounts of Edward Telfair listed as "Muso, Negroe Fellow," who entered the Telfair store on Bay Street nine times during 1773 to buy, on credit, pigtail tobacco, two jackets, a knife, rum, and other minor items.[127]

Reminders of their servile condition were ever present. During 1774, when sales of slaves reached their peak, Savannah saw 1,550 people disembarked from ships directly from Africa, another 1,300 arrive via schooners from the Charles Town market, and about 150 from the Caribbean. The Reverend Henry Muhlenberg recorded that he and his wife sailed from Carolina with ten English passengers, four German women, and "a number of new Negroes who had lately arrived from Africa and had been sold."[128] The total imported to Savannah that year was considerably more than the number who arrived in Antigua and Montserrat and within hailing distance of the 5,700 who came to St. Kitts. Savannah was now the second largest slave market in North America and a significant third-level market along the Caribbean rim. Like Kingston and Charles Town, the town was considerably more than a mere shipping center. The marketing of slaves transformed it into a processing center where enslaved people were landed, bought, sold, and distributed throughout the colony. The colony's most aggressive merchant, John Graham, advertised "Three Sailors, who had been used to go in the schooner and boat," while John Wand casually disposed of his skilled craftsmen when he ran into financial difficulties. When Darling and Company sold five "seasoned" slaves and a schooner, the notice claimed, "Two of them are good boat Negroes and a cooper, the others are very handy as wharf Negroes."[129]

The appalling market for "New Negroes" could bring striking examples of black empowerment. Captain Stephen Dean, an Irishman and slaver who carried 490 West Africans into Georgia, appeared in May 1772 with a free black woman from the small slave-trading town of Kau-Ur on the Gambia River. The former spouse of an Englishman, Fenda Lawrence belonged to an elite of women traders who were active in the commerce for slaves, gum, and textiles, and she had accrued status and capital through the patronage of the *alcati*, the male elite, and connections with the English. Dean described her as "a Considerable trader in the River Gambia," a product of several generations of women slavers in the Senegambia. The kingdom of Saalum, from whose realm she came, enjoyed close ties with the British and included diverse ethnic groups that produced a multicultural population belonging to that larger world of the "Atlantic creole." After Dean delivered over two hundred Africans to Charles Town, she continued the voyage with him to Georgia to apply for a residency permit so she could educate her son, James Lawrence. She also came with five domestic slaves. James Habersham obligingly signed the certificate of residency for this African *signares* who not only possessed wealth but was part of an extensive African network producing slaves.[130] Savannahians were not unaccustomed to such relationships. A mariner, Andrew Elliott, left his estate to Isabella, the daughter of Sylvia Elliott, "a free Negro woman living in Gambia on the coast of Guinea and the reputed daughter of me."[131]

Savannah was a merchants' town with a distinctly Caribbean flavor. From retailers and country factors to Indian traders, export merchants, and brokers, they controlled the waterfront and key segments of property, especially in the front half nearest the bluff. If Savannah bore similarities to towns in the sugar islands, there were notable differences as well. There was a higher percentage of whites to blacks than in the urban centers of the Caribbean, a greater number of white artisans and craftsmen at work, a much stronger middling group that reflected both the legacy of the trustee period and the vigor of the local economy, a larger number of independent merchants, both big and small, a lesser level of social inequality, and the presence of planters who chose to reside in town rather than in Britain, rejecting the practice of their peers in the Caribbean.[132] Nor was Savannah or Georgia the demographic disaster area of that tropical region. Still, the similarities were striking. Georgia's lowcountry came closer to the mono-culture of the Caribbean than any other place on the mainland. While South Carolina shipped a massive amount of indigo along with its barrels of rice and was beginning to tap into the produce of the upcountry, Georgia remained fixated on one commodity: rice. It was a deadly trap. A shipping point for the produce of the lowcountry, Savannah never developed the linkages that could lead the plantation economy down a path of specializa-tion and diversification. In terms of occupational structure, the town more nearly approximated those in the Caribbean than on the mainland.[133] Its waterfront reflected the similarities: the high percentage of black sailors, the number of vessels going to and coming from the West Indies, the hogs-heads of rum being rolled across the docks, the dozens and sometimes hun-dreds of slaves from Caribbean ports being auctioned off, the local mariners who ran stores and speculated in urban property, the sandy streets, and the simple wooden buildings. The rough, arbitrary treatment and the physi-cal threats and beatings that Olaudah Equiano received spoke loudly to the alignment of attitudes with its neighbors to the south. That spiritual kinship, born in the Barbadian plantation model, was sealed by the role of West Indians like Lewis Johnston and Alexander Wylly, who functioned as the heart and soul of the "Christ Church clique" that dominated so much of Georgia's economic and political life. While the merchants of Savannah and Georgia belonged to a web of interlocking connections that spanned the Caribbean and Atlantic, it was a web with roots deep in yet another world, that of the Highlands and Lowlands of Scotland.

The Tannatt Family by Henry Benbridge, ca. 1774. Predominantly Scots, the members of this extended family were part of the emerging elite in colonial Georgia. The elderly woman to the right is Heriot Cunningham Crooke (Mrs. Clement Crooke) who, after her husband died, moved with her family from St. Kitts to Savannah in 1753. Her four daughters married Georgia merchants of Scots origin. The second person from the left is Lady Houstoun, widow of Sir Patrick Houstoun, a Lowland Scot who arrived at the founding of the colony. To her right is Heriot Tannatt, later the wife of William Thomson, son of a leading London merchant in the Georgia trade. Among the men are a nephew of Governor James Wright and the attorney general for the province. Photo © National Gallery of Canada. Courtesy of the National Gallery of Canada, Ottawa. Gift of Jasper H. Nicolls, Ottawa, 1960.

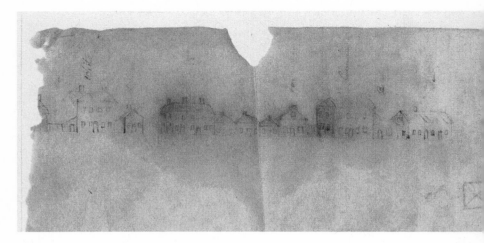

Bay Street, Savannah, 1786. Edward White, the customs house officer of the port of Savannah, created this sketch, which lists the names of the occupants of the buildings. Several of the houses follow the design of cottages shown in a view of the town from 1734. Unlike Charles Town, there are no houses on raised foundations and little indication

that brick was used. The opening in the middle of the drawing appears to be Bull Street. Many of the two-story buildings served as stores as well as residences. MS 2001, Georgia Historical Society, Savannah. Courtesy of the Georgia Historical Society.

James Habersham portrait by Jeremiah Theus, 1772.
Habersham (1715–75) came to Georgia as a schoolteacher and missionary with George Whitefield, built
and managed the Bethesda Orphanage, and then
became the premier merchant in the struggling
colony. During the royal period, he created three
rice plantations and served on the governor's council
and later as the acting governor. He almost single-
handedly shaped the nature of the government and
the economy in the interim period between the
trusteeship and the royal regime. From *The Letters of
Hon. James Habersham, 1756–1775*, vol. 6. Collections
of the Georgia Historical Society, Hargrett Rare
Book and Manuscript Library, University of Georgia
Libraries.

Joseph Clay portrait by Jeremiah Theus, 1772. Clay
(1741–1804) arrived in Georgia at age nineteen and
followed in the footsteps of his uncle James Habersham.
First in partnership with his cousin James Habersham
Jr., then on his own, he exported rice, imported
enslaved Africans, shipped lumber to the West Indies,
and showed himself to be a cautious entrepreneur
well grounded in the art of transatlantic trade. He was
one of the few merchants to embrace the Revolution.
Courtesy of the Society of the Cincinnati in the State
of Georgia.

View of Tiby Lighthouse at the entrance of Savanna River. Georgia. Dec'r, 1764. The lighthouse on Tybee Island marked the entrance to the Savannah River and the beginning of a seventeen-mile journey to Savannah. Watercolor of a drawing in the Crown Collection of Maps in the British Museum. Courtesy of the Hargrett Rare Book and Manuscript Library, University of Georgia Libraries.

View of Cockspur Fort at the entrance of Savanna River in Georgia. Decr. 1764. The government built the small fort after a Spanish vessel raided the Georgia coast at the end of the Seven Years' War. Located at the mouth of the south channel of the Savannah River, it served as an anchorage for incoming vessels awaiting a pilot or for outgoing vessels taking in the last of their cargo from lighters. The fort fell into disuse and was no longer there by 1780. Watercolor of a drawing in the Crown Collection of Maps in the British Museum. Courtesy of the Hargrett Rare Book and Manuscript Library, University of Georgia Libraries.

A Trading Boat Which Sails up to Savannah Town, 200 Miles Higher Up Than Ebenezer. On a trip to Georgia with other colonists from Germany in 1736, Philip von Reck produced some fifty watercolor and pencil sketches of what he saw. This boat was hauling supplies up the Savannah River to the frontier trading post of Savannah Town on the Carolina side of the river. It returned with a cargo of deerskins for Charles Town. Oglethorpe founded Augusta a few months later. Boats continued to be the most common way of transporting skins. CO 5/638, f. 304, NA-UK. Courtesy of National Archives, United Kingdom.

Chapter Five

Merchants in a Creole Society

In the mid-1760s, Savannah would have struck a visitor from Charles Town as a hardworking, sweaty port, without grand buildings or the trappings of wealth but energetically trying to piece together the infrastructure that would allow it to compete. The sights and sounds were familiar, and the Caribbean flavor seemed the natural consequence of exploiting the opportunities nearest at hand. The port was taking on an identity that seemed familiar and comfortable. Georgia was rapidly acquiring the features of older colonies whose populations were elaborating their own versions of British society, producing a blend of traditions, cultures, and practices that set them apart. If the settlers thought of themselves as British and never as creoles, like the Spanish born in the Americas, they knew they were not fully like the English at home and protected their self-esteem by carefully thinking of themselves as "seasoned" to the climate in Georgia and South Carolina. Although their tastes were thoroughly Anglicized, part of the same British American consumer culture that united the mainland, they were beginning to take pride in their distinctiveness. As the royal government established itself and a plantation economy took shape, newly arrived merchants coming from around the Atlantic basin took their place at the center of this emerging society.[1]

Georgians were constructing a society that was merging a variety of cultural inheritances into new forms and shapes. On one level, it was a practical matter of making use of the resources and talents on hand. Artisans in Savannah may have started with architectural plans for Christ Church designed in London and calling for marble, but the finished product spoke to the materials and limitations of their setting, with outside walls overlaid with weatherboard and covered with tar and sand rather than plasterwork.[2] On another level, settlers were fully involved in the process of elaborating a plantation economy modeled on their neighbors'. It was a wrenching change. A Charles Town "Gentleman" writing in the *South Carolina Gazette* as late as 1754 reported hearing Georgians discuss how a "terrible monster, having *twelve* heads of different sizes" had stalked out of the swamps next to the Carolina metropolis making hideous, bellowing noises and attacking nearby plantations. The monster was slavery and, even for those Georgians who accepted the institution and were willing to invest their moral capital in the new order, the overwhelming preponderance of Africans in the Carolina lowcountry bespoke a moral disorder to be avoided at all costs. "It may be a good country in time," the author judged, "but, in my opinion, it can never, never come up to Carolina."[3] The lower middling orders had yet to surrender all of their idealism and remained ambivalent toward the full implications of slavery even while purchasing their first enslaved people to assist in shops, help around the docks, or work in the garden plots outside town.

Trusteeship Georgia had served as the classic example of people reaching out to re-create the same societies they had left, not to create a new one: they included urban dwellers from England, Lutheran refugees from Germany, French Swiss, Lowland Scots with an acquisitive instinct, and Highland Scots speaking Gaelic and wearing tartans. Under the guiding hand of Pastor John Martin Bolzius, the Salzburgers created a farming community modeled after their peasant life in Germany, keeping alive an intense sense of independence that isolated them from the rest of the colony. Offended by the moral and social implications of slavery, Bolzius never tired of pointing to the success of his yeoman farmers who gloried in physical labor under the hot Georgia sun and supplied Savannah with much of its garden produce or of the women weavers who produced most of the colony's small supply of silk. Isolated by location, language, and culture, Ebenezer nevertheless stood very much in the epicenter of the Atlantic world, serving as the nurturer of German culture in the colony. Trunkloads of German books and literature arrived regularly in the remote outpost while Bolzius created a modest orphanage modeled after one in Halle, Germany, sent detailed reports back to Augsburg over three decades, and regularly preached to Germans in other parts of the colony. Yet, once the prohibition on slavery was lifted, the Salzburgers began to purchase one or two Africans; some moved to Savannah to take advantage of new opportunities; and the leading German merchants competed as to who would be the most successful in bringing the world of British merchandise to their co-religionists.[4]

By the 1760s, the lowcountry was no longer that brand-new society. The veterans of the trustee period had been in place for as much as thirty years and saw themselves as Georgians first. Their children had known only the hardships of a frontier colony and were starting to assume significant roles in the life of the colony: successful merchants like John Morel and Samuel Elbert, shopkeepers like Philip Box and the distinctive Abigail Minis, artisans like silversmith Adrian Loyer and carpenter Peter Tondee, planters like the Houstoun brothers, as well as the children of James Habersham and Francis Harris.[5] These young people assumed prominent places in royal Georgia, bringing with them a hard-nosed attitude, as if nothing could be taken for granted but everything was there for the asking, especially if accompanied by enough pluck and determination. Planters from Carolina imparted the long-established ethos and practices nurtured in that eighty-year-old province: their attachment to the Barbadian model of a plantation economy, a readiness to innovate technologically and fuse differing traditions of rice culture, and a hardened attitude toward the use of black labor. And yet Jonathan Bryan, an exemplar of the new plantation elite, showed an ability to work with Creek Indians, a desire to Christianize his enslaved labor, and an openness to the demands of white artisans.[6] Whites, blacks, and natives were bound together in relationships that forced accommodations and created new values and practices. A creole society was taking shape, one that was heavily dependent on the values of the Carolina lowcountry and yet blended disparate cultures into a larger whole. After 1750, the appearance of several dozen merchants, traders, brokers, retailers, and speculators provided a vital ingredient in that search for identity.[7]

If a resident were asked to identify the merchants who took Georgia into the transatlantic world, he or she would have had no difficulty in rattling off the names of a half-dozen men who traded overseas. However, defining those merchants with any rigor was elusive. There were too many shadings of function, too many roles that any one individual could play, and too many outsized ambitions. Most contemporaries in Hanoverian England agreed that a merchant was a wholesale trader who had dealings with foreign countries, someone "who trafficks to remote countries," according to one dictionary.[8] Such a definition did not quite fit the American experience where colonists had a more flexible view. If shopkeepers and skilled artisans had lost any connection to the term, retailers still retained that designation, and the efforts of the ambitious to break into the trading world kept the term a wonderfully supple one. A shopkeeper might be a shopkeeper in legal documents, but when he purchased a piece of land or bought a share in a vessel trading to the West Indies, he suddenly metamorphosed into a "merchant" in the official book of "bonds and miscellaneous deeds." Ambitious sea captains acquired stores on land and kept them supplied primarily with goods from the West Indies and, on occasion, acquired the title "merchant." An occasional planter invested in goods and vessels and styled himself a merchant, sometimes with justification.

Retailers often merited the term, at least those who imported dry goods and other merchandise from Britain on their own credit. With a large store on Oglethorpe Square, Thomas Vincent had as good a claim as any retailer in town. Bitten by the chance of moving up in life, he sold his stationery shop in London, borrowed money from his wife's family, and came to Savannah to import goods on his own account.[9] Country factors, who traded in West Indian goods and sold rice and indigo to the larger merchants, willingly called themselves merchants. With a strategic position on the wharves of Savannah and a small retail store in town, Charles Town resident Thomas Lloyd earned the title but could never break into the ranks of the major factors because he did not command capital. When he wrote to the formidable merchant Henry Laurens for advice on a tempting commercial opportunity, Laurens knowingly replied, "I would advise a Young Gentleman rather to serve as a useful Clerk than to dabble as a petty Merchant."[10] A shopkeeper could borrow the title *merchant* on occasion and a larger retailer could use the term without hesitation, but Georgians knew the men who purchased rice for resale in northern Europe or the West Indies, provided credit, brokered land transactions, and imported a wide range of consumer goods to be offered in wholesale stores. In the period 1763–75, approximately thirty to thirty-five men were involved, not all at the same time and not at the same level, and another twenty to thirty participated in at least some of these functions. Elizabeth Butler and Heriot Crooke, widows of powerful and wealthy planters, functioned in the background as quasi-merchants for a brief time.[11]

Historians typically overlook the fact that trusteeship Georgia made a substantial contribution to royal Georgia in terms of human talent, and in no area was it more apparent than in the composition of the mercantile community: James Habersham and the circle of men around him, Jewish traders struggling to establish their footing, hard-bitten merchants and storekeepers of Augusta who looked to Charles Town rather than Savannah, and men who had grown up during the 1740s. Although it is difficult to generalize about this disparate collection of people, it is possible to detect certain common denominators. They were accustomed to more than their share of setbacks and defeats in life; their spouses came from the same simple backgrounds as they or, in the case of traders in deerskins, from among the Creeks; and as a group they showed a common touch that never left them. There was a sense of humanity, whether in dealing with the enslaved, the less fortunate, or their peers, which bespoke the fading humanitarianism of an earlier age.

At the center stood the towering figure of James Habersham, who almost single-handedly shaped the nature of the government and economy during the transition leading up to the royal period. His advocacy of slavery, an export-based economy, and a share of the Indian trade for Georgia, as well as his high-handed efforts at influencing land distribution, left an enduring legacy. In 1753, he turned over the firm Harris & Habersham to an English merchant; increasingly devoted himself to his rice plantations—Silk Hope, Beverly, and Forest Dean—and acquired almost two hundred slaves to turn his great agricultural complex into an income averaging £2,000 sterling per year. In terms of commercial policy, Habersham retained enormous influence as the chief member of the governor's council.[12] Despite his withdrawal from active trade, he was too much the merchant not to negotiate the sale of his own rice with London correspondents, charter vessels, and make purchases overseas. Although he personified the plantation ethic that the Carolina lowcountry had pioneered, the legacy of the trustee period could still be felt. He remained unusually modest in his personal life. His house in town, while expensive, in no way approached those of lowcountry planters in Charles Town; his clothes were plain; and he rarely attended the grand public events. His wife, Mary Bolton, came from an impecunious family of "respectable" stock in Philadelphia and had no social pretensions. Never losing the religious evangelism that George Whitefield had instilled, he remained faithful to the orphanage at Bethesda, a touchstone in his life. More to the point, he remained committed to the evangelization of Africans in Georgia and wrote to a catechist that there were "many ingenious mechanics among them, and as far as they have had opportunity of being instructed, have discovered as good abilities as usually are found among people of our colour."[13]

A handful of men served him as loyally as he served the governor. Two clerks in the trustees' store, William Spencer and William Russell, became shopkeepers during the 1750s, worked for the interim council under his direction, and, thanks to his sponsorship, were employed as the collector of customs and the naval officer for the port. Habersham's brother-in-law, Robert Bolton, a jack-of-all-trades, ended up as one of two auctioneers for Savannah, providing a valuable service in disposing of surplus goods. The circle was enlarged by the unblinking support of his former partner, Francis Harris, now a rice planter who served alongside Habersham on the governor's council. Habersham pushed his sons into the mercantile arena with mixed success, but the focal point of his attention was a nephew whom he brought over from London at age nineteen, Joseph Clay, son of his deceased sister, Elizabeth. As head of Clay and Habersham and then Joseph Clay and Company, the nephew matured into one of the most astute and productive merchants in the colony.[14]

Jewish shopkeepers and merchants, who scrapped and fought to establish themselves on the lower rungs of the new order, represented another side to the legacy of the trustee period. In the early 1750s, three families remained from the first days. Of those who stayed through the War of Jenkins' Ear, Abraham Minis held a tavern and store on Bay Street and owned coastal sloops that kept Oglethorpe and his regiment at Frederica well supplied. After his death, his wife, Abigail, carried on a small retail shop and managed a plantation until their son, Minis Minis, entered the business to import rum, sugar, candles, soap, butter, and other common items from the North or the West Indies.[15] Like the Minises, Benjamin Sheftall and his family came to Georgia in 1733 aboard the *William and Sarah*, which brought forty-three Jewish people, to the astonishment of Oglethorpe and the trustees. Sheftall was a modest merchant, cautious in his approach, asking for land only seventeen years after arriving, but his two sons, half brothers, were ambitious, scrappy, and constantly in search of opportunity. Financial reversals in later life led Levi Sheftall to resume his original trade of butcher, but the activities of his older brother, Mordecai, the more successful of the two, included cattle raising, tanning, shipping, lumber, sawmill operations, and storekeeping, activities that were characteristic of the trustee period.[16] The Sheftalls demonstrated their acceptance by the ease with which they found partners and capital in their West Indian ventures. Levi married Sarah de la Motta, whom he met on business in St. Croix.[17] Mordecai married the sister of Joshua Hart, a merchant of

Charles Town, and, through him, developed a relationship with Isaac Da Costa, a leading merchant of that same city. It was a tightly knit world, and, although Savannah did not have a congregation between 1740 and 1772, the tiny Jewish community possessed surprising resiliency and staying power, in part through marriages along the Atlantic coast and in the Caribbean.

Other shopkeepers and merchants had grown up in Georgia during the trusteeship period. They understood the dynamics of the new society in a way their elders could not. The mid-eighteenth century in a frontier colony was not the place to hone a particular skill or create a narrow niche; it was a wide-open space that called for flexibility, speed, and an instinct for where opportunity existed. In 1734, John Morel arrived in the colony as a nine-year-old, son of a Swiss father who never made it as a farmer but survived as a tavernkeeper and found prestige of a sort as a drillmaster for German- and French-speaking militia. A naturally gifted entrepreneur, John dabbled in the Indian trade, acquired a wharf, opened a store on the Bay, allied himself with a Scotsman knowledgeable in overseas trade, bought the third-largest island off the coast, raised cattle and indigo, constructed oceangoing ships, and ended up owning three plantations and one hundred fifty-five enslaved people. Among his many initiatives were shipping ventures to the West Indies in which he purchased shares in vessels, an activity that led to building an oceangoing ship on Ossabaw Island with the aid of African craftsmen from Antigua.[18]

In the mid-1750s, Savannah was hungry, almost desperate, for people who had standing outside the colony and offered the kind of legitimacy that was lacking in this outpost of artisans and shopkeepers. Two prominent Charles Town merchants arrived in 1753, were quickly named to the governor's council, and played an important role in the economic and political life of the royal colony. Fleeing his creditors, James Edward Powell had the advantage of inheriting a thousand acres on the Savannah River owned by his father-in-law, a leading Malcontent who had relocated to Beaufort after defeat on the slavery issue. James Read, formerly James Reid, brought new connections to Georgia through his contacts with Liverpool slavers and West Indian sea captains, all the more credible since he began his career on the seas. He too was leaving a troubled background.[19] The fact that these men were reinventing themselves after disastrous financial experiences in Charles Town made them all the more attractive to inhabitants who were emerging from their own financial traumas. Merchants from

South Carolina were important but not as dominant as might have been expected. A pair of Charles Town merchants in the deerskin trade set up branches in Savannah and carried on a vigorous business.[20] However, relocation to an impoverished colony held little interest for Carolina merchants riding an economic boom. Several residents of Charles Town sent a partner to Savannah to test the waters, but most returned after experiencing a lackluster market.[21]

Nor were English merchants plentiful. Retailers like Thomas Vincent and William Handley found a footing, and the ambitious but erratic Button Gwinnett made a brief appearance before pulling together the funds to buy St. Catherines Island.[22] Two Englishmen secured a place as full import-export merchants. As a young entrepreneur, Joseph Clay, nephew of Habersham, developed a careful strategy to maximize political and commercial connections, focusing much of his energies on the West Indies as the best route for creating a profitable, steady business.[23] Nathaniel Hall came from a prominent mercantile family of Bristol and joined with a Scotsman, John Inglis, to form one of the major slave-trading and rice-exporting firms. A young man, he married into the Gibbons family and acquired a major plantation on the Savannah River.[24]

Despite the not insignificant role of these men, the driving force for bringing the colony out of the shadow of South Carolina came from Scotsmen who put a distinctive stamp on the shape of the emerging economic order. They were not as visible as those who had immigrated during the trustee period: Lowlanders who brought indentured servants and led the fight to introduce slavery and the war-like Highlanders who came with Oglethorpe to found the military community of Darien.[25] These men came as individuals or with their families, and their impact was more financial and economic than political or cultural. Despite their inconspicuous profile, they brought an aggressive entrepreneurial spirit, solid commercial know-how, precious access to overseas capital, and invaluable ties with merchant houses in the British Isles and West Indies. The total numbers that came to Georgia may not have been large, but they did not need to be. The new Scots who dominated the merchant community in Savannah, Sunbury, and, to a lesser extent, Augusta became substantial planters throughout the colony, acquired political influence far beyond their numbers, and showed a clannishness that gave them unusual staying power.

Of the twenty-three individuals who advertised in the *Georgia Gazette* in 1768 and merit the term "merchant," twelve came from north Britain. Of the three largest export firms in Savannah, all were in the hands of Scotsmen: John Graham and Company, long a fixture on the Bay; Cowper, Telfairs, created in 1766 and an overnight success; and Gordon & Netherclift, a branch of a Charles Town firm heavily vested in the Indian trade. The firm of Johnston & Wylly, a partnership between emigrants from St. Kitts and Tortola, had gone bankrupt, but the men retained their influence. Below this tier were four firms with access to London capital, all with Scottish connections: Read and Mossman; George Baillie and Company; Samuel Douglass and Company; and Inglis and Hall.[26] To the south, Scots controlled even more decisively the trade coming out of Sunbury, which served a large rice-growing region based on a network of rivers. Their houses included Dunbar, Young, and Simpson; Darling & Munro; and Spalding & Kelsall, with stores in Sunbury, Frederica, and Savannah.[27] Augusta presented a more complex picture. Scots like Lachlan McGillivray and Daniel Clark had long dominated its deerskin trade and newer men became principal suppliers of skins to Savannah firms: Robert Mackay, who came from Jamaica by way of Charles Town, James Grierson, and Andrew McLean.[28]

These Scots sprang from social and professional backgrounds that placed them at a level well above the typical Georgian. Their families included men with landed estates, fathers who were merchants in Edinburgh and Glasgow, a relative who was part of the London Associates trading on a global scale, an uncle who financed the rice trade from London, and the owner of the largest flax mill in Scotland. These were families that commanded both resources and connections. Some hoped to recoup lost fortunes. Others were younger brothers in search of fortune or at least a gentleman's income. Some were on the make. They came as clerks in established partnerships and parlayed their contacts into the foundations for their own enterprises. William and Edward Telfair began as agents in Virginia for Cunningham and Company. Arriving in Savannah, they met the nephew of Captain William Thomson, the Scots sea captain who benefited so handsomely from the business of hauling emigrants to Georgia at trustee expense. In 1764, Thomson had sent his nephew, Basil Cowper, to superintend the work of collecting payments on his extensive property in Georgia and selling bankrupt estates.[29] Two years later, Basil joined William and his brother Edward, newly arrived from Antigua, to found Cowper, Telfairs & Company, soon the dominant firm in the colony. The secret behind their sudden rise was the immense capital that William Thomson commanded, leading Edward Telfair to eulogize: "we all consider [him] more as a Father than a Friend; some debts of Gratitude are to be canceled, but ours never can [be]. . . . labour and fatigue we shall cheerfully spend in his cause."[30] A premier rice trader, the aging Thomson remained the unseen power behind the partnership in London that became Telfair, Cowper, Telfair. Although the Scots could have remained as quintessential outsiders in a society fast developing its own mores and expectations, most walked a fine line as outsiders and insiders: outsiders in terms of their allegiances to the British empire and its Atlantic orientation, insiders by virtue of their integration into the emerging social world.[31]

John Graham personified the creative tension. In 1753, he and his younger brother James left London for Savannah on the promise of financial support and political favors from the metropolitan center. The brothers were already part of the London commercial world, where Graham was "known to some of your Lordships" on the Board of Trade, according to Governor Ellis.[32] Sons of a Presbyterian minister outside Edinburgh, they took the opportunity to change their name from the flat-sounding Pyot to the more recognizable Graham. Early on, progress was measured in painfully small steps.[33] John Graham backed a merchant in the new community of Sunbury only to have the Englishman go bankrupt and flee to Williamsburg. He staked a Scotsman from Jamaica to plantation tools and enslaved people only to watch him fail. He purchased ten slaves on St. Kitts for his mother-in-law, in essence taking the commission on the transaction rather than risking a free sale in Savannah. He pushed his way far enough into the Carolina deerskin trade that the governor named him clerk of accounts and Indian commissary for the colony, but again the volume of deerskins crossing the wharves in Savannah was negligible. He purchased choice tracts of undeveloped land with a remarkably large loan from the Coults brothers of London and Edinburgh. Graham failed to meet the payments but, again, connections proved more powerful than the financial realities of frontier Georgia. Dr. Fothergill, a philanthropist, plant collector, Quaker, and backer of Benjamin Franklin, assumed the payments and extended Graham the privilege of renting the land until he could buy it back.[34]

In 1762, John Graham hammered out a partnership with an influential trader in deerskins, Lachlan McGillivray, a Scot from the trustee period, and John Clark, a prominent factor in London, also a Scot.[35] Although a leading player in the Carolina rice trade, Clark sensed new opportunities in deerskins and willingly sold three-quarters of the partnership to the Graham brothers and McGillivray as the price of gaining a substantial foothold in the business while reducing risk. Four years later, John's brother James married the daughter of the Indian superintendent for the Southern Department and moved to London to coordinate a booming commerce, a position made all the more pivotal by the lucrative contracts his father-in-law deftly sent his way.[36] In Savannah, the operative firm was John Graham and Company; in London, McGillivray, Grahams, Clark. Like most of his peers involved in deerskins, John Graham had a regional view of development. He invested heavily in land in East Florida to take advantage of the boom in indigo and assiduously cultivated the governor, James Grant, a fellow Scot. He used his friendship with the mayor of Lancaster, England, to break into the African slave trade and relied on his relationship with Lachlan McGillivray and Andrew McLean of Augusta to develop an extensive network of trade in Indian territory.[37]

To outward appearances, this leading merchant fit seamlessly into the emerging society. White Georgians were creoles if by that one means simply that they made cultural adaptations to their new environment. Like the Caribbean, creolization was a relative term and not nearly so developed as in the sugar islands where the preponderance of slaves, numerous free blacks, the lavish lifestyle of whites, and the unique features of black life produced a culture distinct from anywhere else. Georgia was a slave society where the worlds of black and white only crossed and mixed fitfully. Brute force and well-defined notions of subordination enabled the two parts to coexist and intermingle at the margins. White Georgians were creole in the limited sense that they put down roots in the lowcountry and showed every intention of accommodating themselves to the circumstances of life there. They came as permanent settlers, unlike so many counterparts in the West Indies who, as soon as they made their fortunes, returned home to become absentee proprietors and enjoy the fruits of their brief sojourns. While thinking of themselves as Englishmen first, Georgians remained firmly anchored to their land.

John Graham was different. For all his success, his ambition was to emulate the sugar barons of the West Indies and become an absentee owner. "Be as it will, I am fully determined to remain where I am till I can leave it on a proper footing," he confided to his friend Governor Grant, "for I must find myself in a situation to spend from 1,000 pounds to 1,500 a year in England, before I will show my face there, and when my plantations will afford this, I won't stay a month longer."[38] This was not the sentiment of Charles Town merchants, who returned to England and transferred their trading skills onto a larger stage. During the final years of the royal period, Graham speculated in land, developed three plantations, and acquired 262 enslaved people to emerge as the wealthiest person in Georgia after the governor and on a level with the kind of fortune some found in the Caribbean.[39] He never followed through on his repeated threats to leave, however. Ultimately, like most of his peers, he integrated himself into the life of the colony. He was an early member of Solomon's Lodge and the Presbyterian Meeting House. He wed one of the four daughters of Clement Crooke, a merchant-planter from St. Kitts, and counted among his brothers-in-law a merchant in the deerskin trade; the politically and commercially influential Alexander Wylly, long-time speaker of the house; and James Mossman, a leading figure in the mercantile world—all of them Scots or with Scottish connections.[40] His sister-in-law Elizabeth Crooke Tannatt Mossman gave him valuable contacts with the Tannatt, Houstoun, and Hume families, all pivotal to Georgia's economy. Appointed to the governor's council in 1764, he became an intimate of James Wright and joined Habersham in managing Wright's eleven plantations. For the royal period, he gave his loyalties to the Atlantic world, supported unpopular measures like the Stamp Act, and weighed carefully his commitments to the creole society emerging in Georgia. Like others of his background, he could never understand why many Americans viewed British rule as oppressive.[41]

By the 1760s, Scottish merchants and storekeepers throughout North America were experiencing a growing wave of resentment and hard feelings at their success and unquestioned loyalty to the British government. Nowhere more was this the case than in the Chesapeake Bay, where the rise of Scottish firms selling tobacco to markets in Europe raised unease and fear on the part of small-time farmers as well as large planters who inhabited a world dominated by questions of debt.[42] Planters who labored under increasing debt and volatile prices saw the stores along coastal rivers as the chief culprits of their plight despite market conditions over which Scottish firms had little control. The strong ties of the Scots to home, their fiercely pro-British stance, and the insular world in which they lived made them seem alien in a land with a growing sense of its own identity. Feelings along the complex river system were uniformly anti-Scottish and anti-merchant. In South Carolina, matters were not so stark. Scots had played critical roles in the early years of the development of that colony, but their successors were experiencing a rise in hostility. By the 1750s, the Charles Town merchant community was broad and deep, drawing on Huguenots, New England sea captains, Sephardic Jews, English, Dutch, Scots, and a rising number of native-born men, and evinced a profound pride in its overall strength, sophistication, and independence. After several weeks in the province, a newly arrived emigrant told his cousin Alexander Ogilvie, "The Scots [as merchants] generally do well which is the Reason the Natives dislike them and bear them so much Envy."[43] He and his peers labored on, supremely indifferent to the resentment generated. When some of the Scots in Charles Town and in Savannah displayed a pro-British attitude during the Stamp Act crisis, a Carolina merchant, Christopher Gadsden, denounced them for being part of "that detestable Stuart race! A race of pedants, pensioners, and tyrants," and he composed a broadside blasting them for being "Strangers, many of them of a very few years standing in this province."[44] Carolinians applauded.

Georgia reflected a world removed to a surprising extent from the larger currents flowing across the North American landscape. It was a world closer to the Caribbean where Scots came as merchants, clerks, attorneys, and managers to make their fortunes and perhaps enter the ranks of planters. Their peers played an important role in the settling of St. Kitts, Jamaica, and Antigua, where a Scottish woman found a "whole company of Scotch people, our language, our manners, our circle of friends and connections, all the same."[45] Since the small white population of the British West Indies was characterized by high turnover as emigrants died or left after making their fortune, the Scots' behavior fit the norm. They never experienced the kind of tension that existed on the mainland.[46] The Scottish traders in Georgia typically came as single men out to make a fortune but, in a society where women were more plentiful than in the West Indies, most found wives and, unlike their peers in the Chesapeake or the Caribbean, showed little inclination to return to the homeland, John Graham notwithstanding. Many acquired plantations and seemed satisfied with the limited social institutions offered. Of twenty merchants who married in Georgia during the colonial period and for whom records can be found, fourteen stayed within their own community but remained in the colony.[47] Two brothers reached out to the larger world in a strategic way. Although Edward and William Telfair were late in marrying, they had their eyes firmly fixed on becoming part of the emerging elite of Georgia. At age forty, William wed Elizabeth Bellinger, the daughter of a wealthy landowner in South Carolina, who bore the exalted title of "landgrave," a carryover from the days of the proprietors. His brother married Sally Gibbons, the daughter of William, a wealthy South Carolina planter who had moved his considerable holdings of slaves across the river to profit from the newly opened rice lands. Thirty-nine years old with a bride of sixteen, Edward was making a bid for power and connections, and yet it was to all appearances a happy marriage, producing nine children and a family name that still echoes in Savannah today.[48]

Increasing one's estate was a central purpose to which most Georgia merchants and planters bent their shoulders. Marriage among the elites was a primary means for adding acreage, expanding slave holdings, and ensuring status and legitimacy as well as barring entrance to outsiders who were always ready to claim a place.[49] Yet the new families that made it into the top echelons of the planting and commercial world were diverse and hardly formed an integrated community. Cultural and ethnic ties were fundamental. For the most part, Scots of a certain station married Scots with similar backgrounds. The same closed approach characterized the Congregationalists who dominated St. John Parish. Those of French or French Swiss origin married one another as did the Irish. Marriages between these groups would later lead to a blending of elites, but at this time the process was still at an early stage.

Socially, the Scots made their way with apparent ease. A merchant and lawyer, Grey Elliott, wrote the constitution for the newly reconstituted Freemasons and became the second provincial grand master of Georgia. The Highlander Lachlan McGillivray, with his Creek wife, Sehoy Marchand, moved with consummate ease in the circles of planters and merchants who traveled about in phaetons and riding chairs, dressed in silk breeches, and raced horses, epitomizing, as his biographer points out, the social revolution taking place in Georgia with men of checkered backgrounds rising into the ranks of Savannah "gentlemen." He became a delegate to the Commons House of Assembly, bred prized Chickasaw horses, and placed his mustee son, Alexander, in a prominent trading house. Public events ratified these developments. When a grand jury was called in Christ Church Parish in 1769, seven of the twelve men were merchants, five of them Scots.

Even where the Scots seemed distinctive, their institutions melded with the established order of things. The members of Independent Presbyterian Church included virtually the whole of the Scottish community in Savannah, but the church had been established by Jonathan Bryan, William Gibbons, and James Edward Powell, as good a slice of the English colonial elite as could be found. When the Scots founded a revitalized St. Andrew's Club in 1764, the reception was decidedly mixed. The columns of the *Georgia Gazette* carried letters expressing concern at the spirit of exclusivity and clannishness of the new organization, fearful it would promote a dreaded "factionalism" in a relatively open society. But the club opened its doors to non-Scots for its annual St. Andrew's dinner.[50]

Politically, the Scots moved into positions of leadership early on. In 1755, Lewis Johnston and Edmund Tannatt entered the Commons House of Assembly. In 1760, Scots were eight of the twenty-one members of the Commons House of Assembly, and in subsequent elections the number varied from five to seven. In each of the elections of 1768 and 1772, four Scottish merchants were returned. During his early years, Governor James Wright built an advisory council heavily Scots in origin. By 1765, its twelve members included four Scottish merchants: John Graham of John Graham and Company; Lewis Johnston of Johnston & Wylly; Grey Elliott of Gordon & Elliott; and James Read, partner in Read and Mossman. Also on the council were Scotsmen James Mackay and Clement Martin, who was still a part-time resident of St. Kitts. As late as 1775, five of the councilors were Scots.[51]

Throughout the royal era, the governor's council remained in a strong position to set commercial policy and found itself better placed than its equivalent in South Carolina, which had lost much of its independence and autonomy to the legislative assembly and the governor during the political battles of the 1750s. The Board of Trade attempted to fill vacancies on the Carolina council with royal placemen, who depended on the Crown for their livelihoods. Political pressures from all sides weakened the prestige of that body and the quality of the people serving as its members.[52] In the West Indies, governors nominated candidates for membership on an island's council but found that the absence of so many wealthy planters, especially on the Leeward Islands, made it difficult to assemble people of "standing." Councils in the Caribbean tended to be recruited from among the ranks of the local assemblies, whose members included plantation managers and shippers rather than owners.[53] The close relationship of Georgia's governor and his council and the cooperation of the Commons House of Assembly on economic issues played a major role in the rapid progress toward the colony's integration into the British Atlantic.

Although the Scots were well integrated into the social order that had emerged by the time of the Revolution, a certain ambiguity underlay their presence. If few shared Graham's intention of leaving the colony, they remained connected to British society, tied to the transatlantic world through the flow of capital and goods, and never understood the growing intensity of the demands for colonial rights and privileges. The Scots of Georgia remained fiercely pro-British in an age of rising hostility to the British government. Although the situation never approached that in South Carolina, much less the Chesapeake Bay, a fissure appeared during the Stamp Act crisis that the economic success of subsequent years could never completely eradicate. In the fall of 1765, American colonists resolutely refused to buy the stamp paper Parliament had approved as a tax on paper documents to help pay for the cost of the British military establishment on the mainland. For North America, the issue was clear. Parliament had not only overstepped its bounds in imposing an "internal" tax on Americans but was taking a step that promised to undermine the independence of their colonial legislatures in matters financial. Riots in Boston and Newport set the stage. Stamp agent after stamp agent across the eastern seaboard resigned his office, diplomatically disappeared, or declared that he could not find the stamp paper. When the enforcement of the act began on November 1, many ports never closed, ships sailed without stamp papers, and governors looked on helplessly. By early 1766, American colonists had effectively nullified the will of the British government, with one lone exception. In January 1766, the merchants of Savannah, a heretofore modest body of men struggling to gain a commercial foothold in the shadow of Charles Town, had committed the unthinkable—they had purchased the detested stamps to send their cargos on their way.[54]

Their complicity was there for all to see. During the fall of 1765, Savannahians had protested the coming enforcement of the Stamp Act in much the same way as elsewhere, through street demonstrations, letters to the *Georgia Gazette*, and anonymous threats to people supposedly appointed as stamp agents.[55] Governor James Wright, master tactician that he was, played a skillful game of concessions and toughness. His master stroke was to persuade the merchants of Savannah to petition the governor's council for permission to recruit a person to act in the place of the stamp agent who had not yet arrived from England. For two weeks, the town was treated to the sight of men of the countinghouse racing around town looking for someone willing to step into the most unpopular position in North America. When the appointed agent arrived from England on January 2, Wright called out a body of forty men to patrol the streets of Savannah while assigning his provincial troops to guard the papers and the agent.[56] Most in this hastily assembled guard were merchants, clerks, and a few sea captains, an extraordinary act of betrayal. Basil Cowper received his baptism of fire in their ranks. By January 7, merchants began purchasing stamp paper and preparing their ships for clearing outward. The radical leader of Charles Town, Christopher Gadsden, never one to mince words, expressed the disgust of fellow Americans when he wrote that Georgians had sold the birthright of Esau, that they were cowards and sissies who had been "deluded and bullied" out of the rights and privileges of Englishmen.[57]

The behavior of Georgia paralleled that of the two largest islands in the British West Indies, which is all the more significant because of the special hardship that the Stamp Act inflicted on the southernmost colonies. The duty on official papers weighed more heavily on these economies, which were almost wholly dependent on shipping; the duty on land grants and wills was double that on the mainland; and the requirement that the duty be paid in cash was more of a problem in the islands, where coins were in short supply. With the duties going to pay the costs of the British military on the mainland, any benefit to the islands was negligible. Nevertheless, Barbados and Jamaica, the powerhouses of the British Caribbean, complied with the Stamp Act. Jamaica paid more stamp duty than the combined total of the rest of the empire. Only the Leeward Islands resisted its implementation, but there the motivation seemed to be their own vulnerability to the economic sanctions by North American merchants.[58] Again, Georgia, or at least a certain slice of Georgia, was more in step with the attitudes and feelings of the southern colonies than those of the mainland.

Although the Stamp Act crisis cast a shadow on the merchants, that shadow did not hover for long. They learned a hard lesson about keeping their heads low, concentrating on the business at hand, and resolutely staying out of the political limelight for the remainder of the royal period.[59] Firmly anchored in a transatlantic community, they assumed that their integration into Georgia's fledgling society signified agreement with their own attitudes. They had reason to think so. As men of a certain social position and wealth, they had been accepted with openness by an increasingly creolized white population; they were beginning to intermarry with prominent local families; they stood at the heart of recognized cultural institutions like the Freemasons and the Presbyterian Meeting House; and they played an outsized role on the political scene. In terms of their daily lives, they were quintessential insiders. Georgians were more than ready to forgive their extravagant behavior in 1765–66 in return for leadership in matters economic.

By the mid-1760s Georgia represented the imperial dream at its best, at least from the perspective of Whitehall. The colony enjoyed a strong governor who made shrewd use of the powers the royal charter gave him in keeping the Commons House of Assembly in check.[60] Financial matters remained relatively calm for most of the period thanks to Parliament's generous annual grant to maintain the civil list. The flow of rice and deerskins to London rather than other markets validated the mercantilist system and created that bilateral flow of commodities and merchandise that British imperialists judged the normal order of things. At a time when London was tightening control of the empire, when conflict over duties and imposts animated political life on both sides of the Atlantic, it was reassuring that Georgia made its fortune by sticking to older models of imperial development, following trade routes established decades earlier by South Carolina, and was not tempted to go along with its neighbor into more profitable venues. Government ministers could appreciate the merchants who saw themselves as citizens of the British Atlantic and seemed to understand economic opportunity better than their peers.

With many of the principal merchants arriving in Georgia during the mid-1760s, the trading community gave its loyalties to the British Atlantic. Hard-headed, forever calculating the relative strength of overseas markets, that community possessed precious connections to sea captains and British slavers, sugar merchants in the West Indies and transatlantic shippers, London correspondents and West African traders, black as well as white. They were too valuable not to earn the renewed confidence of Georgians, and, if any doubts lingered, their role in bringing over seven thousand Africans from Africa and the West Indies into the colony during the last decade of the colonial era gave them a vaunted position within the economy. They were to prove remarkably adept at gaining credibility in the tough world of British slavers and negotiating the subtleties of supply and demand on a transatlantic scale. The question became whether they would be relatively passive agents of a commerce that stretched across three continents or gain a degree of leverage through their manipulation of that demand. Georgia's relationship with South Carolina, the Caribbean, and West Africa came into question as merchants sought to play off sources, one against the other, in response to rapidly changing conditions.

Chapter Six

The Slave Trade in Creating a Black Georgia

Georgia's entry into the market for Africans came during the appalling height of the entire slave trade. In fierce rivalry with the French, Portuguese, and Dutch, the English had long since pushed their way to the forefront of that death-filled commerce and, by the 1730s, become the supreme slaving nation in the Atlantic world. Between 1700 and 1775, its ships delivered more than 1.3 million slaves to the British West Indies and North America. The expansive markets of Jamaica, Barbados, and the Leeward Islands absorbed the vast majority of the newly enslaved people as planters expanded their holdings and the British Caribbean acquired additional islands after the French defeat in 1763. The insatiable demand of the British public for sugar drove the trade while the growing markets for tobacco and rice in Europe added to the demand for Africans in North America. In the late seventeenth century, slavers began sailing to the mainland to supply tobacco planters in Virginia and Maryland and, after 1700, to supply a rising number of rice planters in South Carolina. By the 1730s, Charles Town was importing as many as two to three thousand bondsmen and -women a year, and, although imports all but ceased during the next decade as the colony imposed a high tariff for a short time and rice prices fell during King George's War, expansion of the trade resumed after mid-century. During the third quarter of the eighteenth century, Charles Town imported sixty thousand Africans, the largest slave market in North America.[1]

During the early years, Georgia's commitment to a plantation economy created barely a ripple in the markets of the Caribbean and North America. In the summer of 1750, a newly arrived catechist for Africans reported to his superiors in London that the colony contained "three hundred forty nine working Negroes, two hundred two men, and one hundred forty seven women, besides Children too Young for Labour."[2] To the remaining trustees, James Habersham drove home the point that few residents could afford to purchase slaves directly from Africa and would have to make their acquisitions in Carolina "as their Circumstances will admit."[3] The massive adoption of black slavery, described by Jack Greene as the critical process by which white Georgians developed a positive sense of self, took form only during the last decade of the royal period, 1766–75, when the colony eclipsed Virginia and Maryland in terms of the imports of "New Negroes" and became the second largest market in North America.[4] Over those ten years, as shown in Table 9, Georgia imported 5,349 people from Africa, 2,003 from the many ports in the Caribbean, 2,604 from the booming slave entrepôt of Charles Town, and 500 others from the intercoastal trade. While Charles Town imported 30,100 enslaved people in that ten-year period from Africa and the Caribbean, Georgia brought in a total of 9,956: 7,352 from Africa and the West Indies and 2,604 from the Charles Town market, a total of almost one-third of its neighbor.[5] In light of this dramatic development, questions abound. How far was the Savannah slave market a faithful copy of Charles Town's and how did it differ? To what extent were Savannah's slave factors able to set the agenda for that booming trade as rice exports increased, or was the Georgia market a creature of British slavers and developments in Africa and the Caribbean? In short, what can we learn from this frontier outpost of the components of supply and demand for black slaves in transatlantic markets?

During the eighteenth century, the driving force behind the British transatlantic slave trade was the enormous wealth created by the sugar revolution in the Caribbean, the most valuable part of the empire. By the 1770s, Jamaica had replaced Barbados as the economic powerhouse of the region and become the greatest market for slaves in British America. During the third quarter of the century, Jamaica was the destination of 37 percent of all slave ships sent to British America and 44 percent of all slave vessels dispatched to the British West Indies.[6] It received 258,000 Africans while, for the British West Indies as a whole, Jamaica included, slave vessels brought 548,000.[7] In contrast, Charles Town was the largest slave trading area in British North America during the eighteenth century, gateway to the most expansive plantation economy on the mainland. The slave mart in that town, centralized in a way that had no parallel elsewhere on the continent, had long since displaced that of the Chesapeake Bay region, where the increasing fertility of black women brought about a naturally increasing population and lessened the need for imports. And yet the number of slaves South Carolina imported during the third quarter of the century

TABLE 9   Importation of Enslaved People to Georgia, 1751–75

	1751–55	1756–60	1761–65	1766–70	1771–75	Totals	Percent
Charles Town	174	873	259	58	2,546	3,910	29.9
West Indies	88	264	939	1,323	680	3,294	25.1
Africa	—	—	—	2,896	2,453	5,349	40.8
Intercoastal	—	—	50	100	400	550	4.2
Totals	262	1,137	1,248	4,377	6,079	13,103	100.0
Planters	1,800	706	668	1,115	600	4,889	27.2
						17,992	

Sources: For importations from Charles Town, General Duty Books, vols. B (1748–65) and C (1765–76), South Carolina Department of Archives and History. For the West Indies, O'Malley, "Beyond the Middle Passage," 151. For enslaved people brought directly from Africa, see the Trans-Atlantic Slave Trade Data Base, www.slavevoyages.org, though the author subtracted an estimate for inflated values where numbers were imputed rather than actual. For the intercoastal traffic, shipments from South Carolina in Naval Shipping Lists, CO 5/710, NA-UK, were added to an estimate based on figures in the American Inspector-General's Ledger, 1768–72, Customs 16/1, NA-UK. For enslaved people carried by planters into Georgia, petitions for land, 1751–72, *Colonial Records of the State of Georgia*, vols. 7–11.

was a relatively modest number compared to the Caribbean. Viewing the North American mainland as a secondary market, British slavers treated it accordingly.[8]

By the early 1760s, Carolina planters were in a new phase of expansion, exporting almost a hundred thousand barrels of rice on average and almost four hundred thousand pounds of indigo dye. The small kernels of cereal grain had become the fourth most valuable export commodity in North America while the small bricks of blue-violet dye were the fifth most valuable. Planters could well afford to purchase large numbers of slaves, and over twelve thousand men, women, and children would cross the wharves on the Cooper River between 1761 and 1765.[9] Georgia was in a far different position. Slavers looked for markets generating sufficient income to be able to pay for Africans, and, at the beginning of the decade, its planters were producing a modest three to four thousand barrels of rice a year and little indigo. Money and credit were scarce. "Countries in a state of Infancy & lacking a competent staple commodity every body know cannot raise large Sums of Sterling Money upon demand," Henry Laurens warned an English creditor of a Savannah firm that had purchased Africans, "nor are the debtors in such colonies altogether so easily come at, as if they were in places better established."[10]

The sources for Georgians to secure slaves included the market in Charles Town, the small numbers of Africans coming from the Caribbean, and, most important, enslaved people brought into the colony by migrating planters. Blacks came on wagons and coastal vessels, principally from South Carolina, as their masters sought new rice lands, a dimension that is sometimes overlooked in discussions of the growth of the black population. Georgia benefited in a way that had no parallel in any other colony from the constant infusion of seasoned slaves already inured to the hardships of plantation life, knowledgeable of white ways, and skilled at applying African and European technology to rice cultivation. Carolinians arrived in numbers in the early 1750s with a total of 2,506 black people, or 65 percent of those to enter the colony during that time. In the following decade, another 1,783 arrived, including the slaves of large planters like Henry Laurens, Miles Brewton, Arthur Middleton, and Josiah Tattnall. Over the third quarter of the eighteenth century, 27 percent of the labor force in Georgia came from direct migration, making it the only colony in North America to benefit from so significant a transfer of labor.[11]

Georgia's entry into the slave trade was a slow, gradual process. Purchases of slaves in the Charles Town market averaged a modest thirty-four per year during the first eight years of the 1750s.[12] West Indian merchants scarcely took notice of this young, frontier colony that gave little evidence of becoming a serious plantation economy driven by African labor. Occasional sales were made by sea captains who arrived in port with a small number of enslaved people. Although six ships brought no more than fifty-one Africans during the course of 1755, even the market for that number was extraordinarily thin. When the brig *Pompey* appeared with a load of rum and eighteen enslaved people, the initial effort to sell them went moderately well until a vessel suddenly appeared with twenty "prize" bondsmen taken on the high seas and purchased on the cheap in St. Kitts. The captain related to his partners in Rhode Island that their arrival "has Reduced the Price one third at Least[.] I have Yet six left on hand[.] No Purchasers ofer."[13]

Showing their first serious interest in purchasing slaves, Georgia's planters aggressively entered the Carolina market and bought 811 Africans during 1758–60. Although rice exports had not noticeably increased, signs of a coming boom were apparent. Immigration was strong; the population was growing; and the second governor, Henry Ellis, was an able leader. For the first time, Savannah slave traders appeared in Charles Town: Joseph Wood, a West Indian merchant, Harris & Habersham, Johnston & Wylly, Francis Arthur & Company, Grey Elliott, and James Read. Larger planters like Jonathan Bryan and James Deveaux, originally Carolinians, were expanding their holdings. Major Charles Town firms began to take a position in the Georgia market and send shipments: Smith & Brewton; Austin, Laurens, Appleby; and Da Costa & Farr.[14] But the boomlet of 1759–61 soon petered out and would not resume until 1773. If the number of slaves purchased in Charles Town during a quarter of a century was significant, the timing of those purchases was unusual. South Carolina reexported 8 percent of its slave importations out of the colony, some to North Carolina, others to East Florida, but the main consumer was Georgia.[15] The young colony obtained 3,910 Africans from this market, almost 30 percent of all imports. However, Georgians obtained 72 percent of all those purchased over a period of five years. Remarkably, for twenty of the twenty-five years, Georgia planters and merchants were hardly present in the largest slave market in North America despite all the contacts that linked the two colonies. During 1765, when Carolinians were importing six thousand slaves and the Charles Town market was churning with frantic sales, Georgians remained on the sidelines, taking a total of 60 people.[16] Their absence for so many years suggests a complicated relationship.

The birth of a primary market for slaves in Savannah dates from 1764, when Caribbean merchants discovered the full potential of the colony. Rice exports had expanded from forty-six hundred barrels in 1761 to sixty-five hundred the following year and to seventy-six hundred in 1763, more than sufficient to stoke demand. For the first time, it was apparent to insiders and outsiders alike that Georgia was in the early stages of a boom. Caribbean merchants leapt at the opportunity and emerged as the primary suppliers of slaves, if only for a short time. Of the 3,294 slaves brought into Georgia from the West Indies during the third quarter of the eighteenth century, 1,835 of them came during the period 1764–67, or roughly 56 percent.[17] Viewed from a larger vantage point, Savannah's importation of slaves from the Caribbean during that intense period of activity was probably driven more by supply factors outside Georgia than by the growing demand inside the colony. Slave ships were bringing increasing numbers of Africans to the

sugar islands and merchants were eyeing the rim of the Caribbean for outlets that promised a quick return, especially for human cargo that had not
sold well in the large marts of Kingston, Bridgetown, and Basseterre. The
legislature of South Carolina, concerned over the colony's ability to finance
the growing volume of Africans, was in the process of shutting down the
Charles Town market by imposing a draconian duty on "New Negroes"
for three years, beginning January 1, 1766. As British slavers rushed to send
in their ships in the two years before the deadline, more than 3,000 Africans came through West Indian ports as merchants in the sugar islands
took aim at the Carolina market. Then, that market simply vanished. It is
hardly surprising that Caribbean vessels in 1766 brought into Georgia 547
enslaved people and another 582 the following year. St. Kitts, Jamaica, Grenada, Montserrat, and other ports looked to this once-backward province
to help balance the growing tide of imports from Africa.[18] Georgia was an
indirect and perhaps unintended beneficiary of events.

The preexisting ties to the colonies in the Caribbean were important in
establishing the overall pattern of sources. During the mid-1760s, St. Kitts
sent twenty-one ships with 443 bondspeople, or 24 percent of the total that
can be identified in terms of islands, a fact that speaks to the close relationship with the planters and merchants who migrated from that island.[19] For a
time, St. Kitts displaced Barbados as the distribution point for slaving ships
in the eastern Caribbean. The connection between its capital, Basseterre,
and Savannah was sealed by those who had migrated to Georgia during
the 1750s, merchants and planters like Lewis Johnston, Edmund Tannatt,
and Clement Martin, men who reached influential positions within the
government and society almost from the moment they appeared. Heriot
Crooke, the widow of a merchant-planter on St. Kitts, now a planter on
Bermuda Island, regularly restocked her plantation with people imported
from her former home.[20] Jamaica, the center of the slave trade in British
America, supplied 325 people, or 18 percent. By the turn of the century,
it had overtaken Barbados as the prize colony of the English, producing
more sugar and receiving one-third of slave imports shipped by Britain to
the Americas.[21] Together, the two islands accounted for 42 percent of the
imported slaves whose island origins can be identified. As reflected in Table
10, Montserrat was a distant third, and Grenada in fourth place. The Dutch
islands of St. Croix, Curacao, and St. Eustatius, and the French colony of
Guadeloupe appear in the totals but not for significant amounts. A center

TABLE 10.   Slaves Imported from the West Indies to Georgia, 1764–67

	1764	*1765*	*1766*	*1767*	*Totals*
Anguilla	—	7	—	—	7
Antigua	—	—	37	27	64
Barbados	—	—	20	57	77
Curacao	47	19	—	1	67
Grenada	6	5	62	129	202
Guadelupe	—	2	5	—	7
Cuba	—	—	3	—	3
Jamaica	52	137	91	45	325
Montserrat	26	140	36	13	215
Nevis	—	—	—	16	16
New Providence	—	—	—	14	14
St.Kitts	96	86	188	73	443
St.Croix	—	14	38	12	64
St.Eustatius	—	—	—	16	16
St.Thomas	—	—	1	—	1
St.Vincent	—	—	—	22	22
Tortola	28	—	3	—	31
West Indies	—	41	63	157	261
Totals	255	451	547	582	1835

Sources: For 1764, Donnan, *Documents*, 4:615–16; and Naval Shipping Lists, CO 5/710, NA-UK. For 1765–67, Wax, "New Negroes Are Always in Demand," 202. The table excludes the numbers he included coming from South Carolina and considers those coming from "unknown sources" as from the West Indies. O'Malley, "Beyond the Middle Passage," 151, offers a more accurate picture of the total numbers coming from the West Indies, but Wax provides a careful analysis of individual voyages arriving in Georgia.

of the slave trade like Barbados was barely visible, and small islands like Tortola and St. Vincent made a modest appearance.

Georgians were not slow in taking advantage of the opportunities. Merchants and sea captains based in Savannah owned 25 percent of the slaving voyages in the mid-1760s.[22] With an average cargo size of fourteen enslaved people, entry into the trade was relatively easy. On May 17, 1765, the brig *Charlotte*, with an eight-man crew under the command of Captain Preserved Alger, set sail from Savannah bound for St. Kitts Island and Jamaica. For a vessel owned and operated by two Savannah merchants, James Read and James Mossman, it promised a fair return. In addition to yellow pine lumber and cedar shingles for roofing, the vessel held twenty-six horses, a particularly valuable commodity in the West Indies, forty-two piglets, hay, barrels of beef and pork, rough rice, corn, peas, and a thousand pounds of bacon and ham. Twelve weeks later, Alger returned from Jamaica with thirty "Negroes" to be sold from the deck of his ship.[23] David Montaigut, son of a French Swiss merchant, hauled enslaved people from various points in the Caribbean before he settled into the life of a storekeeper and eventually became naval officer for the port. The governor of Georgia, James Wright, teamed with a Jamaican merchant to import slaves. One woman appears as the partial owner of two voyages that engaged in the trade: Elizabeth Butler, a wealthy widow whose family controlled several plantations on the Ogeechee River.[24] As time went on, the size of the cargos increased. Edward Telfair commissioned his leading sea captain to venture to Jamaica and purchase outright fifty-two Africans for resale in the colony.[25]

That the numbers from the West Indies fell off after 1767 partially reflected the fear of Georgians of being victimized by the practice of island planters in using outports for pawning off enslaved people deemed "rebellious" or too sickly to work on West Indian plantations. Georgia was a backwater market ideal for that purpose. In his celebrated diary, Thomas Thistlewood, the overseer and manager of several plantations in Jamaica, known for his brutality and his intense sexual demands of black women, noted his frustration with Coobah, a woman who repeatedly resisted efforts to break her. She "stole" corn, broke into a house, and refused to work. After she escaped several times and was flogged, he placed her in a collar and chains, sent her to the fields, and starved her. In May 1774, Thistlewood took Coobah to a slave pen and sold her for £40 sterling: "I made Dick take her down to Savanna la Mar, where went myself & delivered her to the Captain of Mr. Lesley's vessel going to Georgia."[26] "As we look on it," Joseph Clay lectured one West Indian merchant, "seasoned" slaves "are thereby the Instrument of introducing so many Rogues or disordered People amongst us As they are commonly sent away either for some incurable disease or their villany [*sic*], nor will one Planter in fifty suffer one of them to set their feet in their Plantations, or buy them on Any Pretense."[27]

During the last fifteen years of the colonial period (1761–75), small vessels in the West Indies carried 27,055 Africans from the larger slaving ports to lesser ports in the Caribbean and North and South America, including the

Chesapeake and the lowcountry, the Bahamas, the Lesser Antilles, Honduras, and Spanish colonies.[28] The trade represented an important strategy for feeding small numbers of Africans into lesser markets throughout the Caribbean rim in the interest of balancing supply and demand. The lowcountry served as the prime outlet. South Carolina received 6,779 people from this intra-American trade, or a quarter of the total, while Georgia accounted for 2,924 bondspeople, or 10.8 percent.[29] The fact that as much as 25 percent of enslaved people carried into the colony came through West Indian ports helped shape the character of the black population. The small shipments of "Negroes" from ports where hundreds of enslaved people were present at any one time typically meant a rich diversity in terms of culture, language, and religion, a diversity that helped mold a new African American identity in Georgia.

The West Indian market provided a ready source that allowed the colony to have a share of the slave trade, but it had serious defects: the smallness of shipments; the problem of timing; the "danger" of seasoned slaves; and the fact that Africans taken off larger slavers often represented a lesser choice in the marts of Kingston and Basseterre. Savannah's merchants hungered after a bigger, more dependable supply with better profits and the chance to command the market. In 1766, Georgia entered the Atlantic slave trade, a turning point for the economy in terms of access to labor, overseas connections, and growing sophistication. It inaugurated the forced migration, under horrific conditions, of 5,345 people, part of the 640,000 enslaved Africans carried to British America in the third quarter of the century. British slavers had been eyeing Savannah and had sent three vessels with Africans the preceding year after stopping at other ports to discharge a few.[30] In a surprise move, the South Carolina legislature opened the door for the entry of Georgia's merchants when it imposed a prohibitive duty on all blacks imported into the colony for three years, beginning January 1, 1766. The ostensible purpose was to allow British merchants the chance to collect outstanding debts from an already high level of imports and to give the province a breathing space to right the growing imbalance between indebtedness and exports.[31] For three years, the wharves, stores, and vessels in Charles Town were free of auctioneers hawking the black people traumatized by the Middle Passage.

From 1766 through 1768, Savannah served as the only significant slave market in the lowcountry, a happenstance that forced its merchants into the kind of intense planning never before undertaken, dealing with hard-nosed slavers in Britain, developing the ability to hold and feed more than one hundred Africans before sale, establishing relationships with planters, and managing a massive outflow of capital. This may well have been the single most important moment in their introduction to the workings of the transatlantic economy, a coming of age in a hard-bitten world. British merchants were less thrilled with the prospects of trading in Georgia, a young, untested market. Rice cultivation was as yet limited; planters were considerably more delinquent in paying their debts; and the merchants of Savannah, for all their contacts in the Atlantic world, operated by a simpler, less sophisticated standard than their brethren in Charles Town.

Between 1766 and 1775, British merchants sent 36 slaving vessels to Savannah, 132 to Charles Town, and 1,270 to the West Indies.[32] Savannah arrived at a moment when competition among British slaving ports was eroding long-established patterns. For the first half of the century, Bristol and London had dominated the trade to Charles Town, with the former supplying more Africans than any other town. Thereafter, Liverpool merchants challenged their control over the trade and Lancaster followed in their wake. Those two towns were responsible for the majority of slaves delivered by British merchants to South Carolina on the eve of the Revolution.[33] Savannah was no exception. That a new era had begun was symbolized by the arrival of the first slave ship in April 1766: the *Mary Brow*, a sixty-ton sloop fresh from Senegal with seventy-eight "New Negroes" ready for sale, an unusually small slave shipment. For the first time, a vessel was coming directly from the west coast of Africa, and the owners, far from speculators, were two of the most experienced men in the Liverpool slave trade, John and Matthew Strong.[34] Savannah was on the eve of a fundamental shift in its source of captives and in that first year secured 802 blacks directly from Africa, the largest number until the last year of the colonial period.[35]

Far from attracting marginal players, Georgia saw some of the most important British slavers interest themselves in the Savannah market, names that dominated the transatlantic traffic: the Strongs of Liverpool; the Campbells of Glasgow; Benjamin Stead, Richard Oswald, Samuel Brailsford, and Robert Mackmillan & Co. of London; William Joliff of Pool; and Thomas Hinde, Miles Barber, and William Watson of Lancaster.[36] Virtually all of them were experienced in the Carolina trade, and several, like Stead and Brailsford, had begun their careers in Charles Town. Savannah's merchants had no difficulty in establishing ties. Joseph Clay used his uncle's good standing to become the correspondent of Benjamin Stead, former Charles Town merchant.[37] John Graham's position as a correspondent of Richard Oswald, a leading trader in London, gave him a decisive head start; and his relationship with Miles Barber, owner of many ships, sealed his position within the Savannah market.[38] James Read of Read and Mossman was described as "well known to Several Gentlemen in Liverpool."[39] Alongside stood the firm of Alexander Inglis and Nathaniel Hall, both relatives of the partners in Inglis, Lloyd and Hall of Charles Town, and with close ties to the Bristol firm of Wraxell, Hall.[40] The long reach of Inglis and Hall enabled them to sell at least one cargo of over two hundred Africans in Charles Town rather than Savannah in response to changing market conditions.[41] Samuel Douglass of Savannah entered into a partnership with Andrew Lord of Charles Town and imported Africans under joint sponsorship. More than a slaving operation, the partnership bought or was granted thousands of acres of land in pursuit of an expansive view of Georgia's development.[42]

British merchants recognized Savannah for what it was, a third-level market that could be milked to best advantage. Miles Barber, "the first African merchant in England," as John Graham assured an interested party, had contacted Graham in December 1766 about handling the arrival of four vessels during the following spring and summer. Graham also learned of a fifth slaver arriving at the same time. The merchant contracted with several Florida planters as well as the governor of that new colony to supply them with their first purchases. As April passed, Graham's tone to the Floridians became defensive, by May impatient, in June artificially optimistic. In September, his tone was abject, and by October, one of Georgia's most successful merchants had reached the point of despair. Barber's agent on the coast of West Africa sent a message that the *Jupiter* had "slaved" much sooner than expected and sailed in December 1766 for another port, the *Gambia* had returned to England after a false start, the *Richmond* was condemned as unsafe on the Gambia River and sold its cargo to different vessels, and the *Hannah* was "still on the coast not half slaved by the middle of August." The one vessel to arrive, the *Dove*, brought ninety-six captives, of whom only thirty-seven lived to be sold "and these such wretches as ever I saw before." Humiliated, the hard-nosed Graham confessed to the governor, "I now wished to God that I never had thought of entering into these engagements."[43] Barber's African agent apparently saw Graham as little more than a useful backup while he tended to more-established markets. Nor was Graham successful with Richard Oswald, who wrote the next year that his plantations in East Florida would have to be supplied through the West Indies "since Georgia failed."[44]

British slavers had other means of applying pressure on Georgia firms. They recruited the London correspondents of Georgia's merchants, who were more than open to participating in the trade. With three vessels on the African coast in 1774, Thomas Shoolbred arranged with the powerful John Nutt, correspondent for leading firms in Charles Town and Georgia, to market the cargos through John Jones & Company of Sunbury and Charles Town. Jones was living and working in Sunbury but still had a business in his former residence. Nutt told Jones that he had "guaranteed" the three vessels for both Jones's Carolina house and Sunbury store, one coming from Gambia for Charles Town, another from Senegal for Sunbury, and a third for Sunbury. He pointedly reminded Jones that his two stores' accounts were "very large and embarrassing," and "If I am not supported with spirit and punctuality, it will be impossible for me to discharge them as they fall due nor can you ever expect that I will exert myself again on your account into a situation of difficulty and danger."[45] The young Georgia merchant was on notice. Only the third vessel landed at Sunbury, with eighty people from Gambia, "prime and healthy."[46] Georgia factors in London duplicated the role of Nutt, acting on behalf of slavers who allowed Georgians little room in the choice of cargo and timing.[47]

For understandable reasons, British slavers remained slow in reacting to the growing possibilities of the Georgia market. Merchants in Liverpool, Lancaster, Bristol, and London assiduously studied reports, judged markets, and made decisions that took months to implement. When slaving vessels were pushing into Charles Town in the early 1770s carrying thousands, few came to Savannah because of the weak demand in the previous two years. When Georgia planters purchased over one thousand Africans in that market in 1773, those merchants reassessed conditions and sent ten ships the next year, bringing fifteen hundred enslaved people, the largest amount to cross the wharves of the town. The fact that South Carolina received significantly fewer Africans in 1774 than the year before may reflect this deployment of resources.

The choice of cargo was important to local merchants, and if one looks at their correspondence, it would appear they had a large voice in the selection. In the spring of 1775, leading traders, together with the governor, issued instructions to an English firm on the composition of a cargo undertaken as a joint venture. Their advice was blunt. The shipment was to "be brought from the Coast of Sena Gambia and from as far down as the Gold Coast." Other people, including the "Ibos, Congas, Cape Mounts" as well as Angola "Negroes" from west central Africa were not to be considered.[48] Again and again, Joseph Clay made the point: "The Windward Coast Negroes say from Gambia to the Gold Coast inclusive are most liked in this country and will afford the best prices and a preference to the Leeward Coast will do tolerable well, Ebo excepted."[49] In the African trade to Georgia between 1766 and 1775, these preferences were met: 40.8 percent came from the Senegambia region (roughly today's Senegal, Gambia, and Guinea), 22.6 percent from Sierra Leone, 22.5 percent from the Windward Coast (Liberia and Ivory Coast), 6.5 percent from the Gold Coast (Ghana), and 7.6 percent from west central Africa (Cameroon, Republic of the Congo, and Angola).[50] The point of origin indicates little more than from what part of the coast the embarkation took place, not whether the captive came from hundreds of miles in the interior or from a coastal community, whether he or she had fallen victim to the long series of Islamic wars among the states of the upper Niger region or was from a stateless, local-governing community. The labels applied to shipments obscured whether a person was from the coastal populations of the Wolof, the Malinke, or the Sereer, or from the Fulbe, who occupied the central and upper valleys of the Senegal River, or from populations deep in the interior, like the Bambara. The heavy presence of Muslims on the coast of Georgia speaks to their role along the river systems reaching deep into the interior. The Upper Guinea, which was the source of a majority of the Africans shipped to Georgia, was a linguistically diverse zone, with different language families, the West Atlantic and the Mande, and enormous ethnic variety.[51]

Many of the enslaved people originated from regions where rice cultivation was well established, and Savannah's slavers were keen on playing up those connections as were their Carolina counterparts. For centuries, West Africans had planted rice in a complex system of production that included the full range of landscapes found in the lowcountry. The parallels between rice cultivation in Africa and the lowcountry were many, including land preparation, sowing, weeding, irrigating, threshing, milling, winnowing, and processing the crop. The *Georgia Gazette* repeatedly made that link clear by advertisements such as the one announcing the arrival of eighty captives from "Sierraleon, a Rice Country on the Coast of Africa."[52] It echoed the dominant theme in advertisements in the Carolina newspapers. A growing body of scholarship argues that West Africans carried with them across the Atlantic not merely the seeds, cultivation skills, and technology but an entire culture built around rice cultivation.[53] The English in particular and Europeans in general had little or no experience with rice culture and with the specific dictates of an irrigation system to provide the right balance in the use of fresh and salt water.

The growth in knowledge about the evolution of the slave trade over the eighteenth century, however, has called into question the degree of African agency in the development of rice in the lowcountry. The appearance of slaves from Senegambia, Sierra Leone, and the Windward Coast in Georgia during the last decade of the colonial era may have had more to do with a major realignment of British trade on the African coast than with planter preference.[54] During the third quarter of the century, British merchants shipped fewer slaves from west central Africa and a dramatically increased number from the Upper Guinea to all North American regions and to the Caribbean. The lowcountry was not the only recipient of Africans who came from rice-growing regions. Louisiana and the Chesapeake Bay saw a significant increase in the proportions of people from this vast area. Moreover, after the Revolution and until the close of the trade, merchants sharply reduced the percentage of slaves from the Upper Guinea to the Lower South, raising the question of why that happened, if their skills were critical. The calculations of British merchants and trading patterns in Africa entered into the picture as well. The bulk of slaves exported during that quarter century still came from the Bight of Benin and Bight of Biafra (Nigeria) as well as west central Africa, where bigger ships carried larger cargos to areas of high consumption, primarily the Caribbean. Slave trading in the Upper Guinea required smaller vessels and the purchase of small groups of Africans. From the standpoint of merchants, the Upper Guinea was a secondary market in Africa as was the lowcountry in the Americas. The connection between the two secondary markets was all the closer because of the shorter distance between the tip of West Africa and the Lower South.

That British slavers set the agenda in Savannah was apparent from the size of the vessels and their cargos, even with the closure of the Carolina market. The African slaving vessels that made their way up the Savannah River ranged from small to very small in terms of tonnage. The *Antelope* was a tiny brig of forty tons carrying 97 Africans who had survived the passage. The newly created partnership of Inglis and Hall advertised their sale: "A Choice Cargo of One Hundred Prime Slaves Just arrived . . . directly from the River Gambia and Sierraleon."[55] The *Woodmanstone*, which had made two previous voyages to Charles Town, was a considerably larger vessel, a ship of two hundred tons transporting 110 Africans from Senegambia.[56] English merchants measured the efficiency of their vessels in terms of the number of enslaved people transported per ton. The *Antelope* reached Savannah with 2.4 blacks per ton; the *Woodmanstone*, with 0.6. The ill effects of the latter's voyage can be judged by the fact that of 22 sailors who started from London, only 13 were left by the time the vessel reached Georgia. The comparison with Charles Town's experience illustrates the extent to which Georgia remained a tertiary market. Over the ten years of the colony's slave trade before the Revolution, ships carried on average 148 Africans versus the 188 of those entering South Carolina.[57] Ten of thirty-six voyages for which there are records transported less than 100 people. It was not a stellar record by the commercial standards of the day. The average number of human beings carried per shipping ton was 1.47 while the figure for its neighbor stood at 2.02, a remarkable number even by Caribbean standards.[58]

Economies of scale ensured that much of the slave trade in both Savannah and Charles Town was concentrated in the hands of relatively few people. While hundreds of merchants, factors, and traders in Charles Town paid duties on imported slaves, eighteen individuals and firms sold 60 percent of the total after 1735.[59] In Savannah, a similar situation prevailed. Participants included country factors and brokers on the waterfront who auctioned off the relatively small consignments that came from the West Indies. They gained the satisfaction of placing small numbers of slaves into the hands of those in need, whether planter, artisan, shopkeeper, or widow. They also gained a financial stake in the game. Nevertheless, the level of concentration was higher in this town than in its neighbor. Over a fifteen-year period, at least fifty-seven men participated, but ten controlled 80 percent of the trade.[60] The inner circle was a tight-knit coterie that cooperated more often than they competed. A factor for a slave cargo in August became the purchaser of Africans from someone else's cargo in October. The dominant firm, Cowper, Telfairs, accounted for the handling and sale of at least fifteen cargos; Inglis and Hall for nine cargos; Joseph Clay and John Graham for most of the rest.[61] These merchants saw the slave trade as fundamental to their efforts to expand their overall businesses. To a Londoner on why the firm had taken on the sale of the cargo of the ship *Francis*, Edward Telfair explained, "we would not have engaged in this adventure had it not been that some of our Considerable Planters would have been drawn from the House had they [the slaves] gone into the hands of any other Merchants here as this is the first Cargo imported this year."[62] Telfair feared that planters would attend to their debt with the slave merchant before repaying the dry goods merchant.[63] Savannah's import-export merchants typically found themselves holding both positions during the course of a trading season, receiving rice from those who had purchased slaves and unable to collect from planters who owed for merchandise alone.

A Charles Town merchant would have found himself at home in negotiating the mechanics of the Savannah market. Like Charles Town's Sullivan Island, Georgia created a quarantine station behind Tybee Island at Lazaretto Creek: a two-story house, made of tabby brick, with low ceilings, few windows, and little ventilation. Conditions were grim; smallpox was a constant worry; and merchants complained of the expense.[64] In town, slave auctions were held at a variety of locations, including on the decks of ships, on wharves, and in holding pens.[65] Some sales took place on nearby plantations like Vale Royal.[66] John Graham maintained a holding pen in the industrial/commercial zone of Yamacraw, where the delivering ship could anchor off the banks of the Savannah River.[67] Other dealers maintained pens in town, probably in the lane between Bay and Bryan streets.[68] As in Charles Town, most vessels arrived between April and October when planters could put the enslaved people to immediate use in rice fields or other agricultural activities. Sales could go quickly, with the bulk of the slaves being purchased the day of the sale, but a dealer could find himself holding a substantial number of bondspeople for several days or even weeks at his cost. Merchants knew the mix of human beings they wanted: two-thirds of a shipment to be males and one-third to be women. In one memorandum, the request was made for the males to include one-third boys, and for the females, one-third girls.[69] Rarely did that profile exist. In fact, gender and age depended on the provenance of cargos. For shipments from the Upper Guinea, men typically outnumbered women by a significant margin, and slave complements had few children, about 6 percent on average. If the overall statistics of the slave trade are considered, planter preferences remained relatively marginal.[70]

Despite the prevalence of Africans from the Upper Guinea, heterogeneity of ethnic origins was a distinguishing feature of the forced migration into Georgia. Most vessels took on enslaved people in small groups at different sites along rivers. Many of the victims came from hundreds of miles in the interior. In Savannah, buyers tended to purchase their slaves in small groups over a period of time and so necessarily chose people from different ethnicities. In October 1774, Cowper, Telfairs sold two cargos totaling 172 people to 50 individuals.[71] Larger purchasers gained the lion's share of the cargos, but small buyers were plentiful. The 12 men who purchased 3 or more slaves accounted for 68 percent of the total; 38 individuals bought 1 or 2 of the remaining. Those percentages were not significantly different from sales in Charles Town, based on a small sample cited by Philip Morgan, or in Kingston, Jamaica, center of the slave trade for the Northern Hemisphere.[72] If the Savannah sales were typical, it suggests how Africans on Georgia plantations came from dozens of ethnic groups spread over thousands of square miles of the continent.

In tackling the financial aspects of the trade, Savannah's merchants operated at a competitive disadvantage. Georgia came relatively late in the day, when the burden of financing the purchase of slaves had shifted from traders in England to local merchants in British America. Under a system that had evolved since the 1730s, the factor in Charles Town and now Savannah remitted in full the net proceeds of the slaves delivered by the ship in either cash, produce, or bills. The bills of exchange were of a specified length of time and to be paid when they fell due, whether in six months, nine months, or longer. If not, interest of 8–10 percent was charged. The local factor took the responsibility for guaranteeing payment of the bill. In a further development, the factor had to send back on the delivering ship some combination of cash, produce, and bills that equaled the full price, a practice that came to be known as "bills in the bottom."[73] The critical difference between the Savannah and Charles Town markets was the ability of Carolinian factors to secure a speedier schedule of payments; typically, their bills were paid within eight to nine months of the sale. Georgians had less currency at hand, less capacity for paying immediately in rice, and needed a portion of the bills to extend beyond twelve months. In October 1774, Edward Telfair and Company sold 83 slaves from the *Philip* for £2,774 sterling. The payment included a bill of exchange at £770 for twelve months and another for sixteen months. Moreover, the sale yielded only £33 per person, a modest amount at a time when prices were higher at Charles Town. In September, a sale of 164 slaves from the *Friend* had produced £5,847 sterling. Telfair sent to England on that slave ship a paltry 250 barrels of rice worth £596, plus bills of exchange, one-third of which were not due until twelve months out.[74]

Obtaining adequate financing was the Achilles' heel of this frontier province. "The Merchants here are not in a situation to give me three years credit for the Negroes and the Country is so poor that there is no money to be borrowed," Robert Baillie told his brother in Edinburgh and speculated whether his family could call on their Scottish connections and persuade two of the greatest slave traders, Richard Oswald and Alexander Grant, to take a mortgage on his estate in return for Africans.[75] Nothing came of the initiative until Baillie's uncle, a London merchant, made a loan of £1,000 sterling. Lachlan McIntosh, brother-in-law to Baillie, requested that his mentor Henry Laurens ask the formidable Oswald to take a mortgage on his estate for forty young Negroes. Laurens's reply was to the point, "With respect to the purchase of '40 Young Slaves to be picked out of a Cargo & at a Moderate price,' upon Mortgage of uncultivated Land in Georgia, I am quite certain none of the Owners of such Cargoes would give me more than one Civil hearing if I should make the Proposition," and declined to act. Laurens, who relied on McIntosh as the agent for his Broughton Island plantation, was not above needling him: "one might say the Swamp Mud of this World hath blinded your Eyes."[76]

The Savannah merchants could not offer the same financing terms as their peers in Charles Town, and indeed this became a point of friction. In January 1768, a slave ship appeared in Charles Town before the onerous duty designed to shut down that market had expired. Henry Laurens did his best to persuade two veteran traders in town, Lachlan McGillivray and Nathaniel Hall, to act as agent for the owner, Smith & Baillies. Viewing the terms of payment as too onerous for the Georgia market, McGillivray refused to consider the proposition. Hall proposed to sell the cargo "upon the best terms of that Market" and remit the proceeds in four, eight, twelve, and sixteen months. The English were accustomed to a more rapid payout, and so Laurens urged the Georgians to consider "the good quality of the

Cargo & the terms upon which I had always sold Negroes, to Wit, to remit according to the times agreed upon with the Purchasers for Payments." The Savannahians stood their ground. Laurens recommended to the local house of Price, Hest & Head that it go to Savannah and undertake the sale "upon Carolina terms." The partners agreed, but when Price reached the town, he discovered there was a duty on transients doing business in the colony which subjected a "stranger" to a 2.5 percent duty on the sale. He withdrew.[77]

Although evidence is hard to come by, it appears that Savannah merchants managed the capital outflow from the slave trade with consummate skill. At the moment of sale, they made a clear profit. At the auction of 164 Africans on the bark *Friend*, Edward Telfair and Company received a healthy £310 in commission at 5 percent, plus additional charges for storage, wharfage, and supplies for the vessel, bringing the return closer to 7 percent. From the proceeds for the trader, the company deducted the cost of feeding the captives until the sale was completed, paid for printing handbills and advertising in the *Georgia Gazette*, and covered the provincial tax on each person sold.[78] Moreover, there was money to be made in collecting payments from planters months after the sale. John Nutt wrote to his agent in Sunbury that he was to be allowed the usual commission of 5 percent for selling and 5 percent for remitting payment.[79] What he did not say was that, if a planter defaulted on his payment, Jones was responsible, and if Jones defaulted or could not make payment on time, Nutt was the ultimate guarantor to the British slaver. Such defaults were apparently limited.[80] The overall accomplishment was formidable. The 5,345 Africans brought into the colony from Africa represented a capital outflow of approximately £187,000 over a ten-year period. Georgia's merchants and their correspondents in London and Bristol supported an increasingly complicated web of credit.[81] If the 3,200 Africans from the West Indies and the 3,900 from Charles Town are added, the total outflow reached over £500,000.

Supply and demand in the Georgia market held surprises. Georgians were not heavily involved in the Charles Town market except for five exceptional years. In years when thousands of Africans were pouring into that town and finding a ready sale, they remained quietly on the sidelines. The reasons are several. Georgians preferred to deal with their own, partly on the basis of personal relationships and partly because of commercial obligations. Second, the Charles Town market seems to have sold slaves at a dearer price than in Savannah. That is difficult to establish given the fact that the latter received cargos that were smaller and probably "inferior" to the larger ones taken to South Carolina and details of sales are hard to come by, but the circumstantial evidence suggests as much. Last, it was possible for a planter stretched to his limit to obtain more favorable terms for his bills of exchange in Savannah than in Charles Town and not have to undertake a purchase "under Carolina terms." But that hesitation disappeared when circumstances changed. At the end of the colonial period, the price of rice shot to unprecedented heights. No more dramatic moment occurred in the whole of slave trading in Georgia than the army of planters and merchants that descended on Charles Town to make purchases in 1773 and 1774. A small-time country factor, Quinton Pooler, came back with twenty-six enslaved people; a new merchant, William Panton, took a risk and purchased seventeen; the irrepressible Button Gwinnett, all but bankrupt, tried to redeem himself by entering the trade with a purchase of sixty men, women, and children. Charles Town traders acted on behalf of Georgia planters and shipped dozens of slaves to Savannah and Sunbury. Georgians purchased 1,099 enslaved people in 1773 and 1,303 in 1774, 61 percent of the total during the third quarter of the century.[82]

The West Indian market held a surprise as well. After such a strong start in 1764–67, the numbers dropped off dramatically. Georgia's rice exports to the Caribbean never took off in the way that South Carolina's did after 1763 and so could not serve as the basis for maintaining those numbers. South Carolina's enormous sales of rice in the West Indies gave its merchants commercial connections that its neighbor could not hope to equal. Then, too, the figures at the beginning were artificially inflated, given the circumstances having to do with Charles Town's closure as a slave market. Finally, Georgia's importation during the 1770s settled at a figure of over 150 people per year on average, one-quarter of the typical number for South Carolina.[83]

"Negro Consignments . . . 'tis a foundation for all other business," Joseph Clay told his London correspondent, and by that he meant the African trade, where profits were to be made, planters' loyalty shaped, and the volume of business in the slaver's store determined.[84] It was also where the greatest risks lay. The commerce bound the Savannah merchant to a new kind of dependence—to British slavers who dictated the terms of trade, to the bewildering patterns of trade on the west coast of Africa, to the domi-

nance of the Caribbean trade in determining the size and direction of shipments, to a new disease environment, and to the state of the rice crop that
determined whether a planter could fulfill his obligations and meet his bills
of exchange. Georgia had little control over the timing of supply or over the
terms of trade. On the reverse side, Edward Telfair, John Graham, Joseph
Clay, and their peers stood in an enviable position in the eyes of most Georgians. They had transformed Savannah into a processing center capable of
handling hundreds of bondspeople during the course of any one year. They
had established working relationships with slavers in British towns, mastered the logistics of moving and holding "New Negroes," worked out a
credit system that functioned reasonably well, and developed a keen knowledge of people and plantations in the lowcountry. The dominance of the
largest merchants did not prevent a number of others from participating
in the benefits and risks. The small retailers and dock masters on the waterfront were eager to provide space for schooners from the West Indies
to vend their half dozen or so captives. Dealers bought blacks at Graham's
Yamacraw pen and turned around and resold them on a secondary market.
The two auctioneers in town, William Ewen and Robert Bolton, were kept
busy disposing of the remainder of human cargos that did not sell.

It was a dirty business. Death was everywhere—on the ships bringing in
the "New Negroes," at the Lazaretto at Tybee, in the holding pens where
the sick and the weak gave up on life, and on plantations where recently
purchased people did not survive the seasoning.[85] Recent research demonstrates that little firm evidence exists about mortality during the "seasoning" period when slaves were adjusting to their new life.[86] Sales of the
enslaved people were only the beginning of a life of uncertainty and frequent separations. Planters and tradesmen who could not meet payments
on their debts surrendered their holdings. Button Gwinnett gave up five
men, four women, and a child to pay off a past due account; the respected
John Milledge surrendered sixteen slaves to creditors. In the colonial wills
that have survived, over a thousand enslaved people were left to family
members and others, in effect new owners who often moved them.[87] As
Trevor Burnard and Kenneth Morgan have written for Jamaica, the common experience for Africans was chaos, movement, and frequent separation from friends, family, and compatriots.[88] An emerging black Georgia
was to bear features that blended the Caribbean and Carolinian experiences in ways that reflected the first stages of people of diverse origins test-

ing the limits of their American setting and creating a new culture along the way. For white planters, the prime consideration was a simpler one: how to deploy the newly arrived labor force in the most efficient way possible and to maximize returns like the early modern capitalists they were, open to experimentation and the imperatives of commerce. As Eugene Genovese has written, it was the beginning of a century-long relationship between whites and blacks in which bitter antagonism existed alongside an organic relationship so complex and ambivalent that neither could express the simplest human feeling without reference to the other.[89] The building of plantations on the Georgia frontier was part of a process that encapsulated the experiences of the Carolina lowcountry and the Caribbean and gave them its own distinctive twist.

Chapter Seven

The Making of the Lowcountry Plantation

In the third quarter of the eighteenth century, important new frontiers for the plantation complex opened up in the British Caribbean as the demand for sugar and Africans surged and the region consolidated its position as the most valuable territory in the empire. The islands that France surrendered at the end of the Seven Years' War—Dominica, St. Vincent, Tobago, and Granada—attracted eager planters who displaced the French and increased sugar production several times over for an insatiable British market. The territories the English had implanted within the Spanish empire, the Mosquito Shore and the Bay of Honduras, took on new life while in Jamaica planters pushed into the interior, expanding the area of cultivation and creating a more diversified economy.[1] One of the largest of the new frontiers lay on the northern edge of this expanding world. Adopting the competitive and exploitative ethos of the Caribbean, a young and feisty Georgia would attempt to create within 25 years a version of the world that the sugar islands had fashioned over 125 years and South Carolina over 80 years. The rise of a plantation economy was considerably more complicated a story than that of a small group of men who made themselves into "rice barons" overnight. That story included small planters who rose to become medium-sized ones and merchants who had choices about plantation models and showed themselves leaders in a highly adaptive economic culture open to agricultural innovation. Simultaneously, how the thirteen thousand Africans imported into the colony and another forty-eight hundred Africans and African Americans brought by their masters would be deployed remained a critical issue. The question of African agency in the development of rice culture took on a different meaning in a colony where one-quarter of the black population came from an adjacent province and were experienced cultivators while the white men who brought them were knowledgeable planters.

In the broadest sense, Georgia would follow the same evolution that the

Caribbean world had undergone in the preceding century: from subsistence farming by small planters to a monoculture based on staples, from small- to large-scale units of production, from low- to high-value output, from free labor to slavery, from a focus on the local market to dependence on external trade. And if its rice plantations fit a lesser scale of things, they acquired their heart and soul from the culture that grew up around the sugar plantations: fields of cane laid out in neat geometric figures; factories built to crush, mill, and boil cane into brown sugar, molasses, and rum; the concentration of hundreds of African slaves in one spot; a brutal work regime; a black-to-white ratio that reached ten to one; reliance on the transatlantic slave trade; and the ecological transformation that accompanied the inevitable deforestation of the islands. The sugar plantations of the West Indies had evolved into one of the most intensive capital enterprises in the world, consumed black people at a frightening rate, and churned out the single most valuable good imported into Great Britain, sugar, worth more than all the exports of the North American mainland. Along with this gargantuan wealth came the most stratified society in British America.[2]

Georgia traced direct descent from this hyperactive and jaundiced culture. First articulated in Barbados during the middle part of the seventeenth century, the practices and attitudes associated with the plantation complex spread to the nearby Leeward Islands in the eastern Caribbean, then to Jamaica after its capture by the English, and from there to the southern part of the North American mainland, all by the end of that century. As historians Jack Greene and Peter Wood have articulated, South Carolina was as much the offspring of Barbados as was Jamaica or other English Caribbean colonies.[3] Its Caribbean connections ran deep: the concentration on a single staple crop, the high ratio of blacks to whites, heavy mortality, the intensely profit-minded and secular attitudes of whites, the massive accumulation of wealth, and the great social disparities within the colony. In the years after its founding in 1670, more than half of the settlers came from Barbados; blacks outnumbered whites by 1710, the first slave society in North America. Carolina's slave code, refashioned after the stunning Stono Rebellion when twenty or more whites were killed by "New Negroes," was the most repressive on the continent.

In the third quarter of the century, Georgia's lowcountry moved from a handful of farms that could be called plantations only by stretching a point to something over three hundred enterprises that were producing for a volatile and often harsh commercial market.[4] Within the space of fifteen years, rice production jumped from twenty-three hundred barrels to twenty-three thousand barrels, although the process was extraordinarily uneven. The Georgia coast was not a single stretch of wetland but a blend of environments and landscapes, sand, mud, and marsh arranged in different configurations, and those configurations called forth different responses.[5] The lowcountry quickly acquired a black face. By the time of the Revolution, the ratio of blacks to whites approached those of the Caribbean and Carolina. For the first half of the eighteenth century, the black-to-white ratio in the British West Indies was six to one and in the years immediately preceding the American Revolution rose to ten to one for the whole of the British Caribbean.[6] In rural parishes in the Carolina lowcountry, the same pattern prevailed. By 1760, fifteen of the eighteen rural parishes were more than 70 percent black, provoking one newly arrived colonist to write to his family in Switzerland that "Carolina looks more like a negro country than like a country settled by white people."[7] According to one study, the Georgia lowcountry had twelve thousand blacks and five thousand whites by 1775 for a ratio of two and a half to one, but inventories and lists of enslaved people indicate the number was closer to six or seven to one in St. Philip and St. John parishes.[8]

The rapid Africanization of the lowcountry was an uneven process. A visitor could find himself or herself in St. Matthew Parish with German peasants and few blacks or travel ten miles to the banks of the Savannah River and be plunged into an almost totally African world. As shown in Table 11, the far ends of the lowcountry, St. Matthew Parish and even St. Andrew Parish, were not fully part of this universe. And in the attempt to compress Carolina's eighty-year experience into a matter of a few years, Georgia's planters simply lacked the energy or resources to move far beyond the Altamaha southward to the St. Marys River. In 1773, William Bartram traveled through southern Georgia and found it a virtual wilderness. After a day's ride, he noted a "sudden transition from rich cultivated settlements, to high pine forests, dark and grassy savannas," and, after a second day's ride, he had "passed the utmost frontier of the white settlements on that border."[9]

The qualities that distinguished the Caribbean planter in the mid-seventeenth century found a distant echo in the Georgia planter of the late colonial era. Most of the sugar islands, which began as raw, crude, and

TABLE 11   Average Size of Plantation by Parish, 1766–77

	Planters	Slaves	Average Number of Slaves
St. Matthew	60	417	7.0
Christ Church	60	2,915	48.6
St. Philip	36	1,081	30.0
St. John	66	1,657	25.1
St. Andrew	49	718	14.7
Totals	271	6,788	25.1

Source: Colonial Inventory Book F, 1755–70; Colonial Inventory Book FF, 1776–77; micro-film of loose inventories in the Georgia Archives; loose inventories in the Telamon Cuyler Collection, University of Georgia; lists of bondsmen in Colonial Bond Books YY and KK. Petitions for land from 1766 to 1772 furnish supporting information. The number of enslaved people in each parish is less significant than the average size of plantations.

unsettled frontier communities, saw ambitious planters push aside smaller planters as they consolidated land to grow sugarcane on a commercial scale and produce the most profitable commodity in the early modern world. Acquisitive, quarrelsome, and often ruthless, they were prone to hard living and heavy drinking and yet were men of enterprise and courage who forged a new culture that applied semi-modern management techniques to agriculture. In a disease environment that made little distinction between black and white, they were also in a race between "quick wealth and a quick death."[10] More than half the planters in the Georgia lowcountry were Carolinians and instinctively shared the values that underlay the Caribbean world. All planters in Georgia, no matter their origin, wanted to become good judges of land quality, to exercise direct managerial authority over their plantations, to plan a season's work, to oversee the flow of supplies to the plantation, and to increase their returns by investing in new technologies. They willingly embraced tying their production to the imperatives of international commerce. They expected to be resident on their plantations and were never enticed by the example of their Caribbean counterparts who treated the islands as little more than temporary abodes before returning to England to enjoy the fruits of their investments.[11] The Georgia planter was a settled person, less ruthless, more devoted to managing his estate onsite but every bit as acquisitive and interested in increasing returns as his peers in the sugar islands.

During the 1750s Georgia began as a place of small planters who on average owned little more than a dozen enslaved people and spent their lives out in the fields of their fledgling plantations, laying the foundations for later success.[12] In this formative period of plantation-building, the most extensive set of rice plantations were to be found south of the Ogeechee River. The governor of Georgia spoke a widely received truth when he relayed to London, "The Southern part of this Province is thicker settled & better improved than near Savannah particularly on the River Medway, where a Town called Sunbury is building."[13] Although diminutive, plantations in that region accounted for more than one-third of the colony's entire slave population (see Tables 2 and 11). Small to middling planters were able to grow impressive amounts of rice in diked swamps with rudimentary drainage systems, a watery world punctuated by sandy ridges and clay bottoms.[14] James Pierce may have been illiterate, as were the men appraising his estate, but his holdings included fourteen enslaved people—seven men and seven women—together with the equipment needed for rice production, one hundred ten head of cattle, fifty hogs, many bushels of Indian corn, and lumber.[15] Valued at £793 sterling, the estate was by no means inconsiderable. John Martin Bolzius estimated that starting a rice plantation would cost about £456 sterling for ten adult slaves, a young boy, overseer's wages, livestock, outbuildings, and tools and advised, "In the beginning one gets along as well as possible," underscoring the essence of small entrepreneurs like Pierce.[16] Along the Medway and Newport rivers and in parts of Christ Church Parish, Georgia more nearly resembled parts of the Carolina lowcountry during the 1720s and 1730s when the possibility of advancement was real and careful management of land and labor could allow a planter slowly to build a work force.[17] Russell Menard's description of the Carolina yeomen of that earlier era as "men of modest means producing provisions, making small crops of rice, raising livestock, slowly building farms and accumulating wealth, and struggling to make their mark in the world and acquire substantial estates" applies equally well here.[18] The initial jump in rice production in the early 1760s came principally from the Southern District.

However, the cultivation techniques upon which the majority of planters relied had major limitations. In the inland swamp method, a planter typically drained swampland next to a freshwater source and cleared off the trees and vegetation. At the top and bottom ends of the newly carved-out field, workers built banks and constructed an impoundment pond at the head. Trunks were inserted into the banks to create a reservoir that enabled water to be released at appropriate moments in the growing cycle.[19] Although the murky water rising out of the swamps was the lifeblood of this method, serious drawbacks accompanied it. Keeping the fields clear of weeds was labor-intensive and costly. The irrigation water that nourished the grain encouraged the growth of weeds so that slaves faced grinding months of toil with a hoe, standing ankle- or even knee-deep in mud. Second, the reservoir of water at the top of a field was often depleted in times of drought and prone to overflow in rainy seasons. From St. Andrew Parish, Robert Baillie complained to his uncle in London about how the blistering heat had dried up the dammed pond: "[Until] we have our Fields under proper Dams & a good reserve of back Water, we can never be certain of a Crop." The next year, flooding wrecked his plans. He had begun constructing the principal dam "when a spell of wet weather has filled the swamps and obliged me to leave off."[20] The technique was capable of increasingly more sophisticated permutations, but the essential limitations remained. For the lowcountry as a whole, plantations using the impoundment method were typically "profitable but not wildly so," in the words of the historian who analyzed Henry Laurens's Wambaw in South Carolina and found that it yielded 9 percent or less.[21]

During the final decade of the colonial era, Savannah's merchants, who had long held back from committing their own resources to planting, transformed themselves into calculating, profit-conscious planters who thought in terms of world markets and new business models. Along with planters like Jonathan Bryan, they introduced a radically different technology to rice cultivation, the tidal flow method, and brought the Savannah River into play after years of relative neglect. In South Carolina during the 1730s, planters began finding ways to harness the tidal flow of coastal rivers to move freshwater onto and off of rice fields through a complicated system of embankments and a network of canals and secondary ditches.[22] By the 1750s, the method was in use along the Santee and Edisto rivers, but the first plantation to introduce the method along the Carolina side of the Savannah River, that of Charles and Jermyn Wright, brothers of Georgia's governor, lost thousands of pounds sterling in a spectacular failure behind Daufuskie Island.[23] Nevertheless, the commercial leaders of Savannah took notice of developments and played the lead role in introducing the innovative but costly technology that reshaped class relations in Georgia.

In the years before 1765, the Savannah River had only been minimally involved in laying the foundation for rice culture. Titles to land conferred by the trustees proved to be a major roadblock. James Oglethorpe had recognized the Yamacraws' claim to a five-mile stretch from the western edge of town at Musgrove Creek to Pipemaker's Creek, some of the most productive soil along the whole of the river.[24] Then, too, the laying out of titles for the early settlers had been a sloppy and inexact process, and paper records had a way of disappearing almost as fast as they were created.[25] The attempts to verify ownership would consume years of effort. However, the question of land titles paled in comparison to the larger issue of water management. To make good on any investment, planters had to find ways to master the treacherous flow of the Savannah; its strong currents wheeled along a distance of 290 miles from the Appalachian hills during the spring rains: trees uprooted, gravel and debris hurrying down, and water overflowing the constantly changing banks.[26] Traditional technology worked poorly. Along the upper part of the river, where fertile land was plentiful, several owners preferred the certainty of timbering to the uncertainty of rice.[27] A few successful rice plantations were functioning by the latter part of the 1750s, including Jonathan Bryan's Walnut Hill, Patrick Graham's Mulberry Grove, and Isaac Young's Orange Valley, but they stood as exceptions.[28]

Along with planters like James Deveaux and Jonathan Bryan, merchants brought the Savannah into play after years of relative neglect. In 1760, only four plantations along the Savannah River were in their hands. By 1775, 60 percent of the principal plantations were under the control of merchants, many of them Scots.[29] Merchants applied the same skills they showed in their Bay Street countinghouses: scrupulous attention to every detail; the ability to mobilize the necessary capital; and a willingness to buy up plantations and drastically reconfigure their physical layouts to create embankments and quarter fields. The reconstruction of the natural environment meant a wholly different order of investment. The well-developed rice plantation, a "huge hydraulic machine" in the words of one Carolina planter, required sufficient manpower to construct floodgates, trunks, canals, embankments several feet high, and ditches, demanding skill and unity of purpose to keep the whole in order.[30] All these elements were present in inland swamp cultivation, but on tidal floodplains they were employed on a much larger scale. Workers had to build a permanent embankment five or six feet high, three to four feet thick at the top, and twelve to fifteen feet thick at the bottom.[31] When the gates flew open at high tide, water flooded the fields. Opened again on the ebb tide, excess water drained away. The enormous investment marked the introduction of a technology that placed power in the hands of the few.

Merchants like John Graham tapped into capital from a range of entrepreneurial activities and invested in slaves, land, rice mills, barns, overseers' houses, and huts. At his newly acquired Mulberry Grove, he sank £4,865 sterling into eighty slaves and a valuable tract of twelve hundred acres—not counting the cost of the built environment.[32] At his second plantation on the river, New Settlement, Graham invested £3,800, not including the cost of the above-ground structures. Following suit, Basil Cowper and Edward Telfair purchased a rice plantation at the site of Mary Musgrove Bosomworth's old trading store, together with its slaves, for £5,816 sterling.[33] In the heady days of the early 1770s, merchant Samuel Douglass bought Annandale from his compatriot Lewis Johnston, who was still cutting timber for the West Indian trade. Douglass transformed one hundred six acres of the unusually difficult swampland into what he described as "the best tide swamp in the highest state of cultivation."[34] In 1774, when the "Intolerable Acts" had fixated the attention of the British public on North America, the London house with the largest investment in the lowcountry, Greenwood & Higginson, established on Ursla Island two settlements with barns and "machines for manufacturing the crop," on three hundred acres banked, drained, ditched, and planted with rice and corn. The Revolution caught the English firm halfway through its ambitious project.[35]

The acquisition of Africans for the Savannah River plantations did not begin in earnest until the late 1760s. Starting with 16 enslaved people in the early 1760s, John Graham put 141 captives on his two Savannah River plantations, over 100 on an inland plantation, Monteith, and a dozen or so in his home in town for a total of 262 people, the second-largest holding in the colony.[36] John Rae, in possession of one of the choicest properties on the river, Rae's Hall, closed his Indian trading post, invested heavily in enslaved people, and drained his commercial house in Savannah of the necessary funds, actions that ended in a spectacular bankruptcy that occupied the courts long after the Revolution.[37] By the early 1770s, other landowners along the Savannah were following suit. "What is the matter that you have bought no Negroes for me this season?" the English politician William Knox asked his agent, James Habersham, about the urgency of converting his plantation from timber to rice: "No pray don't let any of your confounded Punctillio get the better of your good sense and friendship for me in this business. Negroes I must have or I shall never forgive you." The next year, he urged his agent "to complete my number and then I shall look for returns" and made clear that income was not his immediate object: "Whatever the proceeds, invest in Negroes."[38] By the end of the period, the average plantation on the river held 77 workers, with a few estates containing as many as 200. Eighteen plantations held approximately 1,400 slaves on the riverbanks and islands of the Savannah.[39]

The tidal flow method dramatically increased the productivity of the labor force as well as the profitability of plantations.[40] Ultimately, larger planters like John and James Graham and Samuel Douglass looked for a return in the range of 10–15 percent after a successful year of planting and an optimum rate of 15–20 percent in the expectation that a succession of such crops would enable them to pay for additional slaves within four or five years. The annual rate of profit of select planters matched those on the sugar islands, where the returns were well over 10 percent in Barbados and the Leeward Islands and close to 15 percent in Jamaica.[41] Carolina merchants paid close attention. Henry Laurens shifted his labor force from his Wambaw holdings near the Santee River, where the impoundment method was producing mediocre returns, to two plantations at the mouth of the Altamaha River, Broughton Island and New Hope, and put over one hundred enslaved people on them.[42] He incurred heavy initial expenses as workers cleared, leveled, and embanked rice fields to capture the tidal flow of the Altamaha. For the first four years, the returns were either negative or below 5 percent. Once the laborious process of field formation had been completed, yields soared to 550 barrels in 1770 compared to 180 the preceding year and matched his best returns in South Carolina. With the shift to tidal flow, Miles Brewton, among the largest slave traders and exporters in Charles Town, bought Jonathan Bryan's Walnut Hill and made it into an even larger operation called Brewton Hall. An English merchant with Charles Town roots, Benjamin Stead, advanced £3,800 to Rae and Sommerville in return for a mortgage on Rae's Hall, a prime piece of property, and fought a long legal battle to make good his claim.[43]

Most rice plantations continued however with some variation of the impoundment method. Governor James Wright had nine plantations, six on the Ogeechee River and three on the Savannah, but employed the newer

TABLE 12   Percentage of Slaves by Plantation Size: Three Parishes,
1766–77

Parish	1–9	10–19	20–29	30–49	50+	# of Slaves
St. John	6.7	11.3	20.6	29.8	31.6	1,660
St. Philip	6.0	13.6	7.4	57.1	15.9	1,172
Christ Church	2.3	3.5	3.0	14.6	76.6	2,915
3 parishes	4.4	7.8	9.0	27.6	51.2	5,747

Sources: Colonial Inventory Book F, 1755–70; Colonial Inventory Book FF, 1776–77; microfilm of loose inventories in the Georgia Archives; loose inventories in the Telamon Cuyler Collection, University of Georgia; and lists of bondsmen in the Colonial Book of Miscellaneous Bonds YY and KK. Petitions for land from 1766 to 1772 furnish supporting information.

method only on the swifter-flowing Savannah.[44] The torrential rains and flooding of 1771 destroyed all but a few acres of the governor's rice on the Ogeechee, James Habersham noted, and what remained standing was "ragged and much hurt." However, "[h]is rice on his Plantations near this Town look extremely fine and very promising. They are fully in the Tides way, and free from any Damage by Freshes."[45] The tidal flow method had yet to spread to the Ogeechee, even on plantations belonging to the same owner who used it elsewhere.

Christ Church Parish stood alone, a remarkable testimony to the shift to the use of freshwater on the Savannah River. As seen in Table 12, more than 75 percent of the enslaved people in that parish lived and worked on plantations with fifty or more people. In terms of conditions of labor and the search for high returns, these units were the quintessential "factories in the field" in coastal Georgia, an echo of the Caribbean where the geometrically laid-out fields and the capital-intensive sugar mills dominated the scene. The modern era of rice cultivation had arrived, if only for this one river. The initiators were the men most committed to carving out a place for the colony in the transatlantic world. Elsewhere, the pattern was uneven. As suggested by Table 11, St. Matthew Parish remained a society with slaves rather than a slave society. Many farmers, if not the majority, had no slaves and those who did held a modest number on average. Tilling the fields was still a badge of honor among the Germans rather than a mark of poverty. St. Andrew Parish possessed a few large plantations, but most

Scotsmen clung to herding cattle as had their fathers in the Highlands and employed blacks as cowboys rather than as field hands. When John Graham purchased from a Scot in St. Andrew Parish a herd of five hundred cattle for a client in East Florida, the owner agreed to sell "a Negroe fellow, his cowppen keeper who has been bred up from his infancy in this business, and is I am told a very remarkable clever fellow and capable of taking the management of any stock if such a slave is wanted."[46] Plantations in St. John and St. Philip parishes had grown to sizable units with the greatest concentration in the range of thirty to forty-nine slaves. Within the three core parishes of the lowcountry, consolidation moved quickly. By the end of the colonial era, only 12.2 percent of their plantations contained fewer than twenty enslaved people. The distribution of slaves on plantations in St. John, St. Philip, and Christ Church parishes closely matched that for all of South Carolina. The figures are not comparable in the sense that one is based on three parishes and the other on all parishes within Carolina. Nevertheless, Table 13 demonstrates the degree to which the Georgia lowcountry was gaining on the Carolina lowcountry.[47]

The planters of the 1750s may have had few enslaved people on average, but they started with an enormous advantage. During the 1750s, a total of twenty-five hundred blacks had crossed the Savannah River with their masters, a majority of the bondspeople in the province at the end of the decade.[48] It was a labor force accustomed to the rigors of plantation discipline; it was also a labor force in transition. Of those who came with their masters, at least 42 percent had been born in Africa.[49] They had survived the harrowing Middle Passage, the new disease environment, and the trauma of a work routine meant to extract maximum profit. Disoriented and alienated, many still spoke their native tongues, and those who had run away in the first years had been recaptured and subdued, at least outwardly. On the plantation, they found themselves having to interact with Africans from other ethnic groups and to form new associations that demanded a radical rethinking. As Philip Morgan phrased it, they were aliens in a strange land.[50] A majority of the enslaved people brought to Georgia, however, were creoles, born in the New World, more conversant in white ways than the recently transported Africans, and at times at odds with those from across the seas. For the most part, they were the children or grandchildren of those from Africa; their survival rate was higher; families had formed; and their culture was already assimilating elements from the white world. Despite the inevitable fric-

TABLE 13   Distribution of Slaves by Plantation Size: Georgia and South Carolina, 1766–77 (Percent)

Colony	1–9	10–19	20–29	30–49	50+	# of Slaves
Georgia (3 parishes)	4.4	7.8	9.0	27.6	51.2	5,747
South Carolina	7.0	11.0	11.0	19.0	52.0	20,485

Sources: For Georgia, Colonial Inventory Book F, 1755–70; Colonial Inventory Book FF, 1776–77; microfilm of loose inventories in the Georgia Archives; loose inventories in the Telamon Cuyler Collection, University of Georgia; and lists of bondsmen in the Colonial Book of Miscellaneous Bonds YY and KK, Georgia Archives. Petitions for land from 1766 to 1772 furnish supporting information. For South Carolina, P. Morgan, "Plantation Size in South Carolina, 1720–1779: Proportion of Slaves Living on Unit," in his *Slave Counterpoint,* 40. The numbers are for the 1770s.

tion, Africans and creoles learned to cooperate and, in the process, began to evolve a new culture, with distinctly African roots but American in outlook. The enslaved people from South Carolina, whether African or "country born," would lay the seeds of the agricultural revolution that was taking hold of the Georgia lowcountry. Their experience equipped new arrivals with the knowledge and skills to build rice plantations on the frontier.

Many newcomers carried with them an African rice culture rooted in hundreds of years of practice. Rice was an important crop in West Africa, embracing the striking variety of soil and water features on the coast and in inland areas. From the Senegal to the Gambia River, along coastal estuaries in Sierra Leone and the Windward Coast, Africans grew many varieties of *Oryza glaberrima* and *Oryza sativa* in widely differing settings. In Gambia and Senegal, management techniques included placing earthen embankments around the perimeters of inland swamps to hold water. In certain areas, rice culture involved the seasonal rotation of land from rice field to cattle pasture. Ethnic groups like the Baga in the Guinea Conakry region carved out rice fields in the highly saline terrain of red mangrove swamps, which required huge embankments to prevent overspill from tides. A web of canals and dikes was constructed to channel brackish water and freshwater in the right proportions. Mande-speaking people in the uplands cultivated rice on freshwater floodplains. Before coming to Georgia to assist Oglethorpe, Francis Moore described in his journal the practice of growing rice on ridges in these fields nourished by rainfall.[51]

Lowcountry rice plantations followed key principles of West African rice growing to ensure a command of freshwater under varying climatic conditions.[52] Although most blacks from this vast region were from millet-growing or cow-herding regions or were involved in the commercial networks that dominated the river systems, many had experience in the challenges of insulating rice crops against floods, droughts, and salinity by the careful management of water.[53] The parallels between the farming systems on the two continents were clear, from simple techniques like the use of the heel-and-toe method to sow the seed to intricate methods of land preparation and the threshing, winnowing, and milling of the crop. Edda Fields-Black, author of a study of rice production along the Guinea coast, argues that Africans brought not so much the specifics of irrigation techniques to the lowcountry but experience in creating the delicate balance between fresh and brackish water so that rice would grow in tidewater areas.[54] They had knowledge of irrigation technology, including embankments, the plug trunk, and the use of tidal flow for watering fields. In Georgia between 1766 and 1774, 86 percent of the total slaves imported directly from Africa embarked from the coasts of Senegambia, Sierra Leone, and the Windward Coast; and planters and merchants uniformly proclaimed their preference for slaves from this vast area. An advertisement in 1770 for 340 "new Negroes" boosted the sale by claiming they were from "the rice coast."[55] A growing volume of historiography argues for the African sources of American rice cultivation and processing techniques.[56]

For Georgia, qualifications must be made to the idea that significant numbers of Africans familiar with rice came to the colony and tutored European planters who had no previous experience in cultivating the crop. Most blacks from West Africa were involved in the raising of millet or other crops, were herdsmen, or were employed in riverine trade or other occupations. It has been suggested that the dominance of people from Senegambia, Sierra Leone, and the Windward Coast was as much an accident of shifting strategies of British slavers as a response to demand, while the composition of human cargos reflected the wide diversity of people thrown together by war, kidnappings, and the tendency of slavers to buy small numbers at each call along the coast.[57] Moreover, Georgia received 25 percent of its Africans from the West Indies, and their origins typically lay in the Bights of Benin and Biafra, the Gold Coast, and west central Africa, not from rice-growing regions. The small cargos from the sugar islands were composed in a haphazard way that ensured a "more polyglot assortment of African peoples" than those that came directly, people more likely to suffer a higher degree of separation from kin, co-linguists, or shipmates.[58] Of the 27 percent of slaves who came with their owners from South Carolina, a significant percentage were from Angola, other parts of west central Africa, and the bights and lacked knowledge of rice culture on arriving.[59]

Nor were the planters who accompanied their slaves into Georgia eager novices waiting to be taught by their workers. They could build on over fifty years of South Carolina's experience in the inland swamp method, and they could draw on a broad range of English and European precedents to supplement that knowledge. The use of upper and lower dams to establish a field was a method that had long allowed English farmers to enrich their pastures. The techniques for reclaiming wetlands for agriculture were broadly shared among the English and northern Europeans. If Africans had devised the trunk method for transferring water through embankments, planters relied on the hanging floodgates, a device invented by Europeans.[60] As historian Max Edelson suggests, both Africans and Europeans shaped the Georgia and Carolina rice plantation, resulting in a new system of agriculture that was synthetic rather than purely African or British.[61] In reality, the enslaved people on a settlement responded to their driver as much as to the overseer, and that driver was more often than not native-born. Merchant John Graham told Governor James Grant of East Florida that he had purchased "two fine young men their wives and families" for £320 sterling: "the two fellows with their families were born on [Jonathan Bryan's] plantation and in short capable of the management of a plantation themselves." In that same letter, he confessed he had sent "all over Carolina" for overseers but had not succeeded in finding one. He advised the governor that the East Florida planter would do better to save his money as the crop would not bear the expense for the coming season, "and the Negroe I send him is capable to manage all his planting business very well, especially for this year."[62] Graham's appreciation of these black plantation managers speaks to a larger issue. Africans on rice plantations, whatever their origins or prior knowledge, showed themselves innovative, responsive, and calculating in the ways that they went about their work and went on to influence the shape and direction of this vital economy.

During its formative years, Georgia occupied a halfway place between the experiences of South Carolina and the Caribbean, and, if it was closer to the former than to the sugar islands, the fact remained that its black population could not be sustained except through imports. In the West Indies, mortality was high, reaching 2–6 percent annually at mid-century, and fertility was low—so much so that planters in the Leeward Islands and Jamaica spoke of "buying rather than breeding" and emphasized the imports of men until the fourth quarter of the century. About one in four Africans died within the first three years of residence on a plantation.[63] Governor James Wright estimated a mortality rate of 3 percent for blacks in Georgia.[64] For those living on plantations along rivers, the figure was higher. John Graham ventured to guess that he lost 3–4 percent of his slaves per year on his Savannah River plantations, Mulberry Grove and New Settlement, while William De Brahm, the most knowledgeable of Georgians in terms of statistics, thought 5 percent a more appropriate figure.[65] Working knee-deep in marsh took a terrible toll on the workers, and there was also a high incidence of disease. "The Lands Upon the Savanna River, have proved so fatal to the negroes settle[d] upon them . . . that I cannot think of advising you to a Settlement there," wrote Carolina planter Peter Manigault to a friend in 1770.[66]

Gender imbalance was a more significant factor than mortality.[67] According to a historian of slavery in colonial Georgia, Betty Wood, there were 146 men to every 100 women.[68] On larger plantations, the imbalance was greater. Many of the bigger planters made a conscious choice to acquire adult men, not children, and demanded a level of work that undermined family relationships. John Graham's Mulberry Grove and New Settlement plantations contained 84 men, 42 women, and 15 children, and that of his neighbor, William Knox, 68 men, 32 women, and 21 children, for a combined ratio of 185 to 100.[69] As for the all-important fertility of women, Wood considers that the average of 1.17 children per woman in the Carolina of the 1720s held true for this province, reflecting the rigors of field work and the psychological impact of the terrifying transition from Africa to the Americas. The population was only a few steps away from conditions in the West Indies, where the intensive labor of sugar plantations, the deficient diet, the tendency to breast-feed for long periods, and the relative fragility of family life undermined the ability to reproduce.[70] The fact that 75 percent of slaves in Jamaica had been born in Africa confirmed the low levels of fertility.[71] In Georgia, Africans accounted for over 60 percent of the population.[72] The black population of the colony in 1770 provides mute testimony to the repercussions. According to the *Historical Statistics of the United States*, the number stood at 10,625 compared to the 11,400 enslaved people who had come with their masters or been imported by that date.[73]

Plantations in the lowcountry and the Caribbean were built around large numbers of blacks; on a Carolina plantation, thirty to over a hundred enslaved people; and in the West Indies, where the tasks of planting and harvesting sugarcane required exceptionally large work forces, rarely less than a hundred and more typically several hundred.[74] If Georgia's plantations were smaller, the features were similar. Almost all slaves were put to work, some 80 percent in South Carolina and Georgia and 90 percent on the sugar islands, one of the highest labor participation rates anywhere in the world.[75] Women toiled in the fields alongside men. Tasks were performed with hand tools, not plows, while the enslaved people had to master the intricacies of working on capital-intensive units of production that were veritable "factories in the field." In the Lower South, that meant the movement of millions of square feet of marsh mud to build huge embankments, and milling rice in commercially acceptable ways. On the sugar islands, it meant following a rigorously predetermined schedule of furrowing and planting, harvesting the crop in long work days, feeding the cane into grinders, and stirring vats of scalding hot liquid in mills where life and limb were at constant risk.[76] Sugar monoculture involved a particularly intensive and degrading system of chattel bondage.[77] If the lowcountry escaped some of the worst features, the differences were often more of degree than kind.

In the Caribbean, the strongest of the slaves were grouped into gangs to undertake field work, while in South Carolina and Georgia the task system of labor prevailed. Each gang was composed of approximately twenty people under the supervision of a driver and labored from dawn to dusk, with breaks for meals.[78] It was not uncommon for blacks to be in the fields for fifteen hours a day during the planting season and eighteen hours during the harvesting and milling. In the Lower South, the task system set the region apart. Blacks were assigned individual tasks and, when completed, could undertake activities of their own choosing. If a person weeded a quarter acre by the early afternoon, he or she could devote the remaining part of the day to cultivating a garden plot or fishing or hunting small game.[79] The task system had the advantage of setting normative limits on the number of hours demanded of a laborer, but the exact definition of the task resulted from a tug-of-war between slave and owner and typically ended to the latter's advantage.[80] Owners pushed their bondspeople to work ever harder, and if slaves were on occasion compensated for tasks above the regular routine, the infusion of "New Negroes" from Africa put the balance of power firmly in the hands of the owners. In both Georgia and South Carolina, overseers nudged their field hands to spend more hours at work, not only through the spring, summer, and fall but increasingly through the winter to extend and repair the irrigation infrastructure that funneled freshwater onto and off the fields.[81] In reaction, the enslaved people were forever trying to undermine labor discipline and white authority.

Coercion remained at the heart of the plantation complex in the Caribbean and lowcountry. The Barbadian Slave Code of 1661, whose preamble characterized slaves as "an heathenish, brutish and an uncertaine, dangerous kinde of people," unfit to be governed by English law, served as the model for the whole of the West Indies, South Carolina, and eventually Georgia.[82] The whip became the highly personal mechanism of enforcement and, if Georgia plantations saw a less frequent use than those in the West Indies, the records of individual owners, like William Gibbons, are filled with receipts paid for the whipping of recalcitrant slaves at the public gaol. The Barbadian code put police regulations at the heart of the system, prohibited any unauthorized movement of slaves, forbade the use of guns, restricted the right of slaves to gather, and specified an elaborate scale of penalties for transgressions. Animated by this spirit, South Carolina's code was the most repressive on the continent, and in the wake of the Stono Rebellion, it became more so, with heavier surveillance, increased penalties, and rewards for slaves who informed against each other.[83]

In adopting slavery in 1750, Georgia had promulgated a code that showed something of the humanitarian spirit of the trustee period, but replaced it five years later with one largely borrowed from South Carolina's with the aim of making black "misconduct" as difficult and futile as possible. The final code voted by the General Assembly in 1770 contained features that bespoke the changing spirit of Georgians. Capital offenses now included the crime of poisoning, something that had not been mentioned earlier, the rape or attempted rape of a white woman, and breaking into a house for any reason whatsoever.[84] The colony that had begun as a bald repudiation of Carolina's slave society was now giving its mentor a lesson in black-white relations. Although Barbadians were the first group within the Anglo American world to portray blacks as beasts or as beast-like,[85] Georgians were moving uncomfortably close to that spirit. Like Carolinians, they faced security problems comparable to those of the sugar islands and were not slow to digest the implications, as Equiano found to his cost.

As early modern capitalists in the Caribbean mold, all planters shared the mania of their Carolina counterparts for raising rice to buy more blacks and buying blacks to raise more rice. They competed for the best lands, sold and resold property, schemed for ways to acquire more enslaved people, responded to changing local conditions with a practiced eye, and shopped for the best price for their crop among the merchants of Savannah and occasionally Charles Town. White women participated alongside men. They received 70,000 acres of land in the form of grants during the royal period and inherited thousands more. Abigail Minis, an early Jewish settler, successfully managed a plantation with at least sixteen slaves and received grants or purchased tracts of at least 1,000 acres. When her husband died, Elizabeth Butler inherited more than 3,000 acres and 111 enslaved people. From 1763 to 1772, she received twelve grants totaling 5,320 acres, 1,000 of which she intended to use for timbering.[86] These aggressive women and men were engaged in the adaptation of old methods to new challenges and willingly applied a mindset of continual experimentation. They were not simply interested in making better what they were given. Inventive and creative, they brought a new world to coastal Georgia, in terms of both technology and the culture that went with it.[87] At the outset, they were small to medium businesspeople who showed a fierce commitment to hard work, maximizing profits, and assembling as much land as possible.

Entering the Atlantic economy was a novel experience for the early generation of planters and a frequently trying one for later participants. It involved the nature and shape of the rice market in Savannah, the availability and cost of shipping in that port, and the rippling effects of supply and demand in the distant markets of northern Europe. Once again, the export merchant loomed large. Sellers found themselves contending with an international rice market that required flexibility and initiative on the part of merchants, shippers, correspondents, and factors, all of whom had to contend with elaborate legal practices, complex shipping patterns, rapid price fluctuations, shifting demand, and the varied uses of rice in different markets.[88] The distinctive features of that market reflected how the local economy borrowed selectively from the practices of Charles Town to move into the Atlantic economy at breakneck speed. Planters benefited but merchants more so.

Chapter Eight

Georgia's Rice and the Atlantic World

During the 1750s, London slowly awoke to the fact that commercially viable rice was coming out of Georgia. Even the greatest of the Carolina merchants, James Crokatt, missed the first signals. He had stayed long enough in Charles Town to make a fortune in the deerskin trade, retained trading ties with the best merchants in the province, and knew the market intimately because he controlled a significant portion of the growing rice exports. Due to Georgia's checkered history, he and his peers at the Carolina Coffee House had reason to be suspicious of that notoriously difficult colony: the fact that the trustees had forbidden slavery in peremptory fashion, the near bankruptcy of a badly run colonization scheme, and the notorious hostility of the trustees to merchants over a period of two decades. Nor were they impressed with the length of time it had taken Whitehall to replace the failed experiment with royal government. Trustee officials would remain in firm control of the colony until the first governor set foot in Savannah in December 1754 and, even then, continued to exercise considerable power.[1]

Understandably, the rice merchants of London remained profoundly skeptical of the colony's transformation. Establishing a rice plantation in a boggy swamp or tidal marsh promised no quick returns. Blacks working knee-deep in muddy waters, cutting trees and brush to clear fields, and building embankments out of tons of wet earth were among the most vulnerable of laborers in British North America. Indeed the pace was slow and little rice was produced in the early years. By 1755, four years after the introduction of slavery, Georgia had reached a modest take-off point. The port of Savannah saw some 2,291 barrels of rice rolled across its wharves, although only one vessel from Britain carried away a shipment.[2] The dominant figures were merchants of New York, Massachusetts, and Rhode Island, whose vessels transported almost three-quarters of the limited exports. Willing to make quick turnarounds, aggressive Yankees were shipping rice to the Caribbean as well as to their own ports for reexport to Britain. Constantly on the lookout for information about the movement of prices, they were the first to jump into the emerging market in Georgia.[3] Gradually, they had to share their lead. Georgians began taking cargos of rice to New York and Philadelphia in exchange for flour, provisions, and hardware. While most confined their efforts to the coastal trade, the ambitious John Graham quietly dispatched a ship to London with three hundred barrels.[4]

If most British merchants had yet to learn of the game being played out next door to South Carolina, there was an exception. While carrying hundreds of English, Scots, and Germans to trustee Georgia, Captain William Thomson made a considerable fortune as the trustees' most valued sea captain. Skipper of the dependable *Two Brothers*, he received £300 to £600 sterling per voyage by bringing indentured servants and adventurers, who paid their own way. He stuffed cargo into the crowded holds and sold it to the needy settlers already there. When Savannah's public storekeeper ran short of hard currency or sola bills, Thomson financed the store until the trustees reimbursed him. A quiet, unassuming man, he left few records and resolutely maintained a low profile. By 1757, he was in London handling one of the first major shipments of rice coming out of Georgia, over six hundred barrels. A year later, he persuaded a sea captain to carry merchandise to the Medway River, sell the cargo, and bring back the rice grown by the planters in what became St. John Parish. Rather than having to charter the vessel, he contracted with the captain to split the profits on the sale of the rice. Fully loaded, the *Venus* hit a succession of sand bars sailing down the Medway, tore its bottom, and spent several months under repair. The fact that Thomson sent a vessel directly to the most productive region of Georgia even though no port yet existed spoke to his taste for outsized risks as well as his intimate knowledge of the colony.[5]

By the early 1760s, the pattern was changing. Almost a third of exported rice went directly to Britain, another third to northern colonies, and a final third to the West Indies. Once the colony began exporting over 10,000 barrels per year in 1765, London merchants jumped into the game with a vengeance. In that year, the British carried most of Georgia's rice crop, owned twelve of the fourteen vessels sailing to England, and made clear who had the financial muscle.[6] When William Knox, provost marshal of the colony and now a subminister in London, walked into the Carolina Coffee House, he found himself besieged with questions about his Savannah River property: "Pray Mr. Knox how many barrels of Rice did you make last year? 'Upon my word Sir I don't know.' It sold well in Georgia. What price did yours bring? 'Really Sir I can't tell.'" He begged the managers of his estate for more information and better news.[7] By 1772, ships carried away 22,900 barrels to all markets, plus another 2,800 in the intercoastal trade within British North America; presumably most of that went to Charles Town.[8]

Georgia was entering the international rice market at the best possible moment. The international demand for rice had led to a sixfold expansion of South Carolina's production during the 1720s and 1730s and laid the basis for the enormous expansion of its plantation economy. The following two decades had been defined by stagnation in the wake of the War of Jenkins' Ear, the War of the Austrian Succession, and the cataclysmic Seven Years' War. Carolina was producing considerably less rice in 1760 than it had in 1740.[9] But that rapidly changed. Between 1760 and the American Revolution, the volume of rice exported from the Lower South more than doubled. Demand in northern Europe, especially Holland and the German states, was expanding and, although rice was a substitute crop for wheat and other indigenous grains, it was gaining more than a token place in European diets as demographic pressures and a series of poor harvests strained the food supply of western Europe. By mid-century, transportation costs across the Atlantic were falling steadily as ships grew larger and turnaround times shorter, and after mid-century, the British government took a series of steps to ease the duties on colonial rice. Along with the rising volume of exports, the price climbed by over 50 percent between 1760 and 1775. A grain that had had no more than a toehold in the North American landscape at the beginning of the century became one of the most valuable exports.[10] The rising rice market paralleled developments in the West Indies, where the third quarter of the century marked a period of rapid economic growth. Sugar imports rose several times over, reflecting the fast growth of the British population and the rise in sugar consumption per head.[11]

Understandably, London merchants began measuring the worth of the gentlemen of Georgia who had opened a new rice frontier. They assumed planters on the southern side of the Savannah River looked and behaved much like those on the northern side. Georgia owners shared the same aspirations, used the same types of technology, brutally drove their labor forces in the effort to extract maximum profits, and reacted to price levels in much the same way as their neighbors to the north. But there were important differences. As much as 25 percent of the total rice crop was concentrated in the hands of twelve or thirteen planters and merchant-planters, a small group well represented on the governor's council and exercising a firm hand on commercial policy. Never in South Carolina's history had such a high percentage of the crop been in the hands of so few and never had the pool of planters been so narrow and shallow. This small cohort took its cue from Governor James Wright, the largest single producer of rice, who owned 523 slaves distributed over eleven plantations. When an inventory of his estate was taken in January 1777, Patriots found forty-three hundred barrels of rice, mostly stacked in barns and the remainder estimated from the bushels of grain ready to be "beaten out." When Wright had gone to England on leave at the beginning of that decade, James Habersham reported to a London merchant he expected to ship two thousand to three thousand barrels a year of the governor's rice.[12] John Graham announced to the governor of East Florida his expectation of one thousand barrels from three hundred acres and, four years later, claimed twice as much acreage planted in rice.[13] Graham's brother James and his partner, Indian trader Lachlan McGillivray, owner of two premier sites on the Savannah River, together accounted for close to a thousand barrels.[14] Joining this group was former South Carolinian Joseph Butler, who delivered nine hundred sixty-two barrels in early 1775, his cousin James Butler, Jonathan Bryan, William Knox, William and Joseph Gibbons, William McGillivray, James Cuthbert, and Alexander Wright, the governor's son. This small group of friends, who together owned close to fifteen hundred enslaved people, generated roughly six thousand barrels of rice a year at the beginning of the decade and seven thousand or more a year by the time of the Revolution. With the exception of Bryan, they worked closely together, moved in the same circles, shared the same opinions, and shaped the contours of the colony without strong opposition or countervailing forces.[15]

If the top end was distinct, a body of planters with between fifteen and thirty slaves were important participants in the rice trade and fueled the economy of Sunbury in particular. What gave value to the efforts of these more modest planters was the fact that rice was the coin of the realm. Even if someone produced only a few barrels, that person entered into the commercial world. Planters paid off carpenters and other craftsmen with those barrels, bartered for goods in stores in Savannah or Sunbury or on the waterfront, and fed their enslaved people with "rough rice" whose grains had cracked during the milling process. When all sources are added together, the total production was impressive. In addition to the rice exported across the Atlantic, rice shipped in the intercoastal trade in British North America accounted for twenty-eight hundred barrels on average between 1768 and 1772.[16] Most of that was sold in the spot market in Charles Town although some made its way to Philadelphia and perhaps to other northern towns. Rice consumed internally by black and white Georgians added an estimated 10 percent to the total. If 1772 is taken as the base, we can estimate a total crop in the vicinity of twenty-eight thousand barrels.[17] Exports must be qualified in one respect, however. Savannah had become the shipping point for several of the plantations across the Savannah River in South Carolina. Although Henry Laurens sent rice from his Wright Savanna plantation back to Charles Town, others chose the shorter route to Savannah, suggesting that any price differential between the two ports was not significant.[18]

The number of houses that handled rice exports in Savannah was small, probably not more than four or five partnerships at any one time, notably John Graham and Company; Clay and Habersham; Cowper, Telfairs; Read and Mossman; Johnston & Wylly; George Baillie and Company; Douglass and Company; and Inglis and Hall. Ten of these men owned Savannah River plantations, leaders in the fundamental transformation of rice culture in Georgia that opened a profound chasm between middling and large planters.[19] Other partnerships dealt in rice but primarily by brokering that commodity to these same houses. The exporting firms represented people who stood close to the center of power. John Graham, James Read, and Lewis Johnston served on the governor's council. Joseph Clay, nephew of James Habersham, the second most powerful figure in the colony, commanded respect. Basil Cowper was a brother-in-law of the governor's son; Edward Telfair and Nathaniel Hall were married to cousins, Sally Gibbons and Nancy Gibbons, daughters of the powerful Gibbons brothers; and James Mossman, John Graham, and George Baillie were brothers-in-law. Only the Butler family was absent from this interlocking network of families, but Mary, the daughter of the prosperous Elizabeth Butler, married a Charles Town merchant and slave trader and divided her time between Charles Town and four plantations on the Ogeechee.[20]

Export merchants dominated the rice trade in a way reminiscent of

Charles Town in the 1730s. Most contracted directly with individual planters for future deliveries of rice. Merchants supplied the plantation tools,
"Negroe cloth," and a limited amount of credit in return for a commitment
from the planter to deliver the following year's crop. Of several hundred
barrels of rice sold by William Gibbons, the bulk went to merchants for his
yearly supplies, including repaying the cost of four "New Negroes."[21] Direct
purchases of rice from planters by export merchants had dominated the
Charles Town scene during the 1720s and 1730s when the price was moving
dramatically upward. Everyone benefited and few questioned the arrange-
ment. But when the price of rice collapsed during King George's War as
French and Spanish privateers prowled the waters off the lowcountry, the
interests of Carolina planters and merchants diverged. Planters wanted the
independence to seek the highest price in a volatile market and began turning to country, or rice, factors who sold their rice on commission to export
merchants. Those merchants in turn wanted the flexibility to buy rice in advance of the arrival of British ships, which they had chartered for arrival at
a certain time and which needed a prompt departure to ensure a profitable
voyage. They came to prefer purchasing rice for cash or bills of exchange in
the open market.[22]

By the 1760s, country factors in Charles Town had become crucial to
establishing the price. The struggle between the two groups reached the
point that factors formed cartels to keep up prices and push down freight
rates. They typically owned or leased wharves and operated retail stores,
mostly but not always on the wharves, where they exchanged merchandise
of a modest sort for country produce—rice, indigo, corn, peas, and other
provisions—or, more typically, sold that produce for a straight commission,
typically 2.5 percent.[23] By the nature of their functions, a country factor like
Christopher Gadsden, with two stores in Charles Town and smaller stores
in outlying villages, and an export merchant like Henry Laurens engaged
in an annual and often bitter struggle to influence the course of prices. The
former sought high rice prices and low freight rates, all the better to benefit himself and his customers, while the latter wanted low prices and high
freight rates so he could better execute the orders of his British correspondent. Specialization was now the rule in the Carolina port.[24]

In Savannah, the country factor never emerged in the consequential way
he did next door. Prices were rising so there was no immediate incentive to
endow country factors with more power than they possessed. Minor mer-

chants like Thomas Lloyd and William Moore or import merchants like Reid, Storr, and Read and Quinton Pooler announced their modest services through advertisements. After moving from Charles Town to Savannah in 1758, Thomas Lloyd set up a countinghouse near the public market on Ellis Square and simultaneously purchased a "commodious" wharf, together with its stores on the waterfront, advertising the sale of "Country Produce on the usual commissions." Lloyd announced he would make sales for cash "or short credit," in other words no credit above two or three months. William Moore promised he would execute "any commands in the factorage business," charge "low commissions," give good service at his wharf, and offer coffee, rum, cut tobacco, Philadelphia flour, and iron pots at his small store.[25] There was never an equivalent of a Gadsden, much less a cartel with enough force to withhold rice from the market to influence prices. In this quasi-barter system, there was little other than "book" debt, and relatively small amounts of cash or even bills of exchange to change hands. As long as the export merchants imported dry goods for sale in a timely fashion, the old connection remained intact.

Those merchants were in a much stronger position vis-à-vis planters in Georgia than their counterparts in the West Indies. Planters in the low-country negotiated directly with export merchants like Edward Telfair, Joseph Clay, and Nathaniel Hall, who purchased crops on behalf of their London correspondents. Payment was received at the time of the transaction or, as was more likely the case, used to settle outstanding debts for plantation supplies. By way of contrast, planters on a sugar island bypassed the commercial interests in the home port, shipped their sugar directly to British ports, and marketed the crop on their own account and risk. They relied on agents in London to sell their commodity, purchase plantation supplies, extend loans, provide insurance, and tend to the many financial details that arose from the life of a great estate, all in return for a commission. Their agents, who often had West Indian antecedents, were sugar specialists who told their planter clients how to improve the quality of the product, how to pack it for shipment, and what seasons to send it to market. In Savannah, the export merchants performed those functions without having to master as arcane an art as distinguishing the range of quality in the many different types of sugar or negotiate the financial complexities of the London exchange. The merchant in the Lower South was in a much stronger position than his counterpart in the West Indies.[26]

Georgia's merchants were entering the rice market at a moment when sophisticated entrepreneurs throughout the Atlantic had perfected mechanisms for moving that bulky commodity expeditiously to a variety of markets. From his residence in London, William Knox decided that the best moment for his crop to be sold was at the beginning of the season. By December, wheat, rye, and other grains were in short supply in northern Europe, and demand for rice consequently strong. If prices did not rise, he judged, the grain could be stored until the right moment.[27] Habersham's nephew Joseph Clay considered the idea a dubious one. Not only did storage and cooperage add to the cost, but there was the risk of a loss in weight from the drying of the husks, the inevitable leakage of rice onto the warehouse floor, exposure to rats, weevil, and worm, and if this were not enough, the constant danger of destruction by fire in wooden storehouses.[28] While agreeing that the first part of the season was generally best for prices, merchants knew those weeks held a special danger: the early arrival of a chartered vessel with too large a capacity for rice trickling into the port. With a vessel of six-hundred-barrel capacity sitting partially filled at his dock, Edward Telfair was forced to use precious cash and bills of exchange to enter the local market to purchase rice outright at a higher price rather than wait on planters who owed him for previously purchased goods. Merchants strongly expressed their desire for chartered vessels that were smaller rather than larger, would not draw more than twelve or thirteen feet when fully loaded, and had not less than forty working days and sixty running days before having to pay demurrage.[29] That preference reflected the hard fact that Savannah merchants had less control of their purchases than did their Charles Town counterparts because the latter bought on the open market rather than wait for customers to settle their debts.

Although on a long-term movement upward, the actual price of rice was highly volatile, changing in relation to supply, the cost of freight, the market in Charles Town, political developments overseas, and, most important, news of the strength of demand in Atlantic markets. The price could move 15–20 percent or more in the course of one short season.[30] Deep in the summer of 1771, James Habersham learned that the price had reached an unprecedented level in the Carolina port at a time of the year when the market was normally "dull" and trading all but dead in Savannah. With the governor in England on a leave of absence, he gave orders for Wright's rice mills to be put to work beating out one round in the morning and another round in the afternoon until 160 barrels were filled. Slaves on other plantations belonging to Wright were hustled to the Ogeechee River site. An overseer, uneasy about moving twenty prime hands from another plantation during the hot work of midsummer, persuaded Habersham to allow him to give each worker a dram of rum on arrival and a half crown piece when the work was done.[31]

Because of their contacts, Savannah's export merchants enjoyed a crucial advantage in receiving news of price movements on distant European markets. In October 1771, Henry Laurens, who had left Charles Town for business matters in London, advised Habersham of an expected price upswing because of rising demand in northern Europe. He had met with "good Intelligence" that crops in South Carolina and Georgia would find a ready market in the upcoming season and recommended that Habersham not be "hasty in the Sale of your Crop." Laurens and Habersham enjoyed a close relationship over the years so it was only natural that he make clear the personal motive behind his gesture: "And I know that to communicate such intelligence early to a Friend who may have a thousand Barrels or more of his own to sell is my Duty, because I owe him all that is in my Power to do for the Benefit of his own and his Children's Interest." He advised the Georgian to keep the information secret so as not to give away a precious advantage in the market.[32] Despite the six or seven weeks in transit from the moment the letter was written, the information was timely.

The competitiveness of the port became a matter of concern as the Seven Years' War wound down. Responding to the merchant community, the Commons House of Assembly turned its attention to commercial and maritime matters. The rice trade motivated delegates to take badly overdue steps. Between 1763 and 1768, the sadly maintained lighthouse on Tybee Island was rebuilt. Sea captains were to be fined if they gave in to the temptation to dump their heavy stone ballast into the river as they sailed into port. The assembly created a commission to regulate the pilots operating in Savannah and Sunbury, setting the fees and handling complaints about the quality of service. Most important of all was legislation requiring the inspection of rice, wood products, indigo, beef, and pork "to prevent frauds and deceits." At long last, Georgia made an effort to catch up with South Carolina in ensuring basic standards for exports. Other acts set up a special court to hear disputes between mariners and merchants, instituted the process of quarantining ships in case of disease, and created a tax on goods imported for resale in the colony by transients.[33] Within a matter of a half dozen years, Georgia acquired the ability to compete in the Atlantic marketplace, and if the legislation looked better on paper than in the actual execution, it was only a matter of time before the colony caught up.

In 1765, as Georgia's rice market took off, James Habersham and John Graham collaborated in an effort to gain a foothold in the highly competitive market for shipping. Despite the many risks, transatlantic transportation was a profitable undertaking for British shippers who benefited from considerable productivity gains in terms of size of vessel, sailing speed, and efficiency of ports. From the 1750s to the early 1770s, freight charges per ton dropped from 50–55 shillings to 32–38 shillings.[34] Savannah and Charles Town entrepreneurs generally left the shipping trade and its profits to English and Scots merchants. The Lower South had little in the way of shipbuilding, owned few vessels, and preferred to invest its limited capital in safer, less complex activities. In the mid-1760s, almost all of the owners trading with Savannah were from Great Britain, people like the Joliffe family of Poole, Charles Ogilvie from Scotland, the formidable John Nutt of London, and the Scarth family of the small port town of Whitby on the north coast. In constant movement, their vessels entered Savannah from ports on the southeastern coast of England, from London and Bristol, from the West Indies, and a handful from neighboring Charles Town.[35]

In a bold move, Graham and Habersham organized a local syndicate to purchase a prize ship taken during the recent war, hired a captain, and provided a cargo of rice to stake their claim to a recognized place in the international rice market. The syndicate included the elite Savannah exporters: John and James Graham, Joseph Clay, James Habersham Jr., Lachlan McGillivray, James Read, James Mossman, and Alexander Fyffe, together with John Clark, who financed so much of Georgia's rice trade from London. A promising young sea captain had a share as well. A native of Berwick, a few miles south of the Scottish border, George Anderson had grown up sailing the North Atlantic and arrived in New York looking for a bigger world. Giving up on making ends meet in that competitive city, he decamped for Savannah to see what the conclusion of the Seven Years' War meant for that outpost of the commercial world. Although still in his late twenties, he was one of the few local captains (if not the only one) with experience in the transatlantic trade. On July 11, Captain Anderson gave orders to unfurl the topsails of his two-hundred-ton ship, the *Georgia Packet*, and began the slow process of taking it down the river to Cockspur, where lighters loaded the remaining barrels of rice. In addition to deerskins and indigo, the vessel carried 833 barrels of rice, a large shipment by local standards and extraordinary for the summertime when the port of Savannah virtually ceased activity in that market.[36]

Few Georgians attempted to enter the transatlantic shipping trade; even fewer chose to construct vessels for service in the Atlantic. However, one merchant syndicate made a serious foray into large-scale shipbuilding during the 1770s, a high-risk venture where as much money was lost as made. The firm Cowper, Telfairs joined with a former partner, John Morel, now a wealthy planter, in constructing ships of two to three hundred tons capable of carrying a thousand or more barrels of rice. Shipbuilding for the transatlantic trade remained the purview of New Englanders, with their wealth of hardwoods and their tradition of building and operating their own vessels to carry on trade with Britain.[37] The returns on investment in plantation agriculture made the economics of the industry unattractive. The heavy use of slave shipwrights lessened the attractiveness of the industry for skilled white artisans. Vital to this fledgling industry, Africans and African Americans were employed in large numbers in and around Savannah constructing new vessels, repairing and caulking ships, and mending sails.[38] Between 1769 and 1771, nine sloops and schooners were constructed in the colony compared to fifteen in South Carolina. In the latter year, two large, square-rigged ships rolled off the stocks.[39]

John Morel, the original partner of William Telfair, concentrated his energies on Ossabaw Island, where the growth of live oak trees gave him exceptional material for shipbuilding, and on his plantation at Bewlie, where a shipyard turned out schooners.[40] Native to the southern coast, live oak timber offered tremendous tensile strength, a naturally curved grain, and an exceptional resistance to rot. Hard to shape, it nevertheless made for exceptional pieces in the framing of a vessel.[41] In the columns of the *Georgia Gazette*, Morel offered to supply on short notice a "Quantity of sterns, stern posts, transoms, bow timbers, lower, upper and middle futtocks, aprons, knees, etc."[42] Edward Telfair contracted with his Antiguan partner, John Wand, to construct a ship on Ossabaw eighty-four feet in length, twenty-six feet in beam. Wand assumed the financial risk and provided enslaved ship carpenters and blacksmiths for the enterprise. The finished product was a testimony to the skills of the labor on Ossabaw, about thirty men and women newly imported from Africa. The *Elizabeth* sailed with rice for Rotterdam, then to St. Petersburg, and finally to London, where it was sold and the debts paid off. A London merchant had supplied more than £1,000 sterling in hardware, sails, cordage, and other equipment.[43] Next, Cowper, Telfairs commissioned the leading shipwright in the colony, Robert Watts, to build at his yard in Yamacraw the *Butler*, the largest vessel constructed in the colony and capable of carrying eighteen hundred barrels of rice. After its maiden voyage to London, the *Butler* was sold in the secondhand market.[44] The Telfairs had no desire to enter the shipping business. The *Georgia Packet* remained one of the few Georgia-owned vessels in the rice trade.

As a rice port, Savannah played a modest role. In 1772, its neighbor sent four times as many vessels to the British Isles as did Savannah and Sunbury.[45] If we assume a nine-month trading season, an interested citizen could stand on the banks of the Cooper River and watch a British-bound vessel depart every two and a half days while, on the Savannah, he or she had to wait every eleven or twelve days. Nevertheless, Georgia's export merchants could take comfort in other figures. The mean tonnage of departing vessels was almost as great, 130 versus 137 tons, and the number of pounds of rice per ton of vessel was within range of Charles Town's: 2,524 pounds versus 2,950 pounds, demonstrating the efficiency of shipmasters in securing the maximum feasible cargo.[46] A crucial measure of any port's competitiveness was the amount of time it took to unload an incoming vessel, reequip it for another voyage, and find an appropriate cargo. For Savannah, the average turnaround time for ships was longer, forty-nine days compared to thirty-nine days for Charles Town, but that figure may reflect special circumstances having to do with the Stamp Act crisis.[47]

The anomaly in the rice trade was Georgia's failure to follow South Carolina's lead into the Caribbean, as reflected in the statistics in Table 14. In the early 1760s, Georgia was sending a modest two thousand barrels a year to the British West Indies while Carolina was exporting five or six thousand barrels of rice to the region. The end of the Seven Years' War dramatically changed the picture. With the exception of trade with the Iberian Peninsula, English trade laws required that lowcountry planters export their rice directly to England for trans-shipment to non-British colonies and the European continent. An act of 1764 loosened these restrictions and allowed rice shipments to any part of the Americas south of Georgia, in effect opening French and Spanish markets. Carolina's shipments soared

TABLE 14   Rice Exports by Georgia and South Carolina, 1768–72 (# of Barrels)

	Great Britain	Southern Europe	West Indies	Totals
Georgia	14,721	430	2,301	17,452
South Carolina	72,491	25,309	23,489	121,289
Totals	87,212	25,739	25,790	138,741
Georgia as Percent of Total	16.9	1.7	8.9	12.6

Source: Shepherd, "Commodity Exports."

to twenty-five thousand barrels a year on average while Georgia's remained stuck at the same modest level throughout the period. It seems a curious phenomenon when the younger of the two colonies was sending almost as many vessels to the Caribbean as its older neighbor. Georgians were dispatching over a hundred vessels to St. Kitts, Curacao, Antigua, and elsewhere and knew intimately the factors who bought their lumber, horses, and provisions. As historian Kenneth Morgan has pointed out, rice was a relatively cheap, bulky, seasonal, perishable product, subject to wide price fluctuations, and marketable in more than a dozen ports in almost as many countries.[48] The reasons for this failure were purely financial, part of the web of credit that floated the economy. Savannah's and Sunbury's merchants were dependent on their London correspondents, in some cases their own family members, to generate the credit for the huge volume of British imports into Georgia. Those items, reaching £92,000 sterling in 1772, could only be paid for through the sale of rice by the correspondents in Bremen, Amsterdam, and Rotterdam. Remittances of rice remained the principal means for generating the pounds sterling to support the tools and cloth required by a frontier economy. The dependence of these merchants on five or six principal houses in London and one in Bristol seriously limited their flexibility and independence.

The same phenomenon helps explain why Georgia was only marginally involved in regional markets in Europe other than the northern coast. At the beginning of the eighteenth century, rice had been added to the list of enumerated goods, requiring that it be shipped to Britain and duty paid before it could be reexported to Europe. With the lifting of restrictions to the Iberian Peninsula in 1733 after years of lobbying, Carolina dispatched sizable quantities of rice to Spain and Portugal, where it sold well during Lent and when the harvest was poor. In the year after the Stamp Act crisis, South Carolina sent 28,251 barrels to the Iberian Peninsula and 15,238 barrels to the West Indies, almost as much as it shipped to Britain.[49] Charles Town merchants like Henry Laurens sent rice on their own account rather than forwarding it to an English broker and, in so doing, realized a greater return and developed skills valuable for operating in the Atlantic world. Georgia's merchants could never afford the risk of selling rice on their own account nor did they have agents in place in towns like Lisbon and Oporto nor did they possess expertise in chartering ships beyond the conventional route between the colony and England.[50] In choosing the most profitable market, Charles Town's merchants were able to benefit to the fullest extent. Savannah had little choice but to stick with northern European markets.

A more perplexing issue is why Georgians chose to avoid cultivating indigo and never gave the second most valuable crop in the lowcountry a serious chance. The Spanish had grown indigo in Central America with Native American slaves to make a valuable blue dye as early as the sixteenth century, but French plantations on Hispaniola with African labor set the standard of excellence for the quality of dye produced throughout the eighteenth century. Eliza Lucas Pinckney was responsible for the introduction of indigo to British North America when her father, governor of Antigua, moved the family to three plantations near Charles Town. Her innovative experiments matched seed with soil.[51] By the late 1740s, the crop caught on at a moment when the Carolina economy was looking for alternative cash crops in the face of the downturn in the rice market. When the British government provided a bounty, planters moved aggressively into its cultivation, made all the easier because the growing cycle complemented rather than competed with rice. Historians of colonial Georgia typically mention the commodity without comment, although an occasional writer leaves the impression that it was "an economically important crop."[52] It seems inconceivable that a profitable plant requiring less capital or labor than rice would not attract planters who lacked the wherewithal to mount a fully developed plantation or who wanted to supplement their income. In 1772, South Carolina exported 746,000 pounds of blue dye and earned £193,000 sterling. That same year, Georgia shipped a meager 10,600 pounds and earned £2,700, or one shilling less per pound than its neighbor, a surprisingly weak showing.

It was an easy plant to grow. Although an intense process, the actual manufacture of the dye could be done within days, not over weeks or months,
and the bounty provided by the British government guaranteed its profitability. Carolina planters of all stripes were reputed to have pockets "full
of money." The plant needed little care and could be cut after eight to ten
weeks of growth and, on occasion, grown a second time in one season. The
main investment was a series of three vats connected together, made from
wood or metal depending on one's budget. First was the large "steeper"
vat, where bondsmen threw plants into a container of water for a twenty-
four-hour period. The liquid was drained into a "beater" vat, where workers stirred or beat the water to oxygenate the fluid and cause the sludge to
settle to the bottom. In the third vat, the excess liquid was drained. Workers
placed the dark sludge in linen bags to drain and, once that occurred, put the
contents on tables to dry. However, to produce dye of the quality demanded
by the British market was another matter. The work was arduous; the judgments, difficult; the odor of the fermenting plants, noxious; and the thousands of flies that mercilessly swarmed around the vats and drying tables,
maddening. Too much or too little beating could be disastrous. And the
use of oyster shells for lime to oxygenate the water may have adversely affected the results. The fact that Georgia's indigo production sold for 75 percent of South Carolina's speaks to the issue of quality in the eyes of British
buyers, all the more devastating because Carolina indigo was reputed to be
inferior to indigo from the French West Indies and even East Florida.[53]

In 1750, expectations had been widespread that indigo, recently introduced into South Carolina as a commercially viable crop, would soon establish itself in Georgia. Carolina planters attempted its cultivation on
Skidaway Island and the Little Ogeechee River with slave labor but had
been forced to discontinue by Savannah authorities still enforcing the prohibition of slavery.[54] Once the ban was removed, new attempts were made.
In a letter to his father, the young Robert Baillie captured the prevailing
attitude: "I am certain I can make a great deal more in a short time by the
advantageous culture of indigo, the profits accruing from that awful weed
being so great that one Negroe cultivates and makes two acres and a half,
each acre produces at the lowest computation . . . at 4/6 per Lb." Moreover,
he added, the slaves labored only half the year.[55] Indigo was known as a crop
for the "weak-handed" planter, lighter work for the man with little skill or
inclination for rice.[56] Africans had been using indigo for centuries as a sym-

bol of wealth and fertility, and although there is no evidence that they were imported for their knowledge of indigo cultivation, they had prior experience and skills that supported the new economy. Nevertheless, in Georgia, the crop failed to take hold.[57]

The relative inattention to indigo cultivation, so contrary to the experience of Carolinians, gave way to a renewed interest shortly before the Revolution. In 1773, the amount shipped totaled forty-four thousand pounds, a more than 300 percent increase, and the next year expanded to forty-nine thousand.[58] Within a short space of time, the colony had entered into a breakneck race to catch up with its northern neighbor. The province had matured to the point that it could afford the luxury of taking its eye off the main prize and begin to think about secondary crops. The merchants of Savannah and along the coast provided the leadership. Whereas indigo production in South Carolina reflected a broad consensus within the planting class, in Georgia it reflected one small group determined to push the colony into a new stream of revenue and to benefit personally by the commitment. Edward Telfair invested in indigo production on two plantations up the Savannah River, while his partner Basil Cowper planted a remarkable 130 acres with indigo on his plantation along the Savannah. John Morel turned his plantation on Ossabaw Island to indigo manufacture; James Graham kept two sets of vats busy on Hutchinson Island; and Samuel Douglass built five sets of indigo works at his plantation on the Savannah while mounting an extensive operation on Skidaway Island. A merchant of Portuguese origin, John Lucena, constructed four sets of vats on a farm near Augusta. For the last months of 1774, the account books of Edward Telfair record four vessels carrying £6,400 sterling of indigo to England in contrast to the little over £2,000 sterling earned by all Georgia planters only two years before.[59]

Nevertheless, for the colonial era, Georgia came more nearly to being a colony based on monoculture than any in British North America. Its relationship to the Caribbean was closer than that of South Carolina, now a diversified economy with indigo and rice in the lowcountry, tobacco, wheat, and other provisions in the upcountry. For Georgia, indigo played only a modest role, and the deerskin trade, while important to the colony's general economic health, remained confined to a small group of merchants and traders whose exchanges took place in the distant interior out of sight of the coast. Rice remained the foundation for success. The colony came closer to illustrating the "staples thesis" of economic development than any other during the eighteenth century. The central argument of this thesis, most effectively made by John McCusker and Russell Menard, is that the expansion of a staple export determines the rate of economic growth in regions of recent settlement. As that export sector expands in response to demand, there are "spread effects" which induce investment in other parts of the economy, "linkages" in terms of the development of transportation and the processing of commodities.[60] The weaknesses of the thesis are many. It assumes a two-region world, with a metropolis that provides labor and capital and a colony that possesses natural resources. It badly underestimates the growth of an Atlantic economy where the penetrative powers of the price system created markets that spilled over imperial boundaries. It ignores the role of the natural increase in population as the most important force for the expansion of productive capacity. It leaves out of the picture the complexity of peoples and cultures as well as the rapid growth of a sophisticated infrastructure having to do with communication, trade, and the movement of capital that transcended a two-region model. It fits best as an explanation of the initial stages of settlement in the early seventeenth century.[61] Nevertheless, in the case of Georgia for the period 1750–75, the staples thesis retains validity in its simplest sense: the exporting of rice as the driver of expansion in this early stage of growth.

At the end of the colonial period, Georgian planters and merchants had reason to celebrate. From virtually no exports a quarter century before, they accounted for 12.6 percent of the rice exported by the Lower South and 16.9 percent of the amount shipped to Great Britain, as shown in Table 14. At the beginning of the eighteenth century, Parliament had placed rice on an ever-lengthening list of commodities which could be exported only to England and to British colonies and re-exported after paying a duty. By 1764, those policies, rooted in the Navigation Acts of the seventeenth century, had been loosened to the extent of allowing shipments of rice directly to the Iberian Peninsula and to points south of Georgia.[62] In the period 1768–72, 65 percent of the rice exported from the Lower South went to Britain, where it was chiefly re-exported to northern Europe, especially Holland and Germany. The processes of collecting barrels at plantation docks, securing favorable freight rates, seeking competitive insurance, and keeping an eye on the movement of prices demanded a sophisticated knowledge of a world about which Georgians were ignorant only a decade before. Compressing South Carolina's experience into a relatively brief span of time,

TABLE 15   Commodity Exports from Georgia, 1768–72 (Value of Exports, Yearly
Average, in Pounds Sterling)

	Great Britain	Southern Europe	West Indies	Totals	Percent
Rice	33,417	753	4,908	39,078	52.8
Indigo	3,315	—	—	3,315	4.5
Deerskins	19,360	—	—	19,360	26.1
Lumber	219	10	6,438	6,667	9.0
Other	604	13	5,042	5,659	7.6
Totals	56,915	776	16,388	74,079	100.0

Shepherd, "Commodity Exports." The figure for deerskins is based on the number of pounds exported according to Customs 3/68–74, NA-UK, a more reliable source than Customs 16/1, which was used for the Shepherd article. The price per pound of hide comes from Shepherd's tables.

Savannah's merchants achieved a reasonably efficient market by adapting an older model and exercised control of the rice market in a way that their peers in Charles Town had once done but could no longer do. As demonstrated in Table 15, Britain dominated Georgia's trade of rice, deerskins, and indigo, 76 percent of the total value. When the Stamp Act crisis threatened the rice trade at precisely the moment that the Georgia market was poised to take off, the willingness of export merchants to defy opinion in North America is more understandable. As orchestrators of the economic boom, they and their commercial allies were enthusiastic believers in the imperial system and understood the delicate nature of the connections between Georgia, the Caribbean, West Africa, and the British Isles, where the ultimate market was northern Europe. Their confidence was more than vindicated by the unparalleled commercial success of the colony in the decade that followed.

Those merchants enjoyed a privileged position. Planters seemed to understand that, while they were masters on their own plantations commanding the lives of dozens of people, they were marginal participants in the Atlantic economy, subject to unseen forces that set highly visible prices in faraway places. They understood that the marketplace rewarded planting, that the volatile rise and fall of prices during any trading season was an accepted condition for participation, and that the greatest challenge was to stay ahead of creditors and prepare for the next planting season.[63] Antagonism between planter and merchant was minimal for a variety of reasons. Prices were effectively set in Amsterdam, Rotterdam, Bremen, and, to a lesser extent, Charles Town, where the annual battle between planters and country factors, on the one hand, and export merchants, on the other, shaped prices in Savannah. The gradual rise in the overall price for rice during the last years of the colonial era provided a soothing backdrop. The fact that a small group of a dozen or so men around Governor James Wright controlled as much as a quarter of the rice crop placed a concentration of power in their hands that was not duplicated in South Carolina.

That position of power concealed a weakness. Large export merchants like Edward Telfair and John Graham remained the most important purchasers of British goods for the Georgia market and were unable to separate the export trade from the import trade in the way that Carolinians were now doing. They found themselves on an ever-accelerating treadmill of trying to ship sufficient rice to pay off the book debt they owed their London correspondents for British cloth, clothing, tools, chinaware, and the hundreds of other products coming out of the manufactories of Great Britain. The barrels onboard the ships bound for England kept afloat an immense chain of credit that supported the purchase of merchandise in the metropolis of London. Rice and, to a lesser extent, deerskins made possible the creation of a mass market for consumables in this rough-hewn world. How that market came into being and what mix of production and consumer goods it required were problems that London and Savannah had to address on an annual basis. The import trade was crucial to the process by which Georgians would assert their identity.

Chapter Nine

Retailing the "Baubles of Britain"

When the *Antonia de Padua* anchored in Savannah in 1753, tavernkeepers and shopkeepers, many of them women, crowded its deck. They well knew the familiar face of privateer and slave trader Captain Caleb Davis, a rogue who had a knack for finding easy money in the ports of the West Indies. Davis earned the gratitude of his customers by providing goods at a lesser price than those trans-shipped from Charles Town. Mary Morel, the widow of the recently deceased Peter Morel, continued to operate the family's tavern, a popular spot on the Bay. Born in Zurich, Switzerland, and a resident of the town since its founding, Mary Morel walked off the ship with two pipes of wine, a cask of Jamaican rum, and several yards of printed linen. Also present were leading shopkeepers who needed to restock their supplies: Benjamin Sheftall, whose eldest son was to become the highest-ranking Jewish officer in the Revolutionary army; Peter Baillou, a French vintner who had cultivated grapes during the trustee period; and Matthew Roche, a former deerskin trader from South Carolina trying to find his footing in Georgia after a spectacular bankruptcy. The captain of the *Antonia* sold over £500 sterling of mostly rum, brandy, and sugar and earned another £100 from cloth auctioned off at the Vendue House, which was set up for merchandise that could not otherwise be sold.[1]

In the mid-eighteenth century, Savannah was still a frontier town that offered limited choices in goods and little in the way of a social or cultural life. In the same year as the voyage of the *Antonia*, a German emigrant sniffed that the settlement resembled a middle-sized German village: "All the houses look no better than market booths."[2] When a Scotsman from Jamaica stepped off a vessel to set up shop later that same year, his first act was to ask his father to send him the *Gentlemen's Magazine* "as I am now in a Place of the World where there is no such thing as News." He was astonished to see an assembly sitting although there were "scarce twenty gentlemen from the whole of the colony in town" and no more than a handful of tradesmen. "There is yet no diversions & there is not a Fiddle in the whole country," the young man lamented to his brother. "Nor if we had one is there girls enough in the whole town to make a dance." His store lasted a few short months.[3] Outside Savannah in the tiny German village of Ebenezer, John Martin Bolzius described simple farmers and planters who lived like Abraham and the patriarchs, slaughtering and preparing pigs and oxen, baking their cake or bread, brewing a cheap beer made from Indian corn, sugar, syrup, and hops. Life in Ebenezer was cheap by prevailing standards, he emphasized, especially compared to Charles Town, where "the splendor, lust, and opulence" had reached extremes. Bolzius claimed that everything in the way of tables, beds, and other household goods could be had for reasonable money. Typically a shrewd observer, he was gilding the lily in the interest of attracting more Pietists. In fact, unskilled and skilled labor alike cost dearly on the frontier. Savannah, as he admitted elsewhere in his writings, was the most expensive town in the Lower South. A newly arrived immigrant to Ebenezer more accurately reported, "Everything is exceedingly expensive, and there is no money among the people. Hardware and daily wages cost very much."[4]

Arriving in 1757, Governor Henry Ellis mused that there were not five residents worth more than £500 sterling and pointed out to the Board of Trade that Savannah was a town of shopkeepers eking by on the thinnest of margins. In the port of the 1750s, they were jacks-of-all-trades, retailing British merchandise trans-shipped by Charles Town merchants at a stiff premium and buying rum and sugar from the occasional sloop from the West Indies. A member of the colony's small Jewish community, Abraham Minis, had run a shop and tavern on the Bay since the earliest days of the colony. When he died, the inventory of the estate described the layout of his modest dwelling of five rooms, plus garret and kitchen. One of the chambers was a "countinghouse" for his occasional trading operations along the coast; another, his shop, where he offered a limited selection of goods; and a third, the tavern. Boarders found beds scattered throughout every room while seven children squeezed in between. His wife, Abigail Minis, presided over an extensive kitchen, with a large fireplace, bellows, four flatirons, a frying pan, a gridiron, two skillets, pots and pans, tea kettles, and coffeepots.[5] Not all enterprises operated on so primitive a level. Thomas Rasberry had taken over the merchant house of Harris & Habersham on Johnson Square and enjoyed the distinct advantages that came from exporting a small crop of rice and providing supplies for the government. He could afford to order a wide array of goods, from woolen, linen, and cotton cloth to stockings and silk handkerchiefs, from reams of paper and Bibles to nutmeg graters and sugar boxes. Even with these advantages, the lack of direct shipping with London kept his trade at an infant state. He canceled an order for five hundred yards of plain white cloth because the "Persons for whom it was intended cannot wait any longer for it and they'l[l] get supply'd here as a large Quantity is just come up from Charles Town."[6]

Fifteen years later, the colony had become a place where a few large import-export merchants dominated the selling of a considerable volume of merchandise from Great Britain. At a time when Charles Town's export merchants were backing out of the importing business and leaving that branch of commerce to independent retailers, Savannah enshrined the old order. The novelty lay in the way that the import trade increased the mastery of a small group of men over the whole of the economy. Their astonishing success produced an anomalous situation. In the period between 1768 and 1772, Georgians imported goods worth £5.2 sterling per white person, almost as much as white Carolinians at £6.5 per person.[7] It is surprising and unsettling to find a relatively backward colony importing at roughly the same level as the most affluent in North America. The Charles Town District—where average wealth as measured by probate inventories stood at £2,337—was the wealthiest in British North America by a magnitude of several orders.[8] As a colonial mass market came into existence, consumerism had spread in the lowcountry more rapidly than in other regions, and the Carolina elites enjoyed a level of consumption not paralleled elsewhere.[9] In Robert Weir's words, "To a new arrival, Charles Town was 'a very gay place' in which he met merchants whose side tables were furnished with silver 'in such a manner as wou'd not disgrace a nobleman['s] dining room.' In short, the latest fashions, the best wines, the richest furnishings were to be found in every man's home, and even small shopkeepers dressed like gentlemen."[10]

The Carolina lowcountry echoed the exuberant fashions and generous hospitality found in the Caribbean, whose planters had long set an expansive standard in eating, drinking, and other forms of conspicuous consumption within a highly stratified social structure. The richer landowners in the West Indies sought to live in a manner that replicated that of the wealthiest in Great Britain, plowed money into great homes, and entertained on a lavish scale. In the seventeenth century and early eighteenth, the lives of planters and the newly arrived who envisioned quick wealth were often harsh, violent, bawdy, drunken, and promiscuous, as one commentator has written.[11] They proclaimed their status through the number of enslaved people assigned to house duties in town and through the extravagant social and cultural life in larger towns like Kingston and Bridgetown. They were given to outfitting their parlors, halls, and dining rooms with a mounting array of specialized objects that suggested an exaggerated taste compared to the notions of gentility and refinement current in the British Atlantic.[12] But this was a stereotype even in that age, and the image was changing by mid-century as planters showed themselves to be hardworking and thrifty, interested in improving plantation management, while merchants and professional men, including medical doctors, accountants, lawyers, and clerks, were to exert a positive influence in terms of ethics and family life.[13] The sixty-five families who dominated Antiguan gentry at mid-century included local merchants, government officials, doctors, and lawyers who took their professions seriously.[14] The middling and upper middling groups found a place in this world. In Kingston, shopkeepers, retailers, and local wholesalers comprised close to 25 percent of the vocational structure of the town, earning the town the title of the Grand Mart and Magazine of Jamaica.[15]

How white Georgians came close to overtaking their "betters" in South Carolina, at least when viewed from the dry statistics of the Customs Office, raises a fundamental issue—the way a colonial mass market for imported manufactures came into existence in a frontier colony and how it was both different from and like other markets in British North America and the Caribbean. Despite the difference in scale and wealth between the two colonies, the distribution network for dry goods and consumables in Savannah was similar to that in Charles Town. A hierarchy of taverns, shops, and retail and wholesale stores offered goods to a public increasingly able to make decisions about the quality and quantity of their purchases. In the 1760s, there were about fifty-two merchants and shopkeepers who advertised the sale of imported dry goods in the *Georgia Gazette* compared to about one hundred twenty in Charles Town.[16] The comparative figures underscore the fact that Georgia's primary port town enjoyed a surprisingly broad network of people engaged in distributing the valuable cargo that rolled across its docks. Ship captains often sold wares from the decks of their vessels, among them Daniel Waters, a master who offered from his brig *Peggy* an eclectic choice of mackerel, loaf sugar, wine, iron skillets, tea kettles, and bricks.[17] Small stores along the wharves sold food products from the West Indies and northern colonies. Bard and Thompson, ship chandlers, advertised brandy, Jamaican spirits, "northward rum," Madeira, flour, potatoes, hams, and "a few barrels of Northward Pork" along with limited dry goods.[18] Taverns doubled as stores as they did in an earlier time. In 1765, ten people, including Abigail Minis, Abraham's widow, held licenses to keep taverns, but thirsty people could find "all sorts of spirituous liquors" at shops too, including one run by the mother-son combination of Ann Cunningham and James Brooks.[19] Tradesmen served niche markets and freely imported on their own account: a saddler brought saddles from London; a watchmaker and jeweler boasted of his selection of silver-plated buckles, marcasite necklaces and earrings, silver teaspoons, snuff boxes, and gold lockets, "with a variety of other goods too tedious to mention."[20] Several catered to the well-to-do, including the wallpaper hanger who announced "a small but genteel collection of the newest patterns [and] papers," and Mrs. Mary Hughes, who advertised the "newest fashion ribbons, pompoons, French trimmings, . . . and garnet ear-rings and necklaces" imported from London.[21] Henrietta Bourquin, the widow of Dr. Henry Lewis Bourquin, continued her husband's business although in competition with physicians, who handled their own shipments of medicines and made a steady profit on elixirs like Turlington's Balsam of Life: "in great repute all over Europe for disorders of the stomach and bowels."[22]

The principal retailers in Savannah offered broad access to British merchandise.[23] The first serious retailer to open a store was Thomas Vincent, a stationer from London who thought he saw an extraordinary opportunity. Raising money from every quarter he could tap, Vincent called in modest loans made to acquaintances, sold a set of properties in Bristol, borrowed from a tobacconist in London, discounted property he expected to inherit from his parents, and obtained a loan from his wife's father, a silversmith in Middlesex.[24] Flush with several hundred pounds sterling, he convinced the governor's council in 1757 to grant him a public lot on Oglethorpe Square, diagonally across from where the Owens-Thomas House sits today. Savannahians were thrilled to have a successful shopkeeper of London alight in their town and gave him their vote of confidence. Vincent became a delegate to the legislative assembly, a justice of the peace, and a member of Solomon's

Lodge of Freemasons.[25] His was the one store where a person could walk in off the sandy street and expect to find the *Gentlemen's Magazine* or the *Spectator*, Wilkes's *North Briton*, Samuel Richardson's *Clarissa*, and plays by Shakespeare in addition to the usual fare of sermons and religious tracts. Although offering a fairly broad selection, the store became a showcase for a few high-priced items: one large mahogany desk-bookcase for £12 sterling, a complete set of china on a mahogany tea tray, eye-catching silverware, and a small "Japan waiter." Rather than bolts of cloth, the emphasis was on dining ware, furniture, and books, and to these he brought a discriminating taste.[26] In the rear of the store were objects that drew customers with a more practical bent: bridles, hinges, axes, hoes, umbrellas, jelly glasses, rope, and a coffee mill. Vincent never gave in to the urge to join the larger import-export merchants in their extensive trade but succumbed to the desire to enter the ranks of the planters and was virtually bankrupt at the time of his death.[27] The twenty-one slaves he owned were testimony to his frustrated ambition. His widow, Hannah, returned to England and conducted a small-scale business buying goods for a select few families in Savannah.[28]

One English merchant practiced his trade for all of one month in Savannah before moving into a career as a sometime planter and cattle farmer on a barrier island. Ambitious and persuasive, the thirty-year-old Button Gwinnett stepped off the brig *Nancy* in early September 1765. The vessel had sailed from Pensacola in West Florida with a load of dry goods and provisions from England.[29] Gwinnett shared an interest in the cargo with a firm in Liverpool. Without hesitation, he marched into town, rented a well-placed store on the Bay formerly occupied by Johnston & Wylly, and laid out his goods in exemplary fashion. There seems to have been no plan other than the pressing need to find an outlet for the food and merchandise he could not sell in the desolate outpost that was Pensacola. Gwinnett came from a middling social background that placed him on the fringes of gentility. His father was a vicar in a rural village in Gloucestershire, a brother was an officer in the East India Company, and he married the daughter of a grocer in Staffordshire. Gwinnett had experience in shipping goods to Philadelphia, New York, and the West Indies on behalf of English firms.[30] When he arrived in Georgia, he had knowledge of how commerce on the Atlantic stage was conducted and how he could use that information to convince others to bankroll him. Within a month of his arrival, Button Gwinnett responded to an advertisement in the *Georgia Gazette* offering the island of St. Catherines for sale. In an incredible act of legerdemain, he put together the loans necessary to pay the equivalent of £3,000 sterling to Thomas Bosomworth, husband of Mary Musgrove Bosomworth, and moved onto the six thousand acres of upland to reestablish cattle farming and expand into planting. In a matter of three months, he had become one of the largest property owners in Georgia.

In contrast to the individualistic approach of the English, a tight-knit group of Irishmen opened a retail establishment that supplemented English goods with merchandise from Ireland. From a farming family, John Rae captained a boat carrying deerskins from Augusta to Charles Town and, by the 1750s, stood atop the deerskin trade in Georgia.[31] When he moved to Savannah in 1759, he opened a store for the deerskin trade and then, when ambition got the better of him, gradually shifted to becoming a general merchant. He gained a valuable ally when his daughter married the son of Captain Edward Sommerville, who had discovered the advantages of sailing between Ireland and Georgia. Rae joined with his son-in-law to operate a store on Johnson Square.[32] In addition to the usual array of European and East Indian goods, the pair offered Irish linen, Irish beef, Irish butter, oatmeal, and bricks made in Ireland as well as "goods from Baltimore": butter in firkins, potatoes, salmon, salt, and bottled beer.[33] Far from the upscale selection of neighboring stores, the goods attracted a clientele of lesser standing. The bond of kinship tied the two sides of the Atlantic. John Rae persuaded his brother Matthew to recruit tenant farmers in Ireland for a settlement in the backcountry.[34] Two other brothers came to Georgia and entered the trade in Augusta. Incredibly, John Rae became part of the lowcountry elite without having to turn his back on the middling Irish community that had supported him. His daughter Jane married an Irishman; another daughter, Isabella, wed Samuel Elbert, son of a Baptist minister and a formidable figure in the deerskin trade; and a third daughter married Joseph Habersham, son of the powerful James Habersham. In lowcountry Georgia, it was the formula for success: children of a merchant marrying merchants.

Retailers and wholesalers alike needed the services of competent auctioneers, or vendue masters, to retail goods that did not sell. James Habersham counted on a family member to perform this function, a minor figure but not without influence. His brother-in-law, the plainspoken Robert Bolton, became a virtual handyman about town: vendue master, shopkeeper, innkeeper, commissioner of the workhouse, saddler, postmaster, and a pillar of the Presbyterian Church.[35] But Bolton had a hard time scraping by. He had followed his sister from Philadelphia when the Reverend George White-field decided to have the young Habersham marry the sixteen-year-old Mary Bolton. Robert had bounced around occupations and by the mid-1760s was an innkeeper. When the assembly was in session, the population of Savannah temporarily increased, and inns like his were overflowing with delegates and others who journeyed there on business. He worked his way into the position of vendue master, one of two auctioneers who acted as the conduit for the movement of goods and chattel in Savannah. Wholesale and retail merchants, big and small, sent their unsold stock to the exchange to be auctioned off by Bolton and William Ewen, a veteran of the trustee period who eventually earned a seat in the Commons House of Assembly. They were key figures in the secondary slave market in Georgia, selling a few enslaved people at a time for planters, artisans, or traders.[36] And yet, the idiosyncratic Bolton, an object of pity to some, was a deeply convinced Presbyterian who believed Africans deserved to be educated while being told of God's "saving grace." When a cleric came to Savannah to catechize slaves, the young man met with fierce resistance from most quarters. Robert Bolton gave him a room and a place to teach, and while Savannahians made rude remarks in the streets about the "Negro parson," the cleric observed, "I continued to preach in Mr. Bolton's house to white and black all the time."[37] The sometime auctioneer, innkeeper, and saddler was not one to back down from his religious convictions.

Toward the end of the colonial era, there was a noticeable increase in the number of firms breaking into the import trade. Partnerships like Reid, Storr, and Read; John Taylor and Company; George Houstoun and Company; and Moore and Panton staked a serious claim. As the representative of a Glasgow firm, Taylor became the first to bring the store system as it existed in Virginia and Maryland, where one firm supplied the merchandise and its representative in Savannah was an employee. It was the beginning of a new trend seen elsewhere along the seaboard where warehouses of goods were sold "at a low Advance for Cash or short Credit."[38] But the town itself was generating few new retailers; outsiders remained the primary source.

The surprising depth and breadth of the retail sector in Savannah reflected the growing Anglo American "consumer society" that T. H. Breen has described in his writings. American colonists, whether on the mainland or in the Caribbean, called for the latest in British manufactures.[39] In the West Indies, the English became doubly English as a way of preserving their identity in an alien land and requested their London agents to purchase the latest fashions or styles as the most visible symbol of that character.[40] Throughout the British Atlantic, there was an increasing standardization of taste at all levels as a new market took shape, driven by the buying habits not simply of the gentry but of a broad range of people. Tea and the rituals surrounding it extended far down the social scale to the less well-to-do, whether in Boston, Williamsburg, Savannah, or St. John's on Antigua. During the course of the eighteenth century, manufacturing establishments in Britain were churning out increasing quantities of consumer goods, the "Baubles of Britain," to meet demand throughout the British Atlantic. Colonists both in the Caribbean and on the mainland moved closer to the culture of the homeland and embraced the Anglicization of their market.[41]

What distinguished Savannah in this increasingly homogeneous world was the importance of import-export merchants like Edward Telfair, Nathaniel Hall, and John Graham, who stood at the center of the distribution of British goods. At a time when British houses were turning to local, independent retailers elsewhere in North America and when London agents of West Indian planters increasingly handled purchases, their role was becoming anomalous.[42] Although young, ambitious retailers were springing up in Philadelphia and New York to benefit from the generous credit arrangements that English correspondents kept extending, the situation was far different in Georgia. While the inventories of retailers like Thomas Vincent, Alexander Fyffe, and Thomas Lloyd were valued at £300–500 sterling, Edward Telfair and Company valued its inventory at £3,200 and £4,825 in 1772 and 1775, respectively. The firm paid taxes on imported goods worth £13,596 for a turnover that approached four times the merchandise in stock.[43]

In competing advertisements in the *Georgia Gazette*, the leading houses announced a seemingly endless choice of linen, cotton, and woolen fabrics that ranged from the plain and coarse to the sophisticated and elegant. Inglis and Hall touted "a neat assortment of Indian and English chintzes," printed calicoes and linen, persians and taffetas, cambrics and hollands, silk and cotton laces, plain and flowered silk, figured dresden, worsted damask, German serge, and osnaburg cloth. Cowper, Telfairs answered back with bengal check, dyed glazed linen, cotton velvet, shalloons, bombazines, Russian drabs, fine Irish linen, women's calamancoes, blue and red strouds, and "a great variety of superfine broad cloths."[44] In Telfair's store on the Bay, men could find finished clothing, including linen and nankeen waistcoats, worsted and silk breeches, leather gloves, worsted hose, and beaver and felt hats. Elite women could walk in and compare cloaks, mantuas, satin hats, silk hose, "new-fashioned" silk ruffs, neat shoes and pumps, colored silk mitts, quilted petticoats, and blue and white handkerchiefs.[45]

In the great majority of cases, the buyers of goods were retailers who needed to restock their shelves. However, women of a certain station in life could pick out pewter or earthenware dishes for everyday living or fine china and delftware for show. A back row of counters contained corn and coffee mills, castile soap in small boxes, copper tea kettles, bread baskets, and pudding pans. Alongside were condiments like cloves, mace, and black pepper or specialty foods like Spanish olives, almonds, raisins, and other preserved fruits. Hardware was off to the side, barrels of nails, broad axes, awls, and rice sieves, the materials out of which townhouses and plantations were built. "Painted framed mahogany looking glasses" or tea chests were stuck in odd spaces. Paper products were found in profusion: writing paper, account books, and hundreds of quills. Other items were scattered throughout the store: violins and guitars, novels, magazines like the *Spectator*, prints of the king and queen, silver spurs, and "fine Newmarket horsewhips with silver caps." The prime customers were retailers, storekeepers, sea captains refitting their vessels, planters and their spouses, professionals, and widows like Anne Cuthbert, who operated her plantation, sold lumber and rice directly to the Telfairs, and made most of her purchases through their store.[46] Lesser folk found access to credit hard to come by, a deft way of regulating patronage. Nevertheless, the overall network of distribution in Savannah allowed for a broad diffusion of goods, encouraging an openness and fluidity that allowed for myriad opportunities for individual choice.[47] Much of Telfair's offerings ended up on the shelves of retailers and shopkeepers.

Thanks to the strength of its wholesale and retail merchants, Savannah played a similar role to Charles Town in the development of a distinctive consumer culture that set apart their region from the rest of the North American mainland. If all the colonies participated in the same Anglo American cultural system, the lowcountry occupied a unique space. Nowhere else in North America were the boundaries between town and country more fluid and nowhere else was there such a high degree of integration of urban and rural societies. Social, cultural, and political life was concentrated in one town in the colony and in South Carolina.[48] In New England, inhabitants of the many small towns that dotted the region drove the market for the new consumer goods. Over the course of the eighteenth century, residents of small urban centers began demanding items like pottery, glassware, and tea, and if they could not afford large purchases, it was clear their tastes were changing before that of their neighbors in the more rural areas. In Virginia and Maryland, few towns existed and they played a minor role in the "consumer revolution." Rather, the agents for change in the Chesapeake Bay region resided in the "tobacco gentry," who became the first rural social group to adopt new goods. Addiction to short-term fashion and the purchase of the new amenities began with people like William Byrd III, owner of Carter's Grove, and spread downward and outward across the countryside and into towns. Lesser social groups in effect emulated the habits and preferences of the high-status, landed elite. In the lowcountry, it was otherwise. The adoption of goods like tea, silverware, and secular books took place in town and country simultaneously.[49]

The bulk of British manufactured goods entering Georgia came through Savannah, and even though Sunbury was a much more substantial center than Beaufort or Georgetown, it still bought most of its goods in the capital and the rest in Charles Town. In essence, the network of rural suppliers and small-town merchants was exceptionally weak in the lowcountry from the Waccamaw River to the St. Marys.[50] In South Carolina, planters flocked to Charles Town for their purchases and social life,[51] and, if the planters of the Southern District in Georgia tended to avoid Savannah for political and cultural reasons, they were still ordering goods through stores that received their merchandise through the capital. Partnerships like Spalding & Kelsall, Darling & Munro, and Dunbar, Young, and Simpson obtained their credit from Savannah through merchants like John Graham and Company or Cowper, Telfairs. The only other center for the distribution of goods was the German peasant community of Ebenezer. Its two leading merchants, bitter rivals, functioned as economic satellites of the capital. Johann Caspar Wertsch arrived as a baker's apprentice, taught school on plantations, worked in the community store, and did well enough to buy his indenture. He was sufficiently well off that he lent £500 sterling to three Savannah merchants.[52] His challenger, Johann Adam Treutlen, likewise came as an indentured servant from Germany, and after a moment of hesitation, opened a store that Savannah merchants were eager to supply.[53] The sales of British merchandise in this gathering of Pietistic Lutherans and small English planters appear to have been vigorous.

The Georgia and Carolina lowcountries were similar in yet another way.[54] As illustrated in Table 16, they were importing goods in roughly the same proportions. For the period 1771–74, the categories of merchandise brought into the two colonies are almost identical. Consumer goods from England accounted for 83 percent of Carolina's imports, and they stood at 81 percent in Georgia. Cloth and clothing accounted for 59 percent of Carolina's imports, and they represented 62 percent in Georgia. And metal goods like nails, augers, hoes, and axes stood at 7 percent in the northward colony, and they accounted for 6 percent in the southward one.[55] That similarity was no accident. Still a young colony struggling to plant its feet, Georgia was hungry for goods that would allow it to reap the benefits of a plantation society. The Telfair store carried different types of merchandise in almost the same proportion as overall imports from England. Fifty-four percent of the value was in cloth or clothing compared to 62 percent for the colony; producer goods like nails and carpentry tools were 16 percent compared to 19 percent.[56]

As frontier colonists making a large investment in plantation infrastructure, Georgians spent a relatively small amount on producer goods and acted much like Carolinians, who possessed the level of wealth to sustain a society devoted to the consumption of high-status goods. It could be argued that the plain woolen cloth bought for slaves—"Negro cloth"—more clearly belongs with producer goods rather than as an item of consumption, but the same argument holds true for South Carolina. If the overall statistics reflect a broad similarity, a more detailed look shows important differences. By the third quarter of the eighteenth century, taste in cloth was undergoing a profound change. There was a waning demand in North America for woolens, a growing popularity of cotton, and an increasing dominance of linen in purchases.[57] Georgia remained relatively immune to those trends. Some 29 percent of its total imports consisted of the longtime staple of English overseas trade, woolen cloth, whether minikin bays, Welsh plains, flannel, "cloths short," or "stuffs."[58] For Carolinians, only 16 percent of their imports came in the form of woolen products. The bulk of imports to Carolina were linen and cotton products, some 32 percent

TABLE 16   Percent of Total Imports of British Goods: Georgia and
South Carolina, 1771–74

	Georgia	South Carolina
Consumer goods		
Linens, cottons	23	32
Woolens	29	16
Silks	2	3
Clothing, haberdashery	8	8
Subtotal	62	59
Food, drugs	6	6
Domestic hardware	3	2
Silver plate	—	1
Other	10	15
Subtotal	19	24
	81	83
Producer goods		
Metal goods	6	7
Other	13	10
Subtotal	19	17
	100	100

Sources: Imports by Georgia from England, 1771–1774, Inspectors' Ledgers, Ledgers of Imports and Exports, Customs 3, vols. 71–74, NA-UK; Nash, "Domestic Material Culture and Consumer Demand," 351. Nash calls attention to two customs categories, wrought metal goods and the catchall category of "goods several sorts" or "goods unrated," which cannot be readily classified as either consumer or producer goods. He assumed that these goods were divided equally between the two classifications. This table makes the same assumption.

of total imports in comparison to 23 percent for Georgians. Whatever the type, Georgians uniformly chose the coarser, less valuable cloth. For the cheap woolen goods called "cloths short," Georgians bought two and a half times the amount purchased by Carolinians on a per person basis. For a finer woolen fabric called "cloths long," the Carolinians owned that trade. Georgians bought virtually none compared to the roughly £3,500 sterling their neighbors spent on this type in 1771 and again in 1772.

The differences between the qualities of goods purchased by the two colonies appeared in every category. For "Spanish cloth" made from the wool of the prized Merino sheep of Spain, South Carolina imported over £1,000 sterling and Georgia nothing. For wool mixed with cotton to make it lighter and finer, the northern colony was almost the sole consumer. In every category of linen, Carolinians were bringing in almost twice as much per person as came through Savannah and Sunbury. Joseph Clay patiently explained to his correspondent in London that Georgians wanted coarse goods, "such being consumed more generally by the bulk of our white inhabitants as well as our Negroes," and that there was a considerable demand for woolens during the winter months, "such as are suitable for the Indian Trade, cloathing Negroes and for white people in middling circumstances." He asked that woolens arrive between the first of August and the middle of October. Otherwise, other merchants "will have beaten us to the draw. We would have to hold the clothing until the next season, and risk damage by moths."[59]

Georgians were more moderate consumers by instinct and habit than Carolinians or West Indians. Their world was too new and raw and underfunded to adopt the standards of conspicuous consumption across the river. On a per person basis, Charles Town imported three times the number of felt and beaver hats as did its southern neighbor, ordered almost twice the amount of finished clothing, and consumed twice as much refined sugar. As one would expect, South Carolina brought in twenty-eight chariots, seven coaches, and sixty-eight prime steeds for racing and breeding between 1771 and 1774, while only one chariot was purchased for Georgia and no coaches or horses. Rounding out the picture is the fact that the Carolina lowcountry attired itself in twice as much silk per person as did its neighbor. James Habersham defied local practice when he sent a coat and breeches to London as the model for new silk clothing. "All my cloths are miserably spoiled by the Bunglers here, and after repeatedly trying new Hands, I am forced to this Method of getting a decent Garb," he told a correspondent. This master of detail made clear he wanted a decently made coat of silk, fashionable but understated as befitted his age. The order was for a "plain and grave coloured silk coat," a black silk waistcoat without sleeves, a pair of black frame-knit silk stocking breeches, and two pairs of frame-knit black worsted stocking breeches.[60] Carolinians used twice as much Irish linen per person as did Georgians and kept several vessels plying the waters between

Charles Town and the Emerald Isle each year. The latter typically sent one ship owned by the Irish Rae brothers to bring back several tons of bricks and coal, kegs of the "best" herring, and bushels of salt, not Irish linen.[61]

Then, too, Savannah never attracted a planting class that consumed at the level of Charles Town residents. Most planters at the top of the pyramid led gracious lives surrounded by slaves, wilton carpets, and fine furnishings, but they were comparatively few in number and, even among these, a practical attitude prevailed as befitted a colony at the early stages of development. James Habersham, the second most powerful man in the colony, was never one to pass up an opportunity to drive a hard bargain and save a penny. When his enslaved people needed clothing, he found out he could save a 2 percent commission by placing the order in London himself, appreciated that the pea jacket cloth bought by a fellow planter would be too hot for his workers, recommended buying a cloth called "Foul Weather" used for West Country barge men, and thought the cost to be no more than the ten shillings charged for good plains in Georgia.[62] Nor did Savannah attract the whole of the planting elite to town. Planters in the southern part of the colony never built residential houses in town, never created a demand for goods to be consumed onsite, and rarely participated in the social life of Savannah. The residual suspicion of Savannah combined with a growing distrust of the governing elite kept away many. The fault line that lay at the Ogeechee River affected consumption patterns in the colony as a whole.

The preference for a simpler, practical style of living was as much a conscious choice by artisans and lesser merchants whose origins lay in the trustee period as a reflection of a lack of wealth. Carpenters, tavernkeepers, gunsmiths, and cabinetmakers never forgot their roots and never felt comfortable with the conspicuous consumption of Carolinians. In this respect, Savannah differed from the towns of the West Indies. Peter Tondee came to the colony in 1733 as a child. When his father died, he was placed in George Whitefield's Bethesda Orphanage, trained as a carpenter, and became a leading craftsman.[63] In 1750, he joined with Richard Milledge, his partner in carpentry, and Benjamin Sheftall, a shopkeeper, to form the Union Society, initially serving the needs of artisans but evolving to become a charitable endeavor that included a broad cross section of local society.[64] Tondee eventually became a tavernkeeper and acquired an eclectic set of friends who crossed national, religious, and ethnic boundaries. Neighbors included Jews, Germans, Scots, Portuguese, French, Swiss, Italians, and Carolinians. He was the founder of the second Masonic chapter in Georgia, the Unity Lodge. Virtually all of its twenty-five brothers came from the ranks of artisans, including a bricklayer, butcher, tailor, cooper, gunsmith, sailmaker, and clerk.[65] By the 1770s, Tondee owned bondspeople and land and was comfortably off but in no sense a flamboyant consumer. While many of his peers became prosperous serving the needs of the planting and mercantile elites, older artisans like him as well as their children remembered the trustee period not merely as a frustrating and harsh experience but as one from which they still drew a certain pride as survivors. Their marriage partners came from the same humble ranks, and the relative simplicity of life during that time gave them a permanent suspicion of the much talked about "excesses" of Carolinians. Even at a moment when they had embraced the mercantile values of their neighbors, they retained a suspicion of consumption for consumption's sake. This group developed an identity that valued hard work, discipline, and prudence.[66]

The difference in tone compared to Charles Town could be seen in something as simple as the official residence of the governor. In North and South Carolina, those dwellings were meant to impress the populace with their imposing architecture and costly furnishings. Governor James Wright had a much simpler, modest house on St. James Square. Georgians respected its occupant but never held that structure in awe, and in turn Wright chose to live on a much less pretentious scale than his peers. The Reverend John Joachim Zubly regarded the lavishness of Governor William Tryon's palace at New Bern with raised eyebrows, dismissing it as a "sumptuous needless building."[67] Nevertheless, change was in the air. As a stylish resident of Charles Town appointed to public office in Georgia, William Graeme imported the tastes of his upbringing by proudly strutting through the streets in a "full Trimmed sky blew Coat and Waistcoat," a "blue Coat & laced Scarlet Waistcoast," or a red coatee, close-fitting with short tails. On colder days, he wore his bright scarlet frock coat.[68] The most expensive item in his estate consisted of three dozen yards of rich "broad gold lace." Others carried more weight than this political placeman. Dour Scotsman though he was, John Graham set a standard with two elaborately furnished houses in Savannah, skilled slaves who served as tailor, hairdresser, coachman, steward, and "waiting Boys," and a style of living in contrast with his exceptionally modest existence during his first years in the colony.[69] High-status Savannahians were beginning to enjoy making a splash around the squares in their handsome new riding chairs, like the one purchased in Philadelphia and painted a bright green, lined with a light, stone-colored cloth, and with the moldings gilded with the letters G. F. on both sides and in the rear.[70] The ways of the Carolinian and Caribbean elites were reshaping life at the top of the social pyramid.

In the countryside, changing fashions had to overcome the ingrained conservatism of rural communities. In his *History of Georgia* published in 1883, Charles C. Jones Jr. included a telling description of the typical house among the Congregationalists. His account deserves attention because he and his father had grown up in that community and shared friendships and stories with its members. "Strange to say, their dwellings and plantation quarters were invariably located on the edges of the swamps in utter disregard of the manifest laws of health," he began. In essence, the commitment to the inland swamp method in St. John Parish carried a heavy price. Planters spent the entire year in those homes despite the malarial conditions. From the register kept by the society from 1752 to 1772, Jones cited 193 births and 134 deaths among church members, enough to grow the white community but still a high mortality. "[T]heir houses were first built of wood, one story high, with dormer windows in the roofs, small in size, without lights, with no inside linings, and with chimneys of clay."[71] The huts for Africans and African Americans were made of clay or poles. A random sampling of inventories of the estates of the well-off suggests that the same pattern held at a later time. When Joseph Bacon died, twenty-eight slaves plus a small stock of cattle, hogs, and horses accounted for £1,051 of his estate of £1,133, or 93 percent of his worth. The rest consisted of items of modest value: beds and mattresses, pewter plates, crockery, a spinning wheel, a tea kettle, and table linens.[72] As with most in the parish, the principal investment was in slave labor, not furniture or clothing. There were occasional houses like that of the formidable Captain Mark Carr, who was independently wealthy before he arrived in Georgia. When he died on the Newport River, his estate included eighty ounces of silver service, a rich array of clothing, thirty pictures of various kinds, a complete set of china and tea service, and mahogany furniture.[73]

In St. Andrew Parish, the challenges facing a substantial planter kept the home of Robert Baillie, the owner of fifty-three slaves and over three thousand acres, on a modest footing. As the holder of a substantial estate in a poorer part of the colony and as a justice of the peace, Baillie found himself in the awkward position of trying to maintain a gracious and open house for all who passed by while balancing an increasingly tight budget. "My plantation being in a very public Situation," he explained to his mother, "occasions us often to have more Guests than we would chuse, frequently People we never saw before, and often when we have nobody in the Morning but our own Family before Dinner will have five or six extraordinary but this is unavoidable in America without getting such a Character as no Man would willingly have."[74] When high living caught up with him in the 1770s, he scaled back. He told her that wine and other "Superfluitys" had been banished from the house except on extraordinary occasions. "We raise our Own Beef Pork Mutton & the Woods supplys us with Venison & with Fowl such as Turkeys Geese Ducks etc." The river supplied fish. Their bread came from grain grown on the plantation. Their common drink was now grog, a mixture of rum and water, "so you can see our living is not very extravagant." His principal expenses were cloth, clothing, and bed and table linens.

In Christ Church Parish, even a wealthy planter like William Gibbons, now the father-in-law of Edward Telfair, made a deliberate choice in terms of where fashion and style were to be displayed. The contents of his two houses, one on the plantation, the other in town, showed he lived well: several bedsteads with curtains, expensive china, a mahogany grandfather clock, a "handsome" desk, a maple desk, mahogany tables, tea tables, a tea chest, mattresses and blankets, silver shoe buckles, and a silver ladle. The inventory also recorded many ordinary items. Most of the chairs were rush bottom; many of the plates and bowls were earthenware; the blankets were made of duffel; a spinning wheel and cards indicated that the family made some of their clothing from the wool of the sheep he kept. The plantation house was probably modest in its furnishings and the town house full of good furniture. The inventory of his estate summarized his life, well lived but not extravagant, at least by South Carolina standards.[75] Such seeming balance should not obscure what was going on. Like most of his fellow planters in this frontier society, Gibbons was investing heavily in slaves and technology. Whether large or small, planters in the Georgia lowcountry followed the same logic as drove their peers in South Carolina and the Caribbean in generating earnings to afford more slaves to increase total returns.

In one area outside Savannah, a Carolina style of living was rapidly intruding on the older patterns of life. Plantation houses erected in the early 1770s along the Savannah River heralded the arrival of a new aesthetic in the heart of this frontier society. John Graham's elegant home at his newly purchased Mulberry Grove became a showpiece. "We have a coach-house and stables," General Nathanael Greene described his gift of Loyalist property from a grateful state legislature after the Revolution, "a large out-kitchen, and a poultry-house nearly fifty feet long, and twenty wide, parted for different kinds of poultry, with a pigeon-house on top, which will contain not less than a thousand pigeons. Besides these, there are several other buildings convenient for a family, and among the rest, a fine smoke-house. The garden is in ruins, but there are still a great variety of shrubs and flowers in it."[76] At nearby Morton Hall, another merchant, Nathaniel Hall, constructed a house filled with mahogany furniture, expensive mirrors, bedsteads with chintz curtains, silver spoons and ladles, and a "complete" set of "Poncil" tea china. The most palatial of plantation houses was to be found at nearby Thunderbolt, overlooking the calm waters of today's Wilmington River. The brick Georgian house of Josiah Tattnall, a recent immigrant from South Carolina, was one of the largest structures in the colony. The visitor was meant to feel a sense of awe in stepping into the home, and even if the furniture may not have been worth the amount Tattnall claimed as a Loyalist, it represented something beyond the experience of virtually all Georgians. In the hallway was a marble statue, a couch, and a card table; in the common parlor, painted pink, was a mahogany grandfather clock, a bureau, a large mahogany dining room table, a massive looking glass, six expensive chairs, and fenders and tongs for the fireplace. Tattnall intended the dining room to make a statement about status: not one but two mahogany dining tables, fourteen expensive chairs, a large marble statue, three sizable looking glasses, two tea tables, a complete set of imported china, a small round table, a corner buffet table, an elaborate fireplace, and a carpet, presumably a wilton.[77]

Although differing in level of wealth and stage of growth, Georgia and South Carolina shared some but not all of a distinctive consumer culture that diverged significantly from those found in colonies elsewhere. Both funneled the bulk of their export of commodities directly to England; both maintained remarkably high levels of imports per white person; and both had a highly centralized system of distribution in the lowcountry that inhibited the emergence of rural stores. Rural and urban combined in a remarkably fluid way that did much to erase the boundaries of markets that remained separate in other colonies. Profound differences remained, however. During the third quarter of the eighteenth century, Carolina consumers in both the upper and middling groups were purchasing growing quantities of "amenities," like china and silverware, reflecting rapid economic growth and the accompanying prosperity.[78] The colony was wealthier than other colonies, and that wealth was the decisive factor in shaping consumption. Georgia only fitfully shared in the surge of what has been described as "elite consumerism." Although the bulk of its commodities went directly to Britain and a remarkably strong demand for British merchandise existed, importations spoke to differing standards. The purchase of minikin bays, short cloths, and plain whites reflected the continuing desire for woolen products at a time when demand elsewhere was changing in favor of linen, cotton, cotton-linen, and silk fabrics. A few Georgians were wealthy on a level with British planters in the West Indies. Several held one hundred fifty or more enslaved people and claimed a net worth that compared favorably with those in the Leeward Islands, where the average number of Africans per plantation was around two hundred.[79] These planters and planter-merchants were the opening wedge in the creation of a pyramidal society that took full shape only after the Revolution. Most Georgians deferred consumption of high-end items in order to purchase additional Africans. The absolute frenzy in the slave market in Savannah during 1774 bespoke that urge.

Georgians were purchasing great quantities of British merchandise but of a relatively modest value compared to the habits of consumers around the Caribbean rim. Investment in Africans trumped other considerations. The fact that the colony enjoyed a high rate of importation per white person goes to the heart of assembling meaningful statistics for the eighteenth century: how to account for the different types of population that made up the "market." The purchases of white people account in part for the black population, who received clothing from their masters, although an active informal economy existed outside the masters' ken. There was, however, another, less visible reason for the high rate of consumption: the existence of a parallel market composed of thousands of Native Americans, who were increasingly dependent on British goods. The deerskin trade was a significant part of a larger commercial revolution taking place, and if natives seemed a distant, virtually unseen force, they were proving to be knowledgeable consumers who could pick and choose with discernment. That market included no less than 42,000 out of the 162,000 people who lived in the South in 1760.[80] Native Americans had effectively joined the colonial mass market in Georgia and would play a critical role in shaping the colony's demand for British merchandise. Merchants found it necessary to look beyond the lowcountry and take a position in a different commercial world where other rules applied. If trade with the West Indies acted as the primary agent for a booming Georgia, the deerskin trade, although entering a period of decline, emerged as an essential prop to economic development in the lowcountry.

Chapter Ten

The Trade in Deerskins and Rum

The unexpectedly high level of consumption of British goods per capita in Georgia not only reflected the newfound prosperity generated by rice exports but demonstrated the critical importance of the deerskin trade to the colony's economy at a time when South Carolina's had matured well beyond such dependence. Savannah's merchants discovered that, if they were to import consumer goods as well as enslaved people at the high levels they had achieved by the mid-1760s, relying on this seemingly unrelated trade was a necessity. While rice accounted for £33,400 of export earnings to Great Britain in the period 1768–72, deerskins accounted for £19,300, a not insignificant 34 percent of the total value of exports to Britain as reflected in Table 15. In the period between 1760 and 1768, exports of rice and deerskins grew at a phenomenal rate, especially for a colony that had limited experience in marketing either commodity.[1]

Although South Carolina and Georgia were similar in so many ways, they differed in one crucial respect. Carolina had the luxury of developing its principal exports in sequential fashion—deerskin during the first years of the eighteenth century combined with the slave trade in Indians, naval stores occupying an important place for a short while, rice coming into play during the 1720s as Africans were hustled into the lowcountry, and indigo making its fortuitous appearance in the late 1740s. That colony took seventy years to put into place a ruthless and efficient system of staple agriculture while continuing to find ways to exploit a native population that proved stubbornly resistant to Europeans, who had all but wiped out the coastal native people and unbalanced the native polity in the interior. In Georgia, rice and skins went hand in hand, each serving the other. By the mid-1760s, the deerskin trade accounted for approximately 26 percent of the value of all exports, at least as much for imports from Great Britain, and 32 percent of the credit outstanding with London merchants by the time of the Revolution.[2] It is not too much to suggest that deerskins provided the increment that floated an entire economy. Far from an isolated sideshow, that specialized commerce was a prime factor in providing the muscle behind the efforts of Savannah's merchants in creating a consumer economy for the white population as well as contributing capital to the development of lowcountry plantations. Through the increasing importance of rum, the trade was a vital link between Caribbean sugar plantations, native societies, and British consumption of leather clothing and goods.

Savannah arrived at the deerskin trade belatedly.[3] Oglethorpe's efforts to make the frontier post of Augusta the central focus of the commerce had succeeded all too well but that little entrepôt at the crossing of the principal trading paths to the Upper and Lower Creeks came to serve the interests of Charles Town, not Savannah. The deerskin merchants in that town originated in older Carolina firms like McGillivray and Wood and Samuel Eveleigh and Company, conducted their business in Carolina currency, and obtained credit and supplies through Charles Town. They were the pivot point in a supply chain that extended four thousand miles to tie the Old World to native America to the global market system. As Kathryn Braund has written in her seminal work on the deerskin trade, the flow of merchandise began in the towns of Britain where manufacturers produced the guns, wove the cloth, and made the iron tools. It continued in London and Bristol, where merchants assembled the manufactured goods while brokering products from Europe, India, and China. Merchants in Charles Town sold the goods to storekeepers and merchants in Augusta. They in turn sold them to traders, who carried the articles into American Indian towns and villages or sent them to their own stores with traders in their employ. The bargaining for deerskins took place in native towns according to price schedules more often honored in theory than in practice. The skins made their way back to Augusta and there prepared for shipment to Charles Town and on to London and Bristol, where a significant percentage of the relatively small cargo made its way to France. For those at the top, it was a lucrative business; for those at lesser levels there was always the possibility, however improbable, of profitable deals and accumulating enough wealth to become a full-fledged trader.[4]

During the 1750s, Georgia's wealth centered in Augusta, not Savannah. With considerable frustration, James Habersham reported in 1752 that trading boats carried 140,000 pounds of skins past the town to its next-door neighbor, the largest shipping center south of Philadelphia.[5] The requirement imposed by the British government that one-half of traders in the Creek country be licensed by Georgia had never produced the expected results. Carolina had no intention of relaxing its control of the trade, all the more so because deerskins, although less profitable than earlier in the century, still generated the second-largest amount of hard currency earnings for the province until mid-century. During the 1740s, Charles Town shipped on average 250,000 pounds of skins a year, and in the succeeding decade only slightly less, some 220,000 pounds, although with considerable variation from year to year.[6] A dispirited Savannah, possessing few merchants and lacking adequate storage and shipping facilities, never saw more than a token amount unloaded on its waterfront and virtually no transatlantic vessels making a call. In the wake of the calamitous Bosomworth affair of 1749, when Savannah's leadership humiliated Mary Musgrove Bosomworth in front of her native peers, the town magistrates had no standing within the Creek nation and remained isolated and discredited, while Thomas and Mary Bosomworth assumed important missions on behalf of Governor James Glen of South Carolina.[7] Between 1755 and 1759, the town exported an average of 25,000 pounds, a stinging comment on its marginal position.[8] When Glen's successor, Governor William Lyttleton, launched a punitive expedition against Cherokees angered by the treatment of their warriors at the hands of Virginians and by trader abuses and white settlement in Indian country, the colony temporarily benefited. As many as 65,000 pounds were shipped from Savannah as Carolina traders responded to the need to reconfigure lines of supply. The following year, 1761, peace returned to the frontier and the port's share of the trade fell to a minuscule 13,000 pounds and 42,000 the year thereafter. When the government proposed a tax on deerskin exports to finance the building of a fort on Cockspur Island, Savannah's merchants petitioned in protest, citing the fact that the trade was only beginning to come to Georgia and "even this small part is in a very wavering State and far from being Established."[9]

Georgians coveted the growing Creek market for goods and, although ignorant of the culture that evolved out of the merger of disparate native groups, groped for ways to break into an environment that already had a long history. By 1760, the native population in the South was reeling from dramatic demographic and political shifts and shrinking as a consequence. The legacy of the Yamasee War, when the upstart colony of South Carolina was nearly destroyed in a conflict with many of its Indian neighbors, had brought major adjustments to the complex of southeastern Indians. The numerous groups that inhabited the coast and much of the interior of Carolina had dwindled to approximately a thousand people, "settlement Indians" who increasingly drew contempt for their impoverished condition and dependent status.[10] In the mountains north of Georgia, the Cherokee people, recently defeated in a savage war with Carolina, had a population of seventy-five hundred, less than half of what it had been at the opening of the century, and they were struggling to rebuild their towns, homes, and traditional economy. The Muskogees, or Creeks, as the English called them, one of the few native groups whose population was growing, had emerged in the early eighteenth century in the interior with inter-village clan networks coalescing into larger groupings and older towns like Coweta, Cussita, Tuckabatchee, and Okfuskee serving as central cores for smaller, less established towns. Four distinct groups, each with their own language and customs, cultivated strong connections with each other, especially as military allies: the Ochese Muskogees, who lived on the Chattahoochee, and the Tallapoosas, the Abeikas, and the Alabamas, who lived farther west.[11] They occupied a position in the middle of the South, far enough from the coast to maintain a relative freedom from direct white influence and with enough space to pursue their hunting in virtually uninterrupted fashion. Two river systems dominated their lives. The valleys of the Chattahoochee, Flint, and Ocmulgee rivers in modern Georgia sheltered the towns of the eastern segment known as the Lower Creeks. In central Alabama, the watersheds of the Coosa, Tallapoosa, and Alabama rivers served as the home of the Upper Creeks and other ethnic groups.[12]

Even more than geography, the Muskogees benefited from the autonomy enjoyed by each of the over fifty towns and villages that made up their confederation. Of relatively recent origin, the loose confederacy allowed them to live in sedentary or semi-sedentary communities in which the headman or headmen enjoyed considerable power and represented the town at the regional councils held by the Lower and Upper Creeks. The most momentous decisions affecting their lives, notably war or the cession of land to encroaching whites, were a matter of consensus. The network of towns that formed the confederacy may have predated large-scale white intrusion, but newcomers, refugees from the massive upheavals elsewhere, especially from the Yamasee War, were welcomed and quickly incorporated into the existing polity. Located deep in the interior, the Muskogees would show a remarkable capacity to absorb refugees from other groups and regenerate their own communities.[13] By 1760, the Muskogees counted 3,655 fighting men and possibly as many as 13,000 people compared to about 6,000 whites and 3,950 blacks in Georgia, and their numbers would continue to grow.[14] The disparity was more than enough to make the white population aware of its vulnerability; it was also enough to whet the appetite of Georgia's merchants at the possibilities for a lucrative trade.

By the early 1760s, the Muskogee people were fast leaving behind a self-sufficient world where time-honored craftsmanship was passed on from generation to generation and embracing an economy based on commercial hunting and trade. The skin of the white-tail deer became the focus of native life as Carolina and Georgia traders competed to meet a growing demand in Europe for deerskin clothing and leather for articles like bookbinding and harnesses. Muskogees knew the value of their product and negotiated for the best possible terms to obtain the manufactured goods they desired.[15] First and foremost, they wanted the trade guns produced in England, principally Birmingham, which were often engraved with an ornate design to please Indian tastes. They wanted the powder and musket balls to make their hunts successful, all the more important since they had to extend their time in the woods to kill more deer in order to satisfy their growing tastes. They valued the many varieties of colorful cloth offered, from the coarse woolen garments known as duffels, which served as blankets and overcoats, to strouds, a lesser quality woolen cloth made into clothing for both men and women, to worsted fabrics, coarse linens, and bengals, piece goods exported from India. Muskogees had a keen appreciation for the type of iron tools they needed, the hoes, axes, knives, and hatchets necessary for growing crops and hunting in the woods, and the iron pots that could be easily transported. They valued beads made in Venice and Amsterdam as decorative items for necklaces and moccasins. Vermilion made in China became one more vibrant color in the array of war paints. In countless ways, the native Creek was connected to the bazaars of India, the specialty trades of Venice, the cloth manufacturers in France and Germany, the iron manufacturers of northern England, and, most important, the gun manufacturers of Birmingham. Their lives were unquestionably changed by these products. The Muskogees were also transformed as their traditional society came unglued and an uncertain world took shape, where the village chief was losing much of his authority and alcohol exacted a terrible toll.[16]

The treaty that concluded the Seven Years' War in 1763 transformed British North America and in so doing allowed the handful of deerskin merchants of Savannah to seize an important slice of the trade from their competitors in Charles Town. The Peace of Paris required Spain to withdraw from the Florida peninsula in return for Havana, lost in the closing days of the war. As part of the settlement, Georgia received the "debatable lands" that lay between the Altamaha and St. Marys rivers and welcomed two new British colonies, East and West Florida, on its southern boundary. France surrendered all territory west of the Mississippi to Spain and all territory east of the river to Britain, with the exception of New Orleans. The threat of encirclement posed by the French was eliminated; Fort Toulouse in the heart of Upper Creek country disappeared, and the trading path to the Chickasaws and the once-hostile Choctaws lay clear.[17] Upcountry settlers were demanding access to western lands and Governor Wright saw the opportunity to force natives out of enough territory to give the colony a firm footing beyond the narrow strip of coastal land it occupied.

By the Treaty of Augusta in November 1763, Lower Creeks, together with noticeably fewer Upper Creeks, surrendered 2.3 million acres of contested lands east of the Ogeechee River in return for a guaranteed boundary extending north of Augusta to the Little River, west to the Ogeechee River, and down toward the Altamaha.[18] The war had been a disaster for this proud nation. They saw their well-honed talent for playing off three competing empires against one another vanish and the very rationale for their independence effectively compromised. In agreeing to the treaty, natives made the cold calculation that the only way to ensure their hunting grounds while having access to manufactured goods was to surrender the contested land and rely on the British government for enforcement of the new boundary. Georgia's merchants were more sanguine. They saw the treaty as a way to maintain order and stability in the deerskin trade while confining the ever-aggressive backcountry settlers to a well-defined amount of land and carving out for themselves a role in the exploitation of that land.[19]

Four Savannah firms were in a position to take advantage of the new relationships. John Graham and Company, created in 1753, handled purchases for the governor of the official gifts given annually to Creek headmen for distribution in their towns. Graham was appointed clerk of the accounts and Indian commissary by the second governor. John Rae, the Irishman who co-headed the largest firm of merchants in Augusta, moved his part of the operation to Savannah. He had begun his career as the "patroon" of a vessel transporting deerskins to Charles Town, became a principal in the quasi-monopolistic Brown, Rae and Company, possessed licenses to trade in several towns, and owned herds of cattle, grist mills, and thousands of acres in the upcountry.[20] Joining them were two Charles Town firms that had read the signs and decided to make an investment in the future of Savannah. Robertson, Jamieson, and Baillie placed a partner, George Baillie, in town, where he remained until the Revolution. The largest deerskin merchant in South Carolina, John Gordon, who began his career as a young entrepreneur servicing the regiment on St. Simons, set up an operation headed by Thomas Netherclift, son-in-law of his longtime partner, purchased a wharf, invested in shipbuilding facilities, and demonstrated a commitment to activities on a region-wide level that went well beyond the trade itself. He himself continued to operate from South Carolina.[21]

As seen in Table 17, the Treaty of 1763 propelled Georgia into the front ranks of the deerskin trade despite the fact that Carolina merchants were "Exerting themselves and using their utmost Endeavours, not only to prevent the Merchants here from having any further Share in the Said Trade, but also to draw back that which hath with so much difficulty been brought hither."[22] Exports of deerskins from the docks of Savannah jumped from an average of 25,000 pounds per year in the previous decade to a high of 306,500 in 1768. Although exports settled afterward in the vicinity of 275,000 pounds, Savannah was now a major player.[23] The weaknesses of the trade were manifold: the difficulty of operating in another culture, the thinning herds of deer, the flood of newcomers to the trade who were often desperate men on the make, and the mounting debt of the Muskogees. Seemingly oblivious, Savannah's merchants welcomed the emergence of deerskins as a pillar of the new economy and for good reason. The commerce would generate at least £19,300 sterling in earnings between 1768 and 1772 and accounted for roughly 28 percent of the value of all skins exported from British North America, if the figure given by John Lord Sheffield is correct.[24] Deerskins represented 34 percent of the colony's total exports to Great Britain, compared to 59 percent accounted for by rice.[25] The pounds sterling generated by skins supported the cascade of imports during those last years of the colonial era, representing almost one-third the value of British imports at "official" prices to Georgia.[26] That achievement is all the more

TABLE 17   Exports of Deerskins by Port in the Lower South, 1760–74 (lbs.)

	Savannah	Charles Town	Mobile, Pensacola	Totals
1760	65,765	303,610	—	369,375
1768	306,510	158,742	92,346	557,598
1770	284,840	191,959	118,726	595,525
1772	213,475	204,129	199,729	617,333
1774	151,903	233,537	313,656	699,096

Sources: For Savannah for the period 1760–72, William Brown, comptroller, March 1, 1773, in Romans, *A Concise Natural History*, 146; for 1774, Customs 3/74; for South Carolina in 1760, John Stuart, superintendent, to the Board of Trade, March 9, 1764, CO 323, NA-UK; for South Carolina in 1768–74, Customs 3/68–74, NA-UK; for East and West Florida, Customs 3/68–74, NA-UK.

impressive in light of the decline of deerskin prices in international markets from 1733 until 1769 due to the growing flood of deerskins.[27]

For the late colonial era, white Georgians imported close to the same amount in pounds sterling per capita from England as did South Carolinians and more than any other colony by a wide margin. That an economy still finding its feet could indulge in a level of imports that approached that of the wealthiest society in North America is astounding. Embedded in those figures is the value of trading guns, bullets, blankets, woolen clothing, axes, and decorative ornaments. Joseph Clay's observation bears remembering. Georgians wanted coarse goods, "such being consumed more generally by the bulk of our white inhabitants as well as our Negroes," and this meant a considerable demand for woolens, "such as are suitable for the Indian Trade, cloathing Negroes and for white people in middling circumstances."[28] It was not uncommon for native, white, and black to wear clothing made of the same cloth. Twenty-nine percent of Georgia's imports were coarse woolen goods compared to 16 percent for South Carolina; and for cheap woolen goods called "cloths short," Georgians bought two and a half times the amount purchased by Carolinians per white person.[29]

Partnerships in London like McGillivray, Grahams, Clark gained the leverage that came from a higher volume of orders, easier access to credit from manufacturers, and the ability to "trade up" and obtain a higher quality of merchandise for the white population. Those in the deerskin trade in

Savannah benefited equally. They needed a lesser markup on goods coming into the colony either for whites or natives, found themselves in a stronger position to guarantee the debt assumed by planters for the purchase of Africans, and realized a surplus of funds that allowed them to purchase real estate in the lowcountry. According to Graham, the London merchants added 12.5 percent to the price of manufactured goods to cover the cost of shipping, insurance, and commission; the Savannah traders added another 15 percent in selling the goods to merchants and shopkeepers in Augusta and Frederica; the latter charged a 20 percent markup to the men who carried the goods into the interior.[30] They in turn were to follow a price schedule that specified the number of pounds in deerskin hides for each item.[31] Natives could be shrewd buyers and on larger items like duffel blankets insisted on a competitive price. Traders made their profits on lesser items and overcharged and cheated.

Merchants did well; traders and their packhorsemen much less so. John Rae invested in a handsome plantation on the Savannah River while his one-time partner Lachlan McGillivray did likewise in Vale Royal, a premier site outside Savannah.[32] Other deerskin merchants had already made similar purchases, notably Patrick Brown and David Douglass, and others, like Edward Barnard, were to follow suit.[33] After the Revolution, a fellow merchant described John Graham: "Knew Claimant from 1761. He was then in a great way of Mercantile Business. His business was chiefly in the Indian trade. Being worth 5 or 6,000 [pounds] sterling at that time would be esteemed a Man of Fortune."[34] Graham invested heavily in land along the Savannah River and throughout the colony and by the time of the Revolution owned the largest amount of any resident: twenty-six thousand acres, much of that financed by the deerskin trade.

After 1763, Savannah took on some of the characteristics of a town heavily invested in deerskins. Two doors from where Abercorn Street emptied into the Bay, one of the largest deerskin traders of Charles Town, Gordon & Netherclift, had opened a store to carry on business. The patrons were not local citizens but merchants from Augusta and Sunbury, traders from the interior, an occasional Creek headman, and local men of business who needed trade guns and duffels. One occasionally saw the children of traders and their native spouses passing through as their fathers placed them with white families in town to give them a basic education in reading and writing and break them into the world of commerce. In the middle of the block between Drayton and Bull streets was the store of two West Indians, who ran the largest trading firm in Georgia before they spread themselves too thin and went bankrupt. With the Treaty of Paris, they had staked a young Scots trader in the newly acquired seaport of Mobile and underwrote his futile efforts to break into the deerskin trade.[35] Sea captains from the Caribbean frequented their place in search of cargos; traders looked for low prices on staple goods; local residents pressed in to take advantage of the surfeit of European cloths and dry goods. In Ellis Square, the marketplace for the town, the Bristol firm Inglis and Hall advertised wares brought on the brig *Pitt*, including "a neat assortment of dry goods, strouds, trading guns, tomahawks, gunpowder, balls, suitable for the Indian trade," plus a few pipes of Madeira.[36] On the wharves during the spring (after the winter hunt) and increasingly at other times of the year, deerskins were hastily repacked into hogsheads that held five to six hundred pounds or tied into bundles that weighed over one hundred pounds. In his diary, Levi Sheftall told how, as a young teenager with money his father lent him, he bought a few hides to clean: "I found the work very hard and disagreeable, but the money I thought was a full compensation for the hard labour, as I was a strong stripling and cared for no hardships. . . . I thought myself as rich as the Greatest Man."[37]

A resident of the town could not escape the presence of those involved in the trade. Arriving with the first boatload of Jewish settlers, Daniel and Moses Nunes rapidly learned native languages, became traders, and served as interpreters throughout the colonial period.[38] Moses kept an Indian slave and had two children with her, manumitting them only on his death. The most striking figure to walk the streets of Savannah was also one of the wealthiest in the colony, Lachlan McGillivray, who moved his business from Augusta to Savannah in 1762 and merged his deerskin trade with John Graham and Company. Coming as a teenager to newly founded Darien twenty-five years before, this Highlander had a shock of red hair, cut a towering figure, and commanded attention. He held licenses for four major towns among the Upper Creeks, was on intimate terms with most of the leading headmen, served the governors of Georgia and South Carolina on numerous diplomatic missions, and represented a bridge between two cultures. In Little Tallassee, McGillivray had satisfied one of the essential expectations of Muskogee society when he married Sehoy Marchand, daughter of a Creek woman and a French officer and a member of the influential Wind Clan.[39] Together, they raised a son, Alexander, first in Little Tallassee, then in Augusta, and finally in Savannah. The boy received an English education in Charles Town and clerked in the firm Inglis and Hall before he and his mother returned to their native town. Nor were blacks absent from the picture. Michael and Sarah Thomas and their children came out of Indian territory to live in Savannah. Thomas had accompanied a deerskin trader from Pensacola into the Creek nation, made his way to Georgia about 1770, "and was then reputed with his family to be free Negroes."[40] No doubt he spoke one or more native languages and represented a fund of knowledge.

Savannah's sudden thrust onto center stage did not go unanswered. Charles Town recovered lost ground, shipping just over two hundred thousand pounds of deerskins by the 1770s, in part because half of its exports were destined for the luxury markets in France. That port specialized in fully dressed skins carefully prepared, with bristles removed, and softened by soaking in a mash that included the brains of the deer. Those skins were fashioned into elegant gloves and the lesser quality skins into parchment for book bindings. Savannah never tapped into the higher end of the market and paid a price in terms of the revenue per pound of deerskin, 2.3 shillings for Charles Town and 1.7 shillings for Savannah. Although the Cherokee trade still remained the domain of Carolinians like Robert Goudy, Edward Wilkerson, and Edward Keating, it was in an advanced state of decline due to the war and to overhunting. With Carolina traders withdrawing from the trade because of declining profits, it was a time of adjustment.[41]

Both markets faced a growing challenge. In the closing years of the colonial period, the center of the southeastern deerskin trade began to shift to Mobile and Pensacola in West Florida, whose traders attracted hides from the Upper Creeks, Choctaws, and Chickasaws so that Savannah, Charles Town, and West Florida finished on a par with each other in terms of volume of shipments.[42] Kathryn Braund, a historian of the trade, was only partially correct when she judged that the efforts to develop Mobile and Pensacola into major centers of that commerce failed to produce the intended results.[43] The majority of the deerskin trade, she argued, continued in the same channels after 1763. Upper Creeks ultimately found it more convenient to continue working with their old traders in Augusta; extensive commercial networks took time to establish; and West Florida attracted a high percentage of novice traders who tried to muscle their way into the business by loading packhorses with rum rather than manufactured goods. Her argument holds true for the first five years following the creation of British West Florida but not thereafter. After a shaky start, the two towns of West Florida pushed forward. The drop in Georgia's exports in 1774, as shown in Table 17, also reflected the fact that Governor Wright imposed a trade embargo after a bloody incident along the frontier. Traders necessarily diverted a portion of their purchases to Mobile and Pensacola, but there is good reason to think that Savannah remained in a strong position once the embargo was lifted.

Despite the variations in exports, Savannah's merchants retained considerable influence throughout the region. Lachlan McGillivray sent his nephew John McGillivray to Mobile, where he became the leading trader and expanded the family's network to include the Chickasaws and Choctaws as well as Creeks. He coordinated shipments from the Tallassee and Coosa rivers and kept Lachlan McGillivray informed about happenings farther west. William Struthers, another McGillivray partner, split his time between Mobile and Augusta. John Gordon operated in both Charles Town and Savannah, was active in East Florida, and underwrote the activities of the largest trader in the Southeast, George Galphin, dominant in Coweta and other towns in the Chattahoochee Valley.[44] Even Frederica on St. Simons staked a claim to the new trade. On one of his several journeys, the naturalist William Bartram noted that James Spalding had "extensive connections with the Indian tribes of East Florida." The Scotsman set up a store on the St. John's River to tap into the trade of the Seminoles, originally Creeks from the Oconee area, and told Bartram of plans for three more frontier outlets.[45]

Rum had always been an important ingredient in the deerskin trade from the earliest days but, with the expansion that followed the Treaty of 1763, it assumed an ever-growing importance due to easier access, the absence of French competition, and the large number of men who entered the trade after that date. Savannah's merchants played a critical role in this expansion, selling about a third of their total imports of West Indian and New England rum in Indian country. It was an ironic comment on the legacy of the trustee period, when the Georgia Trust persuaded Parliament to forbid the importation of rum into the colony to prevent settlers and natives from imbibing. That act had had little effect and was eventually repealed.[46] In 1757, the Georgia legislature passed a lengthy bill regulating taverns, and buried in the language was a clause banning the sale of alcohol to natives.[47] The South Carolina agent Daniel Pepper noted that Carolina traders carrying rum need not be afraid of Georgia's prohibition, "for I am credibly informed that a good many of the Traders, nay even Indians, are supplied by the Storekeepers in Augusta and New Savannah."[48] After the end of the Seven Years' War, the drink gained a new foothold. In the Proclamation of 1763, the British government declared that "the trade with said Indians shall be free and open to all our subjects whatsoever," provided that every person post a modest bond.[49] With the stroke of a pen, the government overturned decades of existing trading relationships based on the system of licenses issued by governors.

From a commerce regulated by colonial officials, the frontier became a competitive free-for-all.[50] The long-time trader James Adair considered those who entered the trade after that time "the dregs and off-scourings of our colonies," while Governor Grant of East Florida warned "'tis not to be conceived what a set of abandoned wretches live at present in those woods, who wander from one province to another and occasion disturbances everywhere."[51] An adjunct of the Indian superintendent judged the traders in the nation, "excepting a very few, are Composed of Deserters, Horse thieves, half breeds and Negroes."[52] For these new entrants to the trade, rum was cheap, could always be counted on for attracting customers, and could be watered down so that one gallon purchased in Augusta became two gallons in native towns. Often the trading took place outside the traditional framework of a town or village: "in the woods" where a trader could lure Indians and persuade them to do business, buying skins that were "green," or not processed.

However, this traditional portrait misses an important point. The large deerskin merchants and storekeepers in Savannah, Charles Town, and Mobile were as guilty as the rawest, vilest illiterate trader on the frontier in stoking the trade with liquor. They were the linchpin of the Caribbean connection that exchanged lumber, horses, and provisions for rum, sugar, and molasses, and then directed a goodly proportion of that drink into the lands of the Cherokees, Creeks, Chickasaws, and, since the end of the Seven Years' War, Choctaws. They also drew heavily on the distilleries to the north for New England rum that could be purchased more cheaply. A triangular trade tied together West Indians, English, and Native Americans in a close relationship based on the trinity of deerskins, rum, and British manufactured goods. For the sea captain who carried lumber and horses to the West Indies, for the Jamaican merchant who sold the rum, for the merchant who brokered the goods, for the deerskin trader and his pack-horsemen who carried rum into the interior, for all those who participated in the long chain that moved hogsheads, puncheons, and barrels down to the more manageable kegs into the upcountry and then along the trading paths, the business was profitable.

In his work on rum and the American Revolution, John McCusker estimated that between 1768 and 1772, 99,000 gallons were brought into Georgia annually, two-thirds from the West Indies and the remaining third from coastal trade with the distilleries of New England.[53] The figure takes on special interest when the consumers of rum are considered. McCusker estimated that the average white North American consumed 4.2 gallons of rum a year and the average black, 1 gallon.[54] When taken together, the white population and the black population of 1770 consumed 64,175 gallons annually.[55] If so, Native Americans were consuming some 35,000 gallons, approximately one-third of the market in the colony, a figure three and a half times the amount that the Customs Office in Savannah estimated.[56] Georgia did not stand alone. An even greater amount was going through South Carolina, where that colony was importing on average during this period 436,000 gallons of rum, according to McCusker. With a white population of 49,066 and a black population of 75,178 in 1770, the amount consumed internally by whites and blacks, using McCusker's assumptions, would have been 281,255 gallons, leaving a stunning 155,000 gallons unaccounted for. Even if one makes a conservative assumption that one-half of this, or 77,500 gallons, ended up in the deerskin trade, the resulting figure strongly suggests that Charles Town's role had evolved from providing a full array of British merchandise to natives to ceding that ground to Savannah and concentrating on its special position in the Caribbean rum trade. In addition, one must consider the emerging role of Mobile and to a lesser extent Pensacola, where rum flowed northward like a rising tide. Charles Stuart, deputy superintendent at Mobile, asserted that rum and other liquors accounted for four-fifths of the purchases of goods in the surrounding region in West Florida over a twelve-month period.[57] The American Inspector-General's Report for 1768–72 shows that, in an average year, 31,000 gallons of rum were entering the province legally.[58]

When one adds the total amount of rum going to the Creeks, Cherokees, Chickasaws, Choctaws, and other groups and divides by the estimated native population in 1775, the average consumption of rum comes to a staggeringly high figure. Connecting the numbers from Georgia, South Carolina, and West Florida suggests as much as 137,000 gallons were entering native territory on an annual basis.[59] In *Deadly Medicine: Indians and Alcohol in Early America*, Peter Mancall hinted this might be the case and surmised that southeastern Indians were drinking at a significantly higher rate than those in the Northeast. He based his estimate on a statement made in 1776 by John Stuart, superintendent of the Southern Department of Indian Affairs, that 30,000 gallons were consumed in three months in the whole of the South, suggesting a total of 120,000 gallons a year.[60] If Peter Wood's figure is correct for the number of natives present in the South in 1775 (45,200 for those east of the Mississippi), consumption per capita reaches almost 3 gallons. The long-standing problem of West Indian rum had assumed epidemic proportions. "It is certain there is nothing the Indians like better," Charles Stuart, John's brother, observed, "and nothing the traders had rather give."[61] Without any real social prohibition on drunkenness, Muskogees found no reason to restrain themselves. Some historians have suggested that drunkenness reflected a simple desire to escape the tight restrictions placed on native people by clan etiquette, a way to ignore social taboos without being held accountable for their actions. Other scholars have suggested that natives drank because the world they knew was crashing down around them. After the Seven Years' War, the Creeks found themselves suddenly dependent on the English both politically and commercially, victimized by the rush of unscrupulous traders into their lands, and coerced into surrendering territory they did not wish to give up. The phenomenon is all the more puzzling because Muskogees did not have everyday access to rum and other liquors in the way white colonists did.[62]

Leading deerskin merchants were heavily implicated. The inventory of Brown, Struthers, traders and storekeepers in Augusta, contained hundreds of gallons of rum alongside strouds, duffels, and metal objects as did the accounts of the goods that George Galphin sold to traders and others from his Silver Bluff Plantation in the winter of 1766.[63] After Governor Wright imposed a trade embargo on the Creeks because of a violent incident on the frontier, James Spalding of Frederica was discovered selling over a thousand gallons of rum to Creeks flocking in from towns along the Chattahoochee.[64] The extent of rum sales to Creeks and Cherokees appears in the settling of

traders' accounts in the wake of the second Treaty of Augusta, negotiated in
1773. By the terms of that treaty, Creeks and Cherokees agreed to surrender
land north of Augusta in return for cancellation of their heavy debts to traders. Those traders were to receive compensation from the sale of the land by
Georgia to incoming settlers. Before proceeding, Governor Wright called
for a verification of the accounts. After examining the claims, Alexander
Wylly, former speaker of the house and a one-time trader, and Andrew Robertson, a deerskin merchant of Charles Town and partner of George Baillie,
judged the amount to be £77,000 sterling rather than the £111,139 claimed as
debt.[65] Historians have considered the reduction a sign of the overinflating
of prices by deerskin merchants, but the reasons were otherwise.[66] The government disallowed 10 percent from every trade as the cost of doing business
in Indian territory, in effect goods that had been given as presents or used to
buy provisions to live on. It also disallowed any debts incurred for "perishable food," meaning rum. The government had no intention of providing
compensation for alcoholic beverages that violated Georgia law even if that
law had long been a dead letter. The £22,000 disallowed after the deduction
for business costs in all probability represented alcohol.[67]

Thirty-five percent of the claims submitted by George Galphin, arguably the most respected and influential merchant, was likely for rum, the
highest percentage of any trader.[68] A major abuse along the Indian-Georgia
boundary was the presence of trading stores that encouraged young warriors to exchange raw skins for rum. Galphin operated one of the most notorious, Buzzards Roost, an illegal post on the Chattahoochee River about
which a Creek headman, Mad Dog, said it was possible on any given day to
find "great numbers of white and Red people, who had been trading in the
Woods, lying drunk with bottles in their Hands." The store attracted warriors who were anxious to escape the restraining hands of village elders as
well as "disorderly" whites.[69] It is worth noting that small backwoods dealers who traded illicitly for rum do not appear in the figures, so it is easy to
imagine that the amount of trade represented by that drink was even higher.

Merchants found themselves caught in a vise that progressively closed
during the final years of the colonial era. Consumption in Creek country always outstripped production, and natives were forced into increasing
amounts of debt to afford the goods and drink they wanted. In the second
Treaty of Augusta, negotiated in 1773, traders presented their accounts to
claim land ceded by Creeks and Cherokees in exchange for cancellation of

those debts. Natives may have been diligent in satisfying their outstanding debts, but their tastes far outran their ability to produce enough skins. Escalating debt had been a fact of life since the earliest days of the Yamasees when Carolina merchants bullied natives with beatings, kidnappings, and robberies to recover a trade deficit of as much as £10,000 sterling. As the loss of native craftsmanship gained momentum and fewer handmade products were manufactured, the Muskogees became economically dependent on imported goods.

Earlier regulations had forbidden the extension of credit "except for one Pound of Powder and four Pounds of Bullets," and any trader who did so "shall forfeit the Debt due ... from the Indian so trusted or credited and shall also be deemed to have forfeited his Bond."[70] By the 1760s, the usual credit limit was thirty pounds' weight of dressed deerskins per year, with any amount in excess deemed to be unrecoverable. Such regulations remained a dead letter. For minor debts, merchants and traders evolved a system in which a pound of deerskin represented a "chalk." If a trading gun cost sixteen pounds in skins or a shirt four pounds, for example, the trader kept tallies in his Creek store by the use of diagonal lines so that customers could see their credits and debits in terms of the number of chalks recorded. Natives were typically conscientious about trying to discharge their debts, but the mounting financial deficit throughout the nation placed enormous pressure on Creek society to reorient itself around commercial hunting. Kathryn Braund drew the inescapable conclusion, "Economic dependence and individual debt became the most important consequences of Creek participation in the market exchange economy."[71]

Despite the weaknesses of the Creek trade, a handful of London houses were willing to maintain a large credit balance in expectations of a growing market. For the whole of the South, five or six houses controlled that market and never lost faith in their ability to sustain a faltering system. British merchants were addicted to the Georgia market and kept shoveling goods out the doors of their warehouses at an accelerating rate. Secluded in his counting room on Bethlehem Street, John Clark showed an amazing faith in the ability of James Jackson, an Englishman who arrived in Augusta during the late 1750s, to generate the deerskins to support the movement of merchandise across the Atlantic. Beginning as a clerk, Jackson struck out on his own in 1766, buying goods from McGillivray, Grahams, Clark in London and shipping to John Graham and Company in Savannah. The optimism that underlay this trade was unquenchable. In the first five years of their relationship, John Clark sent out £20,150 sterling in goods and received back £13,000 in deerskins. Despite this dismal experience, he forged ahead and over the second five years, from 1771 to 1775, sent more manufactured goods than previously while receiving only a small percentage increase in skins through Savannah, Mobile, and Pensacola.[72]

By the eve of the Revolution, matters had reached a crisis at each level of the credit pyramid. The flow of merchandise from Britain—guns, lead, powder, duffels, strouds, pots, knives, and other prized goods—kept coming through the well-established pipeline that started in the manufacturing centers of Great Britain. That pipeline passed through London and Bristol, on to Savannah and Charles Town, and from there to Augusta, Frederica, and Mobile, where traders carried the goods to native towns and villages. James Jackson & Company, second largest in Georgia with twenty traders fanning out principally to Upper Creek towns, owed John Graham and Company some £19,477, while Spalding & Kelsall in Sunbury owed Graham £9,000, at least one-third of which was deerskin debts. John Graham in turn was indebted to John Clark of London for those sums and more.[73] The formidable George Galphin owed £17,982 sterling to John Gordon and his partner, Thomas Netherclift, and they in turn were indebted to Greenwood & Higginson.[74] In all, Georgia merchants and a handful of Carolina merchants owed £111,139 sterling to their British counterparts. Translated into the weight of deerskins, the Creeks and Cherokees needed to deliver an intimidating 670,000 pounds, or the equivalent of an entire season's hunt by every native group in the Southeast and South. Merchants put pressure on traders for a greater volume of deerskins, but the international market approached saturation. Hunters were killing younger deer; herds were thinned to dangerous levels; and the Creeks and Cherokees found themselves increasingly unable to fulfill their obligations to pay for British goods.[75] The white-tails could not sustain themselves in the face of the booming guns of thousands of natives and the chain of ecological consequences set off by the inevitable overhunting.

Resolution of a kind came when the second Treaty of Augusta forced Creeks and Cherokees to exchange over two million acres of land with the British government for a cancellation of their massive debts to traders and merchants. For once, natives would receive something tangible for their cession; deerskin merchants would be compensated for their investments; and land-hungry settlers would be propitiated, at least for the short term.[76] To Governor Wright, the treaty seemed a neat, clean way of cutting the gordian knot of Indian debt and simultaneously opening fresh lands for rapid development, a balancing act that would not endanger the public peace. He badly underestimated the stakes, however, especially in the size of the debt to be settled. After the deduction of the amount owed for rum, the debt in pounds sterling that came from British merchandise was £85,000 rather than the £45,000 he had guessed, or 32 percent of the £266,200 in total book debt owed by Georgia's merchants to a handful of their correspondents in London.[77] John Clark, formerly of McGillivray, Grahams, Clark, held claims for £69,644; William Thomson, the financial power behind Telfair, Cowper, Telfair, £76,937; the venerable Greenwood & Higginson, largest creditor in South Carolina, £61,185; John Nutt, £30,554; Samuel Brailsford, £13,153; Charles Ogilvie, £10,871; and Benjamin Stead and other merchants, £3,864.[78]

In a colony with little resources, the deerskin trade had mushroomed into a prime constituent of Georgia's overall web of credit, provided by a small group that financed the purchase of Africans and British manufactured goods.[79] The province whose very existence seemed in question as late as the 1740s had received a disproportionately generous inflow of funds from some of the shrewdest minds operating in the transatlantic world in the 1760s and early 1770s. Clearly, the men who plotted financial strategy in Nicholas Lane, Lombard Street, and Old Bethlem saw Georgia as the next South Carolina and were willing to make the necessary investments. The colony absorbed 41 percent of what its neighbor did from the credit lines extended by Londoners, an extraordinary figure in light of the wealth and opportunities that Carolina possessed. In terms of debt per white person, the performance is even more telling: £11.4 per white person in Georgia versus £7.4 in South Carolina.[80]

The Londoners had good reasons for confidence in the explosive growth of this new society.[81] The colony had benefited from a conservatively managed paper currency that traded close to par with the pound sterling. When talk of expanding the supply of paper currency came up in Savannah, Governor Wright described for the Earl of Shelburne his vehement opposition:

> I must say that our Skin Trade which is very considerable, is carried on without money, it is a Barter Trade throughout, The Indians receive no money for their Skins, nor do the Merchants pay any ready money for them, but all the Skins come into their Hands as Payment

or returns made by the Indian Traders for the goods sold or furnished them, for carrying on their trade with the Indians. The chief Articles that money is paid for are Rice & Lumber, and great part of that is paid to the Planters by discount for Negroes dry goods & sold them by the Merchants.[82]

The high level of credit reflected the dependence of merchants on both sides of the Atlantic on the success of the deerskin trade. They had a vested interest in promoting the continued vitality of that trade in the upcountry at the very moment they hoped to further the spread of agriculture while bringing their own land speculation to fruition. That fatal dependence meant an ever-deepening reliance on the rum trade as well as an ever-increasing level of debt. As the vital link between the sugar plantations of the Caribbean, the native towns along the Chattahoochee and Tallapoosa rivers, and the leather shops of London, these merchants forged a connection that fueled the economic expansion of lowcountry Georgia. It was a connection that would not survive the Revolution.

The handwriting was already apparent on the wall before the first events of the American Revolution. The benefits of the Treaty of Augusta with so many partners nursing contradictory expectations unraveled quickly in the upcountry. In late December 1773, a band of Muskogees massacred the Wright and Sherrill families and two African American slaves at the headwaters of the Ogeechee and traumatized not only the region around Augusta but outlying plantations in coastal Georgia as well. Never since its founding had the colony seen this level of violence.[83] The natives' close-up killings of women and children were meant to stun and unnerve, creating a paralyzing fear among people who could only anticipate greater horrors to come. No one could know that the attackers were a desperate band who represented no one but themselves. No one could know whether full-scale warfare was on the brink of breaking out, and even the headmen in Lower Creek towns worried that matters would escalate beyond their powers to rein in emotions. Governor Wright imposed a trade embargo; and Creek leaders, caught off guard by the actions of desperate warriors from the outlaw village of Pucknawheatly, scrambled to regain control.[84] The crisis would merge into the sweeping events of the Revolution in Georgia and redefine the relationship between lowcountry and upcountry, now becoming a more settled land.

Chapter Eleven

Nationalizing the Lowcountry

The traumatic happenings of December 1773 in Boston caught the inhabitants of the Georgia lowcountry off guard. While their attention was drawn to news that a band of renegade Creeks had massacred two white families and their African American slaves along the Ogeechee River, inhabitants missed the significance of what had transpired in Massachusetts. Only the week before the killings in Georgia, about fifty men, "dressed in the Indian manner," faces blackened and bodies wrapped in blankets, had boarded the *Dartmouth*, a ship carrying a load of tea anchored in the harbor, and dumped 342 cases of tea leaves, valued at £10,000 sterling, into the dark waters of Boston harbor to protest the Tea Act of 1773. The action set off a chain of events that led to the American Revolution.[1]

Reflecting the white-hot anger of the British public at what seemed a shockingly criminal deed, Parliament responded accordingly and in the spring of 1774 passed four separate measures. The "Intolerable Acts," as Americans termed the draconian measures, closed the Boston harbor to all but coastal shipping, crippled the power of the Massachusetts Assembly, protected British officials from lawsuits, and made the quartering of troops in private homes a matter of law. To an increasing number of Americans, Britain seemed determined to reduce that colony to servitude. Fixated on their own issues, Georgians were among the few in North America not in an attentive mood. Their focus was shaped not only by the events on the Ogeechee but by their commitment to the British Atlantic world and to the stupendous economic growth that had been realized in so short a time. It would require the full force of the American Revolution to reshape the orientation of the Georgia lowcountry and make that narrow strip of coastal land responsive to the social, cultural, and political life of the emerging American nation.

When a call went out for an intercolonial congress to consider the oppressive measures, all colonies responded except Georgia. A meeting at Peter Tondee's tavern on August 10 was unable to muster a consensus for electing representatives to the forthcoming congress and settled for passing general resolutions that were well within the time-honored tradition of grievances by loyal subjects.[2] Assembling in Philadelphia in September 1774, members of the Continental Congress considered a response and, after lengthy debate, adopted the Continental Association, a voluntary scheme for halting trade with the homeland that called for non-importation, non-exportation, and non-consumption of British goods. After considerable discussion of this complex measure, every colony but Georgia, East and West Florida, Quebec, and the maritime provinces set about creating ad hoc committees to implement a halt to the importation of British goods and the exportation of American commodities to Britain and the West Indies. For the sake of bringing Virginia and South Carolina along, the Continental Congress compromised and extended a nine-month grace period before the terms of the association would be applied to tobacco and rice. Most Georgians remained stubbornly aloof as they had since the non-importation movement against the Townshend duties in 1769.[3] If historian T. H. Breen is correct that consumer politics shaped the movement toward independence, the colony was refusing to take part in one of the most decisive features of the new age of mass politics. Breen considers the consumer boycotts that began with the Stamp Act crisis, accelerated with the protests against the Townshend duties, and climaxed in the Continental Association to be a brilliant American invention that united a dispersed people into a larger whole. The boycotts radicalized American political culture on the eve of independence in ways that no one had foreseen. By 1775, the mere possession of British imports signaled possible disloyalty to the common cause.[4]

Georgians had little liking for the tactic and never participated in the kind of non-importation agreements that forced people to make choices and that provided a means for distinguishing supporters from "the friends of the government." While the mechanics and merchants of Charles Town had come to an uneasy alliance in 1769 that permitted joint participation, the merchants of Savannah gained control of the Patriot movement and adopted a weak resolution that called only for non-importation of those items subject to the Townshend duties.[5] The following year, South Carolina's imports fell by over 50 percent while Georgia's imports shrank by only 3 percent.[6] In failing to join the movement, its colonists never experienced the radical transformation of political life that took place in Charles Town and elsewhere. They never developed the ability to coordinate local protests, to persuade a broad range of people, including women, the poor, and the wealthy, to participate in a huge disruption of the market, nor to experience themselves as a people in much broader, more inclusive terms. The colony missed out on the noisy public forums, the growth of voluntary associations, organized protests, and heated newspaper exchanges that did so much to shape a revolutionary consciousness in other colonies. It was an overwhelming statement of how far removed the colony was from the pulse of the North American mainland.

As William McGillivray phrased it when explaining his state of mind on acquiring a Savannah River plantation in 1774, "There was no apprehension of Danger from the Commotions and they did not enter into the consideration of the purchase."[7] The leadership of the colony was focused on the economic boom that had continued nonstop since 1760, arguably the only province to experience an uninterrupted upswing despite the depression that struck British America after the Seven Years' War. Simply put, hardheaded merchants and planters were intoxicated by the prospect that sustained growth had become a permanent feature of the landscape.[8] Alone among their peers along the eastern seaboard, they determined to forge ahead. Their reaction was understandable. Between 1755 and 1772, the colony saw shipping grow from 52 vessels entering its waters to 218; rice exports rise ten times from 2,200 barrels to 23,000 barrels; the weight of deerskins exported from 49,900 pounds to 270,800 pounds; and lumber from 387,000 feet of board to almost 2.2 million feet.[9] Underlying the explosion in trade was a significant increase in Africans from a modest four hundred blacks to nearly fifteen thousand by 1773, and an equally important advance in the white population, from roughly two thousand to eighteen thousand. By 1775, there were at least seventeen thousand blacks and twenty-two thousand to twenty-three thousand whites.[10] Seeing forty square-rigged vessels in the river before Savannah, the normally reserved James Habersham was moved to scribble to a friend, "this Province is making a rapid increase in her Commerce, Wealth and Population."[11]

Statistical measures speak to the fundamental unity of the coast from the Pee Dee River to the Altamaha, from Georgetown to Darien by 1775. While the Carolina lowcountry contained a population that was 76 percent black, by the end of the royal period the slave population in the Georgia lowcountry was 71 percent and perhaps higher.[12] One could travel through St. Philip and St. John parishes and see little more than plantations with dozens of blacks and only a few white families and overseers. The slave markets in both Savannah and Charles Town were active places in the last years of British rule. In 1774, Georgians imported fifteen hundred captives directly from Africa while buying thirteen hundred of the forty-two hundred Africans sold in the latter town for a total of twenty-eight hundred human beings, an unprecedented number that increased the total black population by around 18 percent.[13] On most plantations, one found similar characteristics: a preponderance of males over females, conditions that inhibited the natural growth of the population, a work regime built around the task system, and a blending of cultures and languages that permitted the survival in much-attenuated form of customs, practices, and beliefs from West Africa. The productivity of these fledgling agricultural units was surprising given their newness. For the period 1768–72, Georgia exported £5.9 sterling per white person compared to £9.4 sterling for South Carolina, and well above that for any other colony in North America.[14] Along Bay Street and through Johnson Square, the talk was about rice, the size of the coming crop, the availability of transportation, and the expected movement of price. Distribution networks throughout both Lowcountries followed the same pattern while the volume of merchandise per white person spoke to the general prosperity throughout the region, well above that of other provinces in British North America.

While Carolinians dug in to defend the "rights of Carolina Englishmen," Georgians had fewer reasons to rebel against British rule than other Americans.[15] For historical reasons, the colony received an annual grant of £3,000 sterling to cover the cost of the civil list, substantially reducing the tax burden of its citizens and making them cautious about any irrevocable step ending that relationship. Nor were Georgians insensitive to the fact that the sparse settlement in the upcountry made them vulnerable to the Creeks, who outnumbered whites until the very end of the period. Reliance on the protection of the British army remained a strong desire even if no British troops were stationed in the colony. If Governor James Wright had used up much of his credit in the political battles of the previous decade, he remained one of the most effective and capable governors in British North America. His part in securing five million additional acres of land from the Creeks earned him accolades from a land-hungry population while his skill at tactical maneuvering in dealing with the Commons House of Assembly slowed the move toward rebellion. On a deeper level, the diversity of the province presented a roadblock to developing a common stance. The Germans around Ebenezer lacked any background in representative government, had found the religious freedom they sought, and tended to support the Crown, at least at the outset. By way of contrast, the Congregationalists of St. John Parish were passionate Whigs and pushed hard for a decisive break with Britain.[16]

However, issues of trade and commerce and, more generally, the very real advantages of the imperial system weighed heavily in people's thinking. Few wanted to risk the economic boom that had carried the colony to new heights. Georgia was very much attached to the benefits of the empire—and the habit of looking to the Caribbean and Britain, rather than to the middle colonies and New England, for sources of inspiration. Led by the coalition of merchants and planters who dominated the colony's political system, residents of Christ Church Parish attempted to navigate the first eighteen months of the Revolution in ways that would not jeopardize continuing economic growth. The leadership vacillated on the question of the Continental Association, with some in favor, others against, but no one willing to embrace it fully. As the colony voted for representatives to a provincial congress in January 1775, the dividing lines became clearer. St. John Parish, dominated by the Congregationalists with their New England ties, and eventually St. Andrew Parish voted for adoption of the Continental Association without reservation, decrying the actions of the British government as a new attempt to enslave America.[17] When the congress met in Savannah on January 18, only five parishes turned up, and they voted in tentative fashion for a watered-down resolution in favor of the association.[18] The document allowed for the import of "Indian goods" to continue, opening a door for merchants to bring in merchandise from Great Britain for all consumers. Nor did it cut off commerce with those colonies that still traded with Great Britain, an omission that permitted Georgia's lucrative commerce with the West Indies to go forward. The prohibition on the export of rice was delayed beyond the time given to South Carolina, and delegates dodged the issue of non-consumption of British goods. In effect, the colony was elevating rum, rice, and deerskins beyond the reach of the Continental Association.[19] In an apologetic letter, the three representatives elected to the Continental Congress confessed that Savannah's merchants flatly opposed the boycott, consumers were divided, most residents remained on the sidelines, and if any effort to impose the boycott were made, civil war threatened. The delegates declined to take their seats in Philadelphia, given "the unworthy part which the Province of Georgia has acted in the great and general contest."[20]

The colony had stamped itself a pariah. In February, the General Committee of South Carolina resolved to have no further trade, dealings, or "intercourse" with its neighbor, branding Georgians as "unworthy of the rights of freemen and as inimical to the liberties of their country."[21] In May, the Continental Congress forbade all commerce with the province for its failure to adopt the association. Parliament provided the most cutting comment of all by not including Georgia on the list of colonies with which it was forbidden to trade.[22] There was a reason. While people in Philadelphia and Charles Town were making painful sacrifices in terms of their standard of living, Savannah's merchants were bringing in a flood of goods. In February, Joseph Clay bluntly told his London supplier that Georgia would never join the association and proceeded to import goods at a higher than normal volume.[23] His colleague Edward Telfair matched him shipment for shipment.[24] Their correspondence throughout the spring reflected the general desire of that community to profit from what seemed a golden opportunity. That they succeeded is reflected in the records of the British Customs Office, showing imports worth £113,000 for 1775 compared to £6,000 for South Carolina.[25] Although the figure is wildly inflated, it underscores both the high volume that poured into the province and the hypocrisy of Savannah's leadership. When news of the bloody events at Lexington and Concord reached Savannah, Clay joined other young "gentlemen" and raided the government's gunpowder arsenal as a protest. Two days later, without the least sense of contradicting himself, he placed an order for eight hundred yards of "Negroe cloth"; a thousand yards of "Negroe white cloth"; three thousand yards of osnaburg cloth; buttons; women's gowns, cloaks, and shoes; men's hats; five thousand needles; two dozen rice mill gouges; and "grubbing" hoes. Whatever their political persuasion, the merchants of Georgia had no intention of seeing the economic boom that had lasted fifteen years come to an end.[26] A significant percentage of lowcountry Georgians shared that state of mind.

The colony was much less tied to the economic, cultural, and political life of the North American continent than was South Carolina. The lack of physical interaction spoke to the issue. In 1772, 81 vessels from New England, New York, and Pennsylvania stopped in South Carolina while 26 called on Georgia, and 129 left South Carolina for northern ports while only 18 did so from Georgia.[27] Those sloops, brigs, and ships carried newspapers, pamphlets, passengers, and gossip, giving Carolinians a much greater sense of the world to the north and bringing them into the momentous debates that roiled the major towns. Savannahians never cultivated those contacts. They did not follow their Carolinian peers to Newport, Rhode Island, and other summer spots far removed from the stultifying heat and the malaria-bearing mosquitoes of the southern seacoast. Very few traveled to the mid-Atlantic colonies for their education and no one, it would appear, went to any institution in New England. The exception was, once again, the indomitable James Habersham, whose faith in the evangelist George Whitefield led him to place James and Joseph at a tutoring school attached to the College of New Jersey in Princeton, where evangelical Presbyterians were educating ministers, young professionals, and the children of merchants.[28]

If few Georgians married Carolinians, virtually no one married someone from elsewhere in the North American mainland. "Northward" brides or grooms were almost never found. Two Jewish merchants found spouses in Philadelphia and Newport, and a leading deerskin merchant in Augusta, Robert Mackay, married the daughter of a wealthy slave trader in Newport whose husband had died in Augusta.[29] The exception to this picture of indifference was the Congregationalists of St. John's, who corresponded with their cousins in Connecticut and welcomed into their midst Dr. Lyman Hall, who studied theology under Yale's president and served as a Congregational minister in New England before becoming a physician. The most vibrant connection to the North was the articulate Dr. John Joachim Zubly, minister of the Presbyterian Meeting House, who spent time in Pennsylvania and continued to correspond with his Lutheran and Presbyterian counterparts there.[30] Although his writings against the Stamp Act and subsequent ministerial abuses were well argued and popular, he represented one of the few such voices in the colony in terms of publications.

The lowcountry's sense of disenfranchisement from the mainland was reinforced by a difficult relationship with the upcountry. The Treaty of 1763 had opened 2.4 million acres for settlement while sparking an explosive growth in the deerskin trade. The export of deerskins reached its high point during the period 1768–72 at the very moment when thousands of settlers were pouring down the Great Wagon Road through Virginia and

North Carolina to claim land at the edge of the frontier and frequently beyond, in native territory. When a noted authority on colonial Georgia, Edward J. Cashin, argued that the Georgia upcountry was so different from the rest of the colony as to constitute a separate province in all but name, he was not exaggerating.[31] To anyone who ventured from the coastal plain to the piedmont, the contrasts were stunning: the deerskin trade with its small coterie of merchants, traders, and packhorsemen compared to the rice cultivation that marshaled thousands of slaves in the most intensive capital investment in North America, natives freely walking the streets of Augusta versus the occasional shepherded delegations that came to Savannah, aggressive settlers and Indian hunters in jarring conflicts over land compared to the silent tug-of-war on plantations between black slaves and white owners over autonomy.

As the upcountry filled up with settlers bent on pushing the Creeks beyond the Oconee River, the contrast shifted focus. The differences revolved around small farmers, often illiterate and untutored, compared to tidewater planters, who had the advantage of contact with a wider world; modest farms versus sizable plantations; a black population of less than 20 percent of the total compared to 70 percent in the lowcountry; the dominance of English as the spoken language versus the linguistic diversity of the lowcountry; hatred of the native versus a continuing reliance on the deerskin trade to finance economic development; and an exaggerated suspicion of authority versus a more deferential attitude. The chief justice of Georgia, Anthony Stokes, may have exaggerated the general feeling of the lowcountry elite but not by much when he accused the "swarm of men" from the back parts of Virginia and North Carolina of being descended from convicts transported to Virginia, and he guessed that these "Crackers" "will in time overrun the rice part of the country, as the Tartars in Asia have done . . . in the southern parts of that country." For the jurist, the stew of people in the upcountry portended the loss of economic, political, and social power by the coastal region.[32]

By the beginning of 1776, Georgia's royal government saw its effective power disappear as Patriots took over the operation of the port, the legal system, and the militia, but the trappings of government remained in place in a strangely choreographed charade. The governor still occupied his house on St. James Square and still met with his council in the appointed assembly room. Each unsure of the other's strength, neither Loyalists nor

Patriots were anxious to push matters to an ultimate confrontation. As late as February 1776, the Council of Safety in Savannah was locked in an intense debate over whether to continue a temporary ban on the export of rice while British naval vessels cruised off Tybee, ready to transport that cargo to feed troops besieged in Boston by George Washington's fledgling army.[33] On March 1, the Council of Safety made a belated decision to extend the ban. The British sent vessels up the river to secure the rice and, with the help of Savannah's merchants and seamen, made off with a dozen vessels and sixteen hundred barrels. John Graham had loaded his workhorse vessel, the *Inverness*, with several hundred barrels of rice and fifty-three hogsheads of deerskins as well as all the records of the Customs Office, at the request of the governor.[34] The shipment was crucial if he were to stave off impending bankruptcy due to his enormous debt to London creditors.[35] In the confused battle, Patriots set the *Inverness* and another vessel afire and sent them drifting toward the rice-filled schooners. Two vessels were destroyed in addition to Graham's ship.[36] Listening to this disheartening news while sitting on the deck of the warship *Scarborough*, the Scotsman bitterly mused that he was paying a high price for no other reason than he would not rebel "against my King & Country: ... My House in town has been attempted to be pulled down, and the next thing I expect to hear is that my Negroes are seized and sold, and my barns and improvements at my plantations destroyed, in short, such is the state we are now reduced to that tho only twelve months ago I deemed my property worth full 40,000 pounds."[37]

The celebrated battle of the rice boats was a minor skirmish but marked a turning point in the expectations of Americans. The Continental Congress in Philadelphia and the Whigs in South Carolina put aside their doubts about the loyalty and seriousness of the Georgians and rushed to offer congratulations. On a more subtle level, the battle initiated a seven-year process by which the American Revolution effectively nationalized the Georgia lowcountry and turned it into a functioning part of the North American mainland. The battle represented the first major step in detaching this small strip of coast from its orientation toward the British Atlantic world and its special connection to the Caribbean.

The leadership of Georgia's economic expansion did not survive the Revolution. After the mock heroics of the battle of the rice boats, the merchant community virtually disappeared from the stage. Joseph Clay, Edward Telfair, Samuel Elbert, Mordecai Sheftall, and a handful of others joined the Patriots as the conservative wing, but most merchants declared for the Crown. A few left with British naval forces. Others headed to St. Augustine. With their estates very much on their minds, several remained in Savannah or on their plantations to gauge changing circumstances and protect their investments. In late June, a revamped Council of Safety arrested forty-three men "whose going at large is dangerous to the liberties of America." Nineteen were merchants, traders, or sea captains. Lewis Johnston mused that government had been thrown into the hands of a set of the most worthless and ignorant men ever to disgrace a country: "Nor could it indeed be expected in a province where every man of Property, Ability, Liberality of sentiment were (with very few exceptions) firm in their loyalty to Government, which was far from being the case in the other Provinces." If Loyalists from Georgia consistently overestimated their support throughout the Revolution, in the spring of 1776 Johnston may not have been far from the mark. A significant number remained committed to an empire that had treated them well.[38]

The ties that bound Georgia to the Caribbean derived much of their strength from the network of contacts linking participants in the trade, especially Scots who populated the port towns of the region. Those once-sturdy links could not withstand political events. Three Scotsmen of St. Andrew Parish and a fourth with a store in Savannah obtained a precious permit during the summer of 1776 to ship rice to Surinam and return with Dutch goods for sale in Georgia. Three of the men were Loyalists, the fourth a member of the revolutionary Council of Safety who used his influence to secure the permit. When the voyage went to Jamaica instead of Surinam and returned with sugar, rum, and coffee for the British garrison in St. Augustine, a political explosion occurred in Savannah. George McIntosh, brother of the revolutionary general Lachlan McIntosh, stood accused of treason.[39] Naively, he pointed out that the St. Andrew Parish Committee, responsible for enforcing the terms of the association, had shown more leniency toward Loyalists than any other parish in hopes that "those we once called our Friends, Neighbours, and nearest Connections" might come to support the cause. Therein lay the problem. Relationships with those friends, neighbors, and nearest connections could not survive the political maelstrom.

Connections with the sugar islands became suspect.[40] Initially, West Indians were bitterly divided over the issue of America, and planters fought

duels over the imperial question.[41] In December 1774, the Jamaican assembly petitioned the Crown in words that repudiated parliamentary sov-
ereignty over the internal affairs of a colony and sounded very much like
the rhetoric used by Patriots in North America. The colonial assemblies
in the Caribbean had long been assertive of their rights and continued to fear
the prerogative powers of the governors. But the prerogative struggle and
the revolutionary movement evolved in radically different directions. The
prolonged contest between Governor Wright and the Commons House
of Assembly more nearly fit the West Indian model of conflict than it did
the revolutionary rhetoric elsewhere in North America, at least in the initial stages.[42] The Jamaican petition was restrained in tone and avoided any
discussion of the merits of the imperial dispute. The West Indian lobby in
London organized to pressure the British government toward a concilia-
tory stance and took a strong stand against the Prohibitory Act, which
proposed to prohibit all trade with the rebel colonies. The effort continued
into 1776, but the underlying motives turned into ones of pure self-interest.
West Indians feared the threat of losing their trade with North America
and envisioned a famine that would provoke a slave insurrection. The great
Jamaican slave rebellion in 1776 effectively ended any efforts in favor of
reconciliation. After initial hesitation, the British West Indies stood forth-
rightly with the Crown in recognition of their overwhelming dependence
on the protected English sugar market and the important role of the British army and navy in securing the Caribbean. As the Revolution unfolded,
the British West Indies would welcome with open arms a steady stream of
Loyalist refugees from North America, many from Georgia.[43]

By the time the Second Provincial Congress assembled in Savannah
in July 1775, a parochial committee, rather than the leading import-export
merchants, was already in control of the docks and the port of Savannah.
Governor Wright informed the Earl of Dartmouth, "One Sheftall a Jew is
Chairman of the Parochial Committee as they call themselves and this Fellow Issues Orders to Captains of Vessels to depart the King's Port without
landing any of their Cargoes legally Imported."[44] A respected merchant,
Mordecai Sheftall was hardly a radical, but he was free of the burden of connections within the governing elite and was considerably more comfortable
in a popular setting. The committee included a fairly representative sample
of the artisans of the town, "a parcel of the lowest people," as the governor
later described them, "chiefly carpenters, shoemakers, blacksmiths, etc."[45]

The constitution adopted on February 5, 1777, placed enormous power in a unicameral legislature and firmly established rule by the consent of the governed, arguably the most democratic of all the constitutions adopted by the thirteen new states. A conservative revolutionary, Joseph Clay had strong opinions on the new constitution, which he found "so very Democratical" because the "Rule & Government has got into the Hands of those whose ability or situation in Life does not intitle them to it."[46] The elites who had controlled Savannah before the Revolution disappeared, the great majority never to return.

Nor did the relationship of the lowcountry with the upcountry survive the Revolution. The year 1775 saw the dominance that deerskin merchants of Savannah and Augusta had long exercised over the upcountry crumble. An aggressive settler society surged to the fore under new leadership that pushed aside the old. That radical change had its origins in the tumultuous aftermath of the Treaty of Augusta and the debate over the acquisition of new lands for farming. The murders of the two families by renegade warriors traumatized the upcountry and in the short term made its residents reluctant to question the legitimacy of the British government. As far away as the lower Altamaha River, planters built defensive stockades.[47] Displaying a firm sense of command, Governor Wright imposed a ban on trade with natives while negotiating a settlement with the headmen. As a condition of peace, settlers widely expected a new land cession that would extend boundaries to the Oconee River, a goal that the deerskin merchants and Governor Wright had shared only two years before. When additional land was not forthcoming and the government agreed to prevent frontiersmen from hunting in the Oconee-Ogeechee strip, a petition by the inhabitants of St. George and St. Paul parishes accused Wright and the merchants of acting out of self-interest and denounced the resumption of the Indian traffic as "of utmost prejudice" to settlers. Wright compounded their sense of alienation when he asked the assembly to pass legislation "to prevent encroachments and trespasses and other irregularities" by "disorderly people" in the ceded lands.[48]

A turning point had been reached. For over twenty-five years, deerskin merchants, who took their lead from Savannah, had exercised oversight and control, both formal and informal, over the affairs of the region. As late as 1772, deerskin merchants still dominated the government of Augusta, occupied most of the positions of justice of the peace in St. Paul Parish, and held two of the three seats in the Commons House of Assembly.[49] Overnight, their leadership in the upcountry crumbled. The Revolution found most traders, but not all, remaining loyal to the Crown and to the vision of a transatlantic world that bound regions and people together in an economic nexus. The revolutionaries who took control of Augusta had no use for natives walking through the streets of an increasingly farming community and were at pains to exclude the traders from positions of leadership. In the clean sweep that followed, new faces appeared in the revolutionary assemblies and as justices of the peace, militia officers, and magistrates. The demotion of the deerskin merchants all but ended their role as cultural brokers between two worlds, an essential link between a hunting culture whose ceremonies and rituals remained opaque to most whites and a farming culture bent on improving all lands and bringing white "civilization" beyond the frontier. With the passing of the Creek trade as an essential element in Georgia's economy, the lowcountry lost its hold over the upcountry, now emerging as a land with farms growing wheat, corn, and tobacco.

By destroying the network of merchants who led Georgia into the Caribbean and Atlantic worlds, the Revolution decapitated the lowcountry of its commercial leadership and cleared the way for the passing of political and economic power to Augusta and the upcountry. The tragedy of the abrupt departure of these merchants was the gaping hole they left in the economic and social life of the new state. Capital, commercial expertise, and invaluable connections disappeared overnight, a much heavier legacy for Savannah to bear than for Charles Town, where no such wholesale turnover occurred. The ensuing vacuum was a major factor in the realignment of power after the Revolution, with the upcountry claiming its due. In a not so subtle revenge, Augusta and the surrounding counties, Richmond, Wilkes, and Burke, stripped Savannah of political and, to a certain extent, economic power. The irony was that the leading merchant of colonial times, the nimble Edward Telfair, one of the few mercantile Scots to embrace the Revolution, transferred his base of operations to the upcountry and assisted his new colleagues in measures against the town that had nourished his early success.[50]

The Caribbean connection reemerged as soon as the war ended; indeed, it had never ceased. Trade with the West Indies continued during the years when Georgia remained free of British control and redoubled after the occupation of Savannah and the reinstitution of royal government under

James Wright.[51] After the evacuation of the British in July 1782, Joseph Clay made contact with correspondents around the region. "We are in every respect the best situated of any state in the union for carrying on an extensive West Indian Trade," he asserted. "Our contiguity to the Islands is a great advantage in our voyages to and from. Our lumber of which we have every kind is in the highest estimation and always commands a preference." He went on to enumerate the other commodities—beef, pork, naval stores, corn, staves, shingles, and masts—that enabled merchants to form a cargo without difficulty.[52] Imports of slaves from the Caribbean resumed; 1,788 people were brought into Georgia by the turn of the century.[53]

In a fit of pique a month after the British evacuation, the state legislature passed a law making it illegal for any native of Scotland to migrate to Georgia or do business. but that was quickly repealed.[54] Scots reappeared as export merchants, including Andrew Low, who established a family dynasty for the better part of the nineteenth century, and Robert Mackay, son of a Creek trader, who was placed with a Scottish relative for his education during the Revolution.[55] James Spalding, a Scot who made a fortune in the deerskin trade, lost it all in the Revolution but, despite his record as a Loyalist, returned to join a handful of others in introducing a new crop on his remaining lands and experimenting with a variety of seeds.[56] Sea Island cotton, a black-seed hybrid created from a variety of plants imported from the West Indies, made its appearance in a way not dissimilar to indigo fifty years earlier.[57] With long, fine, silky fibers that commanded a premium on world markets, the cotton was established in the damp environment of the barrier islands and coastal region. African Americans who had been growing indigo switched with little difficulty. Rice plantations became more like their counterparts in the sugar islands, with fewer planters, more slaves, and larger operations as the tidal flow method spread along the coast. Savannah's profile continued to bear a resemblance to towns of the West Indies, and Georgians continued to visit the islands.

Appearances, though, could be misleading. Although rice and Sea Island cotton provided ever-increasing amounts of wealth to a select few, the coastal region was becoming the handmaiden of the upcountry, which had an expanding economy based on tobacco and wheat, then on short-staple, green-seed cotton. Settlers, who were mostly small property holders from the mid-Atlantic region, carried black slavery into the newly opened lands between the Ogeechee and Oconee rivers, and entered the market economy on their own terms, not on those of the lowcountry gentry. The same types of people that came down the Great Wagon Trail in the 1770s resumed the migration from Virginia and points north. As Joyce Chaplin has written, the upcountry farmers used a model of commercial agriculture other than the one in the lowcountry, a model closer to their experience in the mid-Atlantic. They adapted the gang system of slave labor in contrast to the task system of the coastal region, the plow as a central feature of field work, and tobacco presses for the daunting task of compressing cotton into bales. Eli Whitney's cotton gin reinforced but did not create the conditions necessary for the commercialization of that crop and for the expansion of slavery through the upcountry.[58] Settlers were creating inland plantations with a newer type of organization and management that looked to other sources of inspiration.

By the fourth quarter of the eighteenth century, the lowcountry plantation model seemed to have reached its natural limits and no longer appeared to be a viable model for replication.[59] As short-stemmed cotton flowed into the port of Savannah, the old order of marketing evolved into increasingly sophisticated forms to satisfy the demands of a British textile industry undergoing rapid expansion. In place of the Scots as leaders of economic expansion, a new generation of men from northern states appeared, young, ambitious, and with valuable connections in Boston, New York, and Philadelphia. Arriving in the last two decades of the century, they found ready acceptance and helped make Savannah a recognized part of the cultural corridor that ran from Boston down the eastern seaboard.[60] While the Georgia lowcountry remained tied to the West Indies and to the models it proposed, the aftermath of the American Revolution effectively nationalized this part of the world in terms of structures, connections, and outlook. It was a wrenching change that required seven years of war and at least two decades of adjustment to the realities of the emerging cotton kingdom.

Notes

AO	Audit Office, National Archives, United Kingdom
CGHS	*Collections of the Georgia Historical Society*
CO	Colonial Office, National Archives, United Kingdom
CRG	*Colonial Records of the State of Georgia*
GHS	Georgia Historical Society
LC	Library of Congress
NARA	National Archives and Records Administration
NAS	National Archives of Scotland
NA-UK	National Archives, United Kingdom
PHL	*Papers of Henry Laurens*
RRG	*Revolutionary Records of the State of Georgia*
UGA	University of Georgia

INTRODUCTION

1. P. Morgan, "Lowcountry Georgia and the Early Modern Atlantic World."

2. Greene, "Early Modern Southeastern North America," 525–38; Chestnutt, *South Carolina's Expansion*, esp. 216–30.

3. The last three volumes (2001, 2005, 2009) published in the series *The Carolina Lowcountry and the Atlantic World* set a high standard. However, of the forty-four articles, only one addresses the Georgia lowcountry. See Lounsbury, "Christ Church, Savannah," 58–73. In an important article, Kenneth Morgan considers the colonial rice trade. His attention is necessarily focused on the Charles Town market, not on Savannah's. K. Morgan, "Organization of the Colonial American Rice Trade."

4. Greene, "Travails of an Infant Colony," 132, 133, 140. "[T]he people are so poor & so involved with their neighbours of Carolina; that their utmost industry affords them but a scanty subsistence & a small surplus that goes thither to pay their Debts." Henry Ellis to the Board of Trade, May 5, 1757, *CRG*, 28, pt. 1:24.

5. Marsh, *Georgia's Frontier Women*; B. Wood, *Women's Work, Men's Work*; Stewart,

"*What Nature Suffers to Groe*"; Juricek, *Colonial Georgia and the Creeks*; Sweet, *Negotiating for Georgia*.

6. D. W. Meinig qtd. in Bailyn, *Atlantic History*, 55–56; Horn and Morgan, "Settlers and Slaves," 19–44. Jeffrey Bolster has expanded the concept by pointing out that historians typically neglect the living sea and rarely treat the interactions of human maritime communities with the marine biological communities on which they depend. Bolster, "Putting the Ocean in Atlantic History," 19–47.

7. Hancock, *Oceans of Wine*, xv, xvi; Hancock, *Citizens of the World*, 1–39.

8. Games, "Atlantic History," 741–57; Bailyn, *Atlantic History*, 57–111; Armitage, "Three Concepts of the Atlantic World," 11–30; McCusker and Menard, *The Economy of British America*, 18–34; Coclanis, "In Retrospect: McCusker and Menard's 'Economy of British America,'" 183–97; S. D. Smith, "Reckoning with the Atlantic Economy," 749–64; Nash, "South Carolina and the Atlantic Economy," 677–702; Price, "The Transatlantic Economy," 22–33; Hornsby, *British Atlantic, American Frontier*, 123–25, 223–27.

9. Andrien, "The Spanish Atlantic System," 55–80.

10. Russell-Wood, "The Portuguese Atlantic," 81–110.

11. DuBois, "The French Atlantic," 137–62.

12. Burnard, "The British Atlantic," 111–36; Games, *Migration and the Origins of the English Atlantic World*, 190–216; Zahedieh, "Economy," 51–68; P. Morgan, "The Black Experience in the British Empire," 465.

13. Burnard, "'Prodigious Riches,'" 506–24, esp. 522.

14. Higman, *Concise History of the Caribbean*; Higman, "Economic and Social Development," 1:303.

15. Burnard, "'Prodigious Riches,'" 520.

16. P. Morgan, "Lowcountry Georgia and the Early Modern Atlantic World," 27.

17. The figure of forty thousand or more is based on an estimated eighteen thousand Africans and African Americans and at least twenty-two thousand whites.

18. Stokes, *A View of the Constitution*, 115, 139.

Chapter 1   THE THREE GEORGIAS

1. Harman Verelst to James Oglethorpe, June 17, 1736, in *CRG*, 29:145; Isaac Young to the Trustees, March 29, 1738, in *CRG*, 22, pt. 1:112–14; Entry for March 23, 1741, Journal of the Earl of Egmont, in *CRG*, 5:481; Granger, *Savannah River Plantations*, 282–87. According to a contemporary, the planter in question, Robert Williams, had a settlement on the Savannah River with forty indentured servants and planted for four years until he lost £2,000 sterling; Reese, *The Clamorous Malcontents*, 113.

2. Terms used by the Earl of Egmont, a trustee, to describe the charity settlers sent to Georgia. Ready, *The Castle Builders*, 22.

3. P. Morgan, "Lowcountry Georgia and the Early Modern Atlantic World"; Hornsby, *British Atlantic, American Frontier*, 73–125; Greene, "Travails of an Infant Colony," 113–42; Ready, *The Castle Builders*; Fraser, *Savannah in the Old South*, 1–41; Coleman, *Colonial Georgia*, 1–173.

4. Ready, *The Castle Builders*, 22; Coulter, "A List of the First Shipload of Georgia Settlers," 282–88; Rabac, "Economy and Society in Early Georgia," 126.

5. Compiled from Colonial Conveyance Book C-1, Georgia Archives. On "Mother" Penrose, Marsh, *Georgia's Frontier Women*, 51.

6. Benjamin Martyn to President and Assistants, March 16, 1747, in *CRG*, 31:58–59.

7. James Habersham to the Reverend Mr. Bolzius, September 25, 1747, 14th page, Peter Force Papers, ser. 7E, LC.

8. De Vorsey, *De Brahm's Report*, 141.

9. Kole, *The Minis Family of Georgia*, 3–4; Ready, *The Castle Builders*, 185–86. A former potter from England, William Ewen, left his position at the trustees' public store when that controversial establishment closed, bought goods at discounted prices, and ventured out on his own. Entry of May 1740, Journal of William Stephens, in *CRG*, 4:583; Coleman, *Colonial Georgia*, 130–31. The clerk of the governing magistrates took advantage of his official connections to import sugar from the West Indies. Robert Pringle to Nicholas Rigby, January 4, 1743, in Edgar, *Letterbook of Robert Pringle*, 2:628. These men blended easily into an egalitarian social structure where ambitions were limited.

10. "Journal of the Most Astonishing Journey of Captain Caleb Davis, Eminent Merchant, commencing from the year 1714, Who was, 'till the Year 1741, a very fortunate Trader among the Spaniards, in America, and who was afterwards beguiled and Most shamefully abused by the Tyranny of Army Officers of the Crown of England . . . , From the prison of the Kings Bench," September 15, 1763, Keith Read Collection, Hargrett Library, UGA. Captain Caleb Davis to the Lords Commissioners of the Treasury, February 23, 1762, 150–54, Treasury 1/434, NA-UK.

11. Journal of William Stephens, January 6, 1738, May 29, 1739, September 1739, January 1740, July 19, 1740, in *CRG*, 4:24–29, 64, 343–46, 408–17, 423, 483, 623. Quotation from 344.

12. Lambert, *James Habersham*, 20–25, 33–65; Harden, *A History of Savannah and South Georgia*, 99–101.

13. Cashin, *Beloved Bethesda*, 34–38.

14. Francis Harris shared the basic religious values of James Habersham and found his connections in the wider world complemented Habersham's talent for

handling the financial side of matters. Entry of March 15, 1744, in Coulter, *Journal of William Stephens, 1743–1745*.

15. "Messrs. Grant & Habersham from your Place," a Carolina merchant chided an indebted client in Savannah, "are very Punctual in their Returns & have Established a Very Good Credit in this Place, & money can be no Scarcer to you than to them." Robert Pringle to Nicholas Rigby, January 4, 1743, in Edgar, *Letterbook of Robert Pringle*, 2:628. On John Nicholson, the London correspondent, *CRG*, 25:101, 389–90.

16. William Spencer to Harman Verelst, September 12, 1746, in *CRG*, 25:106–7.

17. On the small commission, Henry Ellis to the Board of Trade, March 11, 1757, in *CRG*, 28, pt. 1:11; James Habersham to the Rev. Mr. Bolzius, September 25, 1747, Peter Force Transcripts, LC.

18. Qtd. in G. Jones, *Detailed Reports on the Salzburger Emigrants*, 7:59.

19. Ready, *The Castle Builders*, 184; Petition of Francis Harris and James Habersham to the President and Assistants, March 29, 1749, in *CRG*, 6:243; James Habersham to Benjamin Martyn, July 7, 1749, in *CRG*, 25:392.

20. Ready, *The Castle Builders*, 110, 123.

21. Harman Verelst to William Stephens, February 6, 1744/45, *CRG*, 30:331–33; Lannen, "James Oglethorpe and the Civil-Military Contest," 211–20; Ivers, *British Drums*, 204–5.

22. Ivers, *British Drums*, 185, 206, 247n6; Logan, "William Logan's Journal," 166–79. On the fate of a free black sold in Frederica, John Dobell to the Trustees, May 1746, in *CRG*, 25:42–48; on reducing the administrative powers of Frederica, Benjamin Martyn to William Stephens, February 6, 1745, in *CRG*, 30:333–35; Juricek, *Colonial Georgia and the Creeks*, 118–19.

23. Ivers, *British Drums*, 78–86, 134, 204–5. On the relationship between the regimental commander and Mary Bosomworth, Juricek, *Colonial Georgia and the Creeks*, 131, 142–50.

24. Reese, *Frederica*; F. Moore, "A Voyage to Georgia"; Scott, *The First Families of Frederica*.

25. Qtd. in Coulter, *Journal of William Stephens, 1741–1743*, 158.

26. Entry of June 14, 1740, Journal of William Stephens, *CRG*, 4:594.

27. Ready, *The Castle Builders*, 312.

28. Juricek, *Colonial Georgia and the Creeks*, 28–29, 51, 96–97, 102–8, 101, 118, 131, 141–44; Sweet, "Mary Musgrove," 11–32; Sweet, *Negotiating for Georgia*, 159–76; Baine, "Myths of Mary Musgrove," 428–35; Fisher, "Mary Musgrove," 163–206; Extracts of Letters between Oglethorpe, Major William Horton, and Lt. Col. Heron to the Rev. and Mrs. Thomas Bosomworth, 1740–51, *CRG*, 27:1–20. On Oglethorpe calling her to Frederica and on contracting debt with Charles Town merchants, "A

Statement of Mrs. Bosomworth's Case," *CRG*, 28, pt. 1:258–59; Thomas Bosomworth's argument, "A Narrative," *CRG*, 27:187–91.

29. Robertson and Robertson, "The Town and Fort of Augusta," 59–74; Weir, *Colonial South Carolina*, 143.

30. Cashin, *Colonial Augusta*; Cashin, *Lachlan McGillivray*, 19–20, 33–34, 48; Braund, *Deerskins & Duffels*, 41–44, 169–70; Coleman, *Colonial Georgia*, 50–51, 215–16.

31. Inventory of Williams Sludders, August 23, 1754; Inventory of Daniel Clark in partnership with Lachlan McGillivray, July 16, 1757; Inventory of John Pettygrew, May 2, 1761; Inventory of store of Lachlan McIntosh and George Johnston, September 9, 1760, Colonial Inventory Book F, 1754–70, Georgia Archives.

32. Cashin, *Lachlan McGillivray*, 104–31, esp. 104–5 and 120.

33. Deposition of Adam Bosomworth, January 24, 1753, in McDowell, *Colonial Records*, 329. As the leading magistrate in Savannah, William Stephens had adopted a cautious position and refused to interfere with the "monopoly" exercised by Brown & Rae. In 1749, the company lost its best advocate when the officer from Oglethorpe's regiment stationed at Augusta returned to England upon the disbanding of that unit. See Cashin, *Lachlan McGillivray*, 101–2.

34. Minutes of the President and Assistants, September 26, 1750, in *CRG*, 6:333. Most of the leading partners had been traders with the old Archibald McGillivray Company of Charles Town: Patrick Brown, William Sludders, George Cussings, Jeremiah Knott, Daniel Clark, Isaac Barksdale, and Lachlan McGillivray. Brown held the license to trade with seven Upper Creek towns but spent most of his time in Augusta. Cashin, *Lachlan McGillivray*, 48–49, 104–20; Braund, *Deerskins & Duffels*, 44; Juricek, *Colonial Georgia and the Creeks*, 182.

35. In 1741, a report cited 1,808 inhabitants. "Number of Inhabitants in Georgia, 1741," in Documents Drawn Up for the Board of Trade, Coe Papers, South Carolina Historical Society. Kenneth Coleman cites a figure of 1,735 inhabitants in 1751, quoted from a Board of Trade report. Coleman, *Colonial Georgia*, 223. The number of blacks is based on Zouberbuhler's figure of 349 adults as well as "children too young to work" present in the summer of 1750 and reduced by a modest amount since slavery was not yet legally established. Figure cited in William Stephens and Assistants to Benjamin Martyn, July 19, 1750, in *CRG*, 26:22.

36. On the mortality rate, Ready, *The Castle Builders*, 55; Cates, "'The Seasoning,'" 146–58; Marsh, *Georgia's Frontier Women*, 26.

37. The Reverend Zouberbuhler reported 613 inhabitants in Savannah in 1748 and 800 in 1750. Zouberbuhler to Rev. Mr. Bearcroft, August 8, 1748, *CRG*, 25:315; Zouberbuhler to Society for the Propagation of the Gospel, December 20, 1750, Edgar W. Knight Collection, ser. 3, Society for the Propagation of the Gospel (Ga.)

Papers, vol. 31, University of North Carolina. Although the inhabitants of Frederica dispersed with the disbanding of the regiment in May 1749, a few remained. Some Scots remained at Darien. Ebenezer maintained its population through immigration. Bigger than any other save Savannah, Augusta was a booming frontier town. Cashin, *Colonial Augusta*. The estimate assumes 700 people in Savannah in 1749, 150 in Ebenezer, 200 in Augusta, and 50 each in Darien and Frederica.

38. In 1749, Georgia had five towns, Frederica (soon to disappear), Darien, Ebenezer, Savannah, and Augusta.

39. Etheridge, "Creating the Shatter Zone," 207–18; Ramsey, *The Yamasee War*; Higman, *Concise History of the Caribbean*, 52–80; Turner, "Indigenous America," 200; Oatis, *A Colonial Complex*, 1–11; Sweet, *Negotiating for Georgia*, 24–39; Gallay, *The Indian Slave Trade*, 338–44, 350–52.

40. Piker, "Colonists and Creeks," 503–40; Juricek, *Colonial Georgia and the Creeks*, 3. Juricek comments that "the area we think of as Georgia was nearly uninhabited." On the Uchees, G. Jones, *The Salzburger Saga*, 98. For an overview, P. Wood, "Circles in the Sand," 5–21.

41. Ramsey, *The Yamasee War*, 219–20; Juricek, *Colonial Georgia and the Creeks*, 38–39.

42. Juricek, *Colonial Georgia and the Creeks*, 156–70; Sweet, *Negotiating for Georgia*, 158–76; Fraser, *Savannah in the Old South*, 35–36; Cashin, *Lachlan McGillivray*, 112–16.

43. Marsh, *Georgia's Frontier Women*, 69–92.

44. Qtd. in Loewald et al., "Johann Martin Bolzius," 253.

45. Landers, *Black Society in Spanish Florida*, 33; Deagan and MacMahon, *Fort Mose*, 20–24.

46. March 1–3, 1738, Journal of the Earl of Egmont, in *CRG*, 5:138–39. A Philadelphia merchant who encountered Captain Davis in Frederica in 1745 thought Davis and his crew "have none but Piratical Principles"; Logan, "William Logan's Journal," 178.

47. Reese, *The Clamorous Malcontents*, 55; "An Act to prevent the Importation and use of Rum and Brandys in the Province of Georgia," April 3, 1735, in *CRG*, 1:48–49; Sirmans, *Colonial South Carolina*, 188; Benjamin Martyn to Samuel Urlsperger, April 13, 1747, in *CRG*, 31:77. The trustees rescinded the ban on rum in 1747 in order to encourage the lumber trade as well as in recognition of its ineffectiveness.

48. "I have some reason to think his Aim is more extensive than appears openly," reported the trust's secretary, William Stephens, "for as he is in Partnership with his Brother & others at St. Hitts & Bristol; who trade much in importing Negroes into the west Indies; tis not hard to conceive what would follow." William Stephens to the Trustees, January 2, 1739, *CRG*, 22, pt. 1:368; Ready, *The Castle Builders*, 183–85. Accounts of Robert Williams and Company with the public store in *CRG*, 29:304,

317, 323, 325, 327. On the political battles involving the debate over slavery and the role of the Malcontents, B. Wood, *Slavery in Colonial Georgia*, 28–56.

49. Benjamin Martyn to the Rev. Samuel Urlsperger, April 13, 1747, in *CRG*, 31:77; G. Jones, *The Salzburger Saga*, 105. The trustees had first seriously considered repealing the ban on rum during the great debate over slavery. Benjamin Martyn to James Oglethorpe, August 10, 1742, in *CRG*, 30:257.

50. James Habersham to the Rev. Mr. Bolzius, September 25, 1747, Peter Force Papers, LC. Sixteen years after its founding, the colony had no commodity to export other than lumber, could barely feed itself, and depended on the inflow of capital from England to cover its needs. The records of the Customs Office present a picture of abject failure: not a single barrel of rice, bundle of deerskins, or pound of indigo exported between 1743 and 1749. Ledgers of Imports and Exports, Customs 3:43–48, NA-UK. Georgians with commodities to export shipped their goods to Charles Town.

51. Chart II A, "Colonists Sent by Trustees, by Nationality, 1732–1752," in Ready, *The Castle Builders*, 22, 43, 51–55, 118. Of the 827 persons sent by the trustees whose occupations are known, only 97 had occupations related to husbandry. Coulter and Saye, *A List of the Early Settlers of Georgia*, ix–xiv.

52. Ready, *The Castle Builders*, 56–57.

53. For a comparison with South Carolina's early experience, Edelson, *Plantation Enterprise*, 53. Edelson describes how the English in South Carolina first viewed the wetlands as unproductive wastes compared to the higher land settlers first claimed. Ready, *The Castle Builders*, 36, 105–11.

54. Ready, *The Castle Builders*, 181.

55. Table 2: "Colonization by Private Sources," in Taylor, "Colonizing Georgia," 123. During the mid-1740s, 45 more adventurers arrived with 243 servants. His analysis works well until the late 1740s. Taylor estimates that between 1733 and 1752, the total number of colonists either sent "on the charity" or who came on their own was 5,604. The figure is too high. For the period 1750–52, Taylor multiplies acreage granted to private individuals by the number of servants they were required to bring according to the old formula. Few such individuals brought indentured servants, most were from Georgia and had little in the way of labor, and those from South Carolina were eager to bring slaves but did not move them until after 1752.

56. If the instability of the work force was legendary, there was another story to be told. Masters fed their servants poorly, housed and clothed them inadequately, and beat them fiercely on occasion. Byrne, "The Burden and the Heat of the Day," 16–36; B. Wood, *Slavery in Colonial Georgia*, 24–25, 94.

57. Table 1: "Public and Private Investment in Georgia, 1732–52," in Taylor, "Colonizing Georgia," 121.

58. W. Heath, "The Early Colonial Money System of Georgia," 145–60; M. Heath, *Constructive Liberalism*, 31–33; Ready, *The Castle Builders*, 310–16. For a typical letter accounting for sola bills and invoices, Harman Verelst to William Stephens, March 7, 1744/45, in *CRG*, 30:337–41. Nor did sola bills function as the only medium of exchange. The trustees continued to accept bills of exchange drawn by magistrates in Georgia as well as certified accounts originating in the public store, a prime reason for the continuing financial difficulties of the colony.

59. Reese, "Harman Verelst," 348–52; Ready, *The Castle Builders*, 310.

60. Minutes of the President and Assistants, June 18, 1746, in *CRG*, 6:156–57.

61. Fant, "Financing the Colonization of Georgia," 29; Taylor, "Colonizing Georgia," 121.

62. Based on information taken from *Proceedings and Debates of the British Parliaments respecting North America*, ed. Leo Francis Stock (Washington, D.C.: Carnegie Institution of Washington, 1924–1941), 4:270, 316, 657; 5:77, 118, 131, 178, 182. Paul Taylor estimated that military expenditures in Georgia between 1736 and 1749 were £314,366 sterling with another possible £99,706. Taylor, "Colonizing Georgia," 122. Payments made personally by James Oglethorpe for the maintenance of troops on St. Simons and for supporting militia, coastal vessels, and Indians were £66,109 sterling from 1738 to 1743. "An account of Oglethorpe's Expenses in America, 1738–1743," in James Oglethorpe Papers, Duke University Library, microfilm, University of Georgia Library. The general issued scrip known as "Oglethorpe's bills," which found ready acceptance given their backing by the War Office. Ready, *The Castle Builders*, 312. The figure for 1743–1747 in the table is based on a report made by Major William Horton, commander of the regiment, in 1746. "Estimate of the charge of one regiment in Georgia and three independent companies, one troop of rangers, one troop of Highland rangers, a marine company, and other extraordinary expenses," Lt. Col. Horton to the War Office, September 1746, in *CRG*, 36:136–38, 198–205, 219–20.

63. Qtd. in G. Jones, *Detailed Reports on the Salzburger Emigrants*, 11:75.

64. James Habersham to Benjamin Martyn, May 24, 1749, in *CRG*, 25:390–91; Harris & Habersham to Benjamin Martyn, July 8, 1749, in *CRG*, 25:397–402.

65. "We shall be glutted with a great quantity of goods and consequently loaded with great debts at a time when little money is circulating in the colony and no produce yet," Harris & Habersham to Benjamin Martyn, July 8, 1749, in *CRG*, 25:397–402 (quotation on 400). For further background, Harris & Habersham to Benjamin Martyn, February 13, 1749, in *CRG*, 25:354–61; Lambert, *James Habersham*, 71–74.

66. Reese, *The Clamorous Malcontents*, 279.

67. Letter from Mr. John Dobell, June 11, 1746, in *CRG*, 25:72; B. Wood, *Slavery in Colonial Georgia*, 74–87.

68. B. Wood and Gray, "The Transition from Indentured to Involuntary Servitude," 356, 364.

69. Simpson, "'She has her country marks very conspicuous in the face,'" 20–51. Local officials were quick to point the finger at one another about harboring Africans. Lt. Col. Heron wrote the trustees that it was "well known to every one in the Colony that Negroes have been in and about Savannah for these several years" and that "the Magistrates knew and winked at it." As a contender for power within Georgia, he had every reason to cast doubt on the integrity of the Savannah magistrates. Heron to Trustees, May 11, 1748, in *CRG*, 25:294–95. B. Wood, "James Edward Oglethorpe," 66–79.

70. Patrick Tailfer estimated "upwards of eighty bondsmen" in Augusta in 1740; it is reasonable to assume that there were at least one hundred by 1749 when the trade had expanded. Reese, *The Clamorous Malcontents*, 118.

71. Stewart, "Whether Wast, Deodand, or Stray," 11, 17, 26.

72. Entry of May 28, 1739, Journal of William Stephens, in *CRG* 4:343–46; Ready, *The Castle Builders*, 295.

73. For maroon colonies on the Savannah, Berlin, *Many Thousands Gone*, 67; G. Jones, *Detailed Reports on the Salzburger Emigrants*, 1:109–11. Bolzius noted small, isolated settlements of runaway slaves along the Georgia–South Carolina coastline in 1734. There is every reason to think such communities continued to survive.

74. For officers and Africans and African Americans, see Ready, *The Castle Builders*, 268; on the slaves held by Thomas Bosomworth, Benjamin Martyn to the President and Assistants, March 16, 1747, in *CRG*, 31:56. On behalf of the trustees, the secretary wanted to know why had Bosomworth not been punished for his violation of the ban on slaves and why had "his Negroes" not been seized.

75. In 1750, the governing magistrates judged the black population to include 349 working adults (202 men and 147 women). William Stephens and Assistants to Benjamin Martyn, July 19, 1750, in *CRG*, 26:22. It is assumed that there were 250–300 adults in the year before the ban on slavery was removed.

76. Berlin, *Many Thousands Gone*, 64–76.

77. Entry of March 21, 1738, Journal of William Stephens, in *CRG* 4:108; Harman Verelst to Thomas Causton, December 14, 1737, *CRG*, 29:248.

78. A slave named John Peter escaped from his master in South Carolina and fled to Savannah. He claimed he was a free man from Dutch Curacao, had been taken by a privateer on the Spanish Main, carried to Philadelphia, and sold to a Georgia merchant. That individual in turn sold him to the Carolina owner. Three Savannahians believed Peter's story, put up a surety payment, and gave him the time to secure a letter confirming his status as a free man. They took out a warrant against the man who had illegally sold him. Although the matter had several layers

of complexity, it is notable that a free man of color could secure such influential backing as late as 1746. John Dobell to the Trustees, May 17, 1746, *CRG*, 25:42–46.

79. Ready, *The Castle Builders*, 295; Byrne, "The Burden and the Heat of the Day," 47; Gallay, "Origins of Slaveholders' Paternalism," 377–79; James Habersham to Hugh Bryan at his plantation at Good Hope near Port Royal, November 30, 1739, Jones Family Papers, GHS; D. Morgan, " Consequences of George White-field's Ministry," 62–82.

80. President and Assistants to Benjamin Martyn, January 10, 1749, in *CRG*, 25:347–51.

81. The President, Assistants and Councilmen to Benjamin Martyn, January 10, 1749, in *CRG*, 25:347–52; the President and Assistants to the Trustees, October 26, 1749, in *CRG*, 25:430–37; B. Wood, *Slavery in Colonial Georgia*, 79–87. "I find that all from the highest to the lowest vote in favor of Negroes and look on me as a Stone in their way toward which they direct all their Spite," John Martin Bolzius to John Dobell, May 20, 1748, in *CRG*, 25:284.

82. Ready, *The Castle Builders*, 235.

Chapter 2. Merging Planting Elites

1. Minutes of the Common Council, March 19, April 11, 1750, in *CRG*, 2:500, 504. On August 8, 1750, the trustees approved a request to the Privy Council to repeal the act that had prohibited slavery in 1735. Neither the Board of Trade nor the Privy Council had time to consider the act before the trustees surrendered their charter in 1752. Coleman, *Colonial Georgia*, 103.

2. As a contemporary later recorded, Georgians remained "in a poor and languishing condition." Hewatt, *An Historical Account*, 2:148–49.

3. "Wylly Family," in *Garrett-Sharpe, Brown-Poindexter and Allied Lines*, 195–222. Wylly's uncle was Frances McCartan, a partner in the firm of McCartan and Campbell in Augusta.

4. Hawes, "Proceedings of the President and Assistants, Part 1," 329. A specially called assembly delivered to the magistrates a list of challenges for the port of Savannah.

5. Wylly encountered the tavern of the popular widow Mary Penrose, the residence of a minor official who imported rum on the side, the store of a sea captain, the shop of a tailor-turned-ship-chandler, and the inn of Abraham Minis, a Jewish trader who had supplied Oglethorpe's troops but was now struggling to make ends meet. Reflecting the modest nature of entrepreneurial endeavor in trusteeship Georgia, Bay Street provided an apt counterpoint to Wylly's ambitions. From the Colonial Conveyance Book, C-1, Georgia Archives.

6. Minutes of the President and Assistants, June 18, 1746, in *CRG*, 6:156–57; James Habersham to Benjamin Martyn, May 24, 1749, in *CRG*, 25:389.

7. Coleman, *Colonial Georgia*, 101–3.

8. The correspondence in *Original Papers, Correspondence, Trustees, General Oglethorpe, and Others, 1745–1750*, *CRG* 25, is the basis for this conclusion. See also Lambert, *James Habersham*, 83. Julie Anne Sweet comes to a gentler conclusion that old age was beginning to catch up. "Stephens was a faithful leader who worked hard, set a good example, and fulfilled his duty. . . . he simply could not keep up even though he wanted to." Sweet, *William Stephens*, 78–80.

9. Benjamin Martyn to James Habersham, July 18, 1750, in *CRG*, 31:200; Lambert, *James Habersham*, 80–81.

10. Benjamin Martyn to William Stephens, July 16, 1750, in *CRG*, 31:190.

11. On his advice, the trustees removed one member, dismissed a clerk, and accepted the resignation of President William Stephens in light of his "Infirmities and confused mind." Minutes of the President and Assistants, April 21, September 26, November 8, December 7, 1750, in *CRG*, 6:315–16, 332, 351, 361. John Martin Bolzius relayed to his Pietist superiors: "Various improvements have been made since Mr. Habersham joined the Council, and several ineffectual and tedious people have been dismissed from their public offices." Bolzius, May 5, 1750, qtd. in G. Jones, *Detailed Reports on the Salzburger Emigrants*, 14:58; Nicholas Rigby to Harman Verelst, July 26, 1750, in *CRG*, 26:40. On Noble Jones, see Coulter, *Wormsloe*.

12. Fraser, *Savannah in the Old South*, 39.

13. Hawes, "Proceedings of the President and Assistants, Part I," 327–28.

14. Minutes of the President and Assistants, January 22, 1751, in Hawes, "Proceedings of the President and Assistants, Part I," 328; President and Assistants to Martyn, February 28, 1751, in *CRG*, 26:172.

15. Parker, *Scottish Highlanders*, 94–98.

16. Cashin, "The Gentlemen of Augusta," 29–56.

17. Taylor, "Colonizing Georgia," 121–22. Based on information taken from Stock, *Proceedings and Debates of the British Parliaments respecting North America*, Taylor estimated that military expenditures in Georgia between 1736 and 1749 were £314,366 sterling with another possible £99,706.

18. Petition of Daniel Demetre, June 4, 1755, in *CRG*, 7:192.

19. Chestnutt, *South Carolina's Expansion*, 53. He based his numbers on the Minutes of the President and Assistants, January 1, 1750–October 30, 1754, in *CRG* 6. The first royal governor, John Reynolds, required all landholders to resubmit their titles. Records in volume 7 of the Colonial Records of Georgia permit verification of the petitions in the preceding volume.

20. The petitioners believed the shabby treatment of Mary Bosomworth by

"malevolent men guided by sinister motives" bespoke a hostile tone to their part of Georgia. As a witness to the deposition, Adam Bosomworth, Mary's brother-in-law, undoubtedly had a hand in its crafting, but the feelings expressed went well beyond his personal agenda. "Memorial and Representation of the state and condition of the southern parts of Georgia from some freeholders," April 18, 1752, in *CRG*, 27:47–52.

21. Jackson, *Lachlan McIntosh*, 1–19.

22. Petition of Hugh, William, and Angus Clark, in Minutes of the President and Assistants, April 4, 1750, in *CRG*, 6:313. Other Scots who received land for cattle farming included Roderick McIntosh, later a deerskin trader, in Minutes, March 3, 1750, in *CRG*, 6:310.

23. The Medway River is occasionally listed as the Midway River on maps and charts. The confusion comes from the nearby town of Midway and the larger community of Midway.

24. Minutes of the Board, June 8, August 20, October 12 and 29, November 3, 1748, in *CRG*, 6:215–27 (quotaton on 215).

25. Carr's first farm had been sacked by the Spanish while he was temporarily posted to Virginia. Letter of Captain Mark Carr, in Minutes of the Board, May 12, 1752, in *CRG*, 6:370. Carr named Sunbury after his ancestral home in Scotland. Groover, *Sweet Land of Liberty*, 8, 9.

26. Harden, "James Mackay of Strathy Hall," 77–98.

27. Colonial Conveyance Book c-1, 397, Georgia Archives; C. Jones, *Dead Towns*, 159–68.

28. Those officers included Raymond Demere, Philip Delegal, Kenneth Baillie, Patrick Sutherland, and William Gray.

29. Shy, *Toward Lexington*, 343–47.

30. For Habersham, Minutes of the Board, April 4, 1750, in *CRG*, 6:313; for Habersham's young son, Minutes, May 12, 1750, in *CRG*, 6:372, and May 12, 1752, in *CRG*, 27:87; for Francis Harris, Habersham's partner and member of the board, Minutes, August 29, 1750, in *CRG*, 6:330; for Harris's son, *CRG*, 6:372; for Jones, Minutes, September 28, 1750, in *CRG*, 6:340; for his son Inigo Jones, *CRG*, 27:80. Also receiving special treatment were Newdigate Stephens, the former president's son, and William Spencer, former clerk to the trustees' store and, briefly, a member of the board.

31. For Henry Parker's son, Minutes, June 9, 1750, in *CRG*, 6:322. Elsewhere, residents who had served the board well were duly rewarded, from the commander of the two scout boats on St. Simons to a clerk of the old trustee store to the keeper of the trustees' cowpen. Daniel Demetre, captain of scout boat, Minutes, May 4, 1750, in *CRG*, 6:318; Jacob Casper Walthour, clerk, trustee store, Minutes, September 27,

1750, in *CRG*, 6:334–35; another clerk of the store, William Russell, Minutes, April 4, 1750, in *CRG*, 6:314; keeper of trustees' cowpen, Minutes, August 29, 1750, in *CRG*, 6:330. Also included were the son of William Stephens, the former president, and William Spencer, a clerk of the store and later comptroller of the port. When two experts on silk cultivation arrived from London to exercise official positions, the board gave them choice tracts on the Savannah River and in one case bestowed another fifteen hundred acres on family members. Pickering Robinson became a member of the board of the president, and Joseph Ottolenghe was named a delegate to the Commons House of Assembly.

32. Petition for land of Peter Baillou, August 1755, in *CRG*, 6:171. Baillou had a wife, two children, and seven "Negroes." Adler, "A Biographical Sketch of John Morel," GHS; Coulter, *Journal of William Stephens, 1743–1745*, 119; Minutes of the President, April 23, 1742, in *CRG*, 6:30.

33. Minutes of the President, March 7, 1751, in Hawes, "Proceedings of the President and Assistants, Part I," 341.

34. Bolzius, March 14, 1751, qtd. in G. Jones, *Detailed Reports on the Salzburger Emigrants*, 15:226.

35. The fact that the governing board would not back a man with his long experience in farming speaks to the restrictive nature of its thinking. Minutes of the President, February 8, 1753, in *CRG*, 6:387.

36. "Rice Exported from Producing Areas: 1698 to 1789," Z 481–85, U.S. Census, *Historical Statistics*, 2:1168.

37. Chestnutt, *South Carolina's Expansion*, 53. He based his numbers on the Minutes of the President and Assistants, January 1, 1750–October 30, 1754, in *CRG*, 6. In addition to those to Georgians and Carolinians, the board made grants to thirty-one German Protestants, twelve West Indians, eight people from other colonies in British North America, and another seven from Scotland, Switzerland, and France.

38. Chestnutt, *South Carolina's Expansion*, 51.

39. De Vorsey, *De Brahm's Report*, 142. The "Spirit of Emigration out of South Carolina became so universal that year," he remembered, "that this and the following year near one thousand Negroes were brought in Georgia, where in 1751 were scarce above three dozen." In fact, it took two to three years for the applicants for land to bring their slaves. Petitions from Carolinians came slowly. According to the petitions listed in *CRG*, 6, only six Carolinians applied for grants in 1750, another four in 1751.

40. Edelson, *Plantation Enterprise*, 52, 74–76, 172–74.

41. Chestnutt, *South Carolina's Expansion*, 83–111; C. Jones, *History of Georgia*, 1:491–95; James Habersham to Benjamin Martyn, August 7, 1752, in *CRG*, 26:374.

The account of Charles C. Jones, written in the 1880s, is of particular interest. He and his family had grown up in the region and were intimately acquainted with the descendants of the first Congregationalists.

42. Gallay, *Formation of a Planter Elite*, 10–11; Sirmans, *Colonial South Carolina*, 80.

43. Chestnutt, *South Carolina's Expansion*, 84.

44. Myers, *Children of Pride*, 8–10.

45. Chestnutt, *South Carolina's Expansion*, 100.

46. Caldwell, "Women Landholders of Colonial Georgia," 190.

47. Myers, *Children of Pride*, 7–9; Sheftall, *Sunbury on the Medway*, 2–19; C. Jones, *Dead Towns*, 149–52.

48. Jackson, "The Carolina Connection," 147–72; Gallay, *Formation of a Planter Elite*, 14–71.

49. Ramsey, *The Yamasee War*, 15–33, 57–61; Oatis, *A Colonial Complex*, 277. Only after a raid on St. Augustine in 1728 did the threat cease and the southernmost part of the Carolina lowcountry become relatively safe for planters and others.

50. Petition for land of Jonathan Bryan, September 20, 1750, in *CRG* 6:333–34; Gallay, *Formation of a Planter Elite*, 1–29, 68, 84.

51. After acquiring Walnut Hill, Bryan began a series of investments in property on the Little and Great Ogeechee rivers and along both sides of the Savannah. He did not overlook the small "garden" and "farm" acreage held by lower middling residents of the town. Bryan was quick to sell property that did not fit with his long-term goal of securing plantations along the major transportation routes. Nevertheless, he was not averse to taking a risk that could yield speculative gains and continually placed bets on land around the Altamaha and Newport rivers, and eventually on Cumberland Island. Gallay, *Formation of a Planter Elite*, 86–87.

52. Jackson, "The Carolina Connection," 148–50; Gallay, *Formation of a Planter Elite*, 84.

53. For the Deveaux and Bull families, Rowland et al., *History of Beaufort County*, 1:132–34, 161–62; Edgar, *South Carolina*, 146; Chestnutt, *South Carolina's Expansion*, 136–40; Edgar and Bailey, *Biographical Directory*, 2:118–19. For Mullryne, Rowland et al., *History of Beaufort County*, 1:116–17, 178; Edgar and Bailey, *Biographical Directory*, 2:188–89. For the Gibbons brothers, Gibbons family folder, Walter Hartridge Collection, GHS; for the Butlers, Chestnutt, *South Carolina's Expansion*, 142–45; and for the Bourquins, Migliazzo, *To Make This Land Our Own*, 91; Bourquin family folder, Walter Hartridge Collection, GHS.

54. Chestnutt, *South Carolina's Expansion*, 151–57. Meriwether, *The Expansion of South Carolina*, 191–96; Edgar and Bailey, *Biographical Directory*, 2:441. James Edward Powell, a Charles Town planter-merchant in financial difficulty, fled his

creditors but found redemption by taking over prime land on the Savannah River from his father-in-law, Robert Williams, a former Malcontent. James Reid, who renamed himself Read, had begun his career as a sea captain in the West Indies, entered the slave trade in Charles Town thanks to "Liverpool contacts," and established a rope walk. Never successful but still solvent, he moved to Savannah where he used his connections in the transatlantic world to establish himself. Other merchants included Matthew Roche and John Francis Triboudet. James Maxwell, a planter and member of the Commons House, was probably the foremost trader among the Cherokees during the 1740s. When he went bankrupt, he left South Carolina "in a hurry selling out for the Colony of Georgia." Qtd in Chestnutt, *South Carolina's Expansion*, 114.

55. Petition of Lewis Johnston before the Board of the President and Assistants, January 11, 1753, in *CRG*, 6:382.

56. Johnston, *Recollections of a Georgia Loyalist*, 5–21.

57. Greene, "Colonial South Carolina and the Caribbean Connection," 78–79; Watts, *The West Indies*, 336–37.

58. "Read a Petition of Lewis Johnson [*sic*] . . . in Behalf of Stephen Adye, Anthony Fahie and Edmund Tannatt all of the island of St. Christophers," January 11, 1753, in *CRG*, 6:382; petitions of Clement Martin and John Hamm, August 6, 1754, in *CRG*, 6:443; H. Davis, *The Fledgling Province*, 162.

59. Robert Baillie to George Baillie, father, February 10, 1754, Baillie Family Papers, NAS.

60. Joseph Ottolenghe to Rev. Mr. Waring, Society for the Propagation [of the Gospel] in Foreign Parts, November 19, 1758, qtd. in B. Wood, *Slavery in Colonial Georgia*, 162.

61. Edelson, *Plantation Enterprise*, 129–35.

62. The families included those of Jonathan Bryan, James Deveaux, John Deveaux, William Gibbons, Joseph Gibbons, Henry Bourquin, Benedict Bourquin, James Read, James Maxwell, James Edward Powell, William Butler Sr., Thomas Butler, William Butler Jr., Elisha Butler, James Butler, and William Elliott.

63. Gallay, *Formation of a Planter Elite*, 66.

64. Of sixty-four Carolinians who migrated to Georgia between 1751 and 1754 and whose petitions for land contained the number of their enslaved people, forty-two brought an average of seven blacks. Petitions for land found in *CRG*, 6.

65. Minutes of the meeting of the President and Assistants in council, October 30, 1754, in *CRG*, 7:9.

66. Lannen, "Liberty and Authority," 212–16; Abbott, *The Royal Governors of Georgia*, 39–56; Coleman, *Colonial Georgia*, 181–84. Edmund Gray, a Quaker who had attempted to establish a settlement near Augusta but had been denied land

by the council, rallied dissidents from every quarter of the colony, including Edward Barnard of Augusta, Captain Mark Carr of Newport River, John Barnard of Wilmington Island, John Farmur and John Harn of the Ogeechee River, Charles Watson and Samuel Mercer of Savannah, and John Mohr McIntosh of Darien. Few Carolinians were prominent in this battle, which shaped the political landscape of Georgia for the rest of the royal period. The *Colonial Records of the State of Georgia* (vols. 7, 13, and 27) remain the best source for understanding the politics of the era.

67. John Reynolds to the Board of Trade, March 29, 1756, in *CRG*, 27:113.

68. Lannen, "Liberty and Authority," 219–21; Abbott, *The Royal Governors of Georgia*, 38–43, 46–53.

69. Samuel Mercer qtd. in Report on the Committee to inquire into the State of the Province, January 24, February 1, 1757, in *CRG*, 13:127–30 (quotation on 128), 147–51; Lannen, "Liberty and Authority," 231–33; Cashin, *Lachlan McGillivray*, 140–43. In the report, Mercer charged that one-fourth of the population along the Savannah River elected three-fourths of the representatives.

70. Lambert, *James Habersham*, 92.

71. Cashin, *Governor Henry Ellis*, 59–72.

72. Gallay, *Formation of a Planter Elite*, 71. As Alan Gallay has pointedly written, the outcome of the Reynolds affair was the most decisive moment in the political history of the colony, paving the way for the council and the next two governors to consolidate power and prevent the emergence of domestic opposition until 1765.

73. Mercantini, *Who Shall Rule at Home?*, 87; Greene, *Quest for Power*, 5.

74. Chestnutt, *South Carolina's Expansion*, 124.

75. From the information contained in land petitions, white Georgians resident before 1750 were masters of at least one-quarter of the black population. James Habersham listed thirty-three bondsmen; Sir Patrick Houstoun, twenty-five; Francis Harris, thirty; Captain Mark Carr, eighteen; Captain Daniel Demetre, twenty-three; and Peter Baillou, a representative shopkeeper, seven. Deerskin merchants and traders in Augusta controlled a significant percentage of the total slaves: Lachlan McGillivray with fifty; John Fitch with forty-seven; John Rae with thirty-six; George Galphin with forty; and John Spencer with thirty.

76. Henry Ellis to the Board of Trade, March 11, 1757, in *CRG*, 28, pt. 1:11. In 1755, there were 52 vessels versus 48 in 1760; 2,299 barrels of rice versus 3,603; 387,849 feet of "timber of all kinds" versus 273,066; 49,995 pounds of deerskin versus 65,765. Report of the Comptroller of the Port of Savannah, 1773, in Romans, *A Concise Natural History*, 146.

77. James Wright to the Board of Trade, January 15, 1762, in *CRG*, 28, pt. 2:186. The population figures were as of April 15, 1761.

78. James Habersham to John Martin Bolzius, September 25, 1747, Peter Force Papers, LC.

Chapter 3. The West Indies, Cornerstone of Trade

1. Hornsby, *British Atlantic, American Frontier*, 43, 54; Sheridan, *Sugar and Slavery*, 314–16; Shepherd, "Commodity Exports," 37–48; Burnard, "'Prodigious Riches,'" 506–24.

2. "Reasons for Establishing the Colony of Georgia, with regard to the Trade of Great Britain, etc., . . . 1733," in *CGHS*, 1:203–38; Reese, *The Most Delightful Country of the Universe*; Ready, *The Castle Builders*, 172–77.

3. James Habersham to John Martin Bolzius, September 25, 1747, Peter Force Papers, ser. 7E, LC.

4. Herndon, "Timber Products," 56–62; Plummer, "18th Century Forests," 1–19; Coclanis, *Shadow of a Dream*, 36; Earley, *Looking for Longleaf*, 7–16.

5. Earley, *Looking for Longleaf*, 7–16; Hickman, *Mississippi Harvest*, 1–10.

6. Romans, *A Concise Natural History*, 146.

7. For the period 1768–72, statistics are derived from Customs 16/1 (1768–72) and the American Inspector-General's Report; and for 1765 and 1766, from the Naval Shipping Lists, CO/710. For Carolina's shipping, Clowse, *Measuring Charleston's Overseas Commerce*.

8. For shipping to the West Indies in 1772, "An Account of the number of vessels which have entered outwards at the several ports in North America," Customs 16/1, NA-UK. Tonnage in the West Indian trade accounted for 50.1 percent in 1768 and 60.2 percent in 1770. For the tonnage in 1770, Macpherson, *Annals of Commerce*, 3:570.

9. James Habersham to William Knox, April 15, 1765, in *CGHS*, 6:30–33.

10. Romans, *A Concise Natural History*, 196.

11. De Vorsey, *De Brahm's Report*, 165.

12. For example, see the petitions of Thomas Morgan, July 1764; Burgon Bond, July 1764; Edward Barnard, December 1764; William Coulson, August 1766; and William Williams, August 1766, in *CRG*, 9:191, 192, 255, 581, 584.

13. Romans, *A Concise Natural History*, 196.

14. Carman, *American Husbandry*, 275.

15. Petitions of Thomas Peacock, August 1764, January 1766, in *CRG*, 9:195, 465; petition of Josiah Tattnell, February 7, 1764, in *CRG*, 9:118.

16. Joseph Clay to John Wertch (Johann Caspar Wertsch), March 16 and 26, November 14, 1773, Letter Book of Joseph Clay and Company, December 19, 1772–March 31, 1774, vol. 1; G. Jones, *The Georgia Dutch*: on Wertsch, 164; on slavery, 270–74.

17. Parker, *Scottish Highlanders*, 56–57, 94–99.

18. Petition of Andrew Griner, August 1764, in *CRG*, 9:199.

19. Marsh, *Georgia's Frontier Women*, 113.

20. Bartram, *The Travels of William Bartram*, 197–98.

21. Stewart, *"What Nature Suffers to Groe,"* 193–216. Stewart focuses on the cutting of the longleaf forests in the Altamaha basin by timber capitalists in the late nineteenth century, but the lessons are suggestive for the earlier period.

22. Order concerning lands to be granted on purchase, in Minutes of the Governor's Council, November 6, 1764, in *CRG*, 9:238–39.

23. Minutes of the Board of the President and Assistants, February 8, 1754, in *CRG*, 6:429; Chestnutt, *South Carolina's Expansion*, 152; Granger, *Savannah River Plantations*, 182, 183, 186.

24. Edelson, "Clearing Swamps, Harvesting Forests," 381–406.

25. Shepherd, "Commodity Exports," Table 4, 37–48.

26. Pendleton, "Short Account," 74; Sheffield, *Observations on the Commerce of the American States*, 68.

27. Johnston & Wylly, Petition of July 1, 1766, in *CRG*, 9:542; Petition of Roger Kelsall and Simon Munro, August 5, 1766, in *CRG*, 9:587.

28. Only one northerner sensed the excitement and moved to this new commercial frontier to exploit timber resources. A merchant, Thomas Eatton came from New York with two nephews, bought land in St. John Parish, and built a wharf in Savannah to ship lumber to the West Indies. Gordon, "Georgia's Debt," 119–34.

29. Herndon, "Timber Products," 58–59; Somerville, Noble and White to Edward Telfair, August 21, 1774, Telfair Papers, Duke University, 519.

30. Joseph Clay to John and William Coppell, April 1, 1784, Letter Book of Joseph Clay and Company, October 25, 1783–September 1, 1784, GHS. The six months from October through March were the ideal months for the lumber industry, although spring floods could make rafting a dicey proposition.

31. Joseph Clay to John Wertch (Johann Caspar Wertsch), March 16 and 26, November 14, 1773, Letter Book of Joseph Clay and Company, December 19, 1772–March 31, 1774, Joseph Clay Papers, GHS; Jones, *The Georgia Dutch*, 164.

32. Sollors, *Interesting Narrative*, 73–77; Sheridan, *Sugar and Slavery*, 172–83.

33. Testimony of "Colonel" John Graham, March 23, 1784, Granville Papers, 30/29/3/10, NA-UK.

34. Naval Shipping Lists, second quarter 1767, CO 5/710.

35. Naval Shipping Lists, 1765–67, CO 5/710.

36. Steele, *The English Atlantic*, 54–55.

37. Samuel Stiles (ca. 1737–1808), Stiles Family Papers, 1825–1919, GHS; Cowper & Telfair to Cap. Sam. Stiles, April 22, 1774, Telfair Family Papers, GHS; Harwell, "William Henry Stiles," 1–7; Ryan and Golson, *Andrew Low*, 14.

38. Rowland et al., *History of Beaufort County*, 139–57.

39. Braddock, *Wooden Ships–Iron Men*, 106–16. The book is a compilation of accounts found in newspapers, the records of colonial governments, and other archival materials.

40. Ibid., 89–90, 141–47, 181–96, 202–13.

41. For example, see the clearance outward of the schooner *Ogeechee*, May 2, 1766, CO 5/710; Petitions for land by William Butler, June 1757, in *CRG*, 7:579. Elizabeth Butler's partner was James Read, also a former Carolinian.

42. "Report of Sir James Wright on the Condition of the Province of Georgia, on 20th Sept. 1773," in *CGHS*, 3:175.

43. Georgia exported livestock valued at £2,873 versus £1,477 for South Carolina on average for the period 1768–72. Shepherd, "Commodity Exports," 46. The earnings from the two thousand barrels of rice sent in an average year was less than the revenue from lumber and was a pittance compared to the earnings from South Carolina's impressive shipments after the end of the Seven Years' War. Savannah's merchants made a conscious choice about giving Britain preference in shipping.

44. *Georgia Gazette*, September 27, October 4, 1764. Georgian planters bred horses known as Chickasaws, after the native breed, and willingly paid stud fees.

45. Shepherd, "Commodity Exports," 46. The number of horses and cattle comes from Shepherd; the figures of the comptroller of the port of Savannah, William Brown, were slightly higher. Romans, *A Concise Natural History*, 146.

46. Stewart, "Whether Wast, Deodand, or Stray," 18–21.

47. Georgia sent on average four hundred forty barrels of beef each year to the West Indies; advertisement by John Morel, Ossabaw Island plantation, *Georgia Gazette*, January 3, 1770.

48. The colony's shipments of beef and pork were about two-thirds of South Carolina's, yet both colonies sent small amounts compared to the long-established suppliers of Virginia, Connecticut, Pennsylvania, and New York. Shepherd, "Commodity Exports," 40–46.

49. Fabel, "British Rule in the Floridas," 134–42; for a detailed view of the colony, see Fabel, *Economy of British West Florida*.

50. Communication of Governor Wright to the governor's council on a talk given by Emisteseegoe, in Minutes, September 5, 1768, in *CRG*, 10:574; Romans, *A Concise Natural History*, 144.

51. John Graham to James Grant, governor of East Florida, January 27, February 10, April 21, May 28, 1767, James Grant Papers, Ballindalloch Muniments, NAS. In the process of discussing the purchase of the stock with Governor Grant, Graham gave a detailed view of the relative merits of cattle raising on the coast and in the backcountry.

52. A. Thompson and William Brown to Governor Wright, October 18, 1773, in *CRG* 38, pt. 1:153. The customs officers, new to Savannah, realized that substantial amounts of rum were being smuggled but had little idea of the actual amount. Their report was intended to convince a skeptical governor.

53. A. Thompson and William Brown to Gov. Wright, October 18, 1773, in *CRG*, 38, pt. 1:153; Tables 8-1 and 8-2 in McCusker, *Rum and the American Revolution*, 2:472, 474.

54. Thompson and Brown, October 18, 1773, in *CRG*, 38, pt. 1:153.

55. James Wright to the Commissioners of Customs, January 14, 1764, in *CRG*, 28, pt. 2:11. Wright defended Spencer for admitting a vessel before the master produced a legal register: "He is an old Man, has a large Family & little or nothing to Subsist on but his Office, has always behaved very well & I believe him to be perfectly honest."

56. McCusker, *Rum and the American Revolution*, 472, 474. John McCusker estimated that 99,000 gallons of rum were carried into Georgia each year in the period 1768–72. Of that number, 65,000 gallons came from the West Indies and 34,000 from the northern colonies. For the period 1769–71, the customs officers reported that 42,226 gallons of rum had been imported from the West Indies and 31,715 from North America for a total of 73,941. The difference between these two totals is 25,059 gallons. The customs officers produced a reasonably accurate picture of the rum coming from North America: 31,000 gallons versus an actual importation of 34,000. That would suggest approximately 21,000 gallons of rum were smuggled into the colony from the Caribbean during this period.

57. Thompson and Brown to Gov. Wright, October 18, 1773, in *CRG*, 38, pt. 1:153.

58. McCusker, *Rum and the American Revolution*, 468–69, 476–77.

59. Ibid., 478.

60. B. Wood, *Women's Work, Men's Work*, 75.

61. McCusker, *Rum and the American Revolution*, 477. McCusker's estimate of the amount of rum consumed by the enslaved population is less well grounded than his estimate for the white population.

62. Mancall, *Deadly Medicine*, 64–77.

63. Adair, *History of the American Indians*, 6.

64. De Vorsey, *De Brahm's Report*, 108.

65. Thompson and Brown, October 18, 1773, in *CRG*, 38, pt. 1:153.

66. John Stuart to Germaine, October 26, 1776, CO 5/72, f. 89, qtd. in Braund, *Deerskins & Duffels*, 105.

67. O'Malley, "Beyond the Middle Passage."

68. Sollors, *Interesting Narrative*, 73–122. In his book, Equiano describes his voyages in the Caribbean and the Lower South for merchant Robert King. On page

86, he recounts how he went "all about the islands upwards of four years, and ever trading as I went."

69. Arrival of the *Prudence*, Captain Farmer, sloop, thirty-two tons, five crew, from Montserrat with seventy slaves, February 11, 1765; arrival of the *Nancy*, Captain Farmer, sloop, sixty tons, six crew, from Guadelupe with five slaves, August 18, 1766, Naval Shipping Lists, CO 5/710.

70. Entries for 1765–67, Naval Shipping Lists, CO 5/710.

71. O'Malley, "Beyond the Middle Passage,"151.

72. Carretta, *Equiano the African*, xvi, 319–20. Carretta's biography amply confirms the accuracy of the details of Equiano's life contained in the autobiography. Nevertheless, the author suggests that Equiano's African identity may have been a rhetorical invention. A baptismal certificate in South Carolina indicates he was born there, as do English naval records for his service for a particular voyage. Equiano's accounts of his enslavement and the Middle Passage may have represented collective memory rather than an individual experience.

73. The information contained in the Naval Shipping Lists and the Colonial Records of Georgia track amazingly well with Equiano's story. The dates are roughly correct as are the types of cargo. For the quotation, Sollors, *Interesting Narrative*, 90; for the numbers of livestock, 109, and Naval Shipping Lists, October 9, 1766, CO 5/710.

74. Sollors, *Interesting Narrative*, 95–96.

75. Hamilton, *Scotland, the Caribbean, and the Atlantic World*, 112–39. Dr. David Byrdie, a physician, borrowed £280 from Basil Cowper and William and Edward Telfair, pledging ten male slaves and six women as security, October 3, 1771, Colonial Bond Book, W 1770–85, Georgia Archives, 61.

76. Sollors, *Interesting Narrative*, 121–22.

Chapter 4. Savannah as a "Caribbean" Town

1. The arrival of the sloop *Prudence*, captained by Thomas Farmer, thirty-two tons, five-man crew, February 11, 1765, together with vessels arriving between January 5 and April 5, 1765, Naval Shipping Lists, CO 5/710.

2. Mereness, *Travels in the American Colonies*, 396.

3. Sellers, *Charleston Business*, 129–30, 217. Although South Carolina and Georgia enjoyed the same export boom based on rice and indigo, Carolina experienced momentary dips after it prohibited slave imports between 1766 and 1769 and with its participation in the non-importation movement as the Revolution approached.

4. Romans, *A Concise Natural History*, 146.

5. De Vorsey, *De Brahm's Report*, 163–65.

6. James Habersham to Henry Ellis, January 27, 1772, in *CGHS*, 6:162. Wilkins, "A View of Savannah," 577–84.

7. Reps, "$C^2 + L^2 = S^2$?"

8. Although Oglethorpe had a hand in planning the design for Savannah, scholars point to Benjamin Martyn, secretary to the Georgia Trust, as the primary author. Reps, "$C^2 + L^2 = S^2$?," 117; Lane, *Savannah Revisited*, 35.

9. Lane, *Savannah Revisited*, 34–48; Fraser, *Savannah in the Old South*, 11; Coleman, *Colonial Georgia*, 27–29; Kornwolf, *Architecture and Town Planning*, 2:928–30.

10. Coclanis, "Sociology of Architecture," 607–23.

11. In the same year, Charles Town had 5,030 whites, 5,833 black slaves, and 24 free blacks; in 1774, Kingston possessed 5,000 whites, 5,000 slaves, and 1,200 "coloureds," including free blacks. The Reverend Samuel Frink to the Society for the Propagation of the Gospel in Foreign Parts, July 8, 1771, London Manuscripts, pkg. 7, pt. 3, ser. C, reel 16, microfilm, UGA Library; P. Morgan, "Black Life in Eighteenth-Century Charleston," 188; C. Clarke, *Kingston, Jamaica*, 13. Morgan estimates a total of 10,887 people in Charles Town in 1770. Peter Coclanis gives a figure of 11,500. Coclanis, *Shadow of a Dream*, 114.

12. For a discussion of towns in the Chesapeake, Kulikoff, *Tobacco and Slaves*, 123–25.

13. Mowat, *East Florida as a British Province*, 64.

14. Robert Raper to James Crockett, January 15, 1760, Robert Raper Letter (photocopy of original in West Sussex Record Office), South Carolina Historical Society, qtd. in Edelson, *Plantation Enterprise*, 137. See also Rowland et al., *History of Beaufort County*, 1:175–94.

15. P. Morgan, "Black Life in Eighteenth-Century Charleston,"188; Coclanis, *Shadow of a Dream*, 74, 76, 113–15; McCusker and Menard, *The Economy of British America*, 185–86; A. Jones, *Wealth of a Nation to Be*, 357. Based on probate records, the average wealth-holder in the Charles Town District was worth £2,337 in 1774, which far exceeded the worth of those in New England and the middle colonies and was well above those in the Chesapeake Bay.

16. Edelson, *Plantation Enterprise*, 126–36; Coclanis, *Shadow of a Dream*, 6–8, 112–13; P. Morgan, "Black Life in Eighteenth-Century Charleston," 188. Russell Menard puts the number of whites in the Carolina lowcountry at 21,500 in 1775. Menard, "Economic and Social Development of the South," 250. In Georgia, at least 1,500 whites lived in Savannah and Sunbury on the Medway River, or approximately 30 percent of the total in the lowcountry. Founded in the late 1750s, Sunbury played a significant role in handling shipping compared to Beaufort or Georgetown but overall its functions remained secondary. In the Carolina lowcountry, there were 19,066 whites, with approximately 6,000 in Charles Town, Georgetown, and Beaufort, or 31 percent.

17. Nash, "Domestic Material Culture and Consumer Demand," 248–50.

18. Watts, *The West Indies*, 378–81; Goveia, *Slave Society*, 240–41; C. Clarke, *Kingston, Jamaica*, 15–16.

19. C. Clarke, *Kingston, Jamaica*, 16–18.

20. Nash, "Urbanization in the Colonial South," 12–14.

21. The Reverend Samuel Frink to the Society for the Propagation of the Gospel in Foreign Parts, July 8, 1771, London Manuscripts, pkg. 7, pt. 3, ser. C, reel 16, microfilm, UGA Library. Savannah's black population included runaways hiding in town, messengers, boatmen, and others from the countryside who formed a transient population.

22. B. Wood, *Women's Work, Men's Work*, 80–86, 101–10; Fraser, *Savannah in the Old South*, 77–80.

23. Based on information supplied by the Reverend Samuel Frink, Anglicans held 2.9 slaves per family; Presbyterians, 1.9; Lutherans, 1.7; and Jewish families, 3.2. Frink to the Society for the Propagation of the Gospel in Foreign Parts, July 8, 1771, London Manuscripts, pkg. 7, pt. 3, ser. C, reel 16, microfilm, UGA Library.

24. P. Morgan, "Black Life in Eighteenth-Century Charleston," 187–232.

25. Berlin and Harris, *Slavery in New York*, 63.

26. C. Clarke, *Kingston, Jamaica*, 13; Goveia, *Slave Society*, 203–4.

27. Henry Ellis to the Board of Trade, January 28, 1759, in *CRG* 28, pt. 1:178. Ellis judged the practice impossible to prevent "in a Country where there are so many inlets, so few Officers, & where every one may export his goods from his own landing place unobserved."

28. In 1760, Savannah handled 37 vessels and Charles Town, 248. "An Aggregate and Valuation of Exports of Produce from the Province of Georgia," in Romans, *A Concise Natural History*, 146. For Charles Town, Clowse, *Measuring Charleston's Overseas Commerce*, 102, 104.

29. "An Account of the Number of Vessels which have cleared outwards at the several ports of North America, 1772," American Inspector-General's Ledger, 1768–72, Customs 16/1, NA-UK.

30. De Vorsey, *De Brahm's Report*, 159; Granger, *Savannah Harbor*, 1–3; "Report of Sir James Wright on the Condition of the Province of Georgia, on September 20th, 1773," in *CGHS*, 3:163–64.

31. James Habersham to Benjamin Martyn, January 24, 1751, in *CRG* 26:137.

32. On Thomas Eatton, Gordon, "Georgia's Debt," 119–34; on William De Brahm's role in constructing the wharves, De Vorsey, *De Brahm's Report*, 158–59. De Brahm had the lumber merchant drive two rows of piles into the river, secure their tops with metal plates, and hammer planks onto the piles with treenails, bits of compressed wood that expanded with moisture. To complete the wharf, the two ends

were blocked with piles connected by metal plates and walls of stone, and the enclosed space was filled with sand.

33. Ownership of wharves was reconstructed from Hemperley, *English Crown Grants*, and Colonial Conveyance Books S, T, U, V, XX, microfilm, GHS. On the west side, there were two mariners involved in the Caribbean trade, a West Indian merchant, a merchant from New York, several Scots merchants, and the Sheftall brothers, veterans of trustee Georgia struggling to break out of the world of petty retailing and finding sweet success in the West Indies.

34. Calculated from information in the American Inspector-General's Ledger, 1768–72, Customs 16/1, NA-UK. For South Carolina, Clowse, *Measuring Charleston's Overseas Commerce*, 105.

35. James Wright to the Board of Trade, February 15, 1762, in *CRG*, 28, pt. 2:183.

36. "An Account of the Number of Vessels, 1772," American Inspector-General's Ledger, 1768–72, Customs 16/1, NA-UK.

37. "Report of Sir James Wright on the Condition of the Province of Georgia, on September 20th, 1773," in *CGHS* 3:165.

38. "An Account of the Number of Vessels, 1772," American Inspector-General's Ledger, 1768–72, Customs 16/1, NA-UK. While Georgia had six fewer vessels returning to the northern colonies than arriving, the latter had twenty-three more. Vessels coming from the northern colonies to the West Indies elected to stop at Charles Town to pick up a return cargo to round out the voyage. Savannah did not figure in that traffic. Less surprising is the fact that Georgia was poorly represented in the slave trade from Africa in that one year, although the two subsequent years saw vigorous activity. No ship came to Savannah or Sunbury from West Africa in that twelve-month period while twenty-four called on their neighbor.

39. *Georgia Gazette*, December 6 and 27, 1764, and January 17, 1765.

40. *Georgia Gazette*, April 14, 1763; Fraser, *Savannah in the Old South*, 63. Other merchants built similar structures. Memorial of Samuel Hunt Jenkins, June 9, 1789, AO 13/35, 438. In reciting his losses to the British government after the Revolution, Samuel Hunt Jenkins claimed a four-story building measuring fifty feet by thirty feet; a small, detached store; a kitchen; and a scale house for weighing goods, the total costing £1,800.

41. Rediker, *Between the Devil and the Deep Blue Sea*, 11.

42. Of the 2,000 people in Savannah in 1771, it is estimated that 25 percent were male adults. The number of blacks and whites involved in maritime activities is assumed to be at least 25 percent of the total population, in line with the percentage for other ports. When boatmen from nearby plantations are added, the number rises.

43. It is assumed that 33 percent of the sailors from vessels sailing from the West Indies were black, that 50 percent of the sailors involved in the Charles Town–

Savannah traffic were black, and that 5 percent of the sailors on ships from Great Britain and from the north were black. For the estimate for the Caribbean, see Bolster, *Black Jacks*, 17–19; Rupert, *Creolization and Contraband*, 141–42; Sollors, *Interesting Narrative*, 85. Captain Samuel Stiles of the Bahamas and Savannah sailed to and from the West Indies with a crew of three blacks and three whites (Sale of the sloop *Sally*, Captain Samuel Stiles, recorded April 28, 1768, Colonial Bond Book R, Georgia Archives). Captain Adam Croddy had a crew of four blacks on his schooner (Estate of Adam Croddy, July 4, 1768, loose papers, Register of Records, drawer 230, box 20, Colonial Inventory Book F, Georgia Archives). For the Charles Town trade, the Reverend Henry Muhlenberg describes coming to Savannah in a schooner with an all-black crew and an Englishman as the captain (Doberstein, *Journals*, 2:594). In his seminal work comparing black culture in the Chesapeake and the lowcountry, Philip Morgan remarks that "all-slave crews increasingly manned South Carolina's river and coastal boats." The shipping traffic from Charles Town to Savannah reflected the high percentage. However, Morgan goes on to argue that maritime slavery was never extensive, "for most slave owners feared the loss of control that seafaring inevitably involved." Morgan, *Slave Counterpoint*, 236–40. In Savannah, sea captains owned most if not all of their black sailors. Given Savannah's more regional pattern of shipping, its waterfront contained a higher percentage of black sailors than Charles Town's.

44. Sollors, *Interesting Narrative*, 85.

45. Welch, *Slave Society in the City*, 85.

46. Bolster, *Black Jacks*, 18.

47. Rupert, *Creolization and Contraband*, 141–42.

48. Bolster, *Black Jacks*, 18.

49. P. Morgan, "Black Society in the Lowcountry," 101, and *Slave Counterpoint*, 239.

50. Bolster, *Black Jacks*, 21–26.

51. Kelly, *Voyage to Jamaica* (1838), qtd. in Welch, *Slave Society in the City*, 5.

52. Bolster, *Black Jacks*, 21.

53. Sollors, *Interesting Narrative*, 102. The *Narrative* mentions his listening to Whitefield preach in Philadelphia, but the dates put the occasion in Savannah.

54. *Georgia Gazette*, July 20, 1768.

55. *Georgia Gazette*, March 9, 1774.

56. *Georgia Gazette*, July 13, 1774.

57. *Georgia Gazette*, July 2, 1766.

58. Sollors, *Interesting Narrative*, 106–9. For details of James Read's career, Chestnutt, *South Carolina's Expansion*, 157–58; Edgar, *Letterbook of Robert Pringle*, 1:xviii, 162; appointment to the governor's council, February 5, 1765, in *CRG* 9:302.

59. In the 1750s, the settlement in Yamacraw took place around a small community called Watson's Free Town, after the store and houses owned by Joseph Watson, an Indian trader confined at one point for his mental instability after a run-in with Mary Musgrove. Petition for land of Joseph Gibbons, October 3, 1758, and petition of William Francis, October 3, 1758, *CRG* 7:815–16, 823. In 1760, the governor put up for sale land on Yamacraw Bluff, where Tomochichi had greeted the first settlers, to raise cash to purchase enslaved people for building fortifications around the town. The first lots on the riverfront went to two deerskin merchants, Daniel Nunes and John Gordon; Grey Elliott, a lawyer and land speculator; and a country factor, Thomas Lloyd, Minutes of the Governor's Council, April 24, 1760, in *CRG*, 8:290–91.

60. Sollors, *Interesting Narrative*, 106–9; Carretta, "I began to feel the happiness of liberty," 92–94.

61. This view is based on an analysis of the Colonial Conveyance Records for the period 1760–75, which is supplemented by information in the *Georgia Gazette* and randomly scattered in secondary works. In its early days, Yamacraw had many sides to its character. Middling families connected with the maritime trade lived there. The lawyer John Glen owned a house that he rented to another lawyer, John Wereat, a major figure during the Revolution. The memorial of John Glen, late of the province of Georgia, 1784, AO 13/35:136. The collector of customs, Alexander Thompson, lived there as well.

62. *Georgia Gazette*, August 10, 1768. Shipwright Robert Watts petitioned for a place for his shipyard in *CRG*, 14:444; George Ancrum, a Charles Town merchant, sold to Joseph Clay two hundred feet on the river, November 11, 1772, Conveyance Book x2, 704, Georgia Archives.

63. *Georgia Gazette*, August 20, 1766.

64. A cleric who took passage on the *Georgia Packet* back to England reported that the crew was shorthanded: "Some had deserted her at Savannah, others had died there, and it was with difficulty any fresh ones could be engaged in the service, owing to the rumour of a Spanish war having broken out." Jay, *Memoirs of the Life and Character of the Late Rev. Cornelius Winter*, 91.

65. Johnston, *Recollections of a Georgia Loyalist*, 40–41.

66. Goveia, *Slave Society*, 230–31; Welch, *Slave Society in the City*, 84.

67. *Georgia Gazette*, July 21, 1763.

68. *Georgia Gazette*, November 16, 1774, October 25, 1775.

69. "An Act to punish seamen or mariners, neglecting or deserting their duty, on board their respective ships or vessels, and for preventing seamen and mariners from being harbored or running in debt," March 6, 1766, in *CRG*, 18:780–85. Tavernkeepers who hid a seaman under contract were to pay a steep fine as were

innkeepers who served a sailor wine, punch, beer, or "any spirituous liquor" above a minimum amount once the contract was signed. Captains were to cover the cost of any imprisonment, a stipulation that all but assured the ineffectiveness of the measure.

70. J. Bartram, "Diary of a Journey," 31.

71. John Ettwein, Notes on a visit to inspect the Moravian lots in Savannah, April 4–5, 1762 (photographic copy of the original in the Moravian Provincial Archives, Bethlehem, Pa.), GHS; De Vorsey, *De Brahm's Report*, 152–53.

72. The drawing of houses on Bay Street was made by Edward White, Customs House officer, in 1786. Kornwolf, *Architecture and Town Planning*, 2:927, 930–31.

73. Mention of piazzas is found in J. Bartram, "Diary of a Journey," 30; a detailed description of the house of the merchant John Graham is in *Georgia Gazette*, December 27, 1763; see also Coclanis, "Sociology of Architecture," 607–23. John Martin Bolzius noted, "In Savannah, one builds with wood and boards, and panels the rooms on the inside, or what is more common, one finishes them with quick-lime. In this way they are very durable and clean, when painted on the outside with oil paint." Loewald et al., "Johann Martin Bolzius," 247. One exception to the rule was John Hume, the attorney general, who constructed an elegant two-story house on Broughton, with brickwork nine feet from the ground, a stable, a kitchen, and a carriage house. Memorial of Hume to the Commissioners for Claims, January 25, 1783, 328, AO 13/35.

74. O'Shaughnessy, *An Empire Divided*, 59–60. In 1773, the total value of exports from the British West Indies to Great Britain reached £2.7 million.

75. Calculated from Table 6.6 in Menard, "Economic and Social Development of the South," 285.

76. Higman, "Jamaican Port Towns," 119. The profile presents a striking contrast with Boston, Philadelphia, and New York, where industrial activities in the form of shipbuilding and the processing of flour, fur, and fish were considerably more developed.

77. Price, "Economic Function and the Growth of American Port Towns," 123–86.

78. Nash, "Urbanization in the Colonial South," 18–21.

79. Price, "Economic Function and the Growth of American Port Towns," 161–63.

80. Fraser, *Charleston! Charleston!*, 129–31; Rogers, *Charleston*, 69–72.

81. Hart, *Building Charleston*, 93.

82. Colonial Conveyance Books, Georgia Archives. Among the buyers of property in Savannah between 1755 and 1772, few names appear of planters residing south of the Little Ogeechee River.

83. Colonial Conveyance Books, Georgia Archives. Based on purchases of property in Savannah between 1755 and 1775, merchants accounted for 30.9 percent in the front half of the town and 13.5 percent in the back half. The figures are compiled from the calculations for Table 8.

84. The analysis of property ownership in Savannah is based on Colonial Conveyance Books c-1 and c-2 for 1755–64, U and V for 1768–71, x-1 and x-2 for 1772–75, Georgia Archives. The information was obtained by reviewing conveyances for all of Georgia and gleaning data on Savannah sites. A laborious process, it had the virtue of not weighting the information toward any one social category.

85. In the mid-1750s, the flavor of the trustee period prevailed. When James Habersham and Francis Harris established the first genuine mercantile store, the array of shops included those of a haberdasher, a victualer doubling as a tavern-keeper, and five artisans. The sounds of hammers and saws were never absent. Habersham and Harris controlled six prime lots for their operations, together with one on Bay Street. Two Scots operated large wholesale establishments while John Rae, a Protestant of Northern Ireland with little education who had fought his way up through the deerskin trade, opened a mercantile house across the way. Although a silversmith practiced his craft and two widows lived on either side of a Habersham property, Johnson Square had lost its connection to the artisanal world. Colonial Conveyance Books, Georgia Archives.

86. G. Jones, "Portrait of an Irish Entrepreneur," 427–47.

87. Rubin, *Third to None*, 2–4, 18–21.

88. H. Davis, *The Fledgling Province*, 69–70; Colonial Conveyance Books U, V, x-1, x-2, Georgia Archives.

89. Kole, *Minis Family*, 8–9.

90. O'Shaughnessy, *An Empire Divided*, 4–5; Higman, *Concise History of the Caribbean*, 120.

91. Sheridan, "Rise of a Colonial Gentry," 342–57.

92. Schaw, *Journal of a Lady of Quality*, 92; O'Shaughnessy, *An Empire Divided*, 4–5; Watts, *The West Indies*, 337.

93. Goveia, *Slave Society*, 204–7, 213.

94. Bolton, *Genealogical and Biographical Account*, 106–11.

95. In his important study of the Georgia lowcountry, Tim Lockley argues that the late colonial period saw a growth of poverty and the creation of a two-tiered society of "indigent subjects" and "men of some substance." His analysis cites the concentration of land grants and slaves in a small percentage of the population. For Savannah, however, a significant number of artisans, craftsmen, and shopkeepers did well in a booming economy although solid information is hard to come by. Lockley, *Lines in the Sand*, 1–28, esp. 21.

96. *Georgia Gazette*, September 6, 1764, May 17, 1775; Cutton, *The Silversmiths in Georgia*, 74.

97. Land grant to Isaac Martin, mariner, and Samuel Pelton, former Indian trader and shopkeeper, Colonial Conveyance Book S, 353, Georgia Archives. David Montaigut's father was Samuel Montaigut, a Huguenot merchant in Purrysburg. G. Jones, *Detailed Reports on the Salzburger Emigrants*, 9:179. After his career as a mariner, David served as justice of the peace and naval officer for the port. Appointments of Montaigut in *CRG*, 7:505, 9:179; Naval Shipping Lists, 1765–67, CO 5/110. Andrew Elton Wells built a distillery fifty-six feet long and forty-six feet wide, "with stills and cisterns capable of making 200 hogsheads of rum per year; also a dry cellar 50 feet long by 18 feet wide, together with a crane and wharf," *Georgia Gazette*, October 19, 1774.

98. Welch, *Slave Society in the City*, 7, 18–19.

99. H. Davis, *The Fledgling Province*, 69–70.

100. B. Wood, *Women's Work, Men's Work*, 84–86.

101. Presentments of the Grand Jurors, June 21 and December 10, 1764, *Georgia Gazette*; B. Wood, *Women's Work, Men's Work*, 82.

102. An Act to Empower certain Commissioners herein appointed to regulate the hire of Porters and Labour of Slaves in the Town of Savannah, in *CRG* 19, pt. 2:23–30.

103. Goveia, *Slave Society*, 226–29; B. Wood, *Women's Work, Men's Work*, 81.

104. Frederic W. N. Bayley, *Four Years' Residence in the West Indies*, 41, qtd. in Welch, *Slave Society in the City*, 18.

105. Goveia, *Slave Society*, 227.

106. Ibid., 238.

107. *South Carolina Gazette*, September 24, 1772, qtd. in Olwell, *Masters, Slaves, and Subjects*, 170–71, 175.

108. P. Morgan, "Black Life in Eighteenth-Century Charles Town," 194–95.

109. B. Wood, *Women's Work, Men's Work*, 83–84.

110. P. Morgan, "Black Life in Eighteenth-Century Charles Town," 194, and "Black Society in the Lowcountry," 123–24.

111. Sollors, *Interesting Narrative*, 86, 92–94.

112. Ibid., 77.

113. Goveia, *Slave Society*, 228.

114. Higman, *Slave Populations of the British Caribbean*, 255–57.

115. Frink to Burton, July 8, 1771, Society for the Propagation of the Gospel, microfilm, UGA Library. Betty Wood points out that the number forty is almost 5 percent of the black population in Savannah. Philip Morgan estimates that it represents 10 percent of Savannah's adult black population. P. Morgan, "British Encounters," 192.

116. For Robert Watts, The Supplementary Memorial of Charles Watts, late of the Province of Georgia, ship carpenter and planter, n.d., AO 13/38. Charles had "4 Negro ship carpenters" and four apprentices or indentured servants.

117. Papers concerning the arbitration in the case of the ship *Elizabeth* between John Wand, owner; William Lang, master; and Cowper, Telfairs of Savannah. John Wand Papers, 1771–72, GHS.

118. "Hypothecation of Ship *Crown Galley*, Webb, to Sawyer, Morel, and Keall," March 31, 1781, Colonial Conveyance Book, KK 2, 251, GHS.

119. B. Wood, *Women's Work, Men's Work*, ch. 5: "Self-Hire in Savannah," 101–21, esp. 108.

120. Circumstantial evidence suggests that Philip D. Morgan's careful reconstruction of black society in the Carolina lowcountry holds true for Georgia. In the neighboring colony, maritime work was the third-largest occupation among males, after agriculture and woodworking. "Watermen," including mariners, rafters, rowers, and fishermen, constituted 20 percent of male slaves belonging to Charles Town residents between 1730 and 1799. P. Morgan, "Black Life in Eighteenth-Century Charleston," 196–200.

121. Estate of Adam Croddy, July 4, 1768, loose papers, Register of Records, drawer 230, box 20, Colonial Inventory Book F, Georgia Archives.

122. Memorial of William Lyford Jr., September 3, 1783, AO 13/36/b:499–502.

123. An Act to Empower certain Commissioners herein appointed to regulate the hire of Porters and Labour of Slaves in the Town of Savannah (1774), in *CRG* 19, pt. 2:23–30; B. Wood, *Women's Work, Men's Work*, 108–10. A second act passed in 1774 fixed rates for the kind of work done by unskilled labor in hopes of preventing slaves from overcharging for their work and having cash to spend on alcohol and other "Evil Courses."

124. Presentments of the Grand Jury, July 6, 1768, *Georgia Gazette*, qtd. in B. Wood, *Women's Work, Men's Work*, 129. For an analysis of the role of black women in marketing in Savannah, see the chapter "Marketing in Savannah," 80–100.

125. Presentments of the Georgia Grand Jury, received by the Governor's Council, February 4, 1772, in *CRG*, 12:214.

126. Sollors, *Interesting Narrative*, 120.

127. Edward Telfair Papers, Duke University, qtd. in Olwell, *Masters, Slaves, and Subjects*, 151.

128. Doberstein, *Journals*, 2:594.

129. *Georgia Gazette*, February 28 and December 6, 1769.

130. Ashcraft-Eason, "She Voluntarily Hath Come," 202–21.

131. Andrew Elliott, September 8, 1771, Colonial Wills Book A, Georgia Archives.

132. Menard, "Economic and Social Development of the South," 277–79.

133. Edelson, *Plantation Enterprise*, 136–37.

Chapter 5. Merchants in a Creole Society

1. Chaplin, "Creoles in British America," 46–65.

2. Lounsbury, "Christ Church, Savannah," 58–73.

3. *South Carolina Gazette*, November 14, 1754; Edelson, *Plantation Enterprise*, 189.

4. G. Jones, *The Salzburger Saga*, 14–81; Bailyn, *Atlantic History*, 38; Marsh, *Georgia's Frontier Women*, 53–61.

5. For John Morel, the Morel file, Walter Hartridge Collection, GHS; for Samuel Elbert, article in *New Georgia Encyclopedia*, http://georgiaencyclopedia.org; for Minis Minis, Kole, *The Minis Family of Georgia*, 31–32; for Peter Tondee, Weeks, *Savannah in the Time of Peter Tondee*; for the Habersham family, Lambert, "Father against Son, and Son against Father," 1–28.

6. Gallay, *Formation of a Planter Elite*, 15, 47–54, 75–77.

7. Chaplin, "Creoles in British America," 46–65. The term "identity" has generated enormous debate among historians of the Atlantic world. Canny and Pagden, *Colonial Identity in the Atlantic World*; Hodson, "Weird Science," 227–32.

8. Hancock, *Citizens of the World*, 8–13.

9. Indenture, June 13, 1754, recorded 1759, Colonial Bond Book J, 166, microfilm, GHS. To secure funds for the move to Georgia, Thomas Vincent borrowed £200 from a tobacconist of London, sold to another person "a Messuage and Tenement" in Bristol that he expected to inherit on the death of his mother and father, and also sold another "messuage, a field and all the other lands of Thomas Vincent in Bristol." He also received £140 from his wife's family.

10. Henry Laurens to Thomas Lloyd, September 7, 1767, *PHL*, 5:299.

11. The numbers are based on biographical material accumulated on merchants, retailers, wholesalers, country factors, brokers, and others involved in trade during the colonial period.

12. Lambert, *James Habersham*, 33–80. For insight into his commercial instincts, James Habersham to William Knox, March 9, 1764, in *CGHS*, 6:16. He was ensconced in the small clique around James Wright, which was increasingly unwilling to listen to other points of view and bent on making the coast a rich man's country.

13. Qtd. in Jay, *Memoirs of the Life and Character of the Late Rev. Cornelius Winter*, 86.

14. For Spencer, *CRG*, 8:40, 88, 348, 505, and 28:192; for Russell, *CRG*, 4:68, 6:105, 7:9–10, 178, and 10:695 as well as the entry for July 24, 1765, Colonial Bond Book R, 51; for Bolton, see R. Bolton, *Genealogical and Biographical Account of the Family of Bolton*; for Clay, *Letters of Joseph Clay*, in *CGHS*, 8.

15. Kole, *The Minis Family of Georgia*, 3–8.

16. The Sheftall diaries, 1733–1808, Keith Read Collection, Hargrett Library, UGA; Levy, *Mordecai Sheftall*, 23–43. On their West Indian ventures and the Jolly Roger affair, October 1, 1763, Colonial Bond Book O, 5–37, microfilm, GHS.

17. Rubin, *Third to None*, 21–22.

18. Morel chose as his wife someone from the same cultural world, the daughter of a French Swiss physician-planter, but when she died he married someone outside the French-speaking community, the daughter of Jonathan Bryan, a strategic move for both families. Adler, "A Biographical Sketch of John Morel," GHS. For one of his West Indian ventures, indenture for the purchase of a sloop in Havana, December 23, 1762, see Colonial Bond Book O, GHS. For the vessel built on Ossabaw, John Wand Papers, GHS.

19. For James Edward Powell, Chestnutt, *South Carolina's Expansion*, 151, 153; Granger, *Savannah River Plantations*, 182; petitions and appointments in *CRG*, 6:429, 27:114. For James Read, Chestnutt, *South Carolina's Expansion*, 157–58; Read and Mossman Letter Book, 1765–66, GHS.

20. John Gordon operated Gordon & Netherclift from 1759 until the Revolution, and George Baillie was a partner in Robertson, Jamieson, and Baillie.

21. Chestnutt, *South Carolina's Expansion*, 154.

22. For Thomas Vincent, indenture, written June 13, 1754, recorded July 1759, Colonial Bond Book J, 166, GHS. For William Handley, advertisements in *Georgia Gazette*, September 13 and October 11, 1764, January 3, 1765. For Button Gwinnett, Jenkins, *Button Gwinnett*, 21–54.

23. For Clay's commercial ventures, see the letter book of Joseph Clay & Company, December 19, 1772–March 31, 1774, vol. 1, microfilm, GHS. In 1773, Clay attempted to recruit a Philadelphia firm to go in with him "to fix a vessel in the West Indies trade in order to provide ourselves with all kinds of West India products which we can take off a very considerable profit annually." Jamaica was the target of choice. Joseph Clay to Bright & Pechin, February 22, 1773, Letter Book, vol. 1, GHS.

24. Nathaniel Hall file, Walter Hartridge Collection, GHS; "an account of the principal and actual losses sustained by Nathaniel Hall," May 7, 1786, AO 13/35.

25. In *Slavery in Colonial Georgia*, 24–30, Betty Wood addresses the role of Lowland Scots. See also Ready, *The Castle Builders*, 32–34. On the role of Highlanders, Jackson, "Darien Antislavery Petition," 618–31; Parker, *Scottish Highlanders*, 82–100.

26. *Georgia Gazette*, 1768. The best single source on Georgia merchants is the information in the petitions for compensation by Loyalists after the Revolution. Pressly, "Scottish Merchants," 139–40; Dobson, *Scots in Georgia*.

27. Petition of John Dunbar, Thomas Young, and John Simpson, February 1763, in *CRG*, 9:25. For Darling & Munro, *Georgia Gazette*, October 4, 1764; for Spald-

ing & Kelsall, "Estimate of Estate and Effects," memorial presented on behalf of Roger Kelsall by John Clark, September 14, 1784, 119–31, AO 13/36a.

28. Cashin, *Lachlan McGillivray*, 104–7, 154–58, 252; "Unfinished Memoirs of Robert Mackay," Robert Mackay, n.d., microfilm, GHS; "Andrew McLean in Current Account with McGillivray, Grahams, Clark," 1765, U.S. Circuit Court, Southern District of Georgia, Savannah, mixed cases, box 57/14A006, NARA.

29. Pressly, "Scottish Merchants," 140–41.

30. "Appointment of 'Edward Telfair of Antigua, Merchant' as true and lawful attorney for Basil Cowper and William Telfair," May 25, 1767, Edward Telfair Papers, reel 10, Duke University; Edward Telfair to Basil Cowper, "My Dear Friend and Partner," Savannah, April 26, 1770, Telfair Papers, reel 12, Duke University; Coulter, "Edward Telfair," 99–124. Basil Cowper and Edward and William Telfair operated under several names. In Savannah, these names included Cowper & Telfairs, William and Edward Telfair, and Edward Telfair and Company; in London, Telfair, Cowper, Telfair.

31. Colley, *Britons*, 128.

32. Governor Henry Ellis to Board of Trade, May 5, 1757, in *CRG*, 28, pt. 1:26. John Graham left a long trail through his memorials to obtain compensation for his losses during the Revolution, numerous entries in the Colonial Records of Georgia, recordings of his business dealings in the Colonial Bond Books, and a detailed listing of his landholdings in Colonial Conveyance Book KK-2, 286–97, GHS, among other places. The best source is the letters written to Governor James Grant of East Florida between 1765 and 1772 in James Grant Papers, Ballindalloch Muniments, NAS. David Graeme, later a provider of foodstuffs to the British armies in Europe and an associate of the inner circle of Scots who dominated international trade, may have been a sponsor. Hancock, *Citizens of the World*, 139; Snapp, *John Stuart*, 25–26.

33. Snapp, *John Stuart*, 25–26.

34. On the Sunbury affair, deposition by John Graham in Walker, *Abstracts of Georgia*, 59; Robert Baillie to his father, February 10, 1754, Baillie Family Papers, GD 1/1155/66, NAS; on purchase of slaves in St. Kitts, Walker, *Abstracts of Georgia*, 53; as Indian commissary, Governor Henry Ellis to Board of Trade, May 5, 1757, in *CRG*, 28, pt. 1:26; on land purchase, Granger, *Savannah River Plantations*, 115; indenture with Dr. Fothergill, Colonial Conveyance Book U, 331, 333, GHS.

35. Graham and his brother James took 50 percent of the company; Lachlan, 25 percent; and Clark, a modest 25 percent, considering the expertise and contacts he brought. John Clark signed the various petitions of "the Merchants of London trading to South Carolina and Georgia" throughout the 1760s and 1770s and testified before Parliament on the rice trade. David and Miriam Milligan to Commissioners,

August 29, 1790, Treasury 79/31, NA-UK; Kellock, "London Merchants and the Pre-1776 American Debts," 121; Snapp, *John Stuart*, 25–26; John Graham to James Grant, December 10, 1765, James Grant Papers, Ballindalloch Muniments, microfilm, NAS.

36. Snapp, *John Stuart*, 51.

37. John Graham to James Grant, April 1, May 28, 1767, James Grant Papers, Ballindalloch Muniments, NAS.

38. John Graham to Gov. James Grant, May 22, 1771, ibid.

39. Minutes of the Governor's Council, August 7, 1764, in *CRG*, 9:193; Minutes of the meeting to consider the case of John Graham, December 20, 1783, 115–20, and John Graham to Gentlemen, May 28, 1788, 121–27, both in AO 12.

40. Crooke Family Papers, Walter Hartridge Collection, GHS. On the Presbyterian Meeting House, H. Davis, *The Fledgling Province*, 203–4.

41. John Graham expressed his political feelings to Governor James Grant in numerous letters in the Ballindalloch collection. For example, Graham to Grant, December 20, 1765, Ballindalloch Papers, NAS.

42. Breen, *Tobacco Culture*, 118–22; Snapp, *John Stuart*, 47.

43. Alexander Cumine to Alexander Ogilvie, April 22, 1763, Ogilvie-Forbes of Boyndlie Papers, Aberdeen University Library, microfilm, South Carolina Historical Society.

44. Godbold and Woody, *Christopher Gadsden*, 60–61, 75, 79; Walsh, *Writings of Christopher Gadsden*, 79.

45. Hamilton, *Scotland, the Caribbean, and the Atlantic World*, 4–5.

46. Rogers, "The East Florida Society," 479–96. Rogers demonstrates how East Florida was another manifestation of the Scottish drive for success. Lord Adam Gordon became the leader of the East Florida Society and spearheaded the movement to acquire large blocks of land.

47. *Georgia Gazette*; Walter Hartridge Collection, GHS; Ingmire, *Colonial Georgia Marriage Records*; Dobson, *Scots in Georgia*.

48. C. Johnson, *Mary Telfair*, 44.

49. Marsh, *Georgia's Frontier Women*, 151–52.

50. W. Clarke, *Early & Historic Freemasonry of Georgia*, 43–47; Solomon's Lodge: Original Minutes Book of the Lodge at Savannah in Georgia, 1756–57, LC, microfilm, GHS; Cashin, *Lachlan McGillivray*, 255–60; *Georgia Gazette*, July 12, 1769, November 1764; H. Davis, *The Fledgling Province*, 203–4; James Habersham to John Clark, November 29, 1771, in *CGHS*, 6:154–55; Snapp, *John Stuart*, 157.

51. Proceedings and Minutes of the Governor and Council, January 7, 1755, *CRG*, 6:89; April 28, 1755, *CRG*, 7:174; May 5, 1757, *CRG*, 28, pt. 1:26; February 14 and 28, 1758, *CRG*, 16:269–70, 290–91; April 21, 1772, *CRG*, 12:314–15; August 18, 1760,

CRG, 13:417–18; November 10, 1768, *CRG*, 14:589–90. Further information is found throughout *CRG*, vols. 9–12.

52. Mercantini, *Who Shall Rule at Home?*, 87.

53. Goveia, *Slave Society*, 53, 71; Dyde, *Out of the Crowded Vagueness*, 89–93.

54. E. Morgan and H. Morgan, *The Stamp Act Crisis*, 163–72. "The Savannah merchants," the Morgans write, "were willing to play the role which those of North Carolina had disdained, and they earned the hatred and contempt of the other colonists for this betrayal of American unity." Fraser, *Savannah in the Old South*, 84–87.

55. James Habersham to William Knox, October 30, December 4, 1765, in *CGHS*, 6:49–50; James Habersham to George Whitefield, January 27, 1766, in *CGHS*, 6:54–55; Roach, "The *Georgia Gazette* and the Stamp Act," 471–91; Miller, "The Stamp Act in Colonial Georgia," 318–31.

56. James Wright to Board of Trade, Savannah, January 15, 1766, in *CRG*, 28, pt. 2:132–34. Suspected stamp agents included George Baillie, commissary for the province, and Simon Munro, both Scottish merchants.

57. Godbold and Woody, *Christopher Gadsden*, 61–62. Appearing in the *South Carolina Gazette*, his fiery words produced a strong reaction. Shortly afterward, the Sons of Liberty stopped two vessels bound for Savannah before they could clear the bar at Charles Town.

58. O'Shaughnessy, *An Empire Divided*, 84–98.

59. Gallay, *Formation of a Planter Elite*, 117–18; C. Jones, *History of Georgia*, 2:112–13. During the non-importation movement, Savannah merchants agreed with Governor Wright that an increase in American manufactures and a decrease in American imports would threaten their interests. A group of these merchants met on September 16, 1769, and passed their own non-importation resolution in an effort to gain leadership of the Patriot movement. They agreed not to import any item subject to the Townshend duties. Jonathan Bryan chaired a meeting three days later of Georgians who went beyond the position of the merchants and called for a general boycott of all non-essential British goods.

60. Abbott, *The Royal Governors of Georgia*, ch. 7.

Chapter 6. The Slave Trade in Creating a Black Georgia

1. Rawley, *Transatlantic Slave Trade*, 149–69; Klein, *Atlantic Slave Trade*, 74–129; O'Malley, "Beyond the Middle Passage," 125–72; Richardson, "The British Slave Trade," 125–72, and "The British Empire and the Atlantic Slave Trade," 440–64; K. Morgan, "Slave Sales in Colonial Charleston," 905–27. The figure of sixty thousand is from the Trans-Atlantic Slave Trade Database at http://slavevoyages.org. See

also Wax, "New Negroes Are Always in Demand," 193–220; B. Wood, *Slavery in Colonial Georgia*, 98–104; Littlefield, "The Slave Trade," 110–41.

2. William Stephens and Assistants to Benjamin Martyn, July 19, 1750, in *CRG*, 26:22.

3. President and Assistants to Benjamin Martyn, February 19, 1751, in *CRG*, 26:156. Habersham typically drafted correspondence touching on commercial issues.

4. Greene, "Travails of an Infant Colony," 141. For statistics on imports to Virginia, Maryland, and Georgia, the Trans-Atlantic Slave Trade Database, http://slavevoyages.org; for imports from the Caribbean to those colonies, Tables 1, 3, and 5 in O'Malley, "Beyond the Middle Passage," 141, 146, 151; on Virginia's imports, K. Morgan, "Slave Sales in Colonial Charleston," 906.

5. The figure of 7,532 includes those people brought directly from Africa (5,349) and those who came through West Indian ports (2,003) between 1766 and 1775. See Table 9. The figure omits the 500 who came through the intercoastal trade.

6. Burnard and Morgan, "Dynamics of the Slave Market," 206.

7. Trans-Atlantic Slave Trade Database, slavevoyages.com.

8. Richardson, "The British Slave Trade," 125–72.

9. Series Z 155–64: Slaves Imported into Charleston, S.C., by Origin, U.S. Census, *Historical Statistics*, 2:1173; Hornsby, *British Atlantic, American Frontier*, 113; K. Morgan, "Slave Sales in Colonial Charleston," 907.

10. Romans, *A Concise Natural History*, 146; Henry Laurens to James Read, March 7, 1763; Laurens to Johnston & Wylly, August 25, 1763; Laurens to William Hodshon, August 26, 1763, all in *PHL*, 3:359–60, 535, 542–45 (quotation at 545).

11. Some of the data in Table 9 were gathered from the petitions for grants of land in "Proceedings and Minutes of the Governor and Council," 1755–72, in *CRG*, vols. 7–12. According to Thomas Statom, there is a close statistical correlation between the inventories of estates and the land petitions, which argues for the validity of using these data in this way. Statom, "Negro Slavery," 167.

12. Herdsmen from St. Andrew Parish looking for one or two men to serve as cowboys joined new planters like James Habersham, who acquired nine people perhaps to resell in the Savannah market but more likely for his plantation, Silk Hope. See List of names of those paying general duty on exported slaves, General Duty Books, vol. B (1748–65), South Carolina Department of Archives and History.

13. Captain Peter Dordin to "Gentlemen," January 30, 1756, folder "Slaves, 1731–1820," Newport Historical Society, qtd. in Wax, "New Negroes Are Always in Demand," 198–200. After the abortive sale, merchant John Graham bought the brig from the hapless captain at a cut-rate price for his own use in the West Indian trade. Walker, *Abstracts of Georgia*, 40.

14. Names of those paying general duty on trans-shipped slaves are in General Duty Books, vol. B (1748–65), South Carolina Department of Archives and History.

15. Of the 8 percent of Africans trans-shipped out of South Carolina, Georgia took 6.4 percent. K. Morgan, "Slave Sales in Colonial Charleston," 911.

16. General Duty Books, vols. B (1748–65) and C (1765–76), South Carolina Department of Archives and History; see Table 9 for the percentage of enslaved people imported from South Carolina.

17. The number of Africans imported through the West Indies comes from the work of Gregory O'Malley, "Beyond the Middle Passage." His figures are based on naval shipping lists from the British West Indies rather than the less complete records of Georgia. Since his figures do not indicate the island of origin, the numbers of imported slaves for the years 1764–67 are taken from the work of Darold Wax, who relied on the naval shipping lists from Georgia and advertisements in the *Georgia Gazette*. Table 3: "Slaves Imported into Georgia from Areas Other than Africa," in Wax, "New Negroes Are Always in Demand," 202. His work relied on Donnan, *Documents*, 4:612–25. Wax labels his table "Slaves Imported into Georgia from Areas Other than Africa, 1765–1775." The numbers include 247 people from unknown sources. It is assumed that these were primarily from the Caribbean.

18. Series Z 155–64: Slaves Imported into Charleston, S.C., by Origin, U.S. Census, *Historical Statistics*, 2:1173.

19. The sources for Table 10 are Donnan, *Documents*, 4:612–25; and Wax, "New Negroes Are Always in Demand," 200. Donnan provides the numbers for the year 1764.

20. "Bill of sale for eight male and two female Negro slaves," May 22, 1756, in Walker, *Abstracts of Georgia*, 53.

21. Burnard and Morgan, "Dynamics of the Slave Market," 205.

22. Entry of vessels to Savannah for 1766, Naval Shipping Lists, Georgia, CO 5/710.

23. Entry of the *Charlotte*, May 16, 1765, Naval Shipping Lists, Georgia, CO 5/710.

24. Entries of vessels, June 18, 1766 (James Wright); July 15, 1766 (David Montaigut); November 20, 1766 (Elizabeth Butler), Naval Shipping Lists, CO 5/710.

25. Cowper, Telfairs to Capt. Sam. Stiles, April 22, 1774, Cowper & Telfairs Letter Book, August 11, 1773–January 3, 1776, Telfair Family Papers, GHS: "As we have for some time past made a small experiment in the purchase of slaves in the West Indies, we have now to recommend a joint purchase by the schooner's return. We entreat that they may be prime and young. The quantity ought to be more than fifty and not exceeding a hundred for the purchase."

26. Qtd. in Hall, *In Miserable Slavery*, 193–95.

27. Clay & Co. to Messrs. Scott, Mackie, and Dover, December 19, 1772, April

22, 1773, Letter Book, December 19, 1772–March 31, 1774, Joseph Clay & Co., GHS. In 1761, the Georgia legislature followed the example of other North American colonies and instituted a duty of £10 on seasoned slaves over ten years of age unless it could be demonstrated by certificate that they had not stayed longer than six months in the islands. Wax, "New Negroes Are Always in Demand," 204; O'Malley, "Beyond the Middle Passage," 136–37; B. Wood, *Slavery in Colonial Georgia*, 104. The problem never disappeared. John Graham received an "unlucky" consignment that included several seasoned people from a merchant in Antigua and promptly dispatched them to the newly emerging market of St. Augustine where buyers were less choosy. John Graham to Governor James Grant, January 6, 1767, James Grant Papers, Ballindalloch Muniments, microfilm, NAS.

28. Calculated from the tables on slave migration from the Caribbean to North America in O'Malley, "Beyond the Middle Passage," 141–42, 146, 149, 151, 153, 156, 160–61, 163, and the tables on estimated slave exports that constituted the intercolonial trade within the Caribbean in O'Malley, "Final Passages," 322, 331, 336, 340.

29. O'Malley, "Beyond the Middle Passage," 142, 151, 166.

30. Wax, "New Negroes Are Always in Demand," 204. The Trans-Atlantic Slave Trade Database does not count these three voyages as part of the direct Atlantic slave trade to Georgia because of their having stopped to discharge a part of the cargo in other ports. Rediker, *The Slave Ship*.

31. B. Wood, *Slavery in Colonial Georgia*, 100; Sellers, *Charleston Business*, 128–30. Sellers states that 5,082 slaves were imported in the first six months of 1765 at an average price of £35. *Historical Statistics* shows a total of 6,500 brought in. With an average price of £35, the total value was over £200,000. The irony is that the massive importations of that year saddled South Carolina with a debt burden conceivably greater than it would have accrued had the market remained open.

32. Trans-Atlantic Slave Trade Database, http://slavevoyages.org.

33. Richardson, "The British Slave Trade," 137–40.

34. *Mary Brow*, April 1766, Naval Shipping Lists, Georgia, CO 5/710; for mention of Matthew and John Strong, Thomas, *The Slave Trade*, 428–29.

35. Trans-Atlantic Slave Trade Database, http://slavevoyages.org.

36. Richardson, "The British Slave Trade," 142–43; Naval Shipping Lists, Georgia, CO 5/710; Cowper & Telfairs Letter Book, August 11, 1773–January 6, 1776, Telfair Family Papers, GHS.

37. Joseph Clay to Benjamin Stead, January 20, 1773, Letter Book, December 19, 1772–March 31, 1774. Clay wrote of the start of the partnership in which "we have agreed and bound ourselves each to the other to continue the same on our joint accounts and risque for five years to commence the first instant."

38. Hancock, *Citizens of the World*, 139.

39. Qtd. in Richardson, "The British Slave Trade," 147.

40. Nathanial Wraxell was among the most prominent Bristol slave traders to South Carolina during the 1750s and 1760s. Richardson, "The British Slave Trade," 142–43.

41. On July 30, 1771, Alexander Inglis and Nathaniel Hall of Savannah sold in the Charles Town market 230 slaves brought from Sierra Leone. Henry Laurens to Felix Warley, Falmouth, October 10, 1771, in *PHL*, 8:5n.

42. "The Memorial of William Greenwood and William Higginson on behalf of themselves and their correspondent, Mr. Samuel Douglass," June 27, 1782, AO 13/34.

43. John Graham to Governor James Grant, April 1, May 28, June 13, September 16, and October 29, 1767, James Grant Papers, Ballindalloch Muniments, microfilm, NAS. The correspondence Graham initially received included copies of instructions sent by Miles Barber to his sea captains, the ports where cargos were to be purchased, and approximate dates for arrival.

44. Richard Oswald to James Grant, February 19, 1768, James Grant Papers, Ballindalloch Muniments, microfilm, NAS.

45. John Nutt to John Jones & Company, Sunbury, February 8, 1774, box 15, Treasury 77, NA-UK.

46. Trans-Atlantic Slave Trade Database, http://slavevoyages.org.

47. John Nutt secured the promise of slaver Richard Oswald that he would use Thomas Loughton Smith of Charles Town as his factor if Henry Laurens ever declined to sell a shipment. Henry Laurens to Samuel Brailsford, Westminster, February 25, 1772, in *PHL*, 8:187–90.

48. Memorandum with the signatures of John Graham, Lachlan McGillivray, William McGillivray, William Struthers, Stephen Dean, and Gov. James Wright, April 1775, James Wright file, box 29, Keith Read Collection, Hargrett Library, UGA. Stephen Dean had been captain of slaving vessels to Savannah. B. Wood, *Slavery in Colonial Georgia*, 103–4.

49. Joseph Clay to unknown correspondent, April 27, 1784, Letter Book: Clay, Telfair & Co., October 25, 1783–September 1, 1784, Clay, Telfair and Company Papers, Joseph Clay Papers, GHS.

50. Trans-Atlantic Slave Trade Database, CD-ROM, 1999, and http://slavevoyages .org. The thirty-six ships that the database records coming to Georgia between 1766 and 1774 brought 5,349 Africans after deductions are made for high estimates. Littlefield, *Rice and Slaves*, 8–21, 33–41; Thornton, *Africa and Africans*, 183–205; Gomez, *Exchanging Our Country Marks*, 45–87. According to Gomez, "Senegambians, along with Africans elsewhere in the continent, were largely responsible for laying the foundations for such ports as Charleston, Savannah, and New Orleans" (44).

51. Littlefield, *Rice and Slaves*, 37–44; Gomez, *Exchanging Our Country Marks*, 44–52; Klein, *Atlantic Slave Trade*, 55–61; Thornton, *Africa and Africans*, 184–89.

52. *Georgia Gazette*, November 30, 1774.

53. Carney, *Black Rice*, ch. 3, "Out of Africa: Rice Culture and African Continuities," and ch. 4, "This Was 'Woman's Wuck,'" 68–141; Carney and Porcher, "Geographies of the Past," 127–47; Fields-Black, *Deep Roots*, 107–15.

54. Eltis, Morgan, and Richardson, "Agency and Diaspora in Atlantic History," 1329–58.

55. *Georgia Gazette*, September 3, 1766; entry of *Antelope*, July 31, 1766, Naval Shipping Lists, Georgia, CO 5/710; Donnan, *Documents*, 620.

56. Joseph Clay and James Habersham Jr. handled the sale. *Georgia Gazette*, October 22, 1766; Entry of *Woodmanstone*, October 20, 1766, Naval Shipping Lists, Georgia, CO 5/710; Donnan, *Documents*, 621. For the details of the voyage and the two voyages to Charles Town, the Trans-Atlantic Slave Trade Database, http://slavevoyages.org.

57. Trans-Atlantic Slave Trade Database, http://slavevoyages.com; Richardson, "The British Slave Trade," 128. The figure of 188 enslaved people per voyage comes from the period 1714–75.

58. Calculations for Georgia come from the statistics found in Trans-Atlantic Slave Trade Database, http://slavevoyages.com; for Charles Town, Littlefield, "The Slave Trade," 76. Shipping tons have not been converted to modern standards.

59. K. Morgan, "Slave Sales in Colonial Charleston," 910.

60. *Georgia Gazette*; Donnan, *Documents*, 612–25; Trans-Atlantic Slave Trade Database, http://slavesvoyages.com; Wax, "New Negroes Are Always in Demand," 202. Virtually all of the African trade was controlled by this coterie of merchants.

61. Of the 954 enslaved people brought into the colony in 1774 and whose broker can be identified, Cowper, Telfairs handled the sale of 637. Wax, "New Negroes are Always in Demand," 206.

62. Edward Telfair to William Thompson [*sic*], August 11, 1773, Cowper & Telfairs Letter Book, August 11, 1773–January 6, 1776, Telfair Family Papers, GHS.

63. Also see Clay & Co. to Messrs. William Fox Jr. & Co., September 1, 1774, Joseph Clay & Co. Papers, Letter Book, vol. 2, 1774–76, Joseph Clay Papers, GHS.

64. Cates, "A Medical History of Georgia," 47–60; H. Davis, *The Fledgling Province*, 90; Minutes of the Governor in Council, February 3, 1767, March 6, 1769, in *CRG*, 10:81, 699–700; "An Act to Prevent the Bringing into and Spreading of Contagious Distempers in this Province," April 7, 1763, in *CRG*, 18:543–52.

65. In 1774, the *Georgia Gazette* carried a notice of sixteen "likely young Negro wenches and fellows" to be sold for cash or barrels of rice on the brig *Prince of Wales* "now lying at Pooler and Parkinson's wharf." *Georgia Gazette*, February 9, 1774.

66. *Georgia Gazette*, November 22, 1764: "Just imported in the schooner *Industry* from St. Kitts, at Mr. McGillivray's plantation, Vale Royal, a cargo of about forty prime new Negroes. Sale begins at 10 A.M."

67. *Georgia Gazette*, August 10, 1768.

68. Barry Sheehy and Cindy Wallace, "Slavery as a Business in Antebellum Savannah, 1855–65" (2009), draft paper in possession of author.

69. The men were not to exceed thirty years of age while none of the women were to be older than twenty-five years. Draft of a Memorandum, April 1775, Keith Read Collection, Hargrett Library, UGA; Wax, "New Negroes Are Always in Demand," 208.

70. P. Morgan, "Africa and the Atlantic c. 1450 to c. 1850."

71. Sale of cargo of the snow *Philip*, October 14, 1774, and of the sloop *Daniel*, October 25, 1774, account book, September 1, 1774–December 31, 1781, box 1, folder 9, Telfair Family Papers, GHS. Most of the young boys brought £30; men, £40–50; and women, £35.

72. Table 18, "The Distribution of Africans among Purchasers in the Chesapeake and Lowcountry, 1689–1786," in P. Morgan, *Slave Counterpoint*, 78; Burnard and Morgan, "Dynamics of the Slave Market," 214.

73. Richardson, "The British Slave Trade," 151–55.

74. Accounts for cargos of the snow *Philip*, October 14, 1774, and of the sloop *Daniel*, October 25, 1774, account book, September 1, 1774–December 31, 1781, box 1, folder 9, Telfair Family Papers, GHS.

75. Robert Baillie to James Baillie, March 6, 1768, GD 1/115/71, NAS.

76. Henry Laurens to Lachlan McIntosh, Westminster, March 13, 1773, in *PHL*, 8:615, 619.

77. Henry Laurens to Smith & Baillies, Charles Town, January 15, 1768, in *PHL*, 5:546–48.

78. Accounts for sales from the bark *Friend*, September 1774, account book, September 1, 1774–December 31, 1781, box 1, folder 9, Telfair Papers, GHS.

79. John Nutt to John Jones & Co., Sunbury, February 8, 1774, Treasury 79/15, NA-UK.

80. The remaining letter books of Cowper, Telfairs make no reference to them.

81. For 1772, Governor Wright reported that the capital outflow for slaves was £20,000 sterling, an average rather than an exceptional year. "Report of Sir James Wright on the Condition of the Province of Georgia, on 20th Sept. 1773," in *CGHS*, 3:165. In 1766, Wright had reported that the cost of "Negroes" was £14,820. James Wright in response to queries made by the Board of Trade, November 29, 1766, in *CRG*, 28, pt. 2:184. The firm Powell, Hopton in Charles Town held £13,000 sterling in obligations from Georgians, all for slaves sold in the last year of the colonial period.

82. Duties entered for 1773 and 1774, General Duty Book, vol. C (1765–76), South Carolina Department of Archives and History.

83. O'Malley, "Beyond the Middle Passage," 151. Gregory O'Malley calculates that between 1771 and 1775 a total of six hundred eighty Africans arrived in Georgia from the West Indies. Darold Wax estimates three hundred ninety for the same time period. O'Malley used information from naval shipping lists from the West Indies. Wax considered information gleaned from the *Georgia Gazette* and other local sources. Nevertheless, when one considers the overall numbers imported between 1766 and 1775, the discrepancy between the two sources is only forty-four people. The ultimate difference is how one divides the time periods.

84. Joseph Clay to James Jackson, March 29, 1784, Letter Book, Clay, Telfair & Co., October 25, 1783–September 1, 1784, vol. 1, Clay, Telfair and Company Papers, Joseph Clay Papers, GHS.

85. In 1774, Edward Telfair reported to his correspondents in Jamaica that of a cargo of thirty-two "New Negroes," ten died before the ship docked at Cockspur, four more passed away on the river to Savannah, and those who survived were "of so mean an appearance, as had not been exposed to Sale in Savannah this Season." Edward Telfair to Somerville, Noble, and White, Jamaica, November 25, 1774, Telfair Letter Book, January 12, 1774–February 20, 1782, box 9, Telfair Family Papers, GHS.

86. Klein, *Atlantic Slave Trade*, 158.

87. Bill of sale between Button Gwinnett and James Read, August 9, 1769, 322, Colonial Bond Book R (1766–72), GHS. The provost marshal seized the slaves of John Milledge to pay off debts to several merchants in town. Milledge arranged to have them not be exposed "to Public Sale but had sold or agreed for the sale in a private way to James Wright for 650 pounds"; February 6, 1770, 325, Colonial Bond Book R (1766–72). For the transfer of enslaved people by wills, see *Abstracts of Colonial Wills*; and Marsh, *Georgia's Frontier Women*, 168.

88. Burnard and Morgan, "Dynamics of the Slave Market," 224.

89. Genovese, *Roll, Jordan, Roll*, 3.

Chapter 7. The Making of the Lowcountry Plantation

1. Higman, *Concise History of the Caribbean*, 114; Higman, "Economic and Social Development," 1:303; Ward, "The British West Indies in the Age of Abolition," 415. To the south of Georgia, British East Florida came into being after the Spanish left in the wake of their defeat in the Seven Years' War. Although it remained unclear how this sandy territory could be integrated into the empire, the British political world poured substantial funds into the effort to tap its resources.

2. Sheridan, "The Formation of Caribbean Plantation Society," 394–95, 403; Higman, *Concise History of the Caribbean*, 98–109; Burnard, "'Prodigious Riches,'" 520.

3. Greene, "Colonial South Carolina and the Caribbean Connection," 73–75; P. Wood, *Black Majority*, 14–17; Edelson, *Plantation Enterprise*, 3–4.

4. The number three hundred was estimated from an analysis of the distribution and frequency of inventories and petitions for land grants. In 1773, Governor Wright reported fourteen hundred farms or plantations in the colony. "Report of Sir James Wright on the Condition of the Province of Georgia, 20th September 1773," in *CGHS*, 3:160.

5. Stewart, *"What Nature Suffers to Groe,"* ch. 3.

6. Tables 7.5 and 7.6 in Watts, *The West Indies*, 311–13; Sheridan, "The Formation of Caribbean Plantation Society," 400. Sheridan's figure for circa 1748 is 5.9 for the British West Indies as a whole and 7.8 for the Leeward Islands. See Table 18.1.

7. Qtd. in P. Morgan, *Slave Counterpoint*, 95.

8. Table 6.1, "Estimated Population of the South in 1775," in Menard, "Economic and Social Development of the South," 250. In 1772, William De Brahm estimated twelve thousand slaves in the Georgia lowcountry. Menard's figures reflect the reality in that year, not in 1775 when many more Africans had been deployed.

9. The Treaty of Paris in 1763 awarded the territory between the Altamaha and the St. Marys rivers, the "debatable lands" long contested by Britain and Spain, to Georgia. At the moment the treaty gave the territory to Great Britain, South Carolina issued warrants for over half a million acres to hundreds of Carolinians in a claim based on dubious charters from another century—and caught Georgia's government off guard. Although the British government recognized Georgia's claim, it did so in a lukewarm fashion and left a degree of uncertainty hanging over land titles. Chestnutt, "South Carolina's Penetration of Georgia," 195–207; Gallay, "Jonathan Bryan's Plantation Empire," 273–74, and *Formation of a Planter Elite*, 102–4. For Bartram's comment, Bartram, *Travels of William Bartram*, 13–14.

10. Sheridan, "The Formation of Caribbean Plantation Society," 404–6; Dunn, *Sugar and Slaves*, 95–106.

11. A visitor found St. Kitts "almost abandoned to overseers and managers, owing to the amazing fortunes that belong to Individuals, who almost all reside in England." O'Shaughnessy, *An Empire Divided*, 4–5.

12. See Table 2; Range, "The Agricultural Revolution," 250–55.

13. Henry Ellis to the Board of Trade, October 27, 1757, in *CRG*, 28, pt. 1:73.

14. Stewart, *"What Nature Suffers to Groe,"* 92–93, 118.

15. Inventory of James Pierce, March 3, 1777, Colonial Book FF, Georgia Archives.

16. Loewald et al., "Johann Martin Bolzius," 234, 261 (quotation).

17. Sheftall, *Sunbury on the Medway*, 12–13; C. Jones, *Dead Towns*, 141–223. The land and tax records bring home the point. In 1763, the amount of land granted in St. John Parish almost equaled that in Christ Church, 81,000 versus 88,100 acres, and the taxes collected amounted to almost half that of Christ Church, which included the large tax base of Savannah. "Total of Quit Rents due to His Majesty," March 25, 1764, in *CRG*, 28, pt. 2:32; "The Produce of the Tax," 1763, 1764, 1765, in *CRG*, 28, pt. 2:34, 196, 198. The amount of quit rents due to the Crown in 1767 showed St. John Parish owing 83 percent of what Christ Church owed. "Total of Quit Rents," March 1767, in *CRG*, 37:79.

18. Menard, "Financing the Lowcountry Export Boom," 665.

19. Wilms, "Development of Rice Culture," 45–57; Carney, *Black Rice*, 86–89; Stewart, *"What Nature Suffers to Groe,"* 92–93.

20. Robert Baillie to Menzies Baillie, July 4, 1774. For additional comments on rice cultivation, see Baillie to his brother James Baillie, August 3, 1773, Baillie Family Papers, NAS.

21. Edelson, *Plantation Enterprise*, 241.

22. Chaplin, *An Anxious Pursuit*, 232.

23. Rowland et al., *History of Beaufort County*, 1:179–80.

24. That section remained effectively closed to development until the Creeks officially transferred title in 1760. In the Treaty of 1739, Oglethorpe had recognized the claim of the Yamacraws to that valuable strip and, after they fell apart as a community and drifted away, the Lower Creeks succeeded to the claim. Juricek, *Colonial Georgia and the Creeks*, 42, 102–7; Sweet, *Negotiating for Georgia*, 36–39, 121–23. White Georgians were hard pressed to do otherwise than acknowledge the transaction, and at one point boards painted red were nailed to posts at the end of town "to show the inhabitants that they could not go over that marsh to cut wood as that Land was the Indians." Autobiography of Levi Sheftall, Sheftall diaries, 1733–1808, Keith Read Collection, Hargrett Library, UGA.

25. "[M]any Lots of the best Land in the Province lie vacant in consequence of claims that are said to exist & were derived from a verbal Cession of Mr. Oglethorpe. The Claimants themselves have not attempted to establish their pretensions nor complied with any one condition in the Royal instruction. They do not reside here nor is it well known where they are but it is probable they are lying at lurch until contiguous lands [are] improved & the value of those they claim raised thereby"; Henry Ellis to the Board of Trade, March 11, 1757, in *CRG*, 28, pt. 1:6. The Augustine family in Charles Town, whose father had lost money in creating a steam-driven sawmill upriver, lived in Charles Town and held out until the mid-1760s, when they sold their acreage at a handsome profit. Granger, *Savannah River Plantations*, 146–47.

26. De Vorsey, *De Brahm's Report*, 159.

27. An immigrant from St. Kitts Island knew the West Indian market and its insatiable appetite for American lumber and had no bolder vision than to satisfy that hunger with his Savannah River plantation. Petition of Lewis Johnston, November 7, 1758, in *CRG*, 7:829; "Memorial of Greenwood & Higginson on behalf of themselves and their correspondent, Mr. Samuel Douglass, merchant of Savannah," June 27, 1782, AO 13/34. Another merchant in Savannah converted his father-in-law's thousand-acre tract into a timbering operation and promptly stripped the land of its trees. Granger, *Savannah River Plantations*, 182.

28. Granger, *Savannah River Plantations*, 42–45, 61–65, 284–85; Gallay, *Formation of a Planter Elite*, 84–86. By the end of the decade, Bryan had acquired adjacent tracts for a total of sixteen hundred acres and stood alone on the east side of the town as a model for what the future held.

29. Most of the twenty plantations that can be identified were owned by merchants, including John Graham, James Graham, Lachlan McGillivray, William McGillivray (patronized by his cousin Lachlan), Nathaniel Hall, Greenwood & Higginson, John Rae, George Kincaid, Samuel Douglass, Edward Telfair, Basil Cowper, John Jamieson, and Lewis Johnston. Others were Jonathan Bryan, Governor James Wright, his son Alexander Wright, James Deveaux, William Knox, Dr. James Cuthbert, James Hume, and Miles Brewton.

30. Doar, *Rice and Rice Planting*, 8.

31. Carney, *Black Rice*, 91–95; Doar, *Rice and Rice Planting*, 9–13; Chaplin, *An Anxious Pursuit*, 231–34.

32. "An account of land, Negroes and other effects[:] the property of John Graham late of Georgia," AO 13/35, 157–60; Minutes of interview of John Graham before the Commission of Claims, December 20, 1783, AO 12, 57–98.

33. Account of Edward Telfair and Company of Georgia with Cowper & Telfair of London, February 2, 1799, Treasury 79/55, document 24, NA-UK.

34. "Memorial of Greenwood & Higginson on behalf of themselves and their correspondent, Mr. Samuel Douglass," June 27, 1782; "An Abstract of the titles to the lands mentioned in the schedule annexed to the memorial of Samuel Douglass," March 16, 1784, AO 13/34.

35. "An Account of the lands of William Higginson and William Greenwood, London merchants," June 17, 1783, AO 13/34; Greenwood and Higginson to Commissioners of American Claims, March 17, 1784, Samuel Douglass to Commissioners of American Claims, March 17, 1784, AO 13/119.

36. "A List of Slaves the property of John Graham, Esq.," January 9, 1781, Colonial Bond Book KK-2, 294–96.

37. *Stead, Pinckney, Mary P. Izard, Elizabeth Izard, executors of Ben. Stead vs. John*

Cobbison and Ann Cobbison, admins. of John Rae and Edward Telfair, executor of John Sommerville, U.S. Circuit Court, Southern District of Georgia, box 89, 55A24, A-3, NARA. The complainants charged that John Rae and John Sommerville, partners in Rae and Sommerville, were indebted on January 1, 1775, for £3,864 sterling for goods supplied and for money lent by Benjamin Stead. "Rae and Sommerville withdrew considerable proportions of the partnership funds which they ought not to have done before payment of their debts and ... each of them invested part of these funds in the purchase of lands, Negroes, etc. as their own separate property."

38. William Knox to James Habersham, March 2, 1768, April 3, 1770, Habersham Papers, GHS.

39. The calculation of the average number of Africans and African Americans on Savannah River plantations has been made from the inventories in Colonial Books F and FF, inventories in the loose papers at the Georgia Archives and the UGA Library, memorials of Loyalists to the Commission on American Claims, inventories taken in 1776 by the new government, and occasional correspondence.

40. While an acre of land at Monteith, Graham's inland plantation, yielded a thousand pounds of rice, an acre at Mulberry Grove produced fifteen hundred. A slave produced in a year as much as six to seven barrels of rice instead of the customary four to five barrels by the impoundment method. Testimony of John Graham before the Claim Commissioners, December 20, 1783, AO 50/115, 12, microfilm, GHS.

41. Watts, *The West Indies*, 276.

42. Edelson, *Plantation Enterprise*, 240–44, esp. 242.

43. Granger, *Savannah River Plantations*, 44–47; *Benjamin Stead versus John Rae estate*, 1790–97, U.S. Circuit Court, Southern District of Georgia, mixed cases, 1790–1860, A/20–1/31, box 3, no. 57/06 A 91, NARA; Granger, *Savannah River Plantations*, 356–57.

44. "Evidence on the memorial of Sir James Wright, Baronet," November 6, 1783, AO 12, microfilm, GHS.

45. James Habersham to Henry Laurens, Savannah, June 3, 1771, in *CGHS*, 6:132–34.

46. John Graham to James Grant, June 2, 1767, James Grant Papers, Ballindalloch Muniments, NAS.

47. Betty Wood established the pattern of slaveholding for the colony as a whole. Of the masters included in the inventories and lists in her study, 6 percent owned more than fifty slaves and accounted for about 45 percent of the slaves, while 56 percent of the masters owned less than ten slaves. *Slavery in Colonial Georgia*, 108.

48. See Table 9.

49. P. Morgan, *Slave Counterpoint*, 61.

50. Ibid., 456–58; Simpson, "'She has her country marks very conspicuous in the face,'" 94–134. For the context of the early days in the development of a plantation economy, B. Wood, *Slavery in Colonial Georgia*, 90–96.

51. Carney, *Black Rice*, 22–23, 31–49. Carney writes, "Rice cultivation is essential to cultural identity throughout much of West Africa" (31). Fields-Black, *Deep Roots*.

52. Carney, *Black Rice*, 69–106; Carney, "From Hands to Tutors"; P. Wood, *Black Majority*, ch. 2; Littlefield, *Rice and Slaves*, ch. 4; Hawthorne, "From 'Black Rice' to 'Brown.'"

53. Edelson, Review of *Black Rice* by Judith Carney, 196–97.

54. Fields-Black, *Deep Roots*, 159.

55. *Georgia Gazette*, May 23, 1770.

56. P. Wood, *Black Majority*, ch. 2; Littlefield, *Rice and Slaves*, ch. 4; Carney, *Black Rice*; Carney, "Landscapes of Technology Transfer," 5–35; G. Hall, "Africa and Africans," 136–50.

57. Eltis, Morgan, and Richardson, "Agency and Diaspora in Atlantic History," 1329–58; Eltis, Morgan, and Richardson, "Black, Brown, or White?," 164–71.

58. O'Malley, "Beyond the Middle Passage," 165–66.

59. Burnard and Morgan, "Dynamics of the Slave Market," 205–28; P. Morgan, *Slave Counterpoint*, 61.

60. Edelson, *Plantation Enterprise*, 74–76; Edelson, Review of *Black Rice* by Judith Carney, 196–97.

61. Edelson, "Beyond 'Black Rice,'" 125–35.

62. John Graham to James Grant, March 1, 1768, James Grant Papers, Ballindalloch Muniments, NAS.

63. P. Morgan, "British Encounters," 161.

64. "Evidence on the Memorial of Sir James Wright, Baronet, Sir James Wright Sworn," October 22, 1783, AO 12, microfilm, Georgia Archives. On the seventh page of Wright's testimony: "He thinks 3 in 100 might die in a year on an average."

65. "An account of lands, Negroes and other effects[:] the property of John Graham," October 3, 1783, AO 13/35, 132; De Vorsey, *De Brahm's Report*, 162.

66. Peter Manigault to Blake, December 24, 1770, Peter Manigault Letter Book, 1763–73, South Carolina Historical Society, qtd. in Stewart, *"What Nature Suffers to Groe,"* 114.

67. P. Morgan, *Slave Counterpoint*, 82–83. In the 1760s, the sex ratio in the Carolina lowcountry was 133 men for every 100 women, but reached parity by the 1790s. P. Morgan, "Black Society in the Lowcountry," 88.

68. B. Wood, *Slavery in Colonial Georgia*, 105.

69. "A List of Slaves the Property of John Graham Esq.," Colonial Bond Book KK, 2:294–97; "A List of William Knox Esq.'s Negroes, Horses, Cattle, Hogs, Rice,

Corn, plantation tools, etc., with value at this time," January 1, 1777, Colonial Bond Book Y, 2:536, Georgia Archives.

70. B. Wood, *Slavery in Colonial Georgia*, 106; P. Morgan, "The Black Experience in the British Empire," 469.

71. Burnard and Morgan, "Dynamics of the Slave Market," 207–8; V. Brown, *The Reaper's Garden*, 17. On mortality rates, scholars point to the Codrington estates in Barbados, where as many as 5 percent of the slaves needed to be replaced every year, and to Nevis, where the annual depletion rate of slaves reached 6.6 percent during the 1730s. Watts, *The West Indies*, 366.

72. Simpson, "'She has her country marks very conspicuous in the face,'" 101. In 1775, the black population was close to eighteen thousand. Approximately thirteen thousand people had come from Africa. Of the slaves carried into the colony from South Carolina, a significant minority were born in Africa.

73. The census typically was done by the end of the first half of the year; slave importations reflect the full calendar year. At the very least, the black population had not yet reached the point of natural increase. Series Z 1–19, U.S. Census, *Historical Statistics*, 2:1168; the total of importations comes from the statistical analysis involved in compiling Table 9.

74. Higman, *Concise History of the Caribbean*, 125; P. Morgan, *Slave Counterpoint*, 35, 39–40; Chaplin, *An Anxious Pursuit*, 230. For the Lower South, thirty slaves was the norm for a settlement working a set of rice fields, but larger plantations had more than one settlement.

75. P. Morgan, "The Black Experience in the British Empire," 470–71.

76. Stewart, *"What Nature Suffers to Groe,"* 90–94; B. Wood, *Slavery in Colonial Georgia*, 108, 135. Betty Wood reinforces the point that the modes of plantation management in Georgia were imported from South Carolina. P. Morgan, "The Black Experience in the British Empire," 472.

77. Craton, "Reluctant Creoles," 315.

78. Higman, *Concise History of the Caribbean*, 125–27.

79. "If the Negroes are Skilful and industrious, they plant something for themselves after the day's work," the Reverend Bolzius observed. They were given as much land as they could handle and, if the amount of time for growing their own food was small, the crops of pumpkins, "water and sugar melons," peanuts, and peas were an important nutritional supplement to their coarse diet of corn, potatoes, and "rough rice." Loewald et al., "Johann Martin Bolzius," 258–60.

80. P. Morgan, "Work and Culture," 563–99, esp. 577–78.

81. Edelson, *Plantation Enterprise*, 84–86, 156. Edelson questions the argument of Judith Carney that slaves received the benefits of the task system in return for teaching planters how to cultivate rice.

82. Dunn, *Sugar and Slaves*, 239.

83. P. Wood, *Black Majority*, 320–25; P. Morgan, *Slave Counterpoint*, 264.

84. "An act for ordering and governing slaves within this province," *CRG*, 19, pt. 1:209–49; B. Wood, *Slavery in Colonial Georgia*, 115, 129.

85. P. Morgan, "British Encounters," 174.

86. Caldwell, "Women Landholders of Colonial Georgia," 189–94; Marsh, *Georgia's Frontier Women*, 112.

87. Chaplin, *An Anxious Pursuit*, 10.

88. K. Morgan, "Organization of the Colonial American Rice Trade," 435; Nash, "Organization of Trade and Finance in the British Atlantic Economy," 96–127.

Chapter 8. Georgia's Rice and the Atlantic World

1. The Naval Shipping Lists for 1755–60 reveal the absence of English merchants in the export of rice, CO 5/709. For a biographical sketch of James Crokatt, *PHL*, 1:2; for the vacuum in government during the early 1750s, Coleman, *Colonial Georgia*, 174–75.

2. Romans, *A Concise Natural History*, 146.

3. Matson, *Merchants & Empire*, 159, 200. Merchants like John van Cortlandt and James Alexander of New York were heavily involved in trade with the Lower South.

4. In 1757, Georgia owners accounted for seven out of nineteen ships with cargos of rice. Naval Shipping Lists for 1757, CO 5/709.

5. "Charter-party with penal bond" between William Cecil, shipmaster, and William Thomson, merchant, January 14, 1758, in Walker, *Abstracts of Georgia*, 139; R. Davis, "American Voyages," 10–16.

6. Fourth-quarter clearances, 1760; first-quarter clearances, 1761 and 1762; all quarters, 1763–65, Naval Shipping Lists, CO 5/709, 710.

7. William Knox to James Habersham, February 9, 1772, James Habersham Papers, GHS.

8. Romans, *A Concise Natural History*, 146; Shepherd and Williamson, "Coastal Trade," 809. The *Historical Statistics* of the U.S. Census gives a slightly different figure for 1772, four hundred fifty more barrels exported than what is shown in the Romans table. Both tables show more than twenty-five thousand barrels exported in 1771.

9. Edgar, *South Carolina*, 146; U.S. Census, *Historical Statistics*, 1192.

10. K. Morgan, "Organization of the Colonial American Rice Trade," 433–52; Dethloff, "The Colonial Rice Trade," 231–43; Hornsby, *British Atlantic, American Frontier*, 111–23; McCusker and Menard, *The Economy of British America*, 176–81.

11. Ward, "The British West Indies in the Age of Abolition," 415–439; Watts, *The West Indies*, 275–76; Hornsby, *British Atlantic, American Frontier*, 43–45.

12. James Habersham to Messrs. Graham, Clark & Company, London, February 15, 1771, in *CGHS*, 6:121.

13. "I this year plant on two plantations 300 acres of Rice. If I am in luck, I ought to make near 1000 Blls[,] less by a couple however will do very well." John Graham to James Grant, Savannah, May 22, 1771, James Grant Papers, Ballindalloch Muniments, microfilm, NAS. Graham claimed six hundred acres under cultivation in "An account of land, Negroes and other effects[:] the property of John Graham, late of Georgia," March 1783, AO 12, 94.

14. "A valuation and appraisement of land, buildings and Negroes on Rice Hope Plantation on Hutchinson Island, belonging to James Graham, Merchant of London," April 1783, AO 1/35, 116–31; Memorial of John McGillivray, May 17, 1784, AO 13/36b, 790; Schedule of Losses, William McGillivray, 1783, AO 12, 19.

15. "Evidence on the Foregoing Memorial of James Butler, March 1, 1784, AO 12, 195. On his principal plantation, he "cleared and planted [500 acres] with Rice and Corn.... He cleared 150 acres of Rice Land & 50 Acres of Corn Land. The remaining 300 acres were without any cultivation. 100 acres of it was for a Reservoir of Water to let in upon Rice Ground. The rest Pine Barren and Hickory Land." His total of three hundred acres of rice produced nine hundred barrels in a typical year. For William Gibbons estate, entry of October 11, 1775, for purchase of rice on November 22, 1774, Telfair Account Book, Telfair Family Papers, box 1, f. 8, GHS; "The memorial of William McGillivray, a Captain in his Majesty's Invalid Forces—Schedule of Losses referred to in the Memorial," 1784, AO 12, NA-UK, microfilm, Georgia Archives.

16. Shepherd and Williamson, "Coastal Trade," Appendix Table 2, 809. The table gives £6,300 as the value of exports of rice to other North American colonies. It is assumed that the average value per barrel was 45 shillings for a total of twenty-eight hundred barrels, shipped primarily to Charles Town.

17. According to the report of the comptroller of the port of Savannah, Georgia exported 23,540 barrels of rice in 1772. Another 2,800 barrels were shipped on average to other North American ports during 1768–72. If 10 percent more was grown for internal consumption, the total was approximately 28,000 barrels of rice. For internal rice consumption, estimates vary. Lewis Gray thought it could account for as much as one-third of the total rice crop. Gray, *History of Agriculture*, 287–90. Coclanis accepts the estimate of Converse Clowse of 10 percent. Coclanis, *Shadow of a Dream*, 256.

18. William Campbell, the last governor of royal South Carolina, purchased a plantation from Basil Cowper and John Smith known as Smithfield. Its rice was

sold through Savannah. "Inventory and appraisement of the Negroes, land etc. of Inverary, plantation on the Savannah River for William Campbell," by John Graham, James Mossman, and John Hume, May 11, 1776, AO 13/119. Others who shipped from Savannah included Cornelius Dupont and the DeSaussure brothers. Rowland et al., *History of Beaufort County*, 1:178–79. Rowland speaks of a tradition of Carolina planters doing business in Charles Town rather than nearby Savannah. Although true after the Revolution, evidence suggests many were using Savannah during the colonial era. Rowland, "Alone on the River," 127.

19. The names of export merchants who dealt in rice have been compiled from advertisements in the *Georgia Gazette*, Loyalist petitions, account ledgers, correspondence, and letter books.

20. Thomas Savage, a Charles Town merchant and slaver, married Mary Elliott Butler, daughter of William and Elizabeth Butler, at one point the largest slavemasters in Georgia. Edgar and Bailey, *Biographical Directory*, 2:596–97.

21. Account Book, 1765–82, Estate of William Gibbons, 1772, Telfair Family Papers, Collection 793, box 12, f. 105, GHS. The records of the estate of Benjamin Farley tell the same story. Of 402 barrels disposed of by the executors, over half went to Rae, Sommerville and Company to cover past-due accounts three years old, and 51 barrels went to Douglass and Company for accounts due from the previous year. No intermediary was involved.

22. Nash, "Organization of Trade and Finance in the Atlantic Economy," 79–81.

23. Godbold and Woody, *Christopher Gadsden*, 12–13.

24. Nash, "Organization of Trade and Finance in the Atlantic Economy," 80–82.

25. For Thomas Lloyd, *Georgia Gazette*, January 17, 1765; for William Moore, *Georgia Gazette*, August 13, 1766.

26. Sheridan, *Sugar and Slavery*, 328–32; Nash, "Organization of Trade and Finance in the Atlantic Economy," 74–81.

27. William Knox to James Habersham, November 6, 1771, James Habersham Papers, GHS.

28. Clay and Co. to Bright and Perkins, February 13, 1774, Letter Book, Joseph Clay and Company, December 19, 1772–March 31, 1774, Joseph Clay Papers, GHS.

29. Joseph Clay to James Jackson, March 29, 1784, Letter Book, Clay, Telfair & Company, October 25, 1783–September 1, 1784, Joseph Clay Papers, GHS.

30. Within a few months in 1772, the price of rice per hundredweight moved from 11 shillings to almost 13 shillings. James Habersham to William Knox, February 11, 1772; James Habersham to James Wright, June 13, July 16, 1772, all in *CGHS*, 6:164, 185, 190.

31. James Habersham to James Wright, July 16, 1772, in *CGHS*, 6:190–92.

32. Henry Laurens to James Habersham, October 12, 1771, in *PHL*, 8:11. Frank Lambert puts this letter in context in *James Habersham*, 122–23.

33. The numerous acts passed by the Commons House of Assembly are in *CRG*, 18:362–785.

34. K. Morgan, " The Organization of the Colonial American Rice Trade," 434; Shepherd and Walton, *Shipping, Maritime Trade, and the Economic Development of Colonial North America*, 73.

35. Eighty-seven percent of owners of vessels entering Savannah were British. Naval Shipping Lists, 1765–67, CO 5/710.

36. *Georgia Packet*, July 11, 1765, British Naval Shipping Lists, CO 5/710.

37. Between 1769 and 1771, Georgians constructed 11 schooners and ships compared to 22 for Carolinians, a small number in relationship to the Upper South where 122 craft were built in the Chesapeake Bay region. "Vessels Built in Thirteen Colonies and West Florida: 1769–1771," Z 516–29, in U.S. Census, *Historical Statistics*, 2:1195.

38. Fleetwood, *Tidecraft*, 47; Goldenberg, *Shipbuilding in Colonial America*, 122.

39. "Vessels Built in Thirteen Colonies and West Florida: 1769–1771," Z 516–29, in U.S. Census, *Historical Statistics*, 2:1195; Clowse, "Shipowning and Shipbuilding."

40. H. Davis, *The Fledgling Province*, 104–5.

41. V. Wood, *Live Oaking*, 11–15.

42. *Georgia Gazette*, October 11, 1775.

43. John Wand Papers, GHS. This collection contains papers concerning the arbitration in the case of the ship *Elizabeth* between John Wand, owner, and Cowper, Telfairs of Savannah.

44. Entry for the ship *Butler*, March 1776, Account Book of William and Edward Telfair and Company, then Edward Telfair Company, Edward Telfair Papers, Duke University.

45. For South Carolina, 121 vessels; for Georgia, 28 vessels. "An Account of the number of vessels which have entered Outwards at the several ports of North America from the 5th January 1772 to the 5th January 1773," American Inspector-General's Report (1768–72), Customs 16/1, NA-UK.

46. Statistics compiled from Naval Shipping Lists, 1765–1766, CO 5/710.

47. The forty-nine days for Savannah comes from information in the naval shipping lists. For South Carolina, Coclanis, *Shadow of a Dream*, 260.

48. Naval Shipping Lists, 1765–66, CO 5/710; Clowse, *Measuring Charleston's Overseas Commerce*, 62; K. Morgan, "The Organization of the Colonial American Rice Trade," 443. British planters in the sugar islands turned to the Lower South to feed their enslaved population. However, J. R. Ward offers little support for this view. Ward, *British West Indian Slavery*, 37, 76- 77.

49. Clowse, *Measuring Charleston's Overseas Commerce*, 60, 62.

50. K. Morgan, "The Organization of the Colonial American Rice Trade," 438, 442.

51. Coon, "Eliza Pinckney," 61–76; Balfour-Paul, *Indigo*, 63–70; Edgar, *South Carolina*, 146–47.

52. Shepherd, "Commodity Exports," 20–21; Weir, *Colonial South Carolina*, 146. Mart Stewart in *"What Nature Suffers to Groe"* calls indigo an economically important crop (89); in *Slavery in Colonial Georgia*, Betty Wood only mentions indigo as a crop grown in the colony; Julia Floyd Smith describes the inferior quality of indigo grown in Georgia and the lack of production in *Slavery and Rice Culture*, 28. For a summary of South Carolina's indigo cultivation, McCusker and Menard, *The Economy of British America*, 187; and Egnal, *New World Economies*, 107–10.

53. Edelson, "The Characters of Commodities," 350–52; Bitler, "Indigo"; Weir, *Colonial South Carolina*, 151.

54. Chestnutt, *South Carolina's Expansion*, 128, 131–32.

55. Robert Baillie to George Baillie, his father, February 10, 1754, Baillie Family Papers, GD 1/1155/66, NAS.

56. Seth John Cuthbert to Lachlan McIntosh, August 9, 1774, Keith Read Collection, Hargrett Library, UGA; Weir, *Colonial South Carolina*, 146, 160.

57. Habersham to the Secretary, June 13, 1751, in *CRG*, 26:235–36. Habersham talks of the initial efforts at indigo planting in Georgia and of Henry Yonge's attempt on Skidaway Island. In 1760, the colony shipped out 11,700 pounds compared to South Carolina's bountiful 507,600. "Indigo and Silk Exported from South Carolina and Georgia: 1747 to 1788," in U.S. Census, *Historical Statistics*, 1189.

58. Imports of indigo from Georgia, 1773 and 1774, Customs 3, 73–74, NA-UK.

59. Romans, *A Concise Natural History*, 146; Memorial of James Graham to the Commissioners, April 1784, AO 13/35; Memorial of Basil Cowper, February 16, 1784, AO 12, 4, NA-UK, microfilm, Georgia Archives; Samuel Douglass to Commissioners, "An Estimate of the Lands which were the sole and entire Property of Samuel Douglass," description of Tweedside and Skidaway Island plantations, June 17, 1783, AO 13/34; John Graham to Governor James Grant, May 22, 1771, James Grant Papers, Ballindalloch Muniments, NAS; John Jamieson to Commissioners, 1785, AO 13/36a; "An Account of the Losses sustained by Thomas Young," December 23, 1783, AO 13. In 1775, the value of the indigo shipped by Young from St. John Parish was an impressive £659.

60. McCusker and Menard, *The Economy of British America*, 18–34. In their classic study, they presented strengths and weaknesses of the staple thesis, speculating that it would allow for a better understanding of regional differences in British America.

61. Coclanis, "In Retrospect: McCusker and Menard's 'Economy of British America,'" 183–97; S. D. Smith, "Reckoning with the Atlantic Economy," 749–64; Nash, "South Carolina and the Atlantic Economy," 677–702; Price, "The Trans-

atlantic Economy," 22–33; Hornsby, *British Atlantic, American Frontier*, 123–25, 223–27.

62. K. Morgan, "Organization of the Colonial American Rice Trade," 438–40. Parliament placed rice on the list of enumerated commodities in two statutes issued in 1705. Rice had to be shipped to Britain, where a duty was collected, before it could be re-exported to Europe.

63. Edelson, *Plantation Enterprise*, 176–86.

Chapter 9. Retailing the "Baubles of Britain"

1. Extracts of a sales account book, 1753–55, voyage of the *Antonia de Padua*, 1753, William Bradley Papers, GHS. When Davis sailed the *Antonia de Padua* into Savannah, naval authorities seized his vessel and touched off a round of petitions and hearings. The voyage was a commercial success.

2. Johann Christoph Bornemann to the Honored Lord Councilor, January 30, 1753, qtd. in G. Jones, "A German Surgeon," 895.

3. Robert Baillie to his father, George Baillie, July 18, 1753, and to his brother James, November 18, 1753, Baillie Family Papers, NAS.

4. Loewald et al., "Johann Martin Bolzius," 229, 243, 245, 247; Weeks, *Savannah in the Time of Peter Tondee*, 100. After his arrival at Ebenezer, Bornemann commented on "the high price of almost all necessities, the lack of money, and useful craftsmen." Johann Christoph Bornemann to Haller, March 11, 1754. Earlier, he had noted, "Everything is exceedingly expensive, and there is no money among the people. Hardware and daily wages cost very much." Bornemann to Councilor, January 30, 1753, both qtd. in G. Jones, "A German Surgeon," 895, 911.

5. Estate of Abraham Minis, June 30, 1757, Inventory Book F, 49–51, Georgia Archives; H. Davis, *The Fledgling Province*, 38–39.

6. Thomas Rasberry to Mr. John Smith, October 10, 1758, Letter Book of Thomas Rasberry, 1758–61, in *CGHS*, 13:16. The clientele of his store represented a narrow range and the volume of goods they purchased was relatively small.

7. The value of imports per white person comes from the average of the official value of imports over a five-year period divided by the estimated population. For 1770, the number of white people was 12,750 for Georgia, and 49,066 for South Carolina, according to U.S. Census, *Historical Statistics*. The yearly average of imports was £66,798 for Georgia and £320,304 for South Carolina.

8. "Wealth by Cluster, All Regions, 1774," in A. Jones, *Wealth of a Nation to Be*, 357.

9. Nash, "Domestic Material Culture and Consumer Demand," 222–23.

10. Weir, *Colonial South Carolina*, 236. By the time of the Revolution, probated

estates in Carolina were worth four times as much as those in Virginia and ten times those in Massachusetts. Nash, "Domestic Material Culture and Consumer Demand," 234.

11. Watts, *The West Indies*, 209, 356–58.

12. Mann, "Becoming Creole," 94–97.

13. Greene, "Society and Economy in the British Caribbean," 1510.

14. Sheridan, *Sugar and Slavery*, 377.

15. Mann, "Becoming Creole," 25–35.

16. For Savannah, the number comes from advertisements in the *Georgia Gazette* and from the Colonial Bond Records at the Georgia Archives. For Charles Town, Calhoun, Zierden, and Paysinger, "Geographic Spread of Charleston's Mercantile Community."

17. *Georgia Gazette*, March 21, 1765.

18. *Georgia Gazette*, March 23, 1774. As ship chandlers, Bard and Thompson offered mostly food products like ship bread, milk, potatoes, butter, and hams. Situated among the staples were "Dry goods as usual."

19. *Georgia Gazette*, January 8, 1764, January 10, 1765.

20. *Georgia Gazette*, July 27, 1774.

21. *Georgia Gazette*, April 15, 1767, October 1, 1766.

22. *Georgia Gazette*, June 9, 1763, October 4, 1769, August 23, 1775.

23. In 1765, twelve people held licenses to retail, including two women. *Georgia Gazette*, January 10, 1765.

24. Bond between Thomas Vincent and Thomas Marlton, London, Colonial Bond Book, June 13, 1754, entered May 25, 1759, in Walker, *Abstracts of Georgia*, 137–38.

25. Solomon's Lodge, no. 1, F. & A.M., Original Minutes Book, the Lodge in Savannah, Georgia, 1756–57, microfilm, GHS.

26. Estate of Thomas Vincent, September 30, 1768, Inventory Book F, 358, Georgia Archives. Although the value of his store goods was modest, he owned twenty-one enslaved people.

27. His early death in 1767 removed a hardworking retailer who brought a measure of sophistication to the town. Vincent owed £3,250 to Edward Telfair and Company, Telfair Account Book, 1774, f. 44, Telfair Family Papers, GHS.

28. Marsh, *Georgia's Frontier Women*, 131–32.

29. Arrival of the *Nancy*, Button Gwinnett, owner, September 7, 1765, Naval Shipping Lists, CO 5/710. Advertisement for the contents of the store he opened is in *Georgia Gazette*, September 12, 1765.

30. Jenkins, *Button Gwinnett*, 21–30.

31. G. Jones, "Portrait of an Irish Entrepreneur," 427–47.

32. *Stead, Pinckney, Mary P., Izard, Elizabeth Izard, executors of Ben. Stead vs. John Cobbison and Ann Cobbison, admins of John Rae and Edward Telfair, executor of John Sommerville*, August 1792, 55A24, A-3, U.S. Circuit Court, Southern District of Georgia, Savannah, mixed cases, 1790–1860, NARA. In 1775, John Rae and John Sommerville were indebted to Benjamin Stead, a merchant in London, for £3,864.

33. See advertisements of Rae and Sommerville, *Georgia Gazette*, November 2 and 9, December 7, 1768, and December 20, 1769. Thomas Sommerville, brother of Edward, handled cargo in Ireland.

34. Dickson, *Ulster Emigration*, 164–69.

35. R. Bolton, *Genealogical and Biographical Account of the Family of Bolton*, 79–104; H. Davis, *The Fledgling Province*, 56–57.

36. *Georgia Gazette*, June 29, 1768: "Five Field Negroes, to be sold at the Exchange in Savannah, for ready money, by Ewen and Bolton, Vendue Masters."

37. Jay, *Memoirs of the Life and Character of the Late Rev. Cornelius Winter*, 73.

38. Petition of Robert Reid, John Storr, and Thomas Read, merchants, to the Commission, June 9, 1786, AO 13/37. A schedule of debts presented claims for £10,304 owed by a broad range of people, including merchant John Graham for £1,013. Memorial of John Buchannan, merchant at Glaenock, February 16, 1784, AO 13/34. William Panton migrated from Scotland to Charles Town to join merchant John Gordon and subsequently came to Savannah to open his own firm with Philip Moore. Coker and Watson, *Indian Traders*, 24–25; "Just Imported by John Foulis," *Georgia Gazette*, March 30, 1774.

39. Breen, "Baubles of Britain," 448–58.

40. Watts, *The West Indies*, 356.

41. Breen, "Baubles of Britain," 452–61.

42. By far the bulk of imported goods that came from Great Britain into Georgia passed through the wholesale stores of Cowper, Telfairs; John Graham and Company; Inglis and Hall; Read and Mossman; Johnston & Wylly; Samuel Douglass and Company; and Clay and Habersham. The largest firm by the time of the Revolution was Cowper, Telfairs, which evolved into William and Edward Telfair Company, then Edward Telfair and Company. An earlier model of the Charles Town merchant who bought rice and imported dry goods is John Guerard, who died in 1764. Nash, "Trade and Business."

43. Estates of Alexander Fyffe, April 13, 1767 (£459), 268; Thomas Vincent, August 15, 1768 (£335 for dry goods), 359, both in Colonial Inventory F, Georgia Archives; Inventory of Goods, Cowper, Telfairs, May 14, 1772; Inventory of Goods, Edward Telfair, January 1, 1775, both in box 1, Telfair Family Papers, 793, GHS; tax on imported goods valued at £13,596, "Copy of Tax Receipt for 1773 in Georgia, Cowper, Telfairs," Edward Telfair, 1780–85, box 3, Duke University.

44. "Inglis and Hall have just imported," *Georgia Gazette*, October 8, 1766; "Cowper and Telfairs have just imported," *Georgia Gazette*, October 8, 1766.

45. Inventory of Goods, January 1, 1775, Edward Telfair and Company, Telfair Family Papers, GHS. The clientele came to the wholesale store through a process of self-selection or through stringent credit requirements for small purchasers.

46. Account Book of Purchases, William and Edward Telfair Company, and Edward Telfair and Company, April 18, 1774–February 2, 1775, Edward Telfair Papers, Duke University.

47. For discussion of the eighteenth-century consumer, Breen, "The Meaning of Things," 249–60.

48. Hart, *Building Charleston*, 1–15. Hart sees the middling groups in Charles Town constituting their own independent force within the system of distribution and consumption in the Carolina lowcountry.

49. Nash, "Domestic Material Culture and Consumer Demand," 221–34.

50. Ibid., 242, 246. Nash argues that consumers in Charles Town at the upper and lower ends of the income spectrum, but not in the middle, demonstrated a greater percentage of holdings of consumer goods than their rural counterparts.

51. For general descriptions of social life in Charles Town, Fraser, *Charleston! Charleston!*, 129–35; Weir, *Colonial South Carolina*, 236–46.

52. Doberstein, *Journals*, 2:667.

53. G. Jones, *The Georgia Dutch*, 174.

54. Nash, "Domestic Material Culture and Consumer Demand," 238, 241. The wealthiest Carolinians were able to increase their investments in slaves and in consumption simultaneously. Circumstantial evidence suggests the same was true for Georgia.

55. Exports to Georgia from England, 1771–74, Ledgers of Imports and Exports, Customs 3, vols. 71–74, NA-UK; Nash, "Domestic Material Culture and Consumer Demand," 251. S. D. Smith explores the challenges of classifying goods between "producer," or capital, goods and consumer goods. Smith, "The Market for Manufactures," 676–708.

56. Inventory of Goods, Edward Telfair and Company, January 1, 1775, box 1, Telfair Family Papers, GHS.

57. DuPlessis, "Cloth and the Emergence of the Atlantic Economy," 72–94. Carolinians were purchasing woolen goods as a higher percentage of total cloth consumption than Philadelphians or New Orleanais.

58. For a discussion of types of clothing and cloth, Styles, *The Dress of the People*, 31–56, 135–52.

59. Joseph Clay to unknown, October 25, 1783, Letter Book, Clay, Telfair & Co., October 25, 1783–September 1, 1784, Joseph Clay Papers, GHS. Clay acknowledged

that linens were wanted, given the hot climate, but the greatest demand was for woolens.

60. James Habersham to William Knox, November 17, 1767, in *CGHS*, 6:61.

61. Edward Telfair to Thomas Somerville [*sic*], April 14, 1774, Telfair Letter Book, Telfair Family Papers, GHS.

62. James Habersham to William Knox, March 9, 1764, in *CGHS*, 6:16.

63. Weeks, *Savannah in the Time of Peter Tondee.*

64. H. Davis, *The Fledgling Province*, 97–98, 169–70.

65. Weeks, *Savannah in the Time of Peter Tondee*, 169; H. Davis, *The Fledgling Province*, 253.

66. Hart, *Building Charleston*, 1–16.

67. Qtd. in H. Davis, *The Fledgling Province*, 62–63.

68. Weeks, *Savannah in the Time of Peter Tondee*, 145.

69. "A List of Slaves the Property of John Graham, Esq.: . . . Negroes Usually Employed and kept about the House," January 10, 1781, Colonial Bond Book KK-2, 297, Georgia Archives.

70. Joseph Clay to Bright & Pechin, February 22, 1773, Letter Book, Joseph Clay and Company, December 19, 1772–March 31, 1774, Joseph Clay Papers, GHS.

71. C. Jones, *History of Georgia*, 1:491–96, quotations on 494.

72. Inventory of the Personal Estate of Joseph Bacon, March 6, 1765, Colonial Inventory Book F, 1755–70, 230, Georgia Archives.

73. Inventory of the estate of Captain Mark Carr, February 27, 1769, Colonial Inventory Book F, 1755–70, Georgia Archives.

74. Robert Baillie to "My Dear Mother," August 4, 1773, Robert Baillie Papers, GD 1/1155/72, NAS.

75. Inventory of the estate of William Gibbons, March 1, 1771, loose papers, drawer 230, reel 21, Georgia Archives.

76. William Johnson, *Sketches of the Life and Correspondence of Nathanael Greene*, 2:411, qtd. in Granger, *Savannah River Plantations*, 72; "An appraisement and valuation of the estate and effects of N. Hall, April 20, 1776," attached to petition of Nathaniel Hall to Commissioners, May 7, 1786, AO 13/35.

77. Petition of Josiah Tattnall, 1783, AO 13/36a.

78. Nash, "Domestic Material Culture and Consumer Demand," 239, 244–46.

79. Governor Wright had 523 enslaved people; John Graham, 262; Lachlan Mc-Gillivray, 197; Jonathan Bryan, a total of 230 during his lifetime; John Morel, 155 at his death; James Habersham, around 200; and John Rae, over 150.

80. Waselkov, Wood, and Hatley, *Powhatan's Mantle*, 60–61. The region includes South Carolina, the Floridas, Georgia, and Creek, Cherokee, Choctaw, and Chickasaw territory.

Chapter 10. The Trade in Deerskins and Rum

1. From 1760 to 1768, rice went from 3,200 to 17,700 barrels and deerskin from 65,700 to 306,500 pounds. "Exports of Produce from the Province of Georgia," in Romans, *A Concise Natural History*, 146.

2. As illustrated in Table 15, deerskins represented £19,360 sterling out of a total of £74,079 in exports. The value of deerskin exports represented 29 percent of the average value of imports (£66,798) between 1768 and 1772 as reported by customs in U.S. Census, *Historical Statistics*, 1176. The amount of book debt in the deerskin trade totaled £85,000 out of £266,000 in book debt by the leading Georgia merchants in 1775.

3. Cashin, *Lachlan McGillivray*, 104–31; Cashin, *Colonial Augusta*, 29–58; Braund, *Deerskins & Duffels*, 121–29; Ready, *The Castle Builders*, 139–71; Sirmans, *Colonial South Carolina*, 188–98.

4. Hudson, *The Packhorseman*. An anthropologist and historian of Native Americans in the Southeast, Hudson produced a historical novel that describes the life of traders and packhorsemen in knowing terms.

5. James Habersham to Benjamin Martyn, February 3, 1752, in *CRG*, 26:337. By the end of the colonial era, Baltimore, Annapolis, Yorktown, and Wilmington had emerged as significant shipping centers but, in a region where stores were scattered along a complex river system, never rivaled Charles Town.

6. "Account of Trade in Deerskins Indian Dressed Exported from Charles Town from Lady Day 1740 to Lady Day 1763 taken from the Custom House Books," John Stuart to the Board of Trade, March 9, 1764, CO 323. A portion of the 220,000 pounds of deerskins came from the Cherokees and generally arrived overland. James Habersham reported 140,000 pounds passed by Savannah in 1751. Charles Town's competitive advantages were many: a well-established merchant community, storage and shipping facilities, capital and credit lines, and correspondents in London and Bristol.

7. Juricek, *Colonial Georgia and the Creeks*, 191; Fraser, *Savannah*, 35–36; Sweet, *Negotiating for Georgia*, 165–71.

8. "Exports of Produce from the Province of Georgia," in Romans, *A Concise Natural History*, 146.

9. Petition of Several Merchants and Shopkeepers, Savannah, December 2, 1761, in *CRG*, 13:617.

10. P. Wood, "The Changing Population of the Colonial South," 57–132; Merrell, *The Indians' New World*, 92–133.

11. Oatis, *A Colonial Complex*, 56–57, 202–3. Called Creeks by the English, the people called themselves the Muskogees or Muscogulges in their native tongue. Braund, *Deerskins & Duffels*, 3.

12. P. Wood, "The Changing Population of the Colonial South," 81–87.

13. Robbie Etheridge points out that Creeks did not exist prehistorically: "Rather, they came into existence sometime in the late seventeenth and early eighteenth centuries in response to the contact between the Old and New Worlds"; Etheridge, *Creek Country*, 22, 26–31, 93. Also see Wright, *Creeks and Seminoles*, 1–40, esp. 2–3; Braund, *Deerskins & Duffels*; Juricek, *Colonial Georgia and the Creeks*; P. Wood, "The Changing Population of the Colonial South," 85.

14. Wood, "The Changing Population of the Colonial South," 85.

15. Waselkov, "The Eighteenth-Century Anglo-Indian Trade," 193–222; Braund, *Deerskins & Duffels*, 121–25; Merrell, *The Indians' New World*, 49–91; Wright, *Creeks and Seminoles*, 53–56.

16. Axtel, *The Indians' New South*, 45–72; Piker, *Okfuskee*, 157–61; Hatley, *The Dividing Paths*, 45–47; Braund, *Deerskins & Duffels*, 121–38; Saunt, *A New Order of Things*, 11–66.

17. Cashin, *Governor Henry Ellis*, 150–69; Anderson, *Crucible of War*, 503–6.

18. De Vorsey, *The Indian Boundary in the Southern Colonies*, 149–57. At the Congress of Augusta, the Creeks took the initiative in making the proposed cession. Why they did so remains a matter of conjecture. Perhaps they recognized the changed dynamics of their situation in the southern interior at the end of the war; perhaps they felt in a weakened position because several traders had been killed the previous spring; and perhaps they were influenced by Lachlan McGillivray and George Galphin, masters of Indian diplomacy. Cashin, *Lachlan McGillivray*, 219–23.

19. Alden, *John Stuart and the Southern Colonial Frontier*, 183–86. The treaty led to increased contact between natives and European Americans that resulted in less, not more, comprehension, according to Joshua Piker in "Colonists and Creeks," 509–21.

20. G. Jones, "Portrait of an Irish Entrepreneur," 427–47.

21. For John Gordon, Chesnutt, *South Carolina's Expansion*, 158–60, and Snapp, *John Stuart*, 24–25; for George Baillie, *PHL*, 3:31, 127, and 5:43. Gordon conducted business from his Charles Town office but steered a considerable part of the deerskin trade through the Savannah office, where the son-in-law of his now-deceased partner, Thomas Netherclift, handled matters. Baillie was a partner in the Charles Town firm Robertson, Jamieson, and Baillie, with an office in Savannah. John Gordon ranked fourth on the list of deerskin exporters from Charles Town for the period 1733–75. His exports extended from 1759 to 1773. W. Moore, "The Largest Exporters of Deerskins," 144–50.

22. Petition of Several Merchants and Shopkeepers, Savannah, December 2, 1761, in *CRG*, 13:617.

23. To establish the level of exports, three main sources were used: the American

Inspector-General's Report for 1768–72, the reporting by the Customs Office for the eighteenth century, and the report compiled by the comptroller of customs in Savannah for the period 1755–72. Although the American Inspector-General's Report is typically the most accurate for commodities, the numbers given for the deerskin trade were off the mark. No exports of deerskins were noted for 1768, and for the other years the figures differ from the other two sources. The average of exports for the period 1768–72 according to the three sources shows that the Customs Office and Savannah figures are within 12 percent of each other while the inspector-general is off by 26 percent of the Customs Office. An average of 242,000–273,000 pounds were shipped annually from Georgia, according to Customs 3 and the report of the collector of the port of Savannah, compared to 177,800 according to the inspector-general.

24. John Lord Sheffield set the value of skins exported from British North America in 1769 at £69,271 sterling. Sheffield, *Observations on the Commerce of the American States*, 102.

25. Shepherd, "Commodity Exports," 11–50. The total average exports from Georgia between 1768 and 1772 were valued at £74,077 sterling. For rice, £39,078; for deerskins, £19,360, according to Customs 3.

26. The "official" values for imports from Great Britain reflected those of the last decade of the seventeenth century and never changed before the Revolution as a matter of convenience for the Customs Office. However, prices in the eighteenth century showed a remarkable stability while the margin of error contained in these figures seems to be less than once thought. Clark, *Guide to English Commercial Statistics*; S. D. Smith, "The Market for Manufactures," 676–708.

27. Braund, *Deerskins & Duffels*, 100.

28. Joseph Clay to unknown, October 25, 1783, Letter Book, Clay, Telfair & Co., October 25, 1783–September 1, 1784, Joseph Clay Papers, GHS.

29. See chapter 9.

30. Response to questionnaire, Governor James Wright to the Board of Trade, November 10, 1764, CO 323/20. Wright consulted with deerskin merchants and traders in Savannah for his information. The total markup of 107 percent over prime cost (the price in Britain plus shipping and insurance) was not as onerous as might appear. Retailers in Savannah typically put a 45–50 percent markup on goods without having to travel hundreds of miles to distribute their merchandise. Wright was giving the official version of things. The actual price paid by Creeks or Cherokees varied with the circumstances. Response to questionnaire, Governor James Grant to Board of Trade, December 1, 1765, CO 323/20. George Galphin's accounts reflect the 20 percent markup charged by merchants and shopkeepers in Augusta. Account Books, 1767–72, George Galphin, microfilm, GHS.

31. For a discussion of price schedules, Braund, *Deerskins & Duffels*, 127–29.

32. G. Jones, "Portrait of an Irish Entrepreneur," 440–41; Cashin, *Lachlan Mc-Gillivray*, 209, 255–56.

33. Granger, *Savannah River Plantations*, 100, 104–5, 178–79, 291, 318.

34. Testimony of Simon Munro on behalf of John Graham, December 23, 1783, Georgia, AO 12, vol. 4, 60/120.

35. Charles Strachan, Letter Book, 1763–70, National Library, Scotland.

36. *Georgia Gazette*, January 4, 1769.

37. Levi Sheftall, Sheftall diaries, 1733–1808, Keith Read Collection, Hargrett Library, UGA.

38. Weeks, *Savannah in the Time of Peter Tondee*, 118–19; Rubin, *Third to None*, 16–21. As early as 1736, Daniel Nunes had assisted in Indian talks at Frederica and Moses Nunes was present at conferences between the Creeks and both Ellis and Wright. Governor Wright appointed Daniel as the official Indian interpreter, lavishing praise on his service, which he described as "of the Utmost Consequence & Indispensably Necessary." Wright to Board of Trade, July 5, 1769, in *CRG*, 28, pt. 2:329.

39. Cashin, *Lachlan McGillivray*, 71–72, 83.

40. Affidavit, August 18, 1779, Colonial Bond Book JJ, Georgia Archives.

41. About half of Charles Town's exports of deerskins went to the ports of Britain for shipment to continental markets. Exports of hides, 1770–74, Customs 3/70–74, NA-UK. The price per pound of deerskin has been derived from Table 1, "Quantities and Estimated Values (in Pounds Sterling) of Selected Commodities Exported from the British North American Colonies to Great Britain, 1768–1772," in Shepherd, "Commodity Exports," 20–21. Hatley, *The Dividing Paths*, 163–66; Alden, *John Stuart and the Southern Colonial Frontier*, 300–302.

42. According to a manuscript in the Bodleian Library, Mobile and Pensacola exported to Britain 116,798 pounds of dressed skins and 87,263 pounds of undressed skins in 1772. The total of 204,061 pounds is close to the 199,729 pounds given in the Customs 3 statistics. Bodleian MS North a. 2. fols. 7, 15–19, cited in Fabel, *Economy of British West Florida*, 54, 246n22.

43. Braund, *Deerskins & Duffels*, 56–57; Wright, *Creeks and Seminoles*, 46; Piker, "'White & Clean' & Contested," 315–47.

44. Fabel, *Economy of British West Florida*, 208; Braund, *Deerskins & Duffels*, 56–57.

45. W. Bartram, *Travels*, 37, 40, 62. Spalding planned for an "upper store" on the St. John's sixty miles higher up, another one fifty miles to the west, and a third near the Bay of Apalachi about one hundred twenty miles distant. Braund, *Deerskins & Duffels*, 135. The partnerships in Charles Town, Savannah, and Mobile relied on

the same correspondents in London. Greenwood & Higginson and McGillivray, Grahams, Clark underwrote the majority of shipments while Charles Ogilvie and Telfair, Cowper, Telfair invested in others. "Merchants' Claims Relating to Lands Ceded by Creeks and Cherokee Indians," AO 13/36, pt. 3, 1782–89, nos. 818–63.

46. Coleman, *Colonial Georgia*, 81, 103; Spalding, *Oglethorpe in America*, 51–55.

47. "Act Regulating Spiritous Liquors, approved July 23, 1757," in *CRG*, 18, pt. 1:223.

48. McDowell, *Colonial Records*, 2:354

49. MacDonald, *Select Charters*, 267–72.

50. General Jeffery Amherst encouraged the new superintendent of Indian affairs, John Stuart, to keep out "worthless people" from the trade but, when asked about granting the superintendent the right to issue licenses, turned him down on the grounds that the idea of licenses was "inconsistent with the freedom and liberty that ought to be indulged to every British subject who conforms to the rules prescribed for carrying on trade in general." Qtd. in Cashin, *Lachlan McGillivray*, 216; Braund, *Deerskins & Duffels*, 103–8.

51. Adair, *History of the American Indians*, 444; James Grant to Board of Trade, December 1, 1764, CO 323/20.

52. David Taitt to John Stuart, March 16, 1772, qtd. in Mereness, *Travels in the American Colonies*, 525.

53. McCusker, *Rum and the American Revolution*, 1:472, 474.

54. Ibid., 1:468–69, 476–77.

55. The white and black populations numbered 12,750 and 10,625, respectively. U.S. Census, *Historical Statistics*, 2:1168.

56. A. Thompson and William Brown to Gov. Wright, October 18, 1773, in *CRG*, 38, pt. 1:153.

57. Charles Stuart to John Stuart, August 26, 1770, CO 5/72, f. 89.

58. American Inspector-General's Report, 1768–72, Customs 16/1, NA-UK.

59. The figure of 137,000 gallons is based on the following assumptions: (1) from John McCusker's calculations, whites consumed on average 4.2 gallons per year and blacks 1 gallon; (2) the populations of Georgia and South Carolina are reflected in U.S. Census, *Historical Statistics*, for 1770; (3) the amount of rum going into Indian territory from Georgia was 35,000 gallons, from West Florida, 25,000, and from South Carolina, 77,000; (4) the total native population for the South from the Mississippi to the Atlantic was 42,500, based on the numbers in Waselkov, Wood, and Hatley, *Powhatan's Mantle*, 60.

60. Mancall, *Deadly Medicine*, 54.

61. Charles Stuart to John Stuart, August 26, 1770, CO 5/72.

62. Mancall, *Deadly Medicine*, 63–84; Braund, *Deerskins & Duffels*, 125–27.

63. Brown, Struthers and Company, February 22, 1766, Colonial Register of Loose Wills, f. 230, Georgia Archives; George Galphin, Account Books, 1767–72, microfilm, GHS.

64. Communication of letters from Governor Patrick Tonyn, East Florida, and from David Taitt, James Grierson, and Edward Barnard, Augusta, Meeting of the Governor's Council, August 30, 1774, in *CRG*, 12:405–10.

65. "State of Accounts, Audited and a Certificate Issued, April–September 1775," AO 13/36/c, 930. There are twenty-two pages of accounts for deerskin merchants and traders. Twenty-five claimants received certificates for claims against the proceeds of the sale of the ceded land to settlers new to Georgia.

66. Snapp, *John Stuart*, 132–33.

67. Minutes of the Governor and Council in Georgia, February 21, 1775, Proceedings and Minutes of Governor and Council, ed. Lilla Hawes, in *CGHS*, 10:13. On the deduction of 10 percent for the cost of doing business: "Whereupon the Board were Unanimously of Opinion That at the Traders Expend part of the Goods which they Carry among the Indians in presents to Head Men and others, and in purchasing provisions during their Residence in the Indian Country, that therefore a deduction of ten p[er] Centum should be made from the Merchts Accounts against the Traders for Indian Goods." On the refusal to pay for items that were not dry goods: "Mr. Robertson and Mr. Wylly laid before the Board a State[ment] of James Greirsons Accounts against his Traders to the Creek and Cherokee Nations, which they had Examined and deducted therefrom every article which appeared to them, not to be goods, usually sent to those Nations to trade amongst them."

68. Claims of George Galphin, "State of Accounts, Audited and a Certificate issued, April–September 1775," AO 13/36c. The accounts showed a claim for £106,777 sterling and a deduction of £38,139 sterling for articles which appeared "not to be goods" or rum.

69. Braund, *Deerskins & Duffels*, 136, 145; Alden, *John Stuart and the Southern Colonial Frontier*, 296. The Mortar and Emistisiguo, eminent leaders of the Upper Creeks, complained bitterly about Buzzards Roost to John Stuart in a meeting in Augusta, October 1769.

70. McDowell, *Colonial Records*, 1:135–36.

71. Braund, *Deerskins & Duffels*, 136–37.

72. Andrew McLean in account current with McGillivray, Grahams, Clark; Messrs. Crooke Mckintosh & Jackson in account with McGillivray, Grahams, Clark, etc., U.S. Circuit Court, Southern District of Georgia, Savannah, mixed cases, box 57/14A006; box 6, Estate of Andrew McLean, NARA. John Clark financed Lachlan McGillivray and John Graham of Savannah and John McGillivray of Mobile. William Thomson and his London partner, William Telfair, supplied capital

to Spalding & Kelsall on St. Simons and James Jackson in Augusta. Greenwood & Higginson, the largest firm trading in the Lower South, stood behind John Gordon of Charles Town and Gordon & Netherclift of Savannah. Charles Ogilvie, a Scotsman who moved from Charles Town to London, financed George Baillie and Company in Savannah and Robertson, Jamieson, and Baillie in Charles Town.

73. Indenture between John Graham and John Clark, June 11, 1783, U.S. Circuit Court, Southern District, NARA; "State of Accounts (of Indian traders), Audited, and a Certificate Issued, April–September, 1775," AO 13/36c. The estimate for pounds of deerskins is based on the figures given in the "State of Accounts." The twenty-two pages of accounts state the figures in pounds of deerskin for all but two merchants.

74. Memorial of William Greenwood and William Higginson, March 17, 1784, AO 13/119.

75. Krech, *Myth and History*, 160–61.

76. Snapp, *John Stuart*, 116–46; Braund, *Deerskins & Duffels*, 151–52; Alden, *John Stuart and the Southern Colonial Frontier*, 310–15.

77. For Wright's estimate of the debt, Snapp, *John Stuart*, 120. The total debt owed to English merchants is based on the £77,000 in accounts accepted by the government, plus £8,000 that had been eliminated as the amount of goods used for presents and to purchase food, in other words, the cost of doing business.

78. Indenture between John Graham, late merchant of Georgia, and John Clark, merchant of London, June 11, 1783, U.S. Circuit Court, oversized, box 8, NARA. Clark had debts owed to him through the three companies that successively handled his business: McGillivray, Grahams, Clark (1762–69), £38,935; Grahams, Clark (1769–74), £22,427; and Clark & Milligan (1776–), £8,282. Indenture made between Basil Cowper and William Telfair, on the one hand, and David Milligan, John Tappenden, Thomas Littler, etc., May 13, 1784, *Telfair vs. Telfair*, 1802, U.S. Circuit Court, NARA. Memorial of William Greenwood and William Higginson, March 17, 1784, AO 13/119. The figures for Nutt, Ogilvie, Stead, and Brailsford are compiled from lawsuits filed in Georgia courts, U.S. Circuit Court, Southern District of Georgia, NARA; Schedule of Assets, Greenwood & Higginson, March 17, 1784, AO 13/119; Memorial of John Buchannan, February 16, 1784, AO 13/34; debts owed to Telfair, Cowper, Telfair, multiple accounts over several years, Treasury 1/79/55; debts due in Georgia to John Nutt, 1797, Treasury 79/5; abstract of the claims of Greenwood & Higginson, n.d., Treasury 79/15, NA-UK.

79. Kellock, "London Merchants and the Pre-1776 American Debts," 116, 121, 124, 126, 137; Chatham Papers, 30/8/343, NA-UK. In 1790, those merchants claimed pre-revolutionary war debts owed by Georgians of £247,781, a figure that placed the

young colony fifth highest in terms of debt owed to Londoners of all colonies that entered the United States.

80. The debt per capita for Georgia and South Carolina is based on the 1770 population figures found in U.S. Census, *Historical Statistics*, 2:116. Citizens of Virginia and Maryland also owed Scotland another £2.6 million, primarily for the tobacco trade; the figures for debts owed to London merchants include interest from 1776 to 1790 of about 41 percent of the total. Price, *Capital and Credit in British Overseas Trade*, 6–8.

81. M. Heath, *Constructive Liberalism*, 57–63.

82. Wright to the Earl of Shelburne, April 6, 1767, in *CRG*, 37:181, manuscript, GHS.

83. Silver, *Our Savage Neighbors*, 58, 64–65, 96.

84. Braund, *Deerskins & Duffels*, 159.

Chapter 11. Nationalizing the Lowcountry

1. Middlekauff, *The Glorious Cause*, 221–31; Schlesinger, *Colonial Merchants and the American Revolution*, 286–90.

2. St. John Parish sent a large delegation to the meeting in hopes of securing a strong commitment to the coming congress. Members from Christ Church Parish and perhaps other parishes as well blocked the attempt. Fraser, *Savannah in the Old South*, 104–5; Coleman, *American Revolution in Georgia*, 40–44; Schlesinger, *Colonial Merchants and the American Revolution*, 381–84.

3. Schlesinger, *Colonial Merchants and the American Revolution*, 393–431.

4. Breen, *The Marketplace of Revolution*, xvi, xvii, 244, 271.

5. Disaffected, the planter Jonathan Bryan presided over a meeting of the public that called for a general boycott of non-essential British goods, including a halt to the slave trade. The merchants carried the day, Bryan's initiative fell flat, and Georgians never engaged in extralegal means to halt British imports. Gallay, *Formation of a Planter Elite*, 117–18; C. Jones, *History of Georgia*, 2:112–15; Piecuch, *Three Peoples, One King*, 20.

6. Value of Exports to and Imports from England to American Colonies and States: 1697–1791, Z 213–26, U.S. Census, *Historical Statistics*, 2:1176.

7. "The memorial of William McGillivray, a Captain in his Majesty's Invalid Forces—Schedule of Losses referred to in the Memorial," 1784, AO 12, NA-UK, microfilm, Georgia Archives.

8. The land grants and purchases showed no signs of slowing down in 1774 and early 1775, even with news of the Battle of Lexington and the slide of royal government into oblivion. James Spalding's requests for land in Hemperley, *English*

Crown Grants, 126–29; memorial of Roger Kelsall, "Estimate of Estate and Effects, 1783," AO 13/361. Others who made purchases included John Graham, Samuel Douglass, Thomas Young, Basil Cowper, and George Baillie.

9. "Exports of Produce from the Province of Georgia, January 5, 1755, to January 5, 1773," in Romans, *A Concise Natural History*, 146.

10. If we accept William De Brahm's figure of 13,000 for the beginning of 1773 and add the purchases in the Charleston market (2,511), the imports from Africa (1,851), those from the West Indies (462), and an estimated figure for the bondspeople brought into the backcountry from North and South Carolina (500) for 1773 and 1774, the total reaches 18,324. The figure must be adjusted for mortality and fertility so this number may be closer to the mid-17,000 range. The white population was estimated by James Wright at 18,000 toward the end of 1773. In 1780, that population had grown to 35,000. It seems reasonable to assume a net growth of 4,000–5,000 in the final two years of the royal period as people moved into the ceded lands north of Augusta.

11. James Habersham to Henry Ellis, January 27, 1772, in *CRG*, 6:162.

12. P. Morgan, *Slave Counterpoint*, 39, 95; Menard, "Economic and Social Development of the South," 250.

13. Trans-Atlantic Slave Trade Database, http://slavevoyages.org; General Duty Book, vol. C (1765–76), South Carolina Department of Archives and History.

14. Shepherd and Walton, *Shipping, Maritime Trade, and the Economic Development of Colonial North America*, 47.

15. Mercantini, *Who Shall Rule at Home?*, 234–58.

16. Hall, *Land and Allegiance*, 7–30; Piecuch, *Three Peoples, One King*, 19–22; Coleman, *American Revolution in Georgia*, 70–75; Abbott, *The Royal Governors of Georgia*, 162–83; Lane, *Savannah Revisited*, 27; C. Jones, *History of Georgia*, 2:169–70.

17. The Parish of St. John expressed its displeasure with events to the Continental Congress in forceful terms. "The Address of the Inhabitants of the Parish of St. John's in the Province of Georgia," April 13, 1775, *Journal of the Continental Congress* (1774–89): 2:45–48.

18. "Association entered into by forty-five of the Deputies assembled in Provincial Congress, at Savannah, in Georgia, on the 18th of January, 1775," in *RRG*, 1:43–48; Hall, *Land and Allegiance*, 21–22; Coleman, *American Revolution in Georgia*, 46–47; Jackson, "Consensus and Conflict," 388–92; Schlesinger, *Colonial Merchants and the American Revolution*, 470–72.

19. "Critique of the Congress' resolution on the Association by the Committee of St. John's Parish," February 9, 1775, in *RRG*, 1:59–60.

20. Noble Wimberly Jones, Archibald Bulloch, John Houstoun to the President of the Continental Congress, Savannah, April 6, 1771, in *RRG*, 1:63.

21. C. Jones, *History of Georgia*, 2:166; Fraser, *Savannah in the Old South*, 107–8; Schlesinger, *Colonial Merchants and the American Revolution*, 529–32.

22. Resolutions adopted by the Second Provincial Congress, July 10, 1775, in *RRG*, 1:248 (final resolution). The Second Provincial Congress adopted the association on July 6 and elected delegates to the Continental Congress on July 8, 1775; Schlesinger, *Colonial Merchants and the American Revolution*, 532, 539. On March 30, 1775, Parliament forbade trade with those colonies that had ratified the association. Left unaffected at this time were Georgia, New York, Delaware, and North Carolina.

23. "[T]here are so many that will not come into the Measure that we apprehend everything relative to it will entirely drop . . . and of course everything in a commercial way will go on as usual"; Joseph Clay to Benjamin Stead, Savannah, February 15, 1775, Letter Book of Joseph Clay and Co., April 11, 1774–May 16, 1776, GHS.

24. Letter Book of Edward Telfair and Company, January 12, 1774–February 20, 1782, box 9, f. 44, Telfair Family Papers, Joseph Clay Papers, GHS.

25. Value of Exports to and Imports from England by American Colonies and States, 1697–1791, Z 213–26, U.S. Census, *Historical Statistics*, 2:1178. The figure for imports is questionable. Edward Telfair wrote to his London correspondent in late June 1775, "It is high time to put a stop to importation till matters are elucidated between your side of the water and ours." Telfair to Telfair, Cowper, Telfair, June 21, 1775, Letter Book, August 11, 1773–May 11, 1776, Telfair Family Papers, GHS. There does not seem to have been any major importation after Georgia entered into the association in July 1775.

26. Joseph Clay to Benjamin Stead, Savannah, May 13, 1775, Letter Book of Joseph Clay and Co., April 11, 1774–May 16, 1776, GHS. For additional examples, see James Spalding's requests for land in Hemperley, *English Crown Grants*, 126–29; and memorial of Roger Kelsall, "Estimate of Estate and Effects, 1783," AO 13/361.

27. "An Account of the Number of Vessels which have cleared outwards at the several ports of North America, 1772," American Inspector-General's Ledger (1768–72), Customs 16/1, NA-UK. In 1769, a mariner from New York, Telamon Cuyler, bought a town house and entered into a partnership with two Savannahians to begin the first regular shipping runs to New York City and the West Indies. The idea never got off the ground. Fraser, *Savannah in the Old South*, 65.

28. Lambert, "Father against Son, and Son against Father," 1–28. The correspondence of Habersham with a teacher at the College of New Jersey indicates that his sons were in a tutoring school attached to the college. The Archives of Princeton University have no record of a Habersham having attended the college before the Revolution. Habersham to the Rev. James Findley, Nassau Hall, Princeton, January 20, 1766, in *CGHS*, 6:53. Lewis Johnston, a devout Presbyterian, sent one son to the College of New Jersey.

29. The sister of Daniel and Moses Nunes, deerskin traders, married Abraham DeLyon, originally from Savannah but later Philadelphia. Their son returned to become a merchant. Other children married into prominent Jewish families in the Northeast. Daniel wed the sister of Boston merchant Moses Michael Hays. Rubin, *Third to None*, 13, 21. Hartridge, *Letters of Robert Mackay to His Wife*, xxiv–xxv.

30. An admirer of John Dickinson's *Letters of a Farmer in Pennsylvania*, he became the one effective pamphleteer in the colony and received region-wide attention at the time of the Stamp Act crisis for his pieces arguing that Parliament did not have the right to tax the colonies. Martin, *John J. Zubly*, 67–70; Greene, *Quest for Power*, 376–77.

31. Cashin, *Governor Henry Ellis*, 61.

32. Stokes, *A View of the Constitution*, 140.

33. The Council of Safety in Charles Town had voted to extend the ban on the exportation of rice in early February. The council in Savannah was split. Basil Cowper, a key player in that body, voted in favor of letting the ban expire. Edward Telfair's role was ambivalent. He chartered two vessels to carry out of the province his stock of goods as well as rice. "Deposition of Thomas Tallemach and James Jones before Archibald Bullock, President and Commander in Chief of the Province aforesaid," May 1, 1776, Edward Telfair Papers, Duke University. Tallemach and Jones were clerks of the Telfair store. The hesitation is evident in the terse minutes of the council in *RRG*, 1:105–13.

34. Deposition of William Brown, comptroller of the port of Savannah, March 21, 1776; Deposition of John McKenzie, late master of the ship *Inverness*, May 1776; Memorial of John Clark and David Milligan, May 10, 1777, all in AO 13/34, 200–217. The Council of Safety, dominated by Savannah merchants and local notables, exercised effective power but without having deposed the governor or created a constitution.

35. "An Account of land, Negroes, and other effects[:] the property of John Graham late of Georgia, April 1776," AO 13/35, 132–40. For Graham's debts, see "Indenture between John Graham, late merchant of Georgia, and John Clark, merchant of London, June 11, 1783," Southern District, U.S. Circuit Court, oversized, NARA.

36. Fraser, *Savannah in the Old South*, 114–18; Jackson, "Battle of the Rice Boats," 229–43.

37. John Graham to James Grant, Cockspur Island, March 26, 1776, James Grant Papers, Ballindalloch Muniments, microfilm, reel 23, 1773–76, NAS.

38. List of those "whose going at large is dangerous to the liberties of America," in Minutes of the Council of Safety, June 26, 1776, in *RRG*, 1:146; Memorandum (thought to be by Lewis Johnston, planter, merchant, member of the governor's council), 1782, Peter Force Papers, ser. 7E, LC; Hall, *Land and Allegiance*, 42–45.

39. The names McIntosh, Baillie, and Houstoun bespoke three influential Scottish families, two of which had played important roles in the life of the colony since the trustee period. Hall, *Land and Allegiance*, 46–49; *The Case of George McIntosh, Esquire*, 1–29; "The Case of George McIntosh," 132–34.

40. John Hancock, President of the Continental Congress, to the President and Council of State of Georgia, January 8, 1777, qtd. in *The Case of George McIntosh, Esquire*, 13.

41. O'Shaughnessy, *An Empire Divided*, 137–43; Higman, *Concise History of the Caribbean*, 144–45.

42. Abbott, *The Royal Governors of Georgia*, 126–44; Greene, *Quest for Power*, 424–36; O'Shaughnessy, *An Empire Divided*, 108–34.

43. Craton, *Testing the Chains*, 172–79; O'Shaughnessy, *An Empire Divided*, 142–47.

44. James Wright to Lord Dartmouth, August 17, 1775, in *CGHS*, 3:208.

45. James Wright to Lord Dartmouth, December 19, 1775, in *CRG*, 38, pt. 1, manuscript, GHS.

46. Joseph Clay to Messrs. Bright & Pechin, July 2, 1777, in *Letters of Joseph Clay*, in *CGHS*, 8:35. For a description of the constitution, Fraser, *Savannah in the Old South*, 120–21; Coleman, *American Revolution in Georgia*, 79–84.

47. A planter to Gentlemen (Edward Telfair and Company), Newport, March 26, 1774, Telfair Papers, Duke University.

48. James Wright's Address to the Assembly, January 18, 1775, *CRG*, 38, pt. 1B:375–79; Cashin, "Sowing the Wind," 233–50, esp. 240–43 (quotation on 243).

49. Edward Barnard functioned as chief magistrate of Augusta and delegate to the Commons House of Assembly, James Grierson as justice of the peace and lieutenant colonel of the Augusta militia (*CRG*, 12:315 and 434); John Rae as a delegate to the Commons House of Assembly and justice of the peace (*CRG*, 11:334); Thomas Waters, Edward Keating, and Timothy Barnard were officers of a newly raised company of rangers and justices of the peace for the ceded lands (*CRG*, 12:390); of the eight justices of the peace for the parishes of St. Paul, St. George, and St. Matthew, at least four were deerskin merchants, including John Francis Williams and James Jackson (*CRG*, 10:429).

50. Lamplugh, *Politics on the Periphery*, 51–52; Pressly, "Scottish Merchants," 167–68.

51. During the Revolution, the commercial letters of Joseph Clay primarily concerned trade with the West Indies. *Letters of Joseph Clay*, in *CGHS*, 8.

52. Joseph Clay to unknown, April 27, 1784, Letter Book, Clay, Telfair & Co., October 25, 1783–September 1, 1784, Joseph Clay Papers, GHS.

53. O'Malley, "Beyond the Middle Passage," 151.

54. "An Act for preventing improper or Disaffected Persons Emigrating from other places," August 5, 1782, in *CRG*, 19, pt. 2:162–66.

55. Ryan and Golson, *Andrew Low*; Hartridge, *Letters of Robert Mackay to His Wife*, xxiii–xxxi.

56. Coulter, *Thomas Spalding of Sapelo*, 1–15.

57. Stephens, "Origin of Sea Island Cotton," 391–99; Chaplin, *An Anxious Pursuit*, 220–23.

58. Chaplin, *An Anxious Pursuit*, 277–80.

59. Greene, "Early Modern Southeastern North America," 536.

60. Pressly, "Northern Roots," 157–99.

Bibliography

PRIMARY SOURCES

Collections of the Georgia Historical Society

Vol. 1. *Collections of the Georgia Historical Society.* Savannah: Georgia Historical
Society, 1840.

Vol. 3. *Letters from General Oglethorpe, Letters from Governor James Wright.*
Savannah: Morning News, 1873.

Vol. 6. *The Letters of the Hon. James Habersham, 1756–1775.* Savannah: Morning
News, 1904.

Vol. 8. *Letters of Joseph Clay, Merchant of Savannah, 1776–1793.* Savannah: Morning
News, 1913.

Vol. 10. *The Proceedings and Minutes of the Governor and Council of Georgia,
October 4, 1774, through November 7, 1775, and September 6, 1779, through
September 20, 1780.* Savannah: Georgia Historical Society, 1952.

Vol. 12. *The Papers of Lachlan McIntosh, 1774–1779.* Edited by Lilla M. Hawes.
Savannah: Georgia Historical Society, 1957.

Vol. 13. *The Letter Book of Thomas Rasberry, 1758–1761.* Edited by Lilla Mills
Hawes. Savannah: Georgia Historical Society, 1959.

Vol. 17. *The Jones Family Papers, 1760–1810.* Edited by John Eddins Simpson.
Savannah: Georgia Historical Society, 1976.

Vol. 19. *Checklist of Eighteenth-Century Manuscripts in the Georgia Historical Society.*
Compiled by Lilla Mills Hawes and Karen Elizabeth Osvald. Savannah:
Georgia Historical Society, 1976.

Colonial Records of the State of Georgia

Vol. 1. *By-Laws and Journal, 1732–1752.* Compiled by Allen D. Candler. Atlanta:
Franklin Printing, 1904.

Vol. 3. *Accounts, Monies and Effects, 1732–1751.* Compiled by Allen D. Candler.
Atlanta: Franklin Printing, 1905.

Vol. 4. *William Stephens' Journal, 1737–1740.* Compiled by Allen D. Candler. Atlanta: Franklin Printing, 1906.

Supplement to vol. 4. *Journal of Colonel William Stephens, 1740–1741.* Compiled by Allen D. Candler. Atlanta: Franklin Printing, 1908.

Vol. 5. *Journal of the Earl of Egmont.* Compiled by Allen D. Candler. Atlanta: Franklin-Turner, 1906.

Vol. 6. *Proceedings of the President and Assistants (October 12, 1741, to October 30, 1754).* Compiled by Allen D. Candler. Atlanta: Franklin Printing, 1906.

Vol. 7. *Proceedings and Minutes of the Governor and Council of His Majesty's Province of Georgia (October 20, 1754–March 6, 1759).* Compiled by Allen D. Candler. Atlanta: Franklin-Turner, 1906.

Vol. 8. *A Journal of the Proceedings and Minutes of the Governor and Council (March 8, 1759–December 31, 1762).* Compiled by Allen D. Candler. Atlanta: Franklin-Turner, 1907.

Vol. 9. *Proceedings and Minutes of the Governor and Council (January 4, 1763, to December 2, 1766).* Compiled by Allen D. Candler. Atlanta: Franklin-Turner, 1907.

Vol. 10. *Proceedings and Minutes of the Governor and Council (January 6, 1767–December 6, 1769).* Compiled by Allen D. Candler. Atlanta: Franklin-Turner, 1907.

Vol. 11. *Proceedings and Minutes of the Governor and Council (April 3, 1770–July 13, 1771).* Compiled by Allen D. Candler. Atlanta: Franklin-Turner, 1907.

Vol. 12. *Proceedings and Minutes of the Governor and Council (August 6, 1771–February 13, 1782).* Compiled by Allen D. Candler. Atlanta: Franklin-Turner, 1907.

Vol. 13. *Journal of the Commons House of Assembly (1755–1762).* Compiled by Allen D. Candler. Atlanta: Franklin-Turner, 1907.

Vol. 14. *Journal of the Commons House of Assembly (1763–1768).* Compiled by Allen D. Candler. Atlanta: Franklin-Turner, 1907.

Vol. 15. *Journal of the Commons House of Assembly (1769–1782).* Compiled by Allen D. Candler. Atlanta: Franklin-Turner, 1907.

Vol. 16. *Journal of the Upper House of the Assembly (1755–1762).* Compiled by Allen D. Candler. Atlanta: Franklin-Turner, 1908.

Vol. 17. *Journal of the Upper House of the Assembly (1763–1774).* Compiled by Allen D. Candler. Atlanta: Franklin-Turner, 1908.

Vol. 18. *Statutes Enacted by the Royal Legislature of Georgia from Its First Session in 1754 to 1768.* Compiled by Allen D. Candler. Atlanta: Chas. P. Byrd, 1910.

Vol. 19, pt. 1. *Statutes, Colonial and Revolutionary, 1768–1773.* Compiled by Allen D. Chandler. Atlanta: Chas. P. Byrd, 1911.

Vol. 19, pt. 2. *Statutes, Colonial and Revolutionary, 1774–1805.* Compiled by Allen D. Candler. Atlanta: Chas. P. Byrd, 1911.

Vol. 20. *Original Papers, Correspondence to the Trustees, James Oglethorpe, and Others, 1732–1735.* Edited by Kenneth Coleman and Milton Ready. Athens: University of Georgia Press, 1977.

Vol. 24. *Original Papers, Correspondence, Trustees, General Oglethorpe, and Others. (1742–1745).* Compiled by Allen D. Candler. Atlanta: Chas. P. Byrd, 1915.

Vol. 25. *Original Papers, Correspondence, Trustees, General Oglethorpe, and Others, 1745–1750.* Compiled by Allen D. Candler. Atlanta: Chas. P. Byrd, 1915.

Vol. 26. *Original Papers, Trustees, President and Assistants, and Others (1750–1752).* Compiled by Allen D. Candler. Atlanta: Chas. P. Byrd, 1916.

Vol. 27. *Original Papers of Governor John Reynolds, 1754–1756.* Edited by Kenneth Coleman and Milton Ready. Athens: University of Georgia Press, 1977.

Vol. 28, pt. 1. *Original Papers of Governors Reynolds, Ellis, Wright and Others, 1757–1763.* Edited by Kenneth Coleman and Milton Ready. Athens: University of Georgia Press, 1976.

Vol. 28, pt. 2. *Original Papers of Governors Reynolds, Ellis, Wright, and Others, 1764–1782.* Edited by Kenneth Coleman and Milton Ready. Athens: University of Georgia Press, 1979.

Vol. 29. *Trustees' Letter Book, 1731–1738.* Edited by Kenneth Coleman and Milton Ready. Athens: University of Georgia Press, 1985.

Vol. 30. *Trustees' Letter Book, 1738–1745.* Edited by Kenneth Coleman and Milton Ready. Athens: University of Georgia Press, 1985.

Vol. 31. *Trustees' Letter Book, 1745–1752.* Edited by Kenneth Coleman and Milton Ready. Athens: University of Georgia Press, 1986.

Vol. 36. "Correspondence, James Oglethorpe, Trustees and Others, 1741–1751." Typescript, Georgia Archives and Georgia Historical Society.

Vol. 37. "Correspondence, Governor James Wright, President James Habersham, etc., 1761–1772." Typescript, Georgia Archives and Georgia Historical Society.

Vol. 38, pt. 1. "Correspondence, Governor James Wright, President James Habersham, etc., 1772–1775." Typescript, Georgia Archives and Georgia Historical Society.

Vol. 39. "Letters, etc., General Oglethorpe and Trustees, Governors Reynolds, Ellis and Wright, 1733–1783." Typescript, Georgia Archives and Georgia Historical Society.

Duke University

William Gibbons Jr. Papers. 1728–1803.

Habersham Family Papers. 1750–1860.

Edward Telfair Papers. 1762–1831.

Georgia Archives

Conveyances: C-1, C-2, S, U, V, X-1, X-2, CC-1, CC-2: 1750–76.
Inventories, F: 1754–70, FF: 1776–77.
Miscellaneous—Bonds: J, O, R, Y-1, Y-2, KK: 1755–78.
Mortgages, Q: 1765–70, W: 1770–75.
Register of Records: Loose Papers and Wills, 1755–80.

Georgia Historical Society

Adler, Emma Morel. "A Biographical Sketch of John Morel, 1733–1776." 1979.
Joseph Vallence Bevan Papers. 1733–1826.
Joseph Clay and Company Papers. 1772–76.
Joseph Clay Papers. 1765–1923.
Clay, Telfair and Company Papers. 1783–95.
Basil Cowper Papers. 1770–79.
Cowper and Telfairs Promissory Notes. 1770–80.
Samuel Douglass Land Plats. 1767–78.
George Galphin Account Books. 1767–72.
John Graham Letter and Claim. 1780.
Habersham Family Papers. 1712–1842.
James Habersham Papers. 1747–75.
Joseph Habersham Papers. 1769–1802.
Walter Hartridge Collection.
Index to Register of Deaths (City of Savannah). 1803–18.
Jones Family Papers. 1723–1936.
Andrew McLean Ledger. 1774–97.
Mossman Read Ledger. 1765–66.
Telfair Family Papers.
Edward Telfair Papers. 1774–1807.
John Wand Papers. 1771–72.

Library of Congress

Peter Force Transcripts. 1742–89.
Habersham Family Papers.

National Archives and Records Administration, Morrow, Ga.

U.S. Circuit Court, Southern District of Georgia, Savannah. Mixed Cases, 1790–1860.

National Archives of Scotland

Baillie Family Papers. 1695–1900.
James Grant Papers: Ballindalloch Muniments.

National Archives, United Kingdom

Audit Office 12: Loyalist Claims Commission.
Audit Office 13: Loyalist Claims Commission.
Chatham Papers.
Colonial Office 5: America and West Indies.
Colonial Office Class 323: Colonies General.
Customs 3 (1696–1780): Ledgers of Imports and Exports.
Customs 16 (1768–72): American Inspector-General's Report.
Granville Papers.
Treasury 1, 77, 79.

National Library, Scotland

Charles Strachan Letter Book. 1763–1770.

Revolutionary Records of the State of Georgia

Vol. 1. *Miscellaneous Papers, Council of Safety, Provincial Congress, etc.* Compiled by Allen D. Candler. Atlanta: Franklin-Turner, 1908.

South Carolina Department of Archives and History

General Duty Books, vols. B (1748–65) and C (1765–76).
Miscellaneous Records: Mortgages and Bonds. 1736–1869.

South Carolina Historical Society

Ogilvie-Forbes of Boyndlie Papers. Microfilm.

University of Georgia, Special Collections

Telamon Cuyler Collection.
DeRenne Manuscripts Collection.
Dismukes, Camillus J., ed. "Colonial Georgia Newspaper Notices: Commercial Advertisers in the Georgia Gazette, 1763–1776." Manuscript. Hargrett Library.

Keith Read Collection.
Society for the Propagation of the Gospel in Foreign Parts. 1701–75. Microfilm.

SECONDARY SOURCES

Abbott, William W. *The Royal Governors of Georgia, 1754–1775*. Chapel Hill: University of North Carolina Press, 1959.

Abstracts of Colonial Wills of the State of Georgia, 1733–1777. Atlanta: Atlanta Town Committee of the National Society, Colonial Dames of America in the State of Georgia, 1962.

Adair, James. *History of the American Indians*. Edited by Samuel Cole Williams. 1930. Reprint, New York: Promontory, 1986.

Alden, John Richard. *John Stuart and the Southern Colonial Frontier: A Study of Indian Relations, War, Trade, and Land Problems in the Southern Wilderness, 1754–1775*. 1944. Reprint, New York: Gordian, 1966.

Anderson, Fred. *Crucible of War: The Seven Years' War and the Fate of Empire in British North America, 1754–1766*. New York: Vintage, 2001.

Andrien, Kenneth J. "The Spanish Atlantic System." In *Atlantic History: A Critical Appraisal*, edited by Jack P. Greene and Philip D. Morgan, 55–80. Oxford: Oxford University Press, 2009.

Armitage, David. "Three Concepts of the Atlantic World." In *The British Atlantic World, 1500–1800*, edited by David Armitage and Michael J. Braddick, 11–30. Basingstoke, England: Palgrave Macmillan, 2002.

Arthur, Linda L. "A New Look at Schooling and Literacy: The Colony of Georgia." *Georgia Historical Quarterly* 84, no. 4 (Winter 2000): 563–88.

Ashcraft-Eason, Lillian. "'She Voluntarily Hath Come': A Gambian Woman Trader in Colonial Georgia in the Eighteenth Century." In *Identity in the Shadow of Slavery*, edited by Paul E. Lovejoy, 202–21. London: Continuum, 2000.

Axley, Lowry. *Holding Aloft the Torch: A History of the Independent Presbyterian Church of Savannah, Georgia*. Savannah: Pigeonhole Press, 1958.

Axtell, James. *The Indians' New South: Cultural Change in the Colonial Southeast*. Baton Rouge: Louisiana State University Press, 1997.

Bailyn, Bernard. *Atlantic History: Concept and Contours*. Cambridge, Mass.: Harvard University Press, 2005.

———. *Voyagers to the West: A Passage in the Peopling of America on the Eve of the Revolution*. New York: Knopf, 1986.

Baine, Rodney M. "Indian Slavery in Colonial Georgia." *Georgia Historical Quarterly* 79, no. 2 (Summer 1995): 418–24.

———. "Myths of Mary Musgrove." *Georgia Historical Quarterly* 76 (Summer 1992): 428–35.

Balfour-Paul, Jenny. *Indigo: From Mummies to Blue Jeans*. London: British Museum Press, 2011.

Bartram, John. "Diary of a Journey through the Carolinas, Georgia, and Florida, from July 1, 1765, to April 10, 1766." Edited by Francis Harper. *Transactions of the American Philosophical Society*, n.s., 33, no. 1 (Dec. 1942): 1–120.

———. "An Extract of Mr. Wm Bartram's Observations in a Journey up the River Savannah in Georgia with his son on discoveries." *Gentleman's Quarterly* 37 (1767): 166–68.

Bartram, William. *The Travels of William Bartram*. Edited by Francis Harper. Athens: University of Georgia Press, 1998.

Beckemeyer, Frances Howell, comp. *Abstracts of Georgia Colonial Conveyance Book, C-1, 1750–1761*. Atlanta: R. J. Taylor Jr. Foundation, 1975.

Behrendt, Stephen D. "Markets, Transaction Cycles, and Profits: Merchant Decision Making in the British Slave Trade." *William and Mary Quarterly*, 3rd ser., 58, no. 1 (Jan. 2001): 171–204.

Bell, Malcolm, Jr. *Major Butler's Legacy: Five Generations of a Slaveholding Family*. Athens: University of Georgia Press, 1987.

Bellot, Leland J. *William Knox: The Life and Thought of an Eighteenth-Century Imperialist*. Austin: University of Texas Press, 1977.

Berlin, Ira. *Many Thousands Gone: The First Two Centuries of Slavery in North America*. Cambridge, Mass.: Belknap, 1998.

Berlin, Ira, and Leslie M. Harris. *Slavery in New York*. New York: New Press, 2005.

Bitler, Jim. "Indigo." www.georgiaencyclopedia.org. 2008.

Bolster, W. Jeffrey. *Black Jacks: African American Seamen in the Age of Sail*. Cambridge, Mass.: Harvard University Press, 1997.

———. "Putting the Ocean in Atlantic History: Maritime Communities and Marine Ecology in the Northwest Atlantic, 1500–1800." *American Historical Review* 113, no. 1 (Feb. 2008): 19–47.

Bolton, Robert. *Genealogical and Biographical Account of the Family of Bolton in England and America, with an Appendix, Memoirs of Robert Bolton*. New York: John A. Gray, 1862.

Braddock, J. G., Sr. *Wooden Ships–Iron Men: Four Master Mariners of the Colonial South*. Charleston, S.C.: VJB Press, 1996.

Braund, Kathryn E. Holland. "The Creek Indians, Blacks, and Slavery." *Journal of Southern History* 57, no. 4 (Nov. 1991): 601–36.

———. *Deerskins & Duffels: Creek Indian Trade with Anglo-America, 1685–1815*. Lincoln: University of Nebraska Press, 1993.

Breen, Timothy H. "Baubles of Britain: The American and Consumer Revolutions of the Eighteenth Century." In *Of Consuming Interests: The Style of Life in the Eighteenth Century*, edited by Cary Carson, Ronald Hoffman, and Peter J. Albert, 444–82. Charlottesville: University of Virginia Press, 1994.

———. "An Empire of Goods: The Anglicization of Colonial America, 1690–1776." *Journal of British Studies* 25, no. 4 (1986): 467–99.

———. *The Marketplace of Revolution: How Consumer Politics Shaped American Independence*. Oxford: Oxford University Press, 2004.

———. "The Meaning of Things: Interpreting the Consumer Economy in the Eighteenth Century." In *Consumption and the World of Goods*, edited by John Brewer and Roy Porter, 249–60. London: Routledge, 1994.

———. *Tobacco Culture: The Mentality of the Great Tidewater Planters on the Eve of the Revolution*. Princeton, N.J.: Princeton University Press, 1985.

Britt, Albert Sidney, Jr., and Anthony Roane Dees, eds. *Selected Eighteenth Century Manuscripts*. Savannah: Georgia Historical Society, 1980.

Brown, Vincent. *The Reaper's Garden: Death and Power in the World of Atlantic Slavery*. Cambridge, Mass.: Harvard University Press, 2008.

Brown, Wallace. *The King's Friends: The Composition and Motives of the American Loyalist Claimants*. Providence, R.I.: Brown University Press, 1965.

Bullard, Mary R. *Cumberland Island: A History*. Athens: University of Georgia Press, 2003.

Bulloch, Joseph G. B. *A History and Genealogy of the Families of Bellinger and Deveaux*. Savannah: Savannah Morning Press, 1895.

Burnard, T. G. "'Prodigious Riches': The Wealth of Jamaica before the American Revolution." *Economic History Review*, n.s., 54, no. 3 (Aug. 2001): 506–24.

Burnard, Trevor. "The British Atlantic." In *Atlantic History: A Critical Appraisal*, edited by Jack P. Greene and Philip D. Morgan, 111–36. Oxford: Oxford University Press, 2009.

Burnard, Trevor, and Kenneth Morgan. "The Dynamics of the Slave Market and Slave Purchasing Patterns in Jamaica, 1655–1788." *William and Mary Quarterly*, 3rd ser., 58, no. 1 (Jan. 2001): 205–28.

Byrd, Alexander X. *Captives and Voyagers: Black Migrants across the Eighteenth-Century British Atlantic World*. Baton Rouge: Louisiana State University Press, 2008.

Byrne, William A. "The Burden and the Heat of the Day: Slavery and Servitude in Savannah, 1733–1865." Ph.D. diss., Florida State University, 1979.

Caldwell, Lee Ann. "Women Landholders of Colonial Georgia." In *Forty Years of Diversity: Essays on Colonial Georgia*, edited by Harvey H. Jackson and Phinizy Spalding, 183–95. Athens: University of Georgia Press, 1984.

Calhoun, Jeanne A., Martha A. Zierden, and Elizabeth A. Paysinger. "The Geographic Spread of Charleston's Mercantile Community, 1732–1767." *South Carolina Historical Magazine* 86 (July 1985): 182–220.

Calloway, Colin G. *The Scratch of a Pen: 1763 and the Transformation of North America.* Oxford: Oxford University Press, 2006.

———. *White People, Indians, and Highlanders: Tribal Peoples and Colonial Encounters in Scotland and America.* Oxford: Oxford University Press, 2008.

Canny, Nicholas, and Anthony Pagden, eds. *Colonial Identity in the Atlantic World, 1500–1800.* Princeton, N.J.: Princeton University Press, 1987.

Carman, Harry J., ed. *American Husbandry.* 1939. Reprint, Port Washington, N.Y.: Kennikat, 1964.

Carney, Judith A. *Black Rice: The African Origins of Rice Cultivation in the Americas.* Cambridge, Mass.: Harvard University Press, 2001.

———. "From Hands to Tutors: African Expertise in the South Carolina Rice Economy." *Agricultural History* 67, no. 3 (Summer 1993): 1–30.

———. "Landscapes of Technology Transfer: Rice Cultivation and African Continuities." *Technology and Culture* 37, no. 1 (Jan. 1996): 5–35.

Carney, Judith A., and Richard Porcher. "Geographies of the Past: Rice, Slaves and Technological Transfer in South Carolina." *Southeastern Geographer* 33, no. 2 (Nov. 1993): 127–47.

Carretta, Vincent. *Equiano the African: Biography of a Self-Made Man.* Athens: University of Georgia Press, 2005.

———. "'I began to feel the happiness of liberty, of which I knew nothing before': Eighteenth-Century Black Accounts of the Lowcountry." In *African American Life in the Georgia Lowcountry: The Atlantic World and the Gullah Geechee,* edited by Philip D. Morgan, 77–102. Athens: University of Georgia Press, 2010.

Carson, Cary, Ronald Hoffman, and Peter J. Albert, eds. *Of Consuming Interests: The Style of Life in the Eighteenth Century.* Charlottesville: University of Virginia Press, 1994.

"The Case of George McIntosh." *Georgia Historical Quarterly* 3 (1919): 131–45.

The Case of George McIntosh, Esquire, a Member of the Late Council and Convention of the State of Georgia with the Proceedings Thereon in the Hon. the Assembly and Council of That State. Savannah, 1777. Reprint, *Photostat Americana,* 2nd ser., no. 16 (Aug. 15, 1942).

Cashin, Edward J. *Beloved Bethesda: A History of George Whitefield's Home for Boys, 1740–2000.* Macon: Mercer University Press, 2001.

———. "The Famous Colonel Wells'[*sic*]: Factionalism in Revolutionary Georgia." *Georgia Historical Quarterly* 58, suppl. (1974): 137–56.

———. "From Creeks to Crackers." In *The Southern Colonial Backcountry: Interdisciplinary Perspectives on Frontier Communities,* edited by David Colin Crass, Steven D. Smith, Martha A. Zierden, and Richard D. Brooks. Knoxville: University of Tennessee Press, 1998.

————. "The Gentlemen of Augusta." In *Colonial Augusta: "Key of the Indian Countrey,"* edited by Edward J. Cashin, 29–58. Macon: Mercer University Press, 1986.

————. *Governor Henry Ellis and the Transformation of British North America.* Athens: University of Georgia Press, 1994.

————. *Guardians of the Valley: Chickasaws in Colonial South Carolina and Georgia.* Columbia: University of South Carolina Press, 2009.

————. *The King's Ranger: Thomas Brown and the American Revolution on the Southern Frontier.* New York: Fordham University Press, 1999.

————. *Lachlan McGillivray, Indian Trader: The Shaping of the Southern Colonial Frontier.* Athens: University of Georgia Press, 1992.

————. *Old Springfield: Race and Religion in Augusta, Georgia.* Augusta: Springfield Village Park Foundation, 1996.

————. "Sowing the Wind: Governor Wright and the Georgia Backcountry on the Eve of the Revolution." In *Forty Years of Diversity: Essays on Colonial Georgia*, edited by Harvey H. Jackson and Phinizy Spalding, 233–50. Athens: University of Georgia Press, 1984.

————. *The Story of Augusta.* Augusta: Richmond County Board of Education, 1980.

Cashin, Edward J., ed. *Colonial Augusta: "Key of the Indian Countrey."* Macon: Mercer University Press, 1986.

Cashin, Edward J., and Heard Robertson. *Augusta and the American Revolution: Events in the Georgia Back Country, 1773–1783.* Darien, Ga.: Ashantilly Press, 1975.

Cates, Gerald Lee. "A Medical History of Georgia: The First Hundred Years, 1733–1833." Ph.D. diss., University of Georgia, 1976.

————. "'The Seasoning': Disease and Death among the First Colonists of Georgia." *Georgia Historical Quarterly* 64, no. 2 (Summer 1980): 146–58.

Chammas, Carole. "Changes in English and Anglo-American Consumption from 1500 to 1800." In *Consumption and the World of Goods*, edited by John Brewer and Roy Porter, 177–205. London: Routledge, 1994.

Chaplin, Joyce E. *An Anxious Pursuit: Agricultural Innovation & Modernity in the Lower South, 1730–1815.* Chapel Hill: University of North Carolina Press, 1993.

————. "Creating a Cotton South in Georgia and South Carolina, 1760–1815." *Journal of Southern History* 55, no. 2 (May 1991): 171–200.

————. "Creoles in British America: From Denial to Acceptance." In *Creolization: History, Ethnography, Theory*, edited by Charles Stewart, 46–65. Walnut Creek, Calif.: Left Coast Press, 2007.

————. "Tidal Rice Cultivation and the Problem of Slavery in South Carolina and Georgia, 1760–1815." *William and Mary Quarterly*, 3rd ser., 49, no. 1 (Jan. 1992): 29–61.

Chestnutt, David R. *South Carolina's Expansion into Colonial Georgia, 1720–1765.* New York: Garland, 1989.

———. "South Carolina's Penetration of Georgia in the 1760s: Henry Laurens as a Case Study." *South Carolina Historical Magazine* 73, no. 4 (Oct. 1972): 194–208.

Clark, G. N. *Guide to English Commercial Statistics, 1696–1782.* London: Offices of the Royal Historical Society, 1938.

Clarke, Colin G. *Kingston, Jamaica: Urban Development and Social Change, 1692–2002.* 1975. Reprint, Kingston, Jamaica: Ian Randle, 2006.

Clarke, William Bordley. *Early & Historic Freemasonry of Georgia, 1733–1800.* Savannah: n.p., 1924.

Clarkson, L. A. "The Organization of the English Leather Industry in the Late Sixteenth and Seventeenth Centuries." *Economic History Review* 13, no. 2 (1960): 245–56.

Clifton, James M., ed. *Life and Labor on Argyle Island: Letters and Documents of a Savannah River Rice Plantation, 1833–1867.* Savannah: Beehive Press, 1978.

Clowse, Converse D. *Measuring Charleston's Overseas Commerce, 1670–1767: Statistics from the Port's Naval Lists.* Washington, D.C.: University Press of America, 1981.

———. "Shipowning and Shipbuilding in Colonial South Carolina: An Overview." *American Neptune* 45 (1985): 221–44.

Coclanis, Peter A. "Global Perspectives on the Early Economic History of South Carolina." *South Carolina Historical Magazine* 106, nos. 2–3 (Apr.–July 2005): 130–45.

———. "The Hydra Head of Merchant Capital: Markets and Merchants in Early South Carolina." In *The Meaning of South Carolina History: Essays in Honor of George C. Rogers Jr.*, edited by David R. Chestnutt and Clyde N. Wilson, 1–18. Columbia: University of South Carolina Press, 1991.

———. "In Retrospect: McCusker and Menard's 'Economy of British America.'" *Reviews in American History* 30, no. 2 (June 2002): 183–97.

———. *The Shadow of a Dream: Economic Life and Death in the South Carolina Low Country, 1670–1920.* New York: Oxford University Press, 1989.

———. "The Sociology of Architecture in Colonial Charleston: Pattern and Process in an Eighteenth-Century Southern City." *Journal of Social History* 18, no. 4 (Summer 1985): 607–23.

Coker, William S., and Thomas D. Watson. *Indian Traders of the Southeastern Spanish Borderlands: Panton, Leslie & Company and John Forbes & Company, 1783–1847.* Pensacola: University of West Florida Press, 1986.

Coleman, Kenneth. *American Revolution in Georgia, 1763–1789.* Athens: University of Georgia Press, 1958.

———. *Colonial Georgia: A History.* New York: Scribner's Sons. 1976. Reprint, Millwood: KTO Press, 1989.

———. "The Founding of Georgia." In *Forty Years of Diversity: Essays on Colonial Georgia*, edited by Harvey H. Jackson and Phinizy Spalding, 4–20. Athens: University of Georgia Press, 1984.

———. "The Southern Frontier: Georgia's Founding and the Expansion of South Carolina." *Georgia Historical Quarterly* 56, no. 2 (Summer 1972): 163–74.

Coleman, Kenneth, and Charles Stephen Gurr, eds. *Dictionary of Georgia Biography*. 2 vols. Athens: University of Georgia Press, 1983.

Colley, Linda. *Britons: Forging the Nation, 1707–1837*. New Haven, Conn.: Yale University Press, 1992.

Coon, David L. "Eliza Lucas Pinckney and the Reintroduction of Indigo Culture in South Carolina." *Journal of Southern History* 42, no. 1 (1976): 61–76.

Corry, John P. "The Houses of Colonial Georgia." *Georgia Historical Quarterly* 14, no. 3 (Sept. 1930): 181–201.

Coulter, E. Merton. "Edward Telfair." *Georgia Historical Quarterly* 20, no. 2 (June 1936): 99–124.

———. "A List of the First Shipload of Georgia Settlers." *Georgia Historical Quarterly* 31, no. 4 (Dec. 1947): 282–88.

———. "Mary Musgrove, 'Queen of the Creeks': A Chapter of Early Georgia Troubles." *Georgia Historical Quarterly* 11, no. 1 (1927): 1–29.

———. *Thomas Spalding of Sapelo*. Baton Rouge: Louisiana State University Press, 1940.

———. *Wormsloe: Two Centuries of a Georgia Family*. Athens: University of Georgia Press, 1955.

Coulter, E. Merton, ed. *The Journal of William Stephens, 1741–1743*. Athens: University of Georgia Press, 1958.

———. *The Journal of William Stephens, 1743–1745*. Athens: University of Georgia Press, 1959.

Coulter, E. Merton, and Albert B. Saye, eds. *A List of the Early Settlers of Georgia*. Athens: University of Georgia Press, 1949.

Crane, Verner W. *The Southern Frontier, 1670–1732*. 1929. Reprint, Ann Arbor: University of Michigan Press, 1959.

Craton, Michael. "Reluctant Creoles: The Planters' World in the British West Indies." In *Strangers within the Realm: Cultural Margins of the First British Empire*, edited by Bernard Bailyn and Philip D. Morgan, 314–62. Chapel Hill: University of North Carolina Press, 1991.

———. *Testing the Chains: Resistance to Slavery in the British West Indies*. 1982. Reprint, Ithaca, N.Y.: Cornell University Press, 2009.

Cutton, George Barton. *The Silversmiths in Georgia: Together with Watchmakers and Jewelers, 1733–1850*. Savannah: Pigeonhole Press, 1958.

Dallimore, Arnold A. *George Whitefield: The Life and Times of the Great Evangelist of the Eighteenth-Century Revival*. 2 vols. London: Banner of Truth Trust, 1995.

Daniel, Marjorie. "Anglicans and Dissenters in Georgia, 1758–1777." *Church History* 7, no. 3 (Sept. 1938): 247–62.

Davis, Harold E. *The Fledgling Province: Social and Cultural Life in Colonial Georgia, 1733–1766*. Chapel Hill: University of North Carolina Press, 1976.

Davis, Robert Scott, Jr. "American Voyages: The Colonial Career of Captain William Thomson and the *Two Brothers*." *Historical Society of Georgia National Guard Journal* 9 (Spring–Summer 2003): 10–16.

Deagan, Kathleen, and Darcie MacMahon. *Fort Mose: Colonial America's Black Fortress of Freedom*. Gainesville: University Press of Florida, 1995.

Dethloff, Henry C. "The Colonial Rice Trade." *Agricultural History* 56, no. 1 (Jan. 1982): 231–43.

De Vorsey, Louis, Jr. "The Colonial Georgia Backcountry." In *Colonial Augusta: "Key of the Indian Countrey,"* edited by Edward J. Cashin, 3–28. Macon: Mercer University Press, 1986.

———. *The Indian Boundary in the Southern Colonies, 1763–1775*. Chapel Hill: University of North Carolina Press, 1966.

De Vorsey, Louis, Jr., ed. *De Brahm's Report of the General Survey in the Southern District of North America*. Columbia: University of South Carolina Press, 1971.

Dickson, R. J. *Ulster Emigration to Colonial America, 1718–1775*. London: Routledge and Kegan Paul, 1966.

Doar, David. *Rice and Rice Planting in the South Carolina Low Country*. 1936. Reprint, Charleston, S.C.: Charleston Museum, 1970.

Doberstein, John W., ed. *Journals of Henry Melchior Muhlenberg*. 3 vols. Translated by John C. Tappet. Philadelphia: Muhlenberg Press, 1945.

Dobson, David. *Scots in Georgia and the Deep South, 1735–1845*. Baltimore: Genealogical Publishing, 2000.

Doerflinger, Thomas M. *A Vigorous Spirit of Enterprise: Merchants and Economic Development in Revolutionary Philadelphia*. Chapel Hill: University of North Carolina Press, 1986.

Donnan, Elizabeth, ed. *Documents Illustrative of the History of the Slave Trade to America*. 4 vols. Washington, D.C.: Carnegie Institution of Washington, 1930–35.

DuBois, Laurent. "The French Atlantic." In *Atlantic History: A Critical Appraisal*, edited by Jack P. Greene and Philip D. Morgan, 137–62. Oxford: Oxford University Press, 2009.

Dunbar, Gary S. "Colonial Carolina Cowpens." *Agricultural History* 35, no. 3 (July 1961): 125–31.

Dunn, Richard. *Sugar and Slaves: The Rise of the Planter Class in the English West Indies, 1624–1713.* Chapel Hill: University of North Carolina Press, 1972.

DuPlessis, Robert S. "Cloth and the Emergence of the Atlantic Economy." In *The Atlantic Economy during the Seventeenth and Eighteenth Centuries: Organization, Operation, Practice, and Personnel,* edited by Peter A. Coclanis, 72–94. Columbia: University of South Carolina Press, 2005.

Dyde, Brian. *Out of the Crowded Vagueness: A History of St. Kitts, Nevis & Anguilla.* Oxford: Macmillan Caribbean, 2005.

Earley, Lawrence S. *Looking for Longleaf: The Fall and Rise of an American Forest.* Chapel Hill: University of North Carolina Press, 2004.

Early Deaths in Savannah, Georgia, 1763–1803. Compiled by the Genealogical Committee of Georgia Historical Society. Savannah: R. J. Taylor Jr. Foundation, 1993.

Edelson, S. Max. "Beyond 'Black Rice': Reconstructing Material and Cultural Contexts for Early Plantation Agriculture." *American Historical Review* 115, no. 1 (Feb. 2010): 125–35.

———. "The Characters of Commodities: The Reputations of South Carolina Rice and Indigo in the Atlantic World." In *The Atlantic Economy during the Seventeenth and Eighteenth Centuries: Organization, Operation, Practice, and Personnel,* edited by Peter A. Coclanis, 344–60. Columbia: University of South Carolina Press, 2005.

———. "Clearing Swamps, Harvesting Forests: Trees and the Making of a Plantation Landscape in the Colonial South Carolina Lowcountry." *Agricultural History* 81, no. 3 (Summer 2007): 381–406.

———. *Plantation Enterprise in Colonial South Carolina.* Cambridge, Mass.: Harvard University Press, 2006.

———. Review of *Black Rice* by Judith Carney. *Journal of American History* 89, no. 1 (June 2001): 196–97.

Edgar, Walter B., ed. *The Letterbook of Robert Pringle.* 2 vols. Columbia: University of South Carolina Press, 1972.

———. *South Carolina: A History.* Columbia: University of South Carolina Press, 1998.

Edgar, Walter B., and N. Louis Bailey, eds. *Biographical Directory of the South Carolina House of Representatives,* vol. 2: *The Commons House of Assembly, 1692–1775.* Columbia: University of South Carolina Press, 1977.

Egnal, Marc. *New World Economies: The Growth of the Thirteen Colonies and Early Canada.* New York: Oxford University Press, 1998.

Elliott, J. H. *Empires of the Atlantic World: Britain and Spain in America, 1492–1830.* New Haven, Conn.: Yale University Press, 2007.

Eltis, David, Philip Morgan, and David Richardson. "Agency and Diaspora in Atlantic History: Reassessing the African Contribution to Rice Cultivation in the Americas." *American Historical Review* 112, no. 5 (Dec. 2007): 1329–58.

———. "Black, Brown, or White?: Color-Coding American Commercial Rice Cultivation with Slave Labor." *American Historical Review* 115, no. 1 (Feb. 2010): 164–71.

Engerman, Stanley L., and Robert E. Gallman, eds. *The Cambridge Economic History of the United States*, vol. 1: *The Colonial Era*. Cambridge: Cambridge University Press, 1996.

Etheridge, Robbie. "Creating the Shatter Zone: Indian Slave Traders and the Collapse of the Southeastern Chiefdoms." In *Light on the Path: The Anthropology and History of the Southeastern Indians*, edited by Thomas J. Pluckhahn and Robbie Etheridge, 207–18. Tuscaloosa: University of Alabama Press, 2006.

———. *Creek Country: The Creek Indians and Their World*. Chapel Hill: University of North Carolina Press, 2003.

Fabel, Robin F. A. "British Rule in the Floridas." In *The New History of Florida*, edited by Michael Gannon, 134–49. Gainesville: University Press of Florida, 1996.

———. *The Economy of British West Florida, 1763–1783*. Tuscaloosa: University of Alabama Press, 1988.

Fant, H. B. "Financing the Colonization of Georgia." *Georgia Historical Quarterly* 20, no. 1 (Mar. 1936): 1–29.

Fields-Black, Edda L. *Deep Roots: Rice Farmers in West Africa and the African Diaspora*. Bloomington: Indiana University Press, 2008.

Fisher, Doris B. "Mary Musgrove: Creek Englishwoman." Ph.D. diss., Emory University, 1990.

Fleetwood, William C. *Tidecraft: The Boats of South Carolina, Georgia and Northeastern Florida, 1550–1950*. Savannah: WBG Marine Press, 1995.

Fraser, Walter J., Jr. *Charleston! Charleston!: The History of a Southern City*. Columbia: University of South Carolina Press, 1991.

———. *Savannah in the Old South*. Athens: University of Georgia Press, 2003.

Frey, Sylvia R. *Water from the Rock: Black Resistance in a Revolutionary Age*. Princeton, N.J.: Princeton University Press, 1991.

Frey, Sylvia R., and Betty Wood. *Coming Shouting to Zion: African American Protestantism in the American South and British Caribbean to 1830*. Chapel Hill: University of North Carolina Press, 1998.

Gallay, Alan. *The Formation of a Planter Elite: Jonathan Bryan and the Southern Colonial Frontier*. Athens: University of Georgia Press, 1989.

———. *The Indian Slave Trade: The Rise of the English Empire in the American South, 1670–1717*. New Haven, Conn.: Yale University Press, 2002.

———. "Jonathan Bryan's Plantation Empire: Land, Politics, and the Formation of a Ruling Class in Colonial Georgia." *William and Mary Quarterly*, 3rd ser., 45, no. 2 (Apr. 1988): 253–79.

———. "The Origins of Slaveholders' Paternalism: George Whitefield, the Bryan Family, and the Great Awakening in the South." *Journal of Southern History* 53, no. 3 (Aug. 1987): 369–94.

Games, Alison. "Atlantic History: Definitions, Challenges, and Opportunities." *American Historical Review* 111, no. 3 (June 2006): 741–57.

———. *Migration and the Origins of the English Atlantic World*. Cambridge, Mass.: Harvard University Press, 1999.

Garrett-Sharpe, Brown-Poindexter and Allied Lines: A Genealogical Study with Biographical Notes. New York: American Historical Company, 1971.

Genovese, Eugene D. *Roll, Jordan, Roll: The World the Slaves Made*. New York: Vintage, 1976.

Gibbes, R. W. *Documentary History of the American Revolution, 1764–1776*, vol. 1. New York: D. Appleton, 1855.

Godbold, E. Stanly, Jr., and Robert H. Woody. *Christopher Gadsden and the American Revolution*. Knoxville: University of Tennessee Press, 1982.

Goldenberg, Joseph A. *Shipbuilding in Colonial America*. Charlottesville: University of Virginia Press, 1976.

Gomez, Michael A. *Exchanging Our Country Marks: The Transformation of African Identities in the Colonial and Antebellum South*. Chapel Hill: University of North Carolina Press, 1998.

Gordon, William W. "Georgia's Debt to Monmouth County, New Jersey." *Georgia Historical Quarterly* 7, no. 2 (June 1923): 119–34.

Goveia, Elsa V. *Slave Society in the British Leeward Islands at the End of the Eighteenth Century*. New Haven, Conn.: Yale University Press, 1965.

Granger, M. L. *Savannah Harbor: Its Origin and Development, 1733–1890*. Savannah: Corps of Engineers, 1968.

Granger, M. L., ed. *Savannah River Plantations*. 1947. Reprint, Savannah: Savannah Writers' Project, Oglethorpe Press, 1997.

Gray, Lewis Cecil. *History of Agriculture in the Southern United States to 1860*. 2 vols. New York: Peter Smith, 1941.

Green, E. R. R. "Queensborough Township: Scotch-Irish Emigration and the Expansion of Georgia, 1763–1776." *William and Mary Quarterly*, 3rd ser., 17, no. 2 (Apr. 1960): 183–99.

Greene, Jack P. "Colonial South Carolina and the Caribbean Connection." In his
Imperatives, Behaviors & Identities: Essays in Early American Cultural History,
68–86. Charlottesville: University of Virginia Press, 1992.

———. "Early Modern Southeastern North America and the Broader Atlantic
Worlds." *Journal of Southern History* 73, no. 3 (Aug. 2007): 525–38.

———. "The Georgia Commons House of Assembly and the Power of
Appointment to Executive Offices, 1765–1775." *Georgia Historical Quarterly* 46,
no. 1 (Mar. 1962): 151–61.

———. "Interpretive Frameworks: The Quest for Intellectual Order in Early
American History." *William and Mary Quarterly*, 3rd ser., 48, no. 4 (Oct. 1991):
515–30.

———. *The Quest for Power: The Lower Houses of Assembly in the Southern
Royal Colonies, 1689–1776*. Chapel Hill: University of North Carolina Press,
1963.

———. "'Society and Economy in the British Caribbean during the Seventeenth
and Eighteenth Centuries': A Review Article." *American Historical Review* 79,
no. 5 (Dec. 1974): 1499–1517.

———. "Travails of an Infant Colony: The Search for Viability, Coherence,
and Identity in Colonial Georgia." In his *Imperatives, Behaviors & Identities:
Essays in Early American Cultural History*, 113–42. Charlottesville: University of
Virginia Press, 1992.

Greene, Jack P., and Philip D. Morgan, eds. *Atlantic History: A Critical Appraisal*.
Oxford: Oxford University Press, 2009.

Greene, Jack P., and J. R. Pole. "Reconstructing British-American Colonial
History: An Introduction." In *Colonial British America: Essays in the New
History of the Early Modern Era*, edited by Jack P. Greene and J. R. Pole, 1–17.
Baltimore: Johns Hopkins University Press, 1984.

Groover, Robert Long. *Sweet Land of Liberty: A History of Liberty County, Georgia*.
Roswell, Ga.: WHW, 1987.

Haggerty, Sheryllynne. *The British-Atlantic Trading Community, 1760–1810: Men,
Women, and the Distribution of Goods*. Leiden: Brill, 2006.

Hahn, Steven C. *The Invention of the Creek Nation, 1670–1763*. Lincoln: University
of Nebraska Press, 2004.

Hall, Douglas. *In Miserable Slavery: Thomas Thistlewood in Jamaica, 1750–86*. 1989.
Reprint, Kingston: University of West Indies Press, 1999.

Hall, Gwendolyn Midlo. "Africa and Africans in the African Diaspora: The Uses of
Relational Databases." *American Historical Review* 115, no. 1 (Feb. 2010): 136–50.

Hall, Leslie. *Land and Allegiance in Revolutionary Georgia*. Athens: University of
Georgia Press, 2001.

Hamalainen, Pekka. "Lost in Transitions: Suffering, Survival, and Belonging in the Early Modern Atlantic World." *William and Mary Quarterly*, 3rd ser., 68, no. 2 (Apr. 2011): 219–23.

Hamilton, Douglas J. *Scotland, the Caribbean, and the Atlantic World, 1750–1820*. Manchester, England: Manchester University Press, 2005.

Hancock, David. *Citizens of the World: London Merchants and the Integration of the British Atlantic Community, 1735–1785*. Cambridge: Cambridge University Press, 1995.

———. *Oceans of Wine: Madeira and the Emergence of American Trade and Taste*. New Haven, Conn.: Yale University Press, 2009.

Harden, William. *A History of Savannah and South Georgia*. 2 vols. 1913. Reprint, Atlanta: Cherokee Publishing, 1981.

———. "James Mackay of Strathy Hall: Comrade in Arms of George Washington." *Georgia Historical Quarterly* 1, no. 2 (June 1917): 77–98.

Harrold, Frances. "Colonial Siblings: Georgia's Relationship with South Carolina during the Pre-Revolutionary Period." *Georgia Historical Quarterly* 73, no. 4 (Winter 1989): 707–44.

Hart, Emma. *Building Charleston: Town and Society in the Eighteenth-Century British Atlantic World*. Charlottesville: University of Virginia Press, 2010.

Hartridge, Walter Charlton. *The Letters of Robert Mackay to His Wife, Written from Ports in America and England, 1795–1816*. Athens: University of Georgia Press, 1949.

Harwell, Christopher Lee. "William Henry Stiles: Georgia Gentleman-Politician." Ph.D. diss., Emory University, 1959.

Hatley, Tom. *The Dividing Paths: Cherokees and South Carolinians through the Era of Revolution*. New York: Oxford University Press, 1993.

Hawes, Lilla M., ed. "Proceedings of the President and Assistants in Council of Georgia, 1749–1751: Part I." *Georgia Historical Quarterly* 35, no. 4 (Dec. 1951): 323–50.

———. "Proceedings of the President and Assistants in Council of Georgia, 1749–1751: Part II." *Georgia Historical Quarterly* 36, no. 1 (Mar. 1952): 46–70.

Hawthorne, Walter. "From 'Black Rice' to 'Brown': Rethinking the History of Risiculture in the Seventeenth and Eighteenth-Century Atlantic." *American Historical Review* 115, no. 1 (Feb. 2010): 151–63.

Heath, Milton S. *Constructive Liberalism: The Role of the State in Economic Development in Georgia to 1860*. Cambridge, Mass.: Harvard University Press, 1954.

Heath, William E. "The Early Colonial Money System of Georgia." *Georgia Historical Quarterly* 19, no. 2 (June 1935): 145–60.

Hemperley, Marion R., ed. and comp. *English Crown Grants in Christ Church Parish, St. Andrew Parish, St. George Parish, St. John Parish, St. Matthew Parish, St. Paul Parish, St. Philip Parish, for Islands in Georgia, and St. David, St. Patrick, St. Thomas, and St. Mary in Georgia, 1755–1775.* Atlanta: Secretary of State Office, 1972–73.

Herndon, G. Melvin. "Naval Stores in Colonial Georgia." *Georgia Historical Quarterly* 52 (Dec. 1968): 426–33.

———. "Timber Products of Colonial Georgia." *Georgia Historical Quarterly* 57 (Spring 1973): 56–62.

Hewatt, Alexander. *An Historical Account of the Rise and Progress of the Colonies of South Carolina and Georgia.* 2 vols. London: Alexander Donaldson, 1779.

Hickman, Nollie. *Mississippi Harvest: Lumbering in the Longleaf Pine Belt, 1840–1915.* Oxford: University Press of Mississippi, 1962.

Higgins, W. Robert. "Charles Town Merchants and Factors Dealing in the External Negro Trade, 1735–1775." *South Carolina Historical Magazine* 65 (1964): 205–17.

Higman, B. W. *A Concise History of the Caribbean.* Cambridge: Cambridge University Press, 2011.

———. "Economic and Social Development of the British West Indies, from Settlement to ca. 1850." In *The Cambridge Economic History of the United States*, vol. 1: *The Colonial Era*, edited by Stanley L. Engerman and Robert E. Gallman, 297–336. Cambridge: Cambridge University Press, 1996.

———. "Jamaican Port Towns in the Early Nineteenth Century." In *Atlantic Port Cities: Economy, Culture, and Society in the Atlantic World, 1650–1850*, edited by Franklin W. Knight and Peggy K. Liss, 117–48. Knoxville: University of Tennessee Press, 1991.

———. *Slave Populations of the British Caribbean.* Mona, Jamaica: University of the West Indies Press, 1995.

———. "The Sugar Revolution." *Economic History Review*, n.s., 53, no. 2 (May 2000): 213–36.

Hodson, Christopher. "Weird Science: Identity in the Atlantic World." *William and Mary Quarterly*, 3rd ser., 68, no. 2 (Apr. 2011): 227–32.

Hoffman, Ronald, John J. McCusker, Russell R. Menard, and Peter J. Albert. *The Economy of Early America: The Revolutionary Period, 1763–1790.* Charlottesville: University of Virginia Press, 1988.

Horn, James, and Philip D. Morgan. "Settlers and Slaves: European and African Migrations to Early Modern British America." In *The Creation of the British Atlantic World*, edited by Elizabeth Mancke and Carole Shammas, 19–44. Baltimore: Johns Hopkins University Press, 2005.

Hornsby, Stephen J. *British Atlantic, American Frontier: Spaces of Power in Early Modern British America.* Hanover, N.H.: University Press of New England, 2005.

Hudson, Charles. *The Packhorseman.* Tuscaloosa: University of Alabama Press, 2009.

Ingmire, Frances T. *Colonial Georgia Marriage Records from 1760–1810.* Signal Mountain, Tenn.: Mountain Press, 1985.

Inscoe, John C., ed. *James Edward Oglethorpe: New Perspectives on His Life and Legacy.* Savannah: Georgia Historical Society, 1997.

Ivers, Larry E. *British Drums on the Southern Frontier: The Military Colonization of Georgia, 1733–1749.* Chapel Hill: University of North Carolina Press, 1974.

Jackson, Harvey H. "The Battle of the Rice Boats: Georgia Joins the Revolution." *Georgia Historical Quarterly* 58, no. 2 (June 1974): 229–43.

———. "Behind the Lines: Savannah during the War of Jenkins's Ear." *Georgia Historical Quarterly* 77 (Fall 1994): 471–92.

———. "The Carolina Connection: Jonathan Bryan, His Brothers, and the Founding of Georgia, 1733–52." *Georgia Historical Quarterly* 68, no. 2 (Summer 1984): 147–72.

———. "Consensus and Conflict: Factional Politics in Revolutionary Georgia, 1774–1777." *Georgia Historical Quarterly* 59, no. 4 (Winter 1975): 388–401.

———. "The Darien Antislavery Petition of 1739 and the Georgia Plan." *William and Mary Quarterly,* 3rd ser., 34, no. 4 (Oct. 1977): 618–31.

———. "Georgia Whiggery: The Origins and Effects of a Many-Faceted Movement." In *Forty Years of Diversity: Essays on Colonial Georgia,* edited by Harvey H. Jackson and Phinizy Spalding, 251–73. Athens: University of Georgia Press, 1984.

———. "Hugh Bryan and the Evangelical Movement in Colonial South Carolina." *William and Mary Quarterly,* 3rd ser., 43, no. 4 (Oct. 1986): 594–614.

———. *Lachlan McIntosh and the Politics of Revolutionary Georgia.* Athens: University of Georgia Press, 1979.

———. "The Rise of the Western Members: Revolutionary Politics and the Georgia Backcountry." In *An Uncivil War: The Southern Backcountry during the American Revolution,* edited by Ronald Hoffman et al., 276–320. Charlottesville: University of Virginia Press, 1985.

Jay, William. *Memoirs of the Life and Character of the Late Rev. Cornelius Winter.* New York: Samuel Whiting, 1811.

Jenkins, Charles Francis. *Button Gwinnett, Signer of the Declaration of Independence.* Garden City, N.Y.: Doubleday, Page, 1926.

Jennison, Watson W. *Cultivating Race: The Expansion of Slavery in Georgia, 1750–1860*. Lexington: University of Kentucky Press, 2012.

Johnson, Charles J., Jr. *Mary Telfair: The Life and Legacy of a Nineteenth-Century Woman*. Savannah: Frederic C. Beil, 2002.

Johnson, James M. *Militiamen, Rangers, and Redcoats: The Military in Georgia, 1754–1776*. Macon: Mercer University Press, 1992.

Johnston, Edith Duncan. *The Houstouns of Georgia*. Athens: University of Georgia Press, 1950.

Johnston, Elizabeth Lichtenstein. *Recollections of a Georgia Loyalist*. Edited by Arthur Eaton. 1901. Reprint, New York: De La More, 1991.

Jones, Alice Hanson. *Wealth of a Nation to Be: the American Colonies on the Eve of the Revolution*. New York: Columbia University Press, 1980.

Jones, Charles C., Jr. *Biographical Sketches of the Delegates from Georgia to the Continental Congress*. Boston: Houghton, Mifflin, 1891.

———. *Dead Towns of Georgia*. 1878. Reprint, Savannah: Oglethorpe Press, 1997.

———. *The History of Georgia*. 2 vols. Boston: Houghton, Mifflin, 1883.

———. *The History of Savannah, Ga.: From Its Settlement to the Close of the Eighteenth Century*. Syracuse, N.Y.: D. Mason, 1890.

Jones, George Fenwick. *The Georgia Dutch: From the Rhine and Danube to the Savannah, 1733–1783*. Athens: University of Georgia Press, 1992.

———. "Portrait of an Irish Entrepreneur in Colonial Augusta: John Rae, 1708–1772." *Georgia Historical Quarterly* 83, no. 3 (Fall 1999): 427–47.

———. *The Salzburger Saga: Religious Exiles and Other Germans along the Savannah*. Athens: University of Georgia Press, 1984.

Jones, George Fenwick, ed. *Detailed Reports on the Salzburger Emigrants Who Settled in America . . . Edited by Samuel Urlsperger*. 17 vols. Athens: University of Georgia Press, 1968–93.

———. "A German Surgeon on the Flora and Fauna of Colonial Georgia: Four Letters of Johann Christoph Bornemann, 1753–1755." *Georgia Historical Quarterly* 76, no. 4 (Winter 1992): 891–914.

———. "Report of Mr. Ettwein's Journey to Georgia and South Carolina, 1765." *South Carolina Historical Magazine* 91, no. 4 (Oct. 1990): 247–60.

Jordon, Winthrop. *White over Black: American Attitudes toward the Negro, 1550–1812*. Baltimore: Penguin, 1969.

Journals of the Continental Congress, 1774–1789. 34 vols. Washington, D.C.: U.S. Government Printing Office, 1904–12.

Juricek, John T. *Colonial Georgia and the Creeks: Anglo-Indian Diplomacy on the Southern Frontier, 1733–1763*. Gainesville: University Press of Florida, 2010.

Karras, Alan L. *Sojourners in the Sun: Scottish Migrants in Jamaica and the Chesapeake, 1740–1800.* Ithaca, N.Y.: Cornell University Press, 1992.

Kellock, Katharine A. "London Merchants and the Pre-1776 American Debts." *Guildhall Studies in London History* 1, no. 3 (Oct. 1974): 109–50.

Klein, Herbert S. *The Atlantic Slave Trade.* Cambridge: Cambridge University Press, 1999.

Kole, Kaye. *The Minis Family of Georgia, 1733–1992.* Savannah: Georgia Historical Society, 1992.

Kornwolf, James D. *Architecture and Town Planning in Colonial North America*, vol. 2: *England in North America, 1585–1867.* Baltimore: Johns Hopkins University Press, 2002.

Krech, Shepard, III. *Myth and History: The Ecological Indian.* New York: Norton, 1999.

Kulikoff, Allan. *Tobacco and Slaves: The Development of Southern Cultures in the Chesapeake, 1680–1800.* Chapel Hill: University of North Carolina Press, 1986.

Lambert, Frank. "Father against Son, and Son against Father: The Habershams of Georgia and the American Revolution." *Georgia Historical Quarterly* 84, no. 1 (Spring 2000): 1–28.

———. *James Habersham: Loyalty, Politics, and Commerce in Colonial Georgia.* Athens: University of Georgia Press, 2005.

———. *"Pedlar in Divinity": George Whitefield and the Transatlantic Revivals, 1737–1770.* Princeton, N.J.: Princeton University Press, 1994.

Lamplugh, George R. *Politics on the Periphery: Factions and Parties in Georgia, 1783–1806.* Newark: University of Delaware Press, 1986.

Landers, Jane. *Black Society in Spanish Florida.* Urbana: University of Illinois Press, 1999.

Lane, Mills. *Savannah Revisited: History & Architecture.* 1969. Reprint, Savannah: Beehive Press, 2001.

Lane, Mills, ed. *General Oglethorpe's Georgia: Colonial Letters, 1733–1745.* 2 vols. Savannah: Beehive Press, 1975.

Lannen, Andrew C. "James Oglethorpe and the Civil-Military Contest for Authority in Colonial Georgia, 1732–1749." *Georgia Historical Quarterly* 95, no. 2 (Summer 2011): 203–31.

———. "Liberty and Authority in Colonial Georgia, 1717–1776." Ph.D. diss., Louisiana State University, 2002.

Lawrence, Alexander A. *Storm over Savannah: The Story of Count d'Estaing and the Siege of the Town in 1779.* Athens: University of Georgia Press, 1951.

LeConte, Joseph. *The Autobiography of Joseph LeConte.* Edited by William Dallam Armes. New York: D. Appleton, 1903.

Levy, B. H. "The Early History of Georgia's Jews." In *Forty Years of Diversity: Essays on Colonial Georgia*, edited by Harvey H. Jackson and Phinizy Spalding, 163–78. Athens: University of Georgia Press, 1984.

———. *Mordecai Sheftall, Jewish Revolutionary Patriot*. Savannah: Georgia Historical Society, 1999.

Littlefield, Daniel C. "Charleston and Internal Slave Redistribution." *South Carolina Historical Magazine* 87, no. 2 (Apr. 1986): 93–105.

———. *Rice and Slaves: Ethnicity and the Slave Trade in Colonial South Carolina*. Baton Rouge: Louisiana State University Press, 1981.

———. "The Slave Trade to Colonial South Carolina: A Profile." *South Carolina Historical Magazine* 101, no. 2 (Apr. 2000): 110–41.

Lockley, Timothy. *Lines in the Sand: Race and Class in Lowcountry Georgia, 1750–1860*. Athens: University of Georgia Press, 2001.

Loewald, Klaus G., Beverly Starika, and Paul S. Taylor, eds. "Johann Martin Bolzius Answers a Questionnaire on Carolina and Georgia." *William and Mary Quarterly*, 3rd ser., 14, no. 2 (Apr. 1957): 218–61.

Logan, William. "William Logan's Journal of a Journey to Georgia, 1745." *Pennsylvania Magazine of History and Biography* 36, no. 1 (1912): 1–16, 162–70.

Lounsbury, Carl. "Christ Church, Savannah: Loopholes in Metropolitan Design on the Frontier." In *Material Culture in Anglo-America: Regional Identity and Urbanity in the Tidewater, Lowcountry, and Caribbean*, edited by David S. Shields, 58–73. Columbia: University of South Carolina Press, 2009.

MacDonald, William. *Select Charters and Other Documents Illustrative of American History, 1606–1775*. New York: Macmillan, 1899.

Mackay, Robert. *The Letters of Robert Mackay to His Wife*. Edited by Walter Charlton Hartridge. Athens: University of Georgia Press, 1949.

Macpherson, David. *Annals of Commerce: Manufactures, Fisheries, and Navigation*. 4 vols. London: Nichols and Son, 1805.

Mancall, Peter C. *Deadly Medicine: Indians and Alcohol in Early America*. Ithaca, N.Y.: Cornell University Press, 1997.

Mancall, Peter C., Joshua L. Rosenbloom, and Thomas Weiss. "Indians and the Economy of Eighteenth-Century Carolina." In *The Atlantic Economy during the Seventeenth and Eighteenth Centuries: Organization, Operation, Practice, and Personnel*, edited by Peter A. Coclanis. 297–322. Columbia: University of South Carolina Press, 2005.

———. "Slave Prices and the South Carolina Economy, 1722–1809." *Journal of Economic History* 61, no. 3 (Sept. 2001): 616–39.

Mann, Douglas F. "Becoming Creole: Material Life and Society in Eighteenth-Century Kingston, Jamaica." Ph.D. diss., University of Georgia, 2005.

Marsh, Ben. *Georgia's Frontier Women: Female Fortunes in a Southern Colony.*
Athens: University of Georgia Press, 2007.

Martin, Roger A. *John J. Zubly, Colonial Georgia Minister.* New York: Arno, 1982.

Martyn, Benjamin. "An Impartial Enquiry into the State and Utility of the
Province of Georgia, 1741." In *The Clamorous Malcontents: Criticisms and
Defenses of the Colony of Georgia, 1741–1743,* edited by Trevor R. Reese, 125–80.
Savannah: Beehive Press, 1973.

Matson, Cathy. *Merchants & Empire: Trading in Colonial New York.* Baltimore:
Johns Hopkins University Press, 1998.

McCusker, John J. "The Current Value of English Exports, 1697–1800." *William
and Mary Quarterly,* 3rd ser., 28, no. 4 (Oct. 1971): 607–28.

———. *Rum and the American Revolution: The Rum Trade and the Balance of
Payments of the Thirteen Continental Colonies.* New York: Garland, 1989.

McCusker, John J., and Russell R. Menard. *The Economy of British America, 1607–
1789.* 1985. Reprint, Chapel Hill: University of North Carolina Press, 1991.

McDowell, William L., Jr., ed. *Colonial Records of South Carolina: Documents
Relating to Indian Affairs, May 21, 1750–August 7, 1754; 1754–1765.* 2 vols.
Columbia: South Carolina Archives Department, 1958.

Menard, Russell R. "Economic and Social Development of the South." In
The Cambridge Economic History of the United States, vol 1: *The Colonial Era,*
edited by Stanley L. Engerman and Robert E. Gallman, 249–95. Cambridge:
Cambridge University Press, 1996.

———. "Financing the Lowcountry Export Boom: Capital and Growth in Early
South Carolina." *William and Mary Quarterly,* 3rd ser., 51 (Oct. 1994): 659–76.

———. "Slave Demography in the Lowcountry, 1670–1740: From Frontier Society
to Plantation Regime." *South Carolina Historical Magazine* 101, no. 3 (July
2000): 190–213.

———. "Slavery, Economic Growth, and Revolutionary Ideology in the South
Carolina Lowcountry." In *The Economy of Early America: The Revolutionary
Period, 1763–1790,* edited by Ronald Hoffman, John J. McCusker, Russell R.
Menard, and Peter J. Albert, 244–74. Charlottesville: University of Virginia
Press, 1988.

Mercantini, Jonathan. *Who Shall Rule at Home?: The Evolution of South Carolina
Political Culture, 1748–1776.* Columbia: University of South Carolina Press,
2007.

Mereness, Newton D., ed. *Travels in the American Colonies.* New York:
Antiquarian Press, 1961.

Meriwether, Robert L. *The Expansion of South Carolina, 1729–1765.* 1940. Reprint,
Philadelphia: Porcupine, 1974.

Meroney, Geraldine. "The London Entrepot Merchants and the Georgia Colony." *William and Mary Quarterly*, 3rd ser., 25, no. 2 (Apr. 1968): 230–44.

Merrell, James H. *The Indians' New World: Catawbas and Their Neighbors from European Contact to the Era of Removal.* New York: Norton, 1989.

Middlekauff, Robert. *The Glorious Cause: The American Revolution, 1763–1789.* Oxford: Oxford University Press, 1982.

Migliazzo, Arlini C. *To Make This Land Our Own: Community, Identity, and Cultural Adaptation in Purrysburg Township, South Carolina, 1732–1865.* Columbia: University of South Carolina Press, 2007.

Miller, Randall M. "The Stamp Act in Colonial Georgia." *Georgia Historical Quarterly* 56, no. 3 (Fall 1972): 318–31.

Moore, Francis. "A Voyage to Georgia Begun in the Year 1735." *Collections of the Georgia Historical Society* 1 (1840): 79–152.

Moore, W. M., Jr. "The Largest Exporters of Deerskins from Charles Town, 1735–1775." *South Carolina Historical Magazine* 74, no. 3 (July 1973): 144–50.

Morgan, David T. "The Consequences of George Whitefield's Ministry in Georgia and the Carolinas, 1739–1740." *Georgia Historical Quarterly* 55, no. 1 (Spring 1971): 62–82.

Morgan, Edmund S., and Helen M. Morgan. *The Stamp Act Crisis: Prologue to Revolution.* 1953. Reprint, Chapel Hill: University of North Carolina Press, 1995.

Morgan, Kenneth. *Bristol & the Atlantic Trade in the Eighteenth Century.* 1993. Reprint, Cambridge: Cambridge University Press, 2003.

———. "The Organization of the Colonial American Rice Trade." *William and Mary Quarterly*, 3rd ser., 52, no. 3 (July 1995): 433–52.

———. "Slave Sales in Colonial Charleston." *English Historical Review* 113 (Sept. 1998): 905–27.

Morgan, Philip D. "Africa and the Atlantic, c. 1450 to c. 1820." In *Atlantic History: A Critical Appraisal*, edited by Jack P. Greene and Philip D. Morgan, 223–48. Oxford: Oxford University Press, 2009.

———. "The Black Experience in the British Empire, 1680–1810." In *The Eighteenth Century*, edited by P. J. Marshall, 465–86. 1998. Reprint, Oxford: Oxford University Press, 2001.

———. "Black Life in Eighteenth-Century Charleston." *Perspectives in American History*, n.s., 1 (1984): 187–232.

———. "Black Society in the Lowcountry, 1760–1810." In *Slavery and Freedom in the Age of the American Revolution*, edited by Ira Berlin and Ronald Hoffman, 83–141. Charlottesville: University of Virginia Press, 1983.

———. "British Encounters with Africans and African-Americans, circa 1600–1780." In *Strangers within the Realm: Cultural Margins of the First British*

Empire, edited by Bernard Bailyn and Philip D. Morgan, 157–219. Chapel Hill: University of North Carolina Press, 1991.

———. "Colonial South Carolina Runaways: Their Significance for Slave Culture." *Out of the House of Bondage: Runaways, Resistance, and Marronage in Africa and the New World*, edited by Gad Heuman, 57–78. London: Frank Cass, 1986.

———. "Lowcountry Georgia and the Early Modern Atlantic World, 1733–ca. 1820." In *African American Life in the Georgia Lowcountry: The Atlantic World and the Gullah Geechee*, edited by Philip D. Morgan, 13–47. Athens: University of Georgia Press, 2010.

———. *Slave Counterpoint: Black Culture in the Eighteenth-Century Chesapeake & Lowcountry*. Chapel Hill: University of North Carolina Press, 1998.

———. "Work and Culture: The Task System and the World of the Lowcountry Blacks, 1700 to 1880." *William and Mary Quarterly*, 3rd ser., 39, no. 4 (1982): 564–99.

Morgan, Philip D., and Jack Greene. "Introduction: The Present State of Atlantic History." In *Atlantic History: A Critical Appraisal*, edited by Jack P. Greene and Philip D. Morgan, 3–33. Oxford: Oxford University Press, 2009.

Mowat, Charles Loch. *East Florida as a British Province, 1763–1784*. Berkeley: University of California Press, 1943.

Myers, Robert Manson, ed. *The Children of Pride: A True Story of Georgia and the Civil War*. New Haven, Conn.: Yale University Press, 1972.

Nash, R. C. "Domestic Material Culture and Consumer Demand in the British Atlantic World: Colonial South Carolina, 1670–1770." In *Material Culture in Anglo-America: Regional Identity and Urbanity in the Tidewater, Lowcountry, and Caribbean*, edited by David S. Shields, 221–66. Columbia: University of South Carolina Press, 2009.

———. "The Organization of Trade and Finance in the Atlantic Economy: Britain and South Carolina, 1670–1775." In *Money, Trade, and Power: The Evolution of Colonial South Carolina's Plantation Society*, edited by Jack P. Greene, Rosemary Brana-Shute, and Randy J. Sparks, 74–107. Columbia: University of South Carolina Press, 2001.

———. "The Organization of Trade and Finance in the British Atlantic Economy, 1600–1830." In *The Atlantic Economy during the Seventeenth and Eighteenth Centuries: Organization, Operation, Practice, and Personnel*, edited by Peter A. Coclanis, 95–151. Columbia: University of South Carolina Press, 2005.

———. "South Carolina and the Atlantic Economy in the Late Seventeenth and Eighteenth Centuries." *Economic History Review*, 2nd ser., 45, no. 4 (1992): 677–702.

———. "Trade and Business in Eighteenth-Century South Carolina: The Career of John Guerard, Merchant and Planter." *South Carolina Historical Magazine* 96, no. 1 (1995): 6–29.

———. "Urbanization in the Colonial South: Charleston, South Carolina, as a Case Study." *Journal of Urban History* 19, no. 1 (1992): 3–39.

Nelson, Paul David. *General James Grant, Scottish Soldier and Royal Governor of East Florida.* Gainesville: University Press of Florida, 1993.

Newman, Eric P. *The Early Paper Money of America.* Iola, Wis.: Krause, 1990.

Nobles, Gregory. "Breaking into the Backcountry: New Approaches to the Early American Frontier, 1750–1800." *William and Mary Quarterly*, 3rd ser., 46, no. 4 (Oct. 1989): 642–70.

Oatis, Steven J. *A Colonial Complex: South Carolina's Frontiers in the Era of the Yamasee War, 1680–1730.* Lincoln: University of Nebraska Press, 2004.

Olwell, Robert. *Masters, Slaves, and Subjects: The Culture of Power in the South Carolina Low Country, 1740–1790.* Ithaca, N.Y.: Cornell University Press, 1998.

O'Malley, Gregory E. "Beyond the Middle Passage: Slave Migration from the Caribbean to North America, 1619–1807." *William and Mary Quarterly*, 3rd ser., 66, no. 1 (Jan. 2009): 125–72.

———. "Final Passages: The British Inter-Colonial Slave Trade, 1619–1807." Ph.D. diss., Johns Hopkins University, 2006.

O'Shaughnessy, Andrew Jackson. *An Empire Divided: The American Revolution and the British Caribbean.* Philadelphia: University of Pennsylvania Press, 2000.

The Papers of Henry Laurens. Edited by George C. Rogers et al. 16 vols. Columbia: South Carolina Historical Society, University of South Carolina Press, 1974–2003.

Pares, Richard. *Yankees and Creoles: The Trade between North America and the West Indies before the American Revolution.* London: Longmans, Green, 1956.

Parker, Anthony W. *Scottish Highlanders in Colonial Georgia: The Recruitment, Emigration, and Settlement at Darien, 1735–1748.* 1997. Reprint, Athens: University of Georgia Press, 2002.

Pendleton, Nathaniel. "Short Account of the Sea Coast of Georgia in Respect to Agriculture, Ship-Building, Navigation, and the Timber Trade." Edited by Theodore Thayer. *Georgia Historical Quarterly* 61 (Mar. 1957): 70–80.

Piecuch, Jim. *Three Peoples, One King: Loyalists, Indians, and Slaves in the Revolutionary South, 1775–1782.* Columbia: University of South Carolina Press, 2008.

Piker, Joshua. "Colonists and Creeks: Rethinking the Pre-Revolutionary Southern Backcountry." *Journal of Southern History* 70, no. 3 (Aug. 2004): 503–40.

———. *Okfuskee: A Creek Indian Town in Colonial America.* Cambridge, Mass.: Harvard University Press, 2004.

———. "'White & Clean' & Contested: Creek Towns and Trading Paths in the Aftermath of the Seven Years' War." *Ethnohistory* 50, no. 2 (Spring 2003): 315–47.

Plummer, Gayther. "18th Century Forests in Georgia." *Bulletin of the Georgia Academy of Science* 33 (Jan. 1975): 1–19.

Pressly, Paul M. "The Northern Roots of Savannah's Antebellum Elite, 1780s–1850s." *Georgia Historical Quarterly* 87, no. 2 (Summer 2005): 157–99.

———. "Scottish Merchants and the Shaping of Colonial Georgia." *Georgia Historical Quarterly* 91, no. 2 (Summer 2007): 135–68.

Price, Jacob M. *Capital and Credit in British Overseas Trade: The View from the Chesapeake, 1700–1776.* Cambridge, Mass.: Harvard University Press, 1980.

———. "Credit in the Slave Trade and Plantation Economies." In *Slavery and the Rise of the Atlantic System,* edited by Barbara L. Solow, 293–339. Cambridge: Cambridge University Press, 1991.

———. "Economic Function and the Growth of American Port Towns in the Eighteenth Century." *Perspectives in American History* 8 (1974): 123–86.

———. "The Transatlantic Economy." In *Colonial British America: Essays in the New History of the Early Modern Era,* edited by Jack P. Greene and J. R. Pole, 18–42. Baltimore: Johns Hopkins University Press, 1984.

———. "What Do Merchants Do?: Reflections on British Overseas Trade, 1660–1790." *Journal of Economic History* 49, no. 2 (June 1989): 267–84.

Rabac, Donna Marie. "Economy and Society in Early Georgia: A Functional Analysis of the Colony's Origins and Evolution." Ph.D diss., University of Michigan, 1978.

Ramsey, William L. *The Yamasee War: A Study of Culture, Economy, and Conflict in the Colonial South.* Lincoln: University of Nebraska Press, 2008.

Range, Willard. "The Agricultural Revolution in Royal Georgia, 1752–1775." *Agricultural History* 21, no. 4 (Oct. 1947): 250–55.

Rawley, James A. *The Transatlantic Slave Trade: A History.* New York: Norton, 1981.

Rea, Robert R. "British West Florida Trade and Commerce in the Customs Records." *Alabama Review* 37, no. 2 (Apr. 1984): 124–57.

Ready, Milton L. *The Castle Builders: Georgia's Economy under the Trustees, 1732–1754.* New York: Arno, 1978.

Rediker, Marcus. *Between the Devil and the Deep Blue Sea: Merchant Seamen, Pirates and the Anglo-American Maritime World, 1700–1750.* Cambridge: Cambridge University Press, 2006.

———. *The Slave Ship: A Human History.* New York: Penguin, 2007.

Reese, Trevor R. *Colonial Georgia: A Study in British Imperial Policy in the Eighteenth Century.* Athens: University of Georgia Press, 1963.

———. *Frederica: Fort and Colonial Town.* St. Simons Island, Ga.: Fort Frederica Association, 1969.

———. "Harman Verelst, Accountant to the Trustees." *Georgia Historical Quarterly* 39 (Dec. 1955): 348–52.

Reese, Trevor R., ed. *The Clamorous Malcontents: Criticisms and Defenses of the Colony of Georgia, 1741–1743.* Savannah: Beehive Press, 1973.

———. *The Most Delightful Country of the Universe: Promotional Literature of the Colony of Georgia, 1717–1734.* Savannah: Beehive Press, 1972.

Register of Deaths in Savannah, Georgia. Compiled by the Genealogical Committee, Georgia Historical Society. Vol. 1: *1803–1807.* Vol. 3: *August 1811–August 1818.* Savannah: R. J. Taylor Jr. Foundation, 1986.

Reps, John W. "C² + L² = S²? Another Look at the Origins of Savannah's Town Plan." In *Forty Years of Diversity: Essays on Colonial Georgia*, edited by Harvey H. Jackson and Phinizy Spalding, 101–51. Athens: University of Georgia Press, 1984.

Richardson, David. "The British Empire and the Atlantic Slave Trade, 1660–1807." In *The Eighteenth Century*, edited by P. J. Marshall, 440–64. 1998. Reprint, Oxford: Oxford University Press, 2001.

———. "The British Slave Trade to Colonial South Carolina." *Slavery and Abolition* 12, no. 3 (Dec. 1991): 125–72.

Roach, S. F., Jr. "The *Georgia Gazette* and the Stamp Act: A Reconsideration." *Georgia Historical Quarterly* 55, no. 4 (Winter 1971): 471–91.

Roberts, William I. "The Losses of a Loyalist Merchant in Georgia during the Revolution." *Georgia Historical Quarterly* 52, no. 3 (Sept. 1968): 270–76.

Robertson, Heard, and Thomas H. Robertson. "The Town and Fort of Augusta." In *Colonial Augusta: "Key of the Indian Countrey,"* edited by Edward J. Cashin, 59–74. Macon: Mercer University Press, 1986.

Rogers, George C., Jr. *Charleston in the Age of the Pinckneys.* 1969. Reprint, Columbia: University of South Carolina Press, 1980.

———. "The East Florida Society of London, 1766–1767." *Florida Historical Quarterly* 54 (Apr. 1976): 479–96.

Romans, Bernard. *A Concise Natural History of East and West Florida.* Edited by Kathlyn E. Holland Braund. Tuscaloosa: University of Alabama Press, 1999.

Rowland, Lawrence S. "'Alone on the River': The Rise and Fall of the Savannah River Rice Plantations of St. Peter's Parish, South Carolina." *South Carolina Historical Magazine* 88 (July 1987): 121–50.

Rowland, Lawrence S., Alexander Moore, and George C. Rogers Jr., eds. *The History of Beaufort County, South Carolina*, vol. 1: *1514–1861*. Columbia: University of South Carolina Press, 1996.

Rubin, Saul Jacob. *Third to None: The Saga of Savannah Jewry, 1733–1983*. Savannah: Congregation Mickve Israel, 1983.

Rupert, Linda M. *Creolization and Contraband: Curacao in the Early Modern Atlantic World*. Athens: University of Georgia Press, 2012.

Russell-Wood, A. J. R. "The Portuguese Atlantic, 1415–1808." In *Atlantic History: A Critical Appraisal*, edited by Jack P. Greene and Philip D. Morgan, 81–110. Oxford: Oxford University Press, 2009.

Ryan, Jennifer Guthrie, and Hugh Stiles Golson. *Andrew Low and the Sign of the Buck: Trade, Triumph, Tragedy at the House of Low*. Savannah: Frederic C. Beil, 2011.

Saunt, Claudio. *A New Order of Things: Property, Power, and the Transformation of the Creek Indians, 1733–1816*. New York: Cambridge University Press, 1999.

Schaw, Janet. *Journal of a Lady of Quality: Being the Narrative of a Journey*. Edited by Evangeline W. Andrews and C. M. Andrews. 1921. Reprint, New Haven, Conn.: Yale University Press, 1923.

Schlesinger, Arthur M. *The Colonial Merchants and the American Revolution, 1763–1776*. 1918. Reprint, New York: Atheneum, 1968.

Scott, J. T. *The First Families of Frederica: Their Lives and Locations*. Athens: n.p., 1985.

Searcy, Martha Condray. *The Georgia-Florida Contest in the American Revolution, 1776–1778*. Tuscaloosa: University of Alabama Press, 1985.

Sellers, Leila. *Charleston Business on the Eve of the American Revolution*. 1934. Reprint, London: Macdonald and Jane's, 1974.

Sheffield, John. *Observations on the Commerce of the American States*. 1784. Reprint, New York: Augustus M. Kelley, 1970.

Sheftall, John Mckay. *Sunbury on the Medway: A Selective History of the Town, Inhabitants, and Fortifications*. 1977. Reprint, Atlanta: Daughters of the American Colonists, Georgia State Chapter, 1995.

Shepherd, James F. "Commodity Exports from the British North American Colonies to Overseas Areas, 1768–1772." *Explorations in Economic History* 8 (1971): 5–76.

Shepherd, James F., and Gary M. Walton. *Shipping, Maritime Trade, and the Economic Development of Colonial North America*. Cambridge: Cambridge University Press, 1972.

———. "Trade, Distribution, and Economic Growth in Colonial America." *Journal of Economic History* 32, no. 1 (Mar. 1972): 128–45.

Shepherd, James F., and S. Williamson. "The Coastal Trade of the British North American Colonies, 1768–1772." *Journal of Economic History* 32, no. 4 (Dec. 1972): 783–810.

Sheridan, Richard B. "The Formation of Caribbean Plantation Society, 1689–1748." In *The Eighteenth Century*, edited by P. J. Marshall, 394–414. 1998. Reprint, Oxford: Oxford University Press, 2001.

———. "The Rise of a Colonial Gentry: A Case Study of Antigua, 1730–1775." *Economic History Review*, n.s., 13, no. 3 (1961): 342–57.

———. *Sugar and Slavery: An Economic History of the British West Indies, 1623–1775.* 1974. Reprint, Kingston, Jamaica: Canoe, 2007.

Shields, David S., ed. *Material Culture in Anglo-America: Regional Identity and Urbanity in the Tidewater, Lowcountry, and Caribbean.* Columbia: University of South Carolina Press, 2009.

Shy, John. *Toward Lexington: The Role of the British Army in the Coming of the American Revolution.* Princeton, N.J.: Princeton University Press, 1965.

Silver, Peter. *Our Savage Neighbors: How Indian War Transformed Early America.* New York: Norton, 2008.

Simpson, Tiwanna M. "'She has her country marks very conspicuous in the face': African Culture and Community in Early Georgia." Ph.D. diss., Ohio State University, 2002.

Sirmans, M. Eugene. *Colonial South Carolina: A Political History, 1663–1763.* Chapel Hill: University of North Carolina Press, 1966.

Smith, David A. "Dependent Urbanization in Colonial America: The Case of Charleston, South Carolina." *Social Forces* 66, no. 1 (Sept. 1987): 1–28.

Smith, Julia Floyd. *Slavery and Rice Culture in Low Country Georgia, 1750–1860.* Knoxville: University of Tennessee Press, 1985.

Smith, S. D. "The Market for Manufactures in the Thirteen Continental Colonies, 1698–1776." *Economic History Review*, n.s., 51, no. 4 (Nov. 1998): 676–708.

———. "Reckoning with the Atlantic Economy." *Historical Journal* 46, no. 3 (Sept. 2003): 749–64.

Smith, W. Calvin. "Georgia Gentlemen: The Habershams of Eighteenth-Century Savannah." Ph.D. diss., University of North Carolina, 1971.

———. "The Habershams: The Merchant Experience in Georgia." In *Forty Years of Diversity: Essays on Colonial Georgia*, edited by Harvey H. Jackson and Phinizy Spalding, 198–216. Athens: University of Georgia Press, 1984.

Snapp, J. Russell. *John Stuart and the Struggle for Empire on the Southern Frontier.* Baton Rouge: Louisiana State University Press, 1996.

Sollors, Werner, ed. *The Interesting Narrative of the Life of Olaudah Equiano, or Gustavus Vassa, the African, Written by Himself.* New York: Norton, 2001.

Spalding, Phinizy. "Georgia and South Carolina during the Oglethorpe Period, 1732–1743." Ph.D. diss., University of North Carolina, 1963.

———. *Oglethorpe in America*. Chicago: University of Chicago Press, 1977.

Statom, Thomas Ral. "Negro Slavery in Eighteenth-Century Georgia." Ph.D. diss., University of Alabama, 1982.

Steele, Ian K. *The English Atlantic: An Exploration of Communication and Community, 1675–1740*. New York: Oxford University Press, 1986.

Stephens, S. G. "The Origin of Sea Island Cotton." *Agricultural History* 50, no. 2 (Apr. 1976): 391–99.

Stevens, William Bacon. *A History of Georgia from Its First Discovery by Europeans to the Adoption of the Present Constitution*. 2 vols. 1847. Reprint, Savannah: Beehive Press, 1972.

Stewart, Mart A. *"What Nature Suffers to Groe": Life, Labor, and Landscape on the Georgia Coast, 1680–1920*. Athens: University of Georgia Press, 1996.

———. "'Whether Wast, Deodand, or Stray': Cattle, Culture, and the Environment in Early Georgia." *Agricultural History* 65, no. 3 (Summer 1991): 1–28.

Stokes, Anthony. *A View of the Constitution of the British Colonies in North America and the West Indies at the Time the Civil War Broke Out on the Continent of America*. London: B. White, 1783.

Stumpf, Stuart O. "The Merchants of Colonial Charleston, 1680–1756." Ph.D. diss., Michigan State University, 1971.

———. "South Carolina Importers of General Merchandise, 1735–1765." *South Carolina Historical Magazine* 84, no. 1 (Jan. 1983): 1–10.

Stumpf, S., and J. Marshall. "Leading Merchants of Charleston's First 'Golden Age.'" *Essays in Economic and Business History* 5 (1986): 38–46.

Styles, John. *The Dress of the People: Everyday Fashion in Eighteenth-Century England*. New Haven, Conn.: Yale University Press, 2007.

Sullivan, Buddy. *Early Days on the Georgia Tidewater: The Story of McIntosh County & Sapelo*. Darien: Darien News, 1992.

Sweet, Julie Anne. "Mary Musgrove." In *Georgia Women: Their Lives and Times*, edited by Ann Short Chirhart and Betty Wood, 11–32. Athens: University of Georgia Press, 2009.

———. *Negotiating for Georgia: British-Creek Relations in the Trustee Era, 1733–1752*. Athens: University of Georgia Press, 2005.

———. *William Stephens: Georgia's Forgotten Founder*. Baton Rouge: Louisiana State University Press, 2010.

Tapper, Oscar J. P. "The Brailsford Debt." *Guildhall Miscellany* 2 (1961): 82–94.

Taylor, Paul. "Colonizing Georgia, 1732–1752: A Statistical Note." *William and Mary Quarterly*, 3rd ser., 22 (Jan. 1965): 119–27.

———. *Georgia Plan: 1732–1752*. Berkeley: University of California, 1972.

Temple, Sarah Gober, and Kenneth Coleman. *Georgia Journeys, 1732–1754*. Athens: University of Georgia Press, 1961.

Thomas, Hugh. *The Slave Trade: The Story of the Atlantic Slave Trade: 1440–1870*. New York: Simon and Schuster, 1997.

Thornton, John. *Africa and Africans in the Making of the Atlantic World, 1400–1800*. 1992. Reprint, Cambridge: Cambridge University Press, 2006.

Turner, Amy Bushnell. "Indigenous America and the Limits of the Atlantic World, 1493–1825." In *Atlantic History: A Critical Appraisal*, edited by Jack P. Greene and Philip D. Morgan, 191–222. Oxford: Oxford University Press, 2009.

U.S. Census. *Historical Statistics of the United States, Colonial Times to 1970*. 2 vols. Washington, D.C.: Government Printing Office, 1975.

Van Horne, John C. "Joseph Solomon Ottolenghe (ca. 1711–1775): Catechist to the Negroes, Superintendent of the Silk Culture, and Public Servant in Colonial Georgia." *Proceedings of the American Philosophical Society* 125, no. 5 (Oct. 1981): 398–409.

Ver Steeg, Clarence. *Origins of a Southern Mosaic*. Athens: University of Georgia Press, 1975.

Walker, George Fuller, comp. *Abstracts of Georgia: Colonial Book J: 1755–1762*. Atlanta: R. J. Taylor Jr. Foundation, 1978.

Walsh, Richard, ed. *Writings of Christopher Gadsden, 1746–1805*. Columbia: University of South Carolina Press, 1966.

Ward, J. R. *British West Indian Slavery, 1750–1834: The Process of Amelioration*. 1988. Reprint, Oxford: Clarendon, 2001.

———. "The British West Indies in the Age of Abolition, 1748–1815." In *The Eighteenth Century*, edited by P. J. Marshall, 415–39. Oxford: Oxford University Press, 2001.

Waselkov, Gregory A. "The Eighteenth-Century Anglo-Indian Trade in Southeastern North America." In *New Faces of the Fur Trade*, edited by Jo-Anne Fiske, Susan Sleeper Smith, and William Wicken, 193–222. East Lansing: Michigan State University, 1998.

Waselkov, Gregory A., Peter H. Wood, and Tom Hatley, eds. *Powhatan's Mantle: Indians in the Colonial Southeast*. Lincoln: University of Nebraska Press, 2006.

Watts, David. *The West Indies: Patterns of Development, Culture, and Environmental Change since 1492*. 1987. Reprint, Cambridge: Cambridge University Press, 1994.

Wax, Darold D. "Georgia and the Negro before the American Revolution."
  Georgia Historical Quarterly 51, no. 1 (Mar. 1967): 63–77.

———. "New Negroes Are Always in Demand: The Slave Trade in Eighteenth-
  Century Georgia." *Georgia Historical Quarterly* 68, no. 2 (Summer 1984):
  193–220.

Weeks, Carl Solana. *Savannah in the Time of Peter Tondee*. Columbia, S.C.:
  Summerhouse, 1997.

Weir, Robert M. *Colonial South Carolina: A History*. Columbia: University of
  South Carolina Press, 1997.

Welch, Pedro L. V. *Slave Society in the City: Bridgetown, Barbados, 1680–1834*.
  Oxford: James Currey, 2004.

White, George. *Historical Collections of Georgia*. New York: Pudney and Russell,
  1855.

Whitefield, George. *An Account of Money Received and Disbursed for the Orphan
  House in Georgia*. London: W. Strahan, 1741.

———. *A Brief Account of the Rise, Progress and Present Situation of the Orphan
  House in Georgia*. Edinburgh: Tho. Lumisden, 1748.

Wilkins, Barratt. "A View of Savannah on the Eve of the Revolution." *Georgia
  Historical Quarterly* 54, no. 4 (Winter 1970): 577–84.

Wilms, Douglas C. "The Development of Rice Culture in 18th Century Georgia."
  Southeastern Geographer 12, no. 1 (Jan. 1972): 45–57.

Windley, Lawrence A, comp. *Runaway Slave Advertisements: A Documentary
  History from the 1730s to 1790*, vol. 4: *Georgia*. Westport, Conn.: Greenwood,
  1983.

Wood, Betty. *Gender, Race, and Rank in a Revolutionary Age: The Georgia
  Lowcountry, 1750–1820*. Athens: University of Georgia Press, 2000.

———. "James Edward Oglethorpe, Race, and Slavery: A Reassessment." In
  Oglethorpe in Perspective: Georgia's Founder after Two Hundred Years, edited by
  Phinizy Spalding and Harvey H. Jackson, 66–79. Tuscaloosa: University of
  Alabama Press, 1989.

———. *Slavery in Colonial Georgia, 1730–1775*. Athens: University of Georgia
  Press, 1984.

———. "Thomas Stephens and the Introduction of Black Slavery in Georgia."
  Georgia Historical Quarterly 59, no. 1 (Spring 1974): 24–40.

———. "'Until He Shall Be Dead, Dead, Dead': The Judicial Treatment of Slaves
  in Eighteenth-Century Georgia." *Georgia Historical Quarterly* 71, no. 3 (Fall
  1987): 377–98.

———. *Women's Work, Men's Work: The Informal Slave Economies of Lowcountry
  Georgia*. Athens: University of Georgia Press, 1995.

Wood, Betty, and Ralph Gray. "The Transition from Indentured to Involuntary Servitude in Colonial Georgia." *Explorations in Economic History* 13 (1976): 353–70.

Wood, Peter H. *Black Majority: Negroes in Colonial South Carolina from 1670 through the Stono Rebellion*. New York: Norton, 1974.

———. "The Changing Population of the Colonial South: An Overview by Race and Region, 1685–1790." In *Powhatan's Mantle: Indians in the Colonial Southeast*, edited by Gregory A. Waselkov, Peter H. Wood, and Tom Hatley, 57–132. Lincoln: University of Nebraska Press, 2006.

———. "Circles in the Sand: Perspectives on the Southern Frontier at the Arrival of James Oglethorpe." In *Oglethorpe in Perspective: Georgia's Founder after Two Hundred Years*, edited by Phinizy Spalding and Harvey H. Jackson, 5–21. Tuscaloosa: University of Alabama Press, 1989.

Wood, Virginia Steele. *Live Oaking: Southern Timber for Tall Ships*. Annapolis, Md.: Naval Institute Press, 1981.

Wood, Virginia Steele, and Mary R. Bullard, eds. *Journal of a Visit to the Georgia Islands . . . in 1753*. Macon: Mercer University Press, 1996.

Wright, J. Leitch, Jr. *Creeks and Seminoles: The Destruction and Regeneration of the Muscogulge People*. Lincoln: University of Nebraska Press, 1990.

———. *Florida in the American Revolution*. Gainesville: University Press of Florida, 1975.

Young, Jeffry Robert. *Domesticating Slavery: The Master Class in Georgia and South Carolina, 1670–1837*. Chapel Hill: University of North Carolina Press, 1999.

Zacek, Natalie A. *Settler Society in the English Leeward Islands, 1670–1776*. Cambridge: Cambridge University Press, 2010.

Zahedieh, Nuala. "Economy." In *The British Atlantic World, 1500–1800*, edited by David Armitage and Michael J. Braddick, 51–68. Basingstoke, England: Palgrave Macmillan, 2002.

Zellar, Gary. *African Creeks: Estelvste and the Creek Nation*. Norman: University of Oklahoma Press, 2007.

Index

The letter *t* following a page number denotes a table.

The map on page xii is missing St. Andrew Parish and should appear as below:

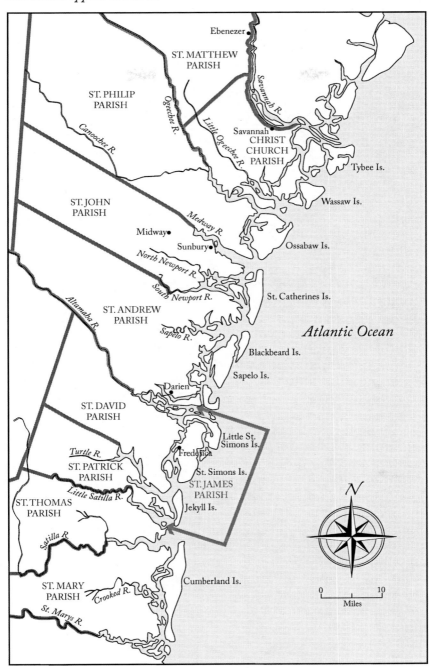

Coastal Georgia, 1775.